A Course on
Cooperative Game Theory

Satya R. Chakravarty
Manipushpak Mitra
Palash Sarkar

CAMBRIDGE
UNIVERSITY PRESS

CAMBRIDGE
UNIVERSITY PRESS

314 to 321, 3rd Floor, Plot No.3, Splendor Forum, Jasola District Centre, New Delhi 110025, India

Cambridge University Press is part of the University of Cambridge.

It furthers the University's mission by disseminating knowledge in the pursuit of education, learning and research at the highest international levels of excellence.

www.cambridge.org
Information on this title: www.cambridge.org/9781107058798

First published 2015
Reprint 2016, 2017, 2018, 2022, 2023

Printed in India by Avantika Printers Pvt. Ltd.

A catalogue record for this publication is available from the British Library

Library of Congress Cataloging-in-Publication Data
Chakravarty, Satya R.
A course on cooperative game theory / Satya R. Chakravarty, Manipushpak Mitra, Palash Sarkar.
pages cm
Includes bibliographical references and index.
Summary: "Deals with real life situations where objectives of the participants are partially cooperative and partially conflicting"-- Provided by publisher.
ISBN 978-1-107-05879-8 (hardback) -- ISBN 978-1-107-69132-2 (pbk.)
1. Game theory. 2. Economics, Mathematical. I. Mitra, Manipushpak. II. Sarkar, Palash, 1969- III. Title.
HB144.C43 2014
519.3--dc23
2014024423

ISBN 978-1-107-05879-8 Hardback
ISBN 978-1-107-69132-2 Paperback

Contents

Preface

The objectives of game theory are to model and analyze interdependent decision-making circumstances. A distinction is made in the literature between cooperative and non-cooperative games in the sense that while for the former, obligatory contracts between the participants, referred to as players, is possible, such a possibility is ruled out for the latter.

Cooperative game theory has become very influential in social sciences in the recent years. This book discusses some highly important issues in cooperative game theory with examples from economics, business and sometimes from politics. The book is divided into two parts. Part 1 is composed of Chapters 1–9. Foundations of game theory and a description of the Chapters 2–13 are presented in Chapter 1. Cooperative games with transferable utility are discussed in Chapters 2–6. Chapter 2 explains some basic concepts, definitions and preliminaries. Chapter 3 analyzes set-valued solution concepts like the core, the dominance core, stable sets and different core catchers. An extensive discussion on the relations between alternative solution concepts is also made in this chapter. Two additional set-valued solution concepts, the bargaining set and the kernel that rely on a coalition structure, are presented in Chapter 4. This chapter also discusses the nucleolus, a one-point solution concept, which has interesting relations with the bargaining set and the kernel. In Chapter 5, we consider a well-known one-point solution concept, the Shapley value. A particular type of transferable-utility cooperative game with some especially attractive properties is a convex game, which has been examined in Chapter 6. Relations between the Weber set, an alternative set-valued solution concept, the core and the Shapley value for such games are also reviewed in detail in this chapter. Chapter 7 presents a systematic analysis of voting games that often arise in interactive decision-making situations. The subject of Chapter 8 is stable matching. We discuss the Gale–Shapley basic model of matching men to women or vice-versa, the concept of stable matching, matching problems in two-sided markets, matching problems when participants from one side do not have preferences and housing exchange problems. An investigation of nontransferable utility games is carried out in Chapter 9. In particular, an analytical discussion on the well-known Nash bargaining model is covered in this chapter.

Each chapter contains at least one numerical example to illustrate a concept or a result. Applied examples are provided in the chapters to indicate real-life applications of the ideas.

The book is well-suited for graduate course in cooperative game theory. However, if desired, only the necessary minimum may be chosen depending on the background of students. For instance, some sections of Chapters 2, 3, 5, 7 and 8 can be used for an undergraduate course in cooperative game theory. The mathematical prerequisites for the book are elementary calculus, real analysis, linear algebra, probability and linear programming. If any result involves advanced mathematics, we have tried to provide a self-contained explanation of the mathematics used. Each of the Chapters 2−13 contains exercises, some of which are quite simple. The difficult exercises are meant for advanced courses.

Several sections of the book were used to teach MSc (Quantitative Economics) students at the Indian Statistical Institute over the years 1998−2013. It is a pleasure to acknowledge the comments and useful suggestions that we received from our students. We are grateful to Rana Barua, Youngsub Chun, Bhaskar Dutta, Marc Fleurbaey, Anirban Kar, Francois Maniquet, Eric S. Maskin, Herve Moulin, Suresh Muthuswami, Sonali Roy, Arunava Sen and William Thomson for their suggestions. Debasmita Basu and Srikanta Kundu (Senior Research Fellows in Economics at the Indian Statistical Institute) drew the figures for Chapter 9 and helped in preparing the bibliography of Chapters 1−9.

The second part of the book (Chapters 10−13) deals with some algorithmic issues arising from investigations into cooperative game theory. This part starts with a chapter providing a brief account of linear programming and its application to the core and the nucleolus. The second chapter provides an overview of the area of algorithms and computationally hard problems and goes on to describe the issues of computational complexity in cooperative game theory. In the third chapter, computational problems related to weighted majority games are considered and dynamic programming based algorithms are carefully developed. The fourth and the final chapter of the second part discusses the Gale−Shapley algorithm in some detail along with optimality considerations and the stable matching polytope. It is hoped that along with the material in the first part, an instructor may choose to expose students to some algorithmic issues discussed in the second part. This will lead to broader insight into the subject. We would like to thank Kishan Chand Gupta and Bhargab Maharaj for reading the initial draft of the four chapters and providing useful comments.

CHAPTER 1

Introduction and Motivation

'Game theory can be defined as the study of mathematical models of conflict and cooperation between intelligent rational decision makers. Game theory provides general mathematical techniques for analyzing situations in which two or more individuals make decisions that will influence one another's welfare' (Myerson 1997, p.1). The underlying idea here is that the decisions of the concerned individuals, who behave rationally, will influence each other's interests/pay-offs. No single person alone can determine the outcome completely. Each person's success depends on the actions of the other concerned individuals as well his own actions. Thus, loosely speaking, game theory deals with the mathematical formulation of a decision-making problem in which the analysis of a competitive situation is developed to determine an optimal course of action for a set of concerned individuals. Aumann (1987; 2008) suggested the alternative term 'interactive decision theory' for this discipline. However, Binmore (1992) argued that a game is played in a situation where rational individuals interact with each other. For instance, price, output, etc. of a firm will be determined by its actions as a decision maker. Game theory here describes how the firm will frame its actions and how these actions will determine the values of the concerned variable. Likewise, when two or more firms collude to gain more power for controlling the market, it is a game.

To understand this more clearly, consider a set of firms in an oligopolistic industry producing a common output. Each firm must not only be concerned with how its own output affects the market price directly; it must also take into consideration how variations in its output will affect the price through its effect on the decisions taken by other firms. Thus, strategic behaviour becomes an essential ingredient of the analysis. A tool that economists employ for modelling this type of situation is non-cooperative game theory.

As a second example, consider a landowner who owns a large piece of land on which some peasants work. The landowner does not work and requires at least one peasant to work on the piece of land to produce some output. On the other hand, the peasants cannot produce anything on their own because they require land. This shows that cooperation between the landowner and peasants is necessary for production of some output, otherwise no production will occur. A situation of this type is modelled by coalition or cooperative game.

In the next section of this introductory chapter, we provide a brief historical sketch of the development of some of the important concepts in game theory. However, we do not claim to present a complete survey of the development in the subject. For further details, an interested reader can see, among others Fudenberg and Tirole (1991), Binmore (1992), Osborne and Rubinstein (1994), Owen (1995), Myerson (1997), Chatterjee and Samuelson (2001) and Peters (2008). We then present a brief introduction to the remaining chapters of the book.

1.1   A Brief Historical Sketch

There are two approaches to the theory of games: the strategic approach and coalitional or cooperative approach. A non- cooperative or procedural game specifies all the possible actions for each individual decision maker, generally referred to as a player. Each course of action open to a player is called a strategy. A strategy is called a pure strategy if it is chosen with certainty, whereas mixed strategy for a player is a probability distribution over his pure strategies.

Modern game theory began with John von Neumann's (1928) classical saddle point theorem for a two-person zero-sum game in which one player's gain is matched by the other player's loss. This was followed by the seminal book by John von Neumann and Oscar Morgenstern (1944), a culmination of rich collaboration between the authors. It provides an excellent treatment of many types of games along with extensive discussions on potential applications of game theory. The book builds up two notions of representation of non-cooperative games: the normal or strategic form and the extensive form. The former specifies the players' strategy sets and their pay-off functions. Each player chooses a strategy and the strategy combination chosen by the players determines a pay-off for each of the players. A game of this type is a single-period or one-shot game. The latter corresponds to presentation of the game in terms of the sequential actions of the players, that is, through a movement of the players and through specification of strategies adopted by each player. Thus, while the former does not take into account the temporal structure of a game, the latter incorporates it explicitly.

von Neumann and Morgenstern's pioneering contribution have inspired researchers to work extensively on the theory of games and its application issues. One such scientist who contributed significantly to both streams of game theory was John F. Nash. In 1951, he developed a general formulation of equilibrium in a non-cooperative game which is now popularly known as the Nash equilibrium. A combination of strategies of the players in a non-cooperative game for which each player maximizes his own pay-off with respect to his own strategy choice, given the strategy choices of the other players, is said to constitute a Nash equilibrium. Equivalently, under Nash equilibrium, holding the strategies of the other players fixed, no player can obtain a higher pay-off by choosing a different strategy. A refinement of the Nash equilibrium was developed by Selten (1975) under the name sub-game perfect equilibrium. A sub-game is a subset of a game which, when considered in isolation, is a game on its own. A strategy combination is called a sub-game perfect equilibrium if it constitutes a Nash equilibrium for each sub-game in the game. Aumann (1974; 1987a) introduced the concept of correlated equilibrium, which is more flexible than the Nash equilibrium. A correlated equilibrium allows statistical dependence among strategies of the players, which is not permissible under the Nash equilibrium. An extensive formal analysis of common knowledge assumption and its implications were investigated by Aumann (1976). A game is characterized by complete information if each player has full knowledge about the characteristics (strategies and pay-offs) of other players. For instance, in a perfectly competitive market, all sellers and buyers possess complete information about the price and quality of the product. John C. Harsanyi developed the concept of Bayesian games in 1967−68. In a Bayesian game, a player does not have complete information on other players' characteristics.

The famous prisoners' dilemma was introduced as an example of non-zero sum game in the 1950s. This dilemma is similar in nature to a situation in an oligopolistic industry where arrangements that benefit the firms in the industry when they act as a cartel, create high incentives for individual firms to deviate from the arrangement. If each firm follows individual interests by deviating from the cartel arrangement, then the arrangement falls apart. The excellent book, *Games and Economic Decisions*, by R.D. Luce and H. Raiffa, which was published in 1957, is one of the first references that provide extensive discussion on the prisoners' dilemma.

The application of game theory to biology is dealt with in John Maynard Smith's book, *Evolution and the Theory of Games*, published in 1982. The main focus was on evolutionary stable strategy, a strategy, which when adopted by all members of a population, over evolutionary time, can withstand any alternative mutant strategy. An evolutionary stable strategy is an example of gradual cooperation representing a Nash equilibrium. Schelling (1960) worked on early examples of gradual cooperation. His famous book, *The Strategy of Conflict*, is regarded as a classical contribution to the understanding of issues like conflict, commitment, and coordination.

Hurwicz (1972; 1973) initiated the mechanism design theory, which was further developed by Maskin (1999) and Myerson (1979; 1981). By a mechanism, we mean a communication system through which players exchange their messages with each other and the messages that together influence the determination of the outcome. An important characteristic, which was formalized by Hurwicz in this context, was incentive compatibility, a requirement which demands that each player knows that his best strategy is guided by the rules, irrespective of what others decide to do.

von Neumann and Morgenstern (1944) considered cooperative games for several players.

> Cooperative theory starts out with a formalization of games (the coalition form) that abstracts away altogether from procedures and ... concentrates, instead, on the possibilities of agreement.... There are several reasons that cooperative game came to be treated separately. One is that when one does build negotiation and enforcement procedures explicitly into the model, then the results of a non-cooperative analysis depend very strongly on the precise form of the procedures, on the order of making offers and counter-offers, and so on. This may be appropriate in voting situations in which precise rules of parliamentary order prevail, where a good strategist can indeed carry the day. But problems of negotiation are usually more amorphous, it is difficult to pin down just what the procedures are. More fundamentally, there is a feeling that procedures are not really all that relevant; that it is the possibilities for

coalition forming, promising and threatening that are decisive, rather than whose turn it is to speak. ... Detail distracts attention from essentials. Some things are seen better from a distance; the Roman camps around Metzada are indiscernible when one is in them, but easily visible from the top of the mountain. (Aumann 1987, p. 463)

Aumann's (1987) argument clearly indicates that essential to the notion of cooperative game is coalition formation. von Neumann and Morgenstern (1944) deal with the patterns of coalition formation under rational behaviour of the players. A coalition is simply a subset of the player set. Cooperative game theory deals with situations where the objectives of the participants of the game are partially cooperative and partially conflicting. It is in the interest of the participants to cooperate, in the sense of making binding agreements, for achieving the maximum possible benefit. When it comes to the distribution of benefit/pay-offs, participants have conflicting interests. Such situations are usually modelled as cooperative games. There is complete information on rules of the game, all available strategies and pay-offs in all possible situations. Participants are free to cooperate, negotiate, bargain, collude, make binding agreements with one another, form coalitions or subgroups, make threats and even withdraw from a coalition. Any subgroup of players can make contractual agreements independently of the remaining players. Therefore, cooperative game theory looks for possible sets of outcomes, investigates what the participants can achieve, which coalitions will form, how the benefits will be divided among the members of a coalition and to what extent the outcomes will be stable.

We may illustrate the situation by an example. Consider a society in which each individual is endowed with a bundle of goods that can be used as inputs in a production process. All production processes are assumed to produce the same output which can be distributed among the individuals. Assume also that the inputs are complementary. Then in order to maximize total output, individuals may need to exchange inputs. This is where cooperation arises. When the problem of distribution of benefits of the cooperation arises, there may be a conflict of individual interests. In other words, the individuals would like to investigate whether there are incentives to cooperate and how to allocate the benefits of cooperation among themselves. In order to resolve the problem, a game theoretic analysis may be quite appropriate. Such a game is called a market game.

Nash (1950) suggested a two-person fixed threat bargaining model using an axiomatic approach for this problem. In this two-person cooperative game, each player obtains a fixed pay-off if the agreement between the players fails. There is a feasible set of outcomes that the players can achieve if they succeed in making an agreement. However, in the absence of an agreement, no player can help or hurt himself or his partner. The unique outcome of the bargaining game is the element of the set of attainable pay-off pairs that maximizes the product of gains from the agreement.

Two pioneering contributions that form important basis in cooperative game theory were from Shapley (1953) and Gillies (1959). Gillies (1959) suggested that the core of cooperative games can be a general solution concept. Shapley (1953) introduced what is known as the 'Shapley value' as a further solution concept. While the core consists of a set of possible allocations satisfying certain conditions, the Shapley value establishes a unique allocation with specific properties. Aumann and Maschler (1964) suggested an alternative method, which has been referred to as the bargaining set. The trend to develop more and more solution concepts possessing varying properties is still an important topic of research in cooperative game theory. We provide an intuitive discussion on several important solution concepts in the next section. More elaborate discussions are presented in subsequent chapters.

We will discuss the history of each solution concept of cooperative games in the corresponding chapter. In order to avoid repetition, we did not discuss it in detail in this chapter. However, the history of non-cooperative games has been presented in detail simply because we do not proceed further with this concept and our presentation will give the reader an idea about the development of the subject.

1.2   An Overview of the Chapters

Cooperative games are divided into two categories: games with transferable utilities and games with non-transferable utilities. By a cooperative game with transferable utilities, we mean a game in which the opportunities available to each coalition is represented by a single number, such as money, interpreted as the pay-off or utility available to the coalition. The members of the coalition are free to divide this amount among themselves in a mutually agreeable manner. That is, the result of cooperation can be numerically quantified and transferred among the members of the coalition involved in the cooperation without any loss or gain. For instance, if the players in a game are firms in a market and utilities/profits of the coalitions are measured in terms of money, then the underlying profit division game is a transferable utility game. Transferability greatly simplifies the analysis. It enables us to define the characteristic function which specifies the worth of any arbitrary coalition. In a non-transferable utility game, the opportunities available at the disposal of a coalition may be represented by a set of vectors rather than by a single number. To understand this, consider an exchange economy consisting of $n \geq 2$ agents. Each agent has an initial endowment of $k \geq 2$ commodities and a preference relation defined on the set of allocation X of k goods to n agents. The initial endowment is an allocation that shows the amount of each good that the consumers bring to the market for exchange. In an exchange economy, the agents, through exchange of their endowments, try to determine some mutually advantageous trade. For any coalition of agents, the value set consists of those elements of X such that the total amount of each good allocated to the members of the coalition equals the total amount of their initial endowments of the good. The agents outside the coalition do not participate in any trading and hold on their initial endowments. For all the agents as a whole, the value set is the set of all feasible allocations. Given prices for different goods, an allocation in this pure exchange economy is a competitive equilibrium if it maximizes the preference for each individual subject to his budget constraint and all the choices are consistent in the sense that equality must hold between total demand and total supply for each good. The first fundamental theorem of Welfare Economics asserts that a competitive equilibrium is in the (Edgeworth) core and hence, it is Pareto efficient. The Edgeworth core is the set of all feasible allocations that cannot be improved upon by any coalition of individuals. An allocation of the fixed quantities of goods in an exchange economy is Pareto efficient if through reallocation of goods no individual can be made better off without making at least one individual worse off. We may refer to trading of goods in this economy as an exchange economy game. In this case, we are not comparing utilities of two agents or transferring utility, and hence this is an example of non-transferable utility game. A two-person bargaining game is also an example of a cooperative game with non-transferable utility. In this book, we will be mainly concerned with transferable utility games. For a substantial discussion on non-transferable utility games, the interested reader can refer to Peleg and Sudhölter (2007).

In cooperative game theory with transferable utility, the pay-off function open to each coalition is described by a characteristic function which associates with each coalition the total utility that the members of the coalition can achieve when they work in concert. Thus, in this case, the focus is on coalitions and their pay-offs. For any coalition, the utility that the characteristic function assigns to it is known as the worth that the coalition can achieve when its members act together. In other words, the worth of a coalition is the amount that the members of the coalition can earn on their own.

We illustrate the concept of characteristic function by giving an example. Suppose person A has an old car to sell which is worthless to him unless he can sell it. Person B, a prospective buyer, values the car at USD 1000, while person C, a second buyer, values it at USD 1050. The game consists of each of the two prospective buyers pricing the car, and the seller accepting the higher price or rejecting both. The general idea here is that by transferring ownership of the car from the seller to one of the buyers, utility is created. The set of coalitions of this 3-person player set is $\{\{A\}, \{B\}, \{C\}, \{A,B\}, \{A,C\}, \{B,C\}, \{A,B,C\}, \varnothing\}$, where $\varnothing$ is the empty set. Thus, coalition $\{A,B\}$ can create 1000 units (dollars) of utility, which the two players can divide between them in any way they choose. For instance, if they decide on a price of USD 550, then person A gains 550 units (he has exchanged a worthless car), while person B gains 450 units (he has obtained a car which he considers of worth USD 1000 for USD 550). Likewise, coalition $\{A,C\}$ can derive 1050 units of utility. The three single player coalitions, $\{A\}$, $\{B\}$ and $\{C\}$, and the coalition $\{B,C\}$ do not obtain any utility because in these cases there is no interaction. Moreover, if the coalition $\{A,B,C\}$ is formed, the best option would be to sell the car to person C and derive a total of 1050 units of utility. Since the empty set does not contain any player, it is a convention that this set creates zero utility. If we denote the characteristic function by v, then we have: $v(\{A\}) = v(\{B\}) = v(\{C\}) = v(\{B,C\}) = 0$, $v(\{A,B\}) = 1000$, $v(\{A,C\}) = v(\{A,B,C\}) = 1050$, and $v(\varnothing) = 0$. In general, for an n-person coalitional (or characteristic function form) game with player set $N = \{A_1, A_2, \ldots, A_n\}$, the characteristic function v is a real valued function defined on the set of all coalitions (subsets of N) satisfying $v(\varnothing) = 0$. The number of possible coalitions here is 2^n.

To illustrate the idea of cooperation further, consider a situation in which there are some potential users of a public service. The cost function determines the cost of providing the service to any group of users in the most efficient way in terms of minimum cost. Cooperation among the service provider and the users, that is, the service provider asks for a payment and the users in exchange of the service agree to make some payment, will ensure the efficient way of serving the users. Consider another example: suppose there are two sellers and one buyer of an indivisible good. Each seller offers to sell one unit of the good and can make the product available at a particular price. The buyer sets a worth on the product and is interested in paying the lowest possible price. He does not want to pay more than his worth valuation. This buyer−seller interaction problem can be modelled as a coalition form game.

Suppose a game is played. A natural question from the players would be how to determine the pay-offs expected from their participation in the game. This is not an easy question to answer and the characteristic function, which determines the joint pay-off of the members of a coalition, does not provide a solution to it. If there are two players in a game, each essentially faces a yes−no question, to cooperate or not to cooperate. However, if there are more than two players, the situation may change substantially. To understand this, let us consider a profit-sharing game in which five persons A_1, A_2, A_3, A_4 and A_5 are partners of a joint business. In this game, there can be $2^5 = 32$ coalitions. Table 1.1, which is taken from Curiel (1997), presents the worth of each possible coalition.

In the above game, each of the partners has contributed some capital and skill to the joint venture. The partners are required to divide an annual profit of USD 100 from the joint venture among them. Therefore, the grand coalition $N = \{A_1, A_2, A_3, A_4, A_5\}$ as a whole earns USD 100. At the outset, the trivial solution of assigning USD 20 to each partner appears to be sensible. However, after a careful analysis, A_4 and A_5 observe that if they work jointly without the other three, they can make a profit of USD 45. Therefore, the equal division allocation will not be acceptable to the coalition $\{A_4, A_5\}$. It turns out that a coalition by A_1, A_2 and A_3 can earn a joint profit of USD 25 only. Hence, these three persons will be quite keen to keep A_4 and A_5 in their coalition. They can decide to give an amount higher than USD 45 (say, USD 46) to A_4 and A_5, and divide the remaining USD 54 equally among themselves. Although this looks like a solution to the problem, after a further analysis, A_3, A_4 and A_5 observe that they can make a joint profit of USD 70. This profit is higher than USD 64 (USD 46+USD 18), which is assigned to them under the second allocation. It, therefore, rules out the possibility of acceptance of the second allocation to the coalition $\{A_3, A_4, A_5\}$. A_1 and A_2 can agree to give USD 70 to A_3, A_4 and A_5, and divide the remaining USD 30 between them. However, if the coalition $\{A_2, A_4, A_5\}$ is formed, its aggregate profit becomes USD 65, which is higher than USD $(2 \times \frac{70}{3} + \frac{30}{2})$, the amount it receives under the last allocation. This implies that A_2, A_4 and A_5 will not be satisfied with this allocation.

Table 1.1   Profit-sharing game

Coalition : S	Worth : v(S)	Coalition : S	Worth : v(S)
$\{A_1\}$	0	$\{A_1, A_2, A_5\}$	40
$\{A_2\}$	0	$\{A_1, A_3, A_4\}$	40
$\{A_3\}$	0	$\{A_1, A_3, A_5\}$	45
$\{A_4\}$	5	$\{A_1, A_4, A_5\}$	55
$\{A_5\}$	10	$\{A_2, A_3, A_4\}$	50
$\{A_1, A_2\}$	0	$\{A_2, A_3, A_5\}$	55
$\{A_1, A_3\}$	5	$\{A_2, A_4, A_5\}$	65
$\{A_1, A_4\}$	15	$\{A_3, A_4, A_5\}$	70
$\{A_1, A_5\}$	20	$\{A_1, A_2, A_3, A_4\}$	60
$\{A_2, A_3\}$	15	$\{A_1, A_2, A_3, A_5\}$	65
$\{A_2, A_4\}$	25	$\{A_1, A_2, A_4, A_5\}$	75
$\{A_2, A_5\}$	30	$\{A_1, A_3, A_4, A_5\}$	80
$\{A_3, A_4\}$	30	$\{A_2, A_3, A_4, A_5\}$	90
$\{A_3, A_5\}$	35	N	100
$\{A_4, A_5\}$	45	$\varnothing$	0
$\{A_1, A_2, A_3\}$	25		
$\{A_1, A_2, A_4\}$	35		

This example clearly indicates that in order to make commitments about the contribution of skill and capital, the partners in a possible coalition will require prior information on the division of profit. A systematic analysis concerning profit division which will clearly consider how much each coalition can acquire, is necessary. The focus of interest will be the partners' bargaining power over the division of profit. A player has to decide which of the many possible coalitions to join. He will also have to take into account the extent to which players outside his coalition will coordinate their actions. Loosely speaking, 'who needs whom more?' For instance, if A_2 forms coalitions with A_4 and A_5

respectively, these coalitions can earn USD 25 and USD 30 on their own. If A_1 joins the former coalition and A_3 joins the latter, then the worths increase respectively to USD 35 and USD 55. Given that a player prefers more to less, A_2 has to look at the possibilities of different coalitions, rule of division of the worths of the coalitions and so on.

There is no generally accepted theory to determine a unique solution to a coalition form game. Each solution concept has its own advantages and disadvantages. This will be discussed in the subsequent chapters in further details.

Let us represent a division of the money in the profit-sharing example by $x = (x_{A_1}, x_{A_2}, x_{A_3}, x_{A_4}, x_{A_5})$, which we refer to as a pay-off vector or an allocation. Here, x_{A_i} stands for the pay-off received by person A_i under the vector x. It is plausible to assume that no player will accept less than what he could earn on his own (acting alone), that is, $x_{A_i} \geq v(\{A_i\})$ for all $A_i \in N$. This is known as individual rationality. We can also assume that players are able to come to an agreement that they will share the total available utility so that $\sum_{A_i \in N} x_{A_i} = v(N) = 100$, where $\sum_{A_i} x_{A_i}$ is the total amount assigned to all the players under x. This is a Pareto efficiency condition; given the total utility $v(N)$, the pay-off of one player cannot be increased without reducing that of another player. In a coalitional form game, a pay-off vector satisfying these two conditions is called an imputation. The set of imputations in a coalition form game is a convex set, that is, if x and y are any two imputations in an n-person game, then any convex combination $\lambda x + (1 - \lambda) y$ is also an imputation of the game, where $0 \leq \lambda \leq 1$ is a scalar.

If an imputation x also satisfies a stability condition which says that for all coalitions S, $\sum_{A_i \in S} x_{A_i} \geq v(S)$, then x is called a core allocation in the sense of Gillies (1959), where $\sum_{A_i \in S} x_{A_i}$ means that the sum is taken over the pay-offs of all the persons who are in the coalition S. Equivalently, an imputation is in the core if no coalition can deviate and obtain an allocation which turns out to be better for its members. For a core allocation x, the possibility $\sum_{A_i \in S} x_{A_i} < v(S)$ is ruled out for any coalition S. In other words, a core allocation is not blocked by any subgroup of players, where blocking requires that players in the subgroup can improve their pay-off by working on their own. Clearly, the essential idea underlying the core in cooperative game theory is in the spirit of that in Edgeworth's exchange economy model with non-transferable utility. Thus, Edgewoth's analysis of the trading situation in an exchange economy is an important forerunner of cooperative game theory.

In Chapter 2 of the book, we present the background material in detail and illustrate the concepts using examples. A rigorous analysis of the core and some related issues are presented in Chapter 3. Although the core is probably the most intuitive solution concept in cooperative game theory, one shortcoming of the core is that it may be empty. The Bondareva–Shapley theorem, which we present rigorously and illustrate using examples, provides necessary and sufficient conditions for the core of a game to be non-empty. Some variants of the core are also discussed in the chapter using examples.

A very highly relevant concept in the study of cooperative games is domination—the power a coalition can exert to go on its own. Of two imputations x and y, y is dominated by x via a coalition S if x gives more to each member of S than y (that is, $x_{A_i} > y_{A_i}$ for all $A_i \in S$) and S can achieve at least its portion of x (that is, $\sum_{A_i \in S} x_{A_i} \leq v(S)$). The dominance core, which is closely related to the core, of a game is the set of all imputations that are not dominated via any coalition.

The stable set or the von Neumann set, proposed by von Neumann and Morgenstern (1944), tries to reduce the number of acceptable allocations using some intuitive conditions. Like the core, it is based on dominations. A stable set of a game is a subset of the set of imputations whose elements satisfy two stability conditions: (i) external and (ii) internal. By external stability, we mean that each imputation outside a stable set is dominated by an imputation in the stable set. By internal stability, we mean that no imputation in the stable set is dominated by another stable set imputation. Evidently, all imputations in a stable set are 'equal' in terms of un-domination. In Chapter 3, we will establish the relationship between the core, the dominance core and the stable set. The conditions for these three solution concepts to coincide are also investigated in the chapter.

As we have argued, bargaining among the players will determine the division of overall profit. Often in this context, it becomes necessary to look at the marginal contribution of a player in the grand coalition—the amount by which the overall value will reduce if the player leaves the game. We may also look at the minimum right pay-off of a player, which is the least amount the player has reasons to ask. In fact, the amount a player receives under a core allocation is bounded between his minimum right pay-off and his marginal contribution. This boundedness property, which is also analyzed in Chapter 3, seems quite plausible. A section of the chapter is devoted to illustration of basic concepts and results. One of the examples we provide in the section is the cooperative game theoretic approach to the 'Coase theorem', which demands that given any imperfection in the market that gives rise to an inefficient allocation, costless negotiations between the concerned agents will lead to the attainment of a Pareto efficient allocation. For instance, the two parties involved here may be a chemical factory dumping wastes into a river and a laundry using river water for cleaning clothes. The Coase theorem may be regarded as an analytical starting point for the economic analysis of the law. As a second example, we provide an analytical discussion on a market game.

The core has often been criticized on the ground that it has a strong static flavour, it does not incorporate the real dynamics of a bargaining process. This was one of the major reasons that led Aumann and Maschler (1964) to define the bargaining set. This set explicitly takes into account the fact that a negotiation process is a multi-criteria phenomenon. Players in a game definitely try to maximize their pay-offs, but their natural objective is also to enter into a stable situation. Quite often, players intentionally give up parts of their pay-offs to join a coalition which has fewer chances to break down. A dynamic process of 'objections' and 'counter- objections' is employed to model this behaviour. The player set is divided into several non-overlapping coalitions. Such a division of the player set is called a coalition structure Ω. An individually rational pay-off vector x where each coalition gets exactly its portion of x is called a pay-off configuration. Thus, if $\Omega = \{S_1, S_2, \ldots, S_k\}$ is a coalition structure, then the individually rational pay-off vector x is a pay-off configuration paired with $\Omega = \{S_1, S_2, \ldots, S_k\}$ if $\sum_{A_i \in S_l} x_{A_i} = v(S_l)$ for all S_l in $\Omega = \{S_1, S_2, \ldots, S_k\}$. We often write (Ω, x) to denote this. The equality $\sum_{A_i \in S_l} x_{A_i} = v(S_l)$ for all S_l in $\Omega = \{S_1, S_2, \ldots, S_k\}$ is often referred to as group rationality.

Given (Ω, x), an objection of a player A_i against another player A_j at x, where both A_i and A_j belong to the same coalition S of Ω, consists of a coalition S', which contains A_i but not A_j, paired with a pay-off configuration y under which A_i will get more than what he was getting under x, and each of the other members of S' get at least as much as he gets under x. Informally, an objection or threat of a player A_i against A_j is based on A_i's assumption that A_j is getting too much in their partnership S and if he can take his business elsewhere by joining other members of S', he will get more. A counter-objection is a proposal of A_j which is similar to an objection. More precisely, in a counter-objection, a coalition $\hat{S}$, containing A_j but not A_i, is paired with a pay-off configuration z that protects the shares of all those who are in $\hat{S}$ but not in S', including A_j himself, under the configuration x. Furthermore, each of those members of $\hat{S}$ who were also in the partnership S' will get at least as much as he was getting when he was in S'. Therefore, in counter-objection or counter-threat, A_j does not find A_i's objection convincing and forms a new partnership without A_i by which he can protect his share. A pay-off vector is in the bargaining set if every objection against it has a counter-objection. That is, a bargaining process has been stabilized on a given coalition structure and some pay-off vector. It then follows that for this coalition structure, the conditions of the bargaining set have been fulfilled. The bargaining set is always non-empty and contains the core. An analytical discussion on the bargaining set is presented in Section 2 of Chapter 4.

Pre-kernels and kernels are solution concepts in the class of objection−counter-objection variants. Precise definitions of these two concepts rely on the surplus of a player against another player. Given a cooperative game v with n players, the excess of a coalition S with respect to a pay-off vector x is the difference $e(S,x) = v(S) - \sum_{A_i \in S} x_{A_i}$. This excess $e(S,x)$ can be taken as a measure of the dissatisfaction (or unhappiness) of the coalition S with the vector x in the sense that the higher is the value of the excess $e(S,x)$, the lower is the amount obtained by S under x. It determines the exact amount by which the members of the coalition can improve their combined pay-off over what they receive under x. If the excess is positive, then the coalition receives less than its worth, and the pay-off vector is outside the core. If the excess is negative, then it is acceptable but the coalition is interested in the smallest possible excess. We can as well say that this excess represents the total gain (or loss) that the members of the coalition will receive if they decide not to accept x and constitute their own coalition.

Given a coalition structure $\Omega = \{S_1, S_2, \ldots, S_k\}$, a game v, $S_l \in \Omega$ and $A_i, A_j \in S_l \in \Omega$, the surplus of a player A_i against A_j at x, which we denote by $s_{A_i A_j}(x)$, is the maximum excess over all coalitions S which contain A_i but not A_j. This surplus represents the bargaining power of A_i over A_j in the sense that it is the maximum gain (minimum loss in case of negativity) that player A_i can obtain if he does not accept x and forms a coalition with other members of the coalition except A_j and all these other members are satisfied with what they receive under x. The pre-kernel is then defined as the set of all pay-off configurations x which assign equal bargaining powers to all pairs of players, that is, it is the set of all pay-off configurations x that satisfy $s_{A_i A_j}(x) = s_{A_j A_i}(x)$ for all $S_l \in \Omega$ and every A_i and A_j in S_l. On the other hand, the kernel is the set of all pay-off configurations x such that either $s_{A_i A_j}(x) \leq s_{A_j A_i}(x)$ or $x_{A_j} = v(\{A_j\})$ for all $S_l \in \Omega$ and every A_i and A_j in S_l. If A_j is at his personal minimum, that is, $x_{A_j} = v(\{A_j\})$, then A_i cannot have a convincing objection against A_j because an objection will now require that A_j's payment is reduced to a level which is below his personal minimum $v(\{A_j\})$, which he can get on his own. If $s_{A_i A_j}(x) > s_{A_j A_i}(x)$ then, A_i outweighs A_j, that is, A_i has more bargaining power than A_j, and hence cannot have any convincing objection against A_j. The kernel and pre-kernel are always non-empty. The kernel is a subset of the bargaining set. We analyze kernel and pre-kernel in detail in Section 3 of Chapter 4. For super-additive games, the kernel and pre-kernel coincide. Super-additivity requires that for any two disjoint coalitions, the worth of the union of the coalitions is at least as large as that of the sum of the worths of the constituting coalitions. Loosely speaking, super-additivity says that larger coalitions have larger worth.

We begin Section 4.4 with a discussion on the concept of nucleolus. For each imputation x, we compute all excesses, that is, we calculate $e(S, x)$ for all non-empty $S \subseteq N$. We then identify those imputations for which the maximum excesses are the smallest. If this smallest value corresponds to a unique imputation, then this imputation constitutes the nucleolus. In case of non-uniqueness here, we identify all those imputations for which the second maximum excesses are the smallest. If this is associated with a unique imputation, then this imputation is the nucleolus. Otherwise, we continue until a unique imputation is obtained, which is the nucleolus. Thus, in the nucleolus, the excesses associated with the pay-off vector are made as small as possible for all coalitions. In other words, the nucleolus is the imputation that lexicographically minimizes the maximal excess.

The pre-nucleolus of a game is defined as the nucleolus of the game with respect to the set of feasible pay-off vectors, where feasibility of a pay-off vector requires that the worth of the grand coalition, the set of all players N, is at least as large as the total amount assigned to them under the pay-off vector $(v(N) \geq \sum_{A_i \in N} x_{A_i})$. Aumann and Maschler (1985) showed interesting applications of the kernel and nucleolus to bankruptcy problems, distributional problems arising in the context of allocation of a fixed amount of a good among some persons, particularly, when the total available amount is insufficient to meet the demands of the concerned persons. Examples are distribution of river water among farmers in the summer, division of an estate among heirs and sharing of financial responsibilities of a liquidated firm by its partners. We present a more elaborate discussion on this issue in Section 4.5.

A summary statistic of a complex probability distribution over a diverse set of alternatives is known as the Shapley value. It can be interpreted in terms of an expected pay-off from participation in a game. To understand this more explicitly, note that corresponding to each ordering of players in an n-player game, there is a marginal contribution pay-off vector of the players. For an n-player game, there will be $n!$ $(\equiv n.(n-1).....2.1)$ ordering of the players, and hence $n!$ marginal contribution pay-off vectors. For any specific ordering, the marginal contribution pay-off vector can be formed as follows: Let the players join an organization one by one in the particular ordering. Then each player can be given the marginal contribution he creates by joining the organization. It is assumed that all orders of formation of the grand coalition are equally probable. Then the expected value of the marginal contributions that a player makes in different orders of the grand coalition formation is his Shapley value. Existence and uniqueness of the Shapley value and its interpretation from alternative perspectives will be the subject of Chapter 5. Consider the problem of distribution of an amount of revenue in a fair way, given the legitimate claims of various individuals. A related problem is taxation—in the budget how should one design a tax schedule? The two most important cooperative game-theoretic solutions to revenue allocation problems are the Shapley value and the nucleolus.

The smallest convex set containing all the marginal contribution pay-off vectors is the Weber set of a game. Thus, it can be regarded as a set valued extension of the Shapley value. The Weber set is a core catcher in the sense that the core is a subset of the Weber set. However, they coincide if the game is convex. The converse is also true. That is, if the Weber set and the core coincide, then the game is convex. Convexity of a game demands that if two coalitions (disjoint or non-disjoint) join, then the sum of the worths of the union and the intersection of the coalitions is at least as large as the sum of the worths of the two coalitions. In other words, a convex game gives rise to large economies of scale. Clearly, a convex game is super-additive. While for a general game, the Shapley value need not be an element of the non-empty core of a game, for a convex game, the Shapley value is in the core. Thus, for convex games, the Shapley value is an attractive core allocation. Chapter 6 of the book presents rigorous discussions on these issues.

A highly important concept of political science is power. Chapter 7 of the book provides a formal treatment of power, as it is reflected in a formal voting system. If in a voting situation, each voter has only one vote and a resolution is accepted if it is supported by a majority of voters, then everyone has the same type of power in the voting body. However, if some voters have more votes than others, then they are in a position to influence the voting outcome by exercising their additional votes. Consequently, rigorous approaches to the quantification of power of a member of a voting body have been suggested in literature. Examples of collective bodies where decisions are taken by votes of the members are: The United Nations Security Council, The International Monetary Fund, The United States Federal System, The Council of Ministers in the European Union, Nassau County in the State of New York, the board room of any corporate house etc. In Chapter 7, after presenting the necessary background material, we formally define an individual voting power measure, and discuss some well-known measures. Then we present some reasonable postulates for an individual power measure. Some characteristics of the voting body as a whole are also presented. A few applications where these measures have been used are considered as well.

The concern of Chapter 8 is mathematical matching. A matching is a function from one set of elements to elements belonging to another set. An example of matching is a marriage problem, in which each person (a man or woman) has preferences over the set of persons of the opposite sex. A matching is called stable if there does not exist any man−woman pair such that both of the pair are individually better off than they would be with the elements assigned under the matching. We study the marriage problem under alternative assumptions about the numbers of men and women, the core of a marriage problem and the Gale−Shapley (1962) algorithm for a stable matching. Some additional issues like firm−worker matching and matching when one side does not have preferences (for example, assigning rooms to pair of students) are also investigated.

In Chapter 9, we briefly discuss cooperative games with non-transferable utility. Two applications of such games that we discuss in this chapter are the Nash (1950) bargaining model and an exchange economy.

Chapters 10−13 take a look at the different computational issues related to the different concepts introduced in the earlier chapters. While identifying/characterizing a key notion is important, practical considerations require the ability to compute the notion for it to be useful. Towards this end, Chapter 9 starts with a brief outline of what it means for a quantity to be computed efficiently and sketches the boundary between problems that are computationally tractable and those that are not. This is followed by computational issues specific to the core, the nucleolus, the Shapley value and the number of swings in a voting game. Computational approaches to the first two concepts are essentially based on algorithms to solve the linear programming problem and necessitate a study of this fundamental problem. The Shapley value while being a useful concept can be time-consuming to compute and these issues are discussed. Finally, we will show how the number of swings may be computed using the method of dynamic programming.

CHAPTER 2

Basics and Preliminaries

2.1 Introduction

As we have seen in the discussion of the profit-sharing game in Chapter 1, if all the players in a game decide to work together, there arises a natural question concerning the division of profit among themselves. We have also observed that if some of the players in a coalition object to a proposed allocation, they can decide to leave the coalition. In order to understand this formally, a rigorous treatment of the worth of different coalitions of players and the marginal contribution of a player to a coalition is necessary. Often, some structural assumptions about a game, for instance, whether the game is additive, super-additive or sub-additive, make the analysis convenient. Moreover, in some situations, study of issues like equivalence between two games becomes relevant. This chapter makes a formal presentation of such preliminary concepts and analyzes their implications.

2.2 Preliminaries

In this section, we present and explain some preliminary concepts and look at their implications. We assume that $N = \{A_1, A_2, \ldots, A_n\}$ is a finite set of players, where $n \geq 2$ is a positive integer. The players are decision makers in the game and we will call any subset S of N, a coalition. The entire set of players N is called the grand coalition. The collection of all coalitions of N is denoted by 2^N; each coalition has certain strategies which it can employ. Each coalition also knows how best to use these strategies in order to maximize the amount of pay-off received by all its members. For any coalition S, the complement of S in N, which is denoted by $N \setminus S$, is the set of all players who are in N but not in S. For any coalition S, $|S|$ stands for the number of players in S.

An n-person cooperative game assigns to each coalition S, the pay-off that it can achieve without the help of other players. It is a convention to define the pay-off of the empty coalition $\varnothing$ as zero. Formally,

---

Definition 1 A cooperative game in characteristic function form (or *coalition form*) consists of a finite set of players N and a function $v : 2^N \to \Re$ such that $v(\varnothing) = 0$, where $\Re$ is the set of real numbers.

The function v is often referred to as a characteristic or coalition function. The interpretation of v is that for every non-empty coalition S, it assigns a real number $v(S)$, the worth of the coalition S. In other words, coalition S can guarantee the value $v(S)$ for itself by coordinating the strategies of its members without the help of other players. It is the best outcome for the players in S if they cooperate without the help of the players in the complement set $N \setminus S$. The worth $v(S)$ of a coalition can be regarded as the amount of money or utility that the coalition can divide among its members. It is the maximum value created when the members of S come together and interact. For any player A_i, $v(\{A_i\})$ is his personal minimum, since he can guarantee this amount to himself without joining any coalition. For the grand coalition N, the players will want to divide $v(N)$ among themselves. The outcome of this division will depend on the power structure in the grand coalition. A player's power is represented by his ability to help or hurt any group of players by agreeing or refusing to cooperate. A cooperative game in characteristic function form is usually referred to as a transferable utility game. Unless specified, it will be assumed throughout the book that the games we are considering are cooperative games with transferable utility. We will write G^N for the set of all characteristic form games with the player set N. Thus, v in Definition 1 is an element of G^N.

A player's power in the bargaining among the players will depend on the extent to which other players need him. It will be determined by the amount he is able to contribute to the worth of a coalition when he joins it. This amount is simply the marginal contribution of the player to a coalition.

Formally,

Definition 2 Given a game $v \in G^N$, for any player $A_i \in N$ and for any coalition $S \subseteq N \setminus \{A_i\}$, the *marginal contribution* that A_i makes to the expanded coalition $S \cup \{A_i\}$ by joining S is $v(S \cup \{A_i\}) - v(S)$.

If we denote $S \cup \{A_i\}$ by $\hat{S}$, then $v(S \cup \{A_i\}) - v(S)$ can be rewritten as $v(\hat{S}) - v(\hat{S} \setminus \{A_i\})$, where, by definition, $\hat{S} \subseteq N$. This is the marginal contribution of a player to a coalition containing him. It can be regarded as the amount by which the worth of the coalition would shrink if the player in question decides to leave the coalition. Since this is an alternative way of stating Definition 2, the two notions of marginal contributions are the same.

The following definition specifies a property that provides incentives for forming larger coalitions.

Definition 3 A game $v \in G^N$ is called *super-additive* if $v(S \cup T) \geq v(S) + v(T)$ for all $S, T \subset N$ such that $S \cap T = \emptyset$.

Super-additivity means that the worth of cooperation is higher than the worth of working independently. In other words, in a super-additive game, cooperation is always advantageous, and hence creates incentives. It parallels the concept of economies of scale—the increase in efficiency of production in terms of lower per unit cost that a firm generates by increasing the scale of production. A super-additive game is *cohesive*, where cohesiveness means that $v(N) \geq \sum_{j=1}^{k} v(S_j)$ for every partition $\{S_1, \ldots, S_k\}$ of N, that is, $\cup_{j=1}^{k} S_j = N$ and $S_i \cap S_j = \emptyset$ if $i \neq j$. In particular, we have $v(N) \geq \sum_{i=1}^{n} v(\{A_i\})$. Cohesiveness guarantees that the grand coalition should form.

In the context of games where costs are used instead of pay-offs, the notion of sub-additivity is used.

Definition 4 A game $c \in G^N$ is called *sub-additive* if $c(S \cup T) \leq c(S) + c(T)$ for all $S, T \subset N$ such that $S \cap T = \emptyset$. Equivalently, c is sub-additive if $-c$ is super-additive.

Sub-additivity is an appropriate property for cost-sharing games. Here, the coalition function c is the cost function. The player set N represents the set of customers of some public goods or service, and for any coalition S, $c(S)$ is the least cost of providing the service to the members of S.

Sub-additivity demands that for any two disjoint coalitions S and T, the cost of serving the members of the merged coalition $S \cup T$ is not higher than the cost of serving the members of the coalitions S and T independently. It bears similarity with economies of scope, which is based on the concept that it is cheaper to produce two or more products jointly than separately. It is also customary to transform a cost-sharing game into a cost-savings game defined as $v(S) = \sum_{A_i \in S} c(\{A_i\}) - c(S)$. The characteristic function v indicates the saving in the cost of serving the members of a coalition $S \subseteq N$ instead of serving the members independently. Sub-additivity of the cost-sharing game implies that saving is non-negative. Often it may be convenient to make the transformation using a dual game.

Definition 5   A game $u \in G^N$ is called the *dual* of a game $v \in G^N$ if $u(S) = v(N) - v(N \setminus S)$ for all $S \subseteq N$.

We may now define a cost-sharing game as $c(S) = v(N) - v(N \setminus S)$ for all $S \subseteq N$. The amount $c(S)$ can be interpreted as the cost that the coalition S imposes by not joining the coalition $N \setminus S$ to form the grand coalition N.

An example of a cost-sharing game is a municipal cost-sharing problem. Let there be n municipalities in a city. Each municipality requires a minimum amount of water, which it can supply from its own distribution system or from a system that can be shared by some or all of the other municipalities. Then for any coalition S of the municipalities, $c(S)$ stands for the minimum cost of supplying water to the members of S. Games of this type have been investigated, among others, by Suzuki and Nakayama (1976) and Young, Okada and Hashimoto (1982).

Definition 6   A game $v \in G^N$ is called *additive* if $v(S \cup T) = v(S) + v(T)$ for all $S, T \subset N$ such that $S \cap T = \emptyset$.

For any $A_i \in S \subseteq N$, by additivity, $v(S) = v(S \setminus \{A_i\}) + v(\{A_i\})$. Continuing this way, we can show that $v(S) = \sum_{A_i \in S} v(\{A_i\})$, where $\sum_{A_i \in S}$ means that the sum is taken over all players in S.

Definition 7   A game $v \in G^N$ is called *inessential* if $v(N) = \sum_{A_i \in N} v(\{A_i\})$.

Clearly, an additive game is an inessential game. The following proposition specifies a sufficient condition for an inessential game to be additive.

Proposition 1   If an inessential game $v \in G^N$ is super-additive, then it is additive.

Proof: Assume that the assertion is false, that is, there exists an inessential and super-additive game $v \in G^N$ which is not additive. Then there exist two non-empty and mutually exclusive coalitions S and T such that $v(S \cup T) > v(S) + v(T)$. By super-additivity, $v(N) \geq v(S \cup T) + v(N \setminus (S \cup T))$. This along with the previous inequality gives $v(N) > v(S) + v(T) + v(N \setminus (S \cup T))$. Now, applying super-additivity repeatedly to the players in S, we get $v(S) = v(\cup_{A_i \in S} \{A_i\}) \geq \sum_{A_i \in S} v(\{A_i\})$. Similarly, using super- additivity, it also follows that $v(T) \geq \sum_{A_i \in T} v(\{A_i\})$ and $v(N \setminus (S \cup T)) \geq \sum_{A_i \in N \setminus (S \cup T)} v(\{A_i\})$. Hence, $v(S) + v(T) + v(N \setminus (S \cup T)) \geq \sum_{A_i \in N} v(\{A_i\})$. Combining this inequality with $v(N) > v(S) + v(T) + v(N \setminus (S \cup T))$, we get $v(N) > \sum_{A_i \in N} v(\{A_i\})$. However, this contradicts the definition of inessentiality. Hence, the assertion stated in the proposition is true. □

In an inessential game, there is no problem in dividing $v(N)$, and hence there is no necessity for coalition formation. Consequently, such games are not very interesting from a strategic point of view.

Definition 8   A game $v \in G^N$ is called *essential* if $v(N) > \sum_{A_i \in N} v(\{A_i\})$.

Since in an essential game, the worth $v(N)$ of the grand coalition is higher than the sum of the personal minimums of the players, there are incentives for the players to form the grand coalition. The profit-sharing game considered in Chapter 1 is essential. As we will see, each essential game can be identified with a game possessing some special characteristics. Definitions 7 and 8 do not consider the possibility of $v(N) < \sum_{A_i \in N} v(\{A_i\})$, which says that the worth of the grand coalition is less than the sum of the personal minimums of the players. Since this situation does not provide any incentive to form a grand coalition, we will not consider this counter-intuitive possibility in our future discussion.

Given any two games $u, v \in G^N$, a natural issue of investigation is the relationship between them.

Definition 9   Consider two arbitrary games $u, v \in G^N$. Then the game u is *strategically equivalent* to the game v if there exists a scalar $q > 0$ and $\alpha = (\alpha(A_1), \alpha(A_2), \ldots, \alpha(A_n)) \in \mathfrak{R}^n$ such that $u(S) = qv(S) + \sum_{A_i \in S} \alpha(A_i)$ for all non-empty $S \subseteq N$, where $\mathfrak{R}^n$ stands for the n-dimensional Euclidean space.

The switch from u to v simply amounts to changing the unit of pay-off using the exchange rate q and providing a subsidy (if $\alpha(A_i) > 0$) or imposing a fee (if $\alpha(A_i) < 0$).

In Definition 9, if we set $q = 1$ and $\alpha(A_i) = 0$ for all $A_i \in N$, then v becomes strategically equivalent to itself. Thus, strategic equivalence is a reflexive relation. Next, note that we can rewrite the above definition as $v(S) = (1/q)u(S) - \sum_{A_i \in S}[\alpha(A_i)/q]$. This means that if u is strategically equivalent to v, then v is strategically equivalent to u. That is, strategic equivalence is a symmetric relation. Finally, let u be strategically equivalent to v and $\hat{u}$ be strategically equivalent to u. Then for all non-empty subsets S of N, $u(S) = qv(S) + \sum_{A_i \in S} \alpha(A_i)$ and $\hat{u}(S) = ru(S) + \sum_{A_i \in S} \hat{\alpha}(A_i)$, where $r > 0$ is a scalar and $\hat{\alpha}(A_i)$s are real numbers. It now follows that $\hat{u}(S) = rqv(S) + (r\sum_{A_i \in S} \alpha(A_i) + \sum_{A_i \in S} \hat{\alpha}(A_i))$. This demonstrates that $\hat{u}$ is strategically equivalent to v, which in turn shows that strategic equivalence is a transitive relation. Since a relation satisfying reflexivity, symmetry and transitivity is called an equivalence relation, we can summarize the above discussion as follows.

Observation 1: Given a player set N, strategic equivalence is an equivalence relation on the set G^N.

The operation strategic equivalence does not change anything essentially. The study of one game in each class of strategically equivalent games is sufficient. In order to establish the strategic equivalence property of an essential game, we need the following.

Definition 10 A game $v \in G^N$ is called $(0 - 1)$ *normalized or reduced form* if $v(\{A_i\}) = 0$ for all $A_i \in N$ and $v(N) = 1$.

Evidently, a normalized game is essential. With two players, the $(0 - 1)$ normalized game may be referred to as a two-person bargaining game. The outcome $(v(\{A_1\}), v(\{A_2\})) = (0,0)$, which may be regarded as the threat point, arises if there is no cooperation between the players. On the other hand, if the players make binding agreements, decide to cooperate and form the coalition $N = \{A_1, A_2\}$, then they can create a value $v(N) = 1$, which they can divide between them in an unambiguous way. This game is also known as the divide the dollar game.

Proposition 2 Each essential game $v \in G^N$ is uniquely strategically equivalent to a $(0 - 1)$ normalized game $u \in G^N$.

Proof: Given an essential game $v \in G^N$, it is necessary to construct a unique game u such that $u(S) = qv(S) + \sum_{A_i \in S} \alpha(A_i)$ for all non-empty S, for some $q > 0$ and real numbers $\alpha(A_i)$, $1 \leq i \leq n$, where $u(\{A_i\}) = 0$ for all $A_i \in N$ and $u(N) = 1$. If $S = \{A_i\}$, then it is necessary that $0 = u(\{A_i\}) = qv(\{A_i\}) + \alpha(A_i)$. Hence, it is necessary that

$$\alpha(A_i) = -qv(\{A_i\}) \ \forall \ A_i \in N. \tag{2.1}$$

If $S = N$, then $1 = u(N) = qv(N) + \sum_{A_i \in N} \alpha(A_i)$, and using (2.1), we get $1 = u(N) = q[v(N) - \sum_{A_i \in N} v(\{A_i\})]$. Hence, we get $q = (1/[v(N) - \sum_{A_i \in N} v(\{A_i\})])$, which is obviously unique given v, and given essentiality of v, $q > 0$. Substituting this value of q in (2.1), we uniquely get $\alpha(A_i) = ([-v(\{A_i\})]/[v(N) - \sum_{A_i \in N} v(\{A_i\})])$ for each $A_i \in N$. Using q and the numbers $\alpha(A_i)$ for each $A_i \in N$, we get that for each coalition $S \subseteq N$, if we define $u(S) = ([v(S) - \sum_{A_i \in S} v(\{A_i\})]/[v(N) - \sum_{A_i \in N} v(\{A_i\})])$, then u is $(0-1)$ normalized. Further, given the essential game $v \in G^N$, $u \in G^N$ is unique and strategically equivalent to v. This completes the proof of the proposition. □

Proposition 2 establishes that an essential game has a unique representation in terms of a $(0-1)$ normalized game through strategic equivalence. For two $(0-1)$ normalized games that are strategically equivalent, the following result holds.

Proposition 3 If the game $u \in G^N$ is strategically equivalent to the game $v \in G^N$ and they are $(0-1)$ normalized, then $u = v$.

Proof: Let the $(0-1)$ normalized game $u \in G^N$ be strategically equivalent to the $(0-1)$ normalized game $v \in G^N$. By strategic equivalence, $u(S) = qv(S) + \sum_{A_i \in S} \alpha(A_i)$ for each $S \subseteq N$ and by $(0-1)$ normalization, $u(\{A_i\}) = v(\{A_i\}) = 0$ for all $A_i \in N$. Taking $S = \{A_i\}$ in the definition of strategic equivalence, where $A_i \in N$ is arbitrary, we get $\alpha(A_i) = 0$ for all $A_i \in N$. By $(0-1)$ normalization again, $u(N) = v(N)$. Therefore, for $S = N$, the definition of strategic equivalence along with $\alpha(A_i) = 0$ for all $A_i \in N$ gives $q = 1$. Hence, $u = v$. □

Proposition 3 demonstrates that two strategically equivalent $(0-1)$ normalized games are identical. For both essential and inessential games, we have the following result in terms of strategic equivalence.

Proposition 4 If the game $u \in G^N$ is strategically equivalent to $v \in G^N$ and one of them is essential (inessential), the other is essential (inessential) as well.

Proof: Let $v \in G^N$ be a game and $u \in G^N$ be strategically equivalent to v. Then by definition, $u(S) = qv(S) + \sum_{A_i \in S} \alpha(A_i)$ for all non-empty S, where $q > 0$. If v is essential, then we get $u(N) = qv(N) + \sum_{A_i \in N} \alpha(A_i) > q \sum_{A_i \in N} v(\{A_i\}) + \sum_{A_i \in N} \alpha(A_i) = \sum_{A_i \in N}[qv(\{A_i\}) + \alpha(A_i)] = \sum_{A_i \in N} u(\{A_i\})$ implying essentiality of u. If u is essential, then $v(N) = (1/q) u(N) - \sum_{A_i \in N}(\alpha(A_i)/q) > \sum_{A_i \in N} (u(\{A_i\})/q) - \sum_{A_i \in N} (\alpha(A_i)/q) = (1/q)\sum_{A_i \in N} [u(\{A_i\}) - \alpha(A_i)] = \sum_{A_i \in N} v(\{A_i\})$ implying that v is essential as well. For the inessential case, the proof is similar except that all the strict inequalities in the above proof are replaced by equalities. □

The following result shows that in the two-player case, either inessentiality or strategic equivalence characterizes the game.

Proposition 5 Let u be a two-player coalition form game. Then it is either inessential or strategically equivalent to the two-player reduced form game.

Proof: Let the two-player game u be defined as $u(\{A_1\}) = \theta_1, u(\{A_2\}) = \theta_2$ and $u(\{A_1, A_2\}) = \theta_{12}$. Then either $\theta_{12} > \theta_1 + \theta_2$ or $\theta_{12} = \theta_1 + \theta_2$, which means that the game is either essential or inessential.[1] Let v be the $(0-1)$ normalized game so that $v(\{A_1\}) = v(\{A_2\}) = 0$ and $v(\{A_1, A_2\}) = 1$. For the essential game u to be strategically equivalent to v, it is necessary to find $q > 0$ and real numbers $\alpha(A_i), i \in \{1,2\}$, where $\theta_i = u(\{A_i\} = qv(\{A_i\}) + \alpha(A_i)$ implies that $\theta_i = \alpha(A_i)$ for each $i \in \{1,2\}$ and $\theta_{12} = u(\{A_1, A_2\} = qv(\{A_1, A_2\}) + \alpha(A_1) + \alpha(A_2)$ implies that $\theta_{12} = q + \theta_1 + \theta_2$, which in turn implies that $q = \theta_{12} - \theta_1 - \theta_2$. Since $\theta_{12} > \theta_1 + \theta_2$, it follows that we get $q = \theta_{12} - \theta_1 - \theta_2 > 0$ and real numbers $\alpha(A_1) = \theta_1$ and $\alpha(A_2) = \theta_2$ for any essential game u such that the $(0-1)$ normalized game v, thus obtained, is strategically equivalent to u. This completes the proof of the proposition. □

Often in a game, coalitions with the same number of players have the same worth. Such games are called symmetric.

> **Definition 11** A game $v \in G^N$ is called *symmetric* if for any $S, T \subseteq N$ with $|S| = |T|$, we have $v(S) = v(T)$.

Thus, in a symmetric game, equality of the numbers of players across the coalitions implies equality of values of the coalitions. Note that the coalitions under consideration may be disjoint. Clearly, the personal

---

[1] Recall that we have ruled out the possibility that $u(\{A_1, A_2\}) < u(\{A_1\}) + u(\{A_2\})$. In particular, see the discussion after Definition 8.

minimums in a symmetric game are equal. In a symmetric game, identities of the players are unimportant. They can be changed without changing the equality of pay-offs. For instance, if one player in the coalition S moves to the coalition T and one player in T moves to S, then symmetry demands that the pay-offs of the newly formed coalitions are also equal.

The following definition will also be useful in some contexts.

Definition 12 A game $v \in G^N$ is called *monotonic* if $S \subseteq T \subseteq N$ implies that $v(S) \leq v(T)$.

For monotonic games, any sub-coalition of a coalition cannot have higher pay-off than that of the coalition itself. Note that monotonicity does not mean that $|S| < |T|$ implies $v(S) \leq v(T)$. For instance, in the profit-sharing game of Chapter 1, if $S = \{A_2, A_5\}$ and $T = \{A_1, A_2, A_3\}$, then $|S| < |T|$. However, $v(S) = 30 > 25 = v(T)$. This game is monotonic but not symmetric.

If the worth of a coalition and the worth of its complement add up to the total value created by the grand coalition, then it is called a constant-sum game.

Definition 13 A game $v \in G^N$ is called *constant-sum* if for all $S \subseteq N$, $v(S) + v(N \setminus S) = v(N)$.

Very often, political games are constant-sum games. For instance, the total number of seats in the parliament of a country is fixed and a seat won by one political party cannot be won by another party. One party's win is another party's loss. Such a situation also often arises in sporting events. Constant-sum games have been studied extensively by von Neumann and Morgenstern (1953).

The following proposition, the structure of whose proof is similar to that of Proposition 5, establishes a property of a three-player constant-sum game in terms of inessentiality/strategic equivalence.

Proposition 6 Let u be a three-player constant-sum coalition form game. Then it is either inessential or strategically equivalent to a three-player game v, where

$$v(S) = \begin{cases} 1, & \text{if } |S| \geq 2, \\ 0, & \text{otherwise.} \end{cases} \tag{2.2}$$

Since in the game v considered in Proposition 6 a positive utility is created only when a majority of the players cooperate, it is often referred to as the three-player majority game.

2.3   Illustrative Examples

The objective of this section is to illustrate the concept of a coalition form game using two examples.

Example 1 Let the player set $N = \{A_1, A_2, \ldots, A_n\}$ be divided into two disjoint subsets L and R, that is, $L \cup R = N$ and $L \cap R = \emptyset$. Each member of R has one right shoe and each member of L has one left shoe. The shoes are identical in all respects except for the left–right difference. A single shoe has no value, whereas a left–right pair is worth 1 unit. We wish to model this situation as a cooperative game. For simplicity, let $N = \{A_1, A_2, \ldots, A_7\}$, $R = \{A_1, A_4, A_7\}$ and $L = \{A_2, A_3, A_5, A_6\}$. Consider the subset $S = \{A_1, A_3, A_6\}$ of N. Then $S \cap R = \{A_1\}$ and $S \cap L = \{A_3, A_6\}$. Thus, the player in $S \cap R$ has a right shoe, whereas the two players in $S \cap L$ have two left shoes. If there is cooperation among the players of S, it is possible to have one pair of left–right shoe. The number 1 (representing one pair of left–right shoe) is the minimum of the number of shoes in $S \cap R$ and $S \cap L$. In general, given the players $N = \{A_1, A_2, \ldots, A_n\}$, the characteristic function $v : 2^N \to \Re$ is defined as

$$v(S) = \begin{cases} 0, & \text{if } |S| \in \{0, 1\}, \\ \min\{|S \cap R|, |S \cap L|\}, & \text{if } |S| \geq 2. \end{cases} \tag{2.3}$$

Clearly, $v(N) = \min\{|R|, |L|\}$.

Example 2 There are two sellers and two buyers of a product. Each seller has one unit of the good whose worth for him is USD 150. Each buyer, who does not have the good, wants to buy one unit of it. The worth of it for him is USD 200. We wish to determine the characteristic function of this game.

The player set is $N = \{A_1, A_2, A_3, A_4\}$, where $\{A_1, A_2\}$ is the set of sellers and $\{A_3, A_4\}$ is the set of buyers. In view of the information provided, $v(\{A_1\}) = v(\{A_2\}) = 150$, but $v(\{A_3\}) = v(\{A_4\}) = 0$. Likewise, $v(\{A_1, A_2\}) = v(\{A_3, A_4\}) = 0$ since these cases do not involve a buyer–seller interaction. Now, suppose A_1 has decided to sell the good to A_3 or A_4 at a price p_1. The deal will be made only when it becomes profitable to both parties so that p_1 must be greater than 150 (seller's perspective) and less than 200 (buyer's perspective). That is, $150 < p_1 < 200$. If the deal materializes, A_1 has USD p_1 and A_3 or A_4 has the good which has a worth of USD 200 to him but for which he has paid a lower amount, that is, he has USD 200 minus USD p_1, the amount he has paid for the good. If the good has been sold to A_3, the worth of the coalition $\{A_1, A_3\}$ is $v(\{A_1, A_3\}) = p_1 + 200 - p_1 = 200$. By the same argument, $v(\{A_1, A_4\}) = 200$. Likewise, $v(\{A_2, A_3\}) = v(\{A_2, A_4\}) = 200$. Next, suppose both A_1 and A_2 are interested in selling the good to A_3, who needs only 1 unit of the good. In this case, A_1 can offer a bribe of p_2 to A_2 for not participating in the selling business. Then, A_1 will sell the good to A_3 at a price of $p_3 > p_2$. Therefore, under this transaction, the amounts received by A_1, A_2 and A_3 are respectively $(p_3 - p_2)$, $(p_2 + 150)$ and $(200 - p_3)$. Hence, $v(\{A_1, A_2, A_3\}) = (p_3 - p_2) + (p_2 + 150) + (200 - p_3) = 350$. By the same reasoning, $v(\{A_1, A_2, A_4\}) = 350$. If both A_3 and A_4 want to buy the good from A_1, then A_3 can offer a bribe of $p_4 > 0$ to A_4 to quit the game. A_1 will sell the product to A_3 at a price of $p_5 > 0$. Under this deal, the amounts received by A_1, A_3 and A_4 are respectively p_5, p_4 and $(200 - p_4 - p_5)$. Hence, $v(\{A_1, A_3, A_4\}) = 200 - p_4 - p_5 + p_4 + p_5 = 200$. Similarly, $v(\{A_1, A_3, A_4\}) = 200$. Finally, we can establish that $v(\{A_1, A_2, A_3, A_4\}) = 400$.

Exercises

2.1 A building in the centre of a city is worth USD 2000 per month to its owner, a grocery shop. A cloth merchant is ready to pay a monthly rent of USD 2500 for the building, whereas a bank offers to pay USD 3000 per month as rent for opening its any-time-money counter in the building. Formulate the characteristic function of this building rental game.

2.2 Let $v \in G^N$ be a coalition form game. Identify a necessary and sufficient condition for v to be strategically equivalent to a $0 - 1$ normalized game.

2.3 In the buyer–seller game considered in Section 2.3, suppose each seller offers to sell the product at a price of USD 200 and each buyer considers the product to be worth USD 250. What is the characteristic function of this game?

2.4 Give an example of a game which is (i) additive, (ii) super-additive.

2.5 In a horse market game, player A_1 (the seller) has a horse which is worthless to him, unless he can sell it. Players A_2 and A_3 (the buyers) value the horse at USD 100 and USD 110, respectively. Verify whether the game is monotonic and super-additive.

2.6 Assume that for the landowner−peasants game considered in Chapter 1, the production function is given by $\ln(1 + k)$, where k is the number of peasants working on the land. What is the characteristic function of this game?

CHAPTER 3

The Core and Some Related Solutions

3.1 Introduction

As discussed earlier, if all the players in a game decide to work together, there arises a natural question concerning the division of profit among themselves. Moreover, if some of the players in a coalition object to a proposed allocation, they can decide to leave the coalition. The core is one of the most important solution concepts to such problems in cooperative game theory. It combines the property of Pareto efficiency with individual rationality. A core allocation is based on the idea that no set of players will leave the coalition and take a collective action that will make them better off. An allocation in the core assures that each player is better off in the grand coalition, the coalition of all players of the game. According to Myerson (1997), the core is very appealing since it includes Pareto efficient allocations and reflects the power of the players, as represented by the characteristic function—the function that specifies the worth of any coalition.

After defining and illustrating the core, and looking at some implications of the definition in the next section, we will discuss the relationship between the core and the dominance core in Section 3.3. The topic of discussion in Section 3.4 is the Bondareva (1963)−Shapley(1967) theorem, which provides a necessary and sufficient condition for the core to be non-empty. In Section 3.5, we provide a treatment of two core catchers that contain the core as a subset. Some variants of the core are analyzed in Section 3.6. The von Neumann−Morgenstern solution or stable set, a solution concept closely related to the core, is presented in Section 3.7. Some real-life applications of the core are shown in Section 3.8.

3.2   Concepts and Definitions

In this section, we will define the core formally and study some of its properties. The core is probably the most prominent solution concept for allocating pay-offs (or costs) in problems of cooperative game theory. The central idea behind the core is a stability condition which says that a pay-off vector is in the core if no deviation is profitable. As before, we assume that $N = \{A_1, \ldots, A_n\}$ is the finite set of players, where $n \geq 2$ is a positive integer. To define the core formally, we need to define some preliminary terms.

Definition 14 Given a game $v \in G^N$, an *outcome* of the game or an allocation (a pay-off vector) is an n-coordinated vector $x = (x_{A_1}, x_{A_2}, \ldots, x_{A_n})$.

Here x_{A_i}, the ith coordinate of the pay-off vector x, is the amount received by player A_i. For any pay-off vector $x = (x_{A_1}, x_{A_2}, \ldots, x_{A_n})$ and any coalition $S \subseteq N$, $x(S)$ denotes the sum of pay-offs assigned to the players in S, that is, $x(S) = \sum_{A_i \in S} x_{A_i}$. In evaluating a pay-off vector, a player will compare how much he is getting under the proposed vector with his personal minimum. If the comparison is not favourable, he will prefer to remain satisfied with his personal minimum and work alone. This in turn rules out the possibility of forming the grand coalition. If the comparison turns out to be favourable to him, the pay-off vector is called individually rational.

Definition 15 Given a game $v \in G^N$, a pay-off vector x is called *individually rational* if $x_{A_i} \geq v(\{A_i\})$ for all $A_i \in N$.

It is also desirable that the aggregate amount generated under a pay-off vector is equal to the amount earned by the grand coalition, that is, $x(N) = v(N)$. This condition is called total rationality or Pareto efficiency.

Definition 16 Given a game $v \in G^N$, a pay-off vector x is called *totally rational or Pareto efficient* if $x(N) = v(N)$.

The Pareto efficiency condition can be broken down into two conditions: $x(N) \leq v(N)$ and $x(N) \geq v(N)$. The first inequality is a feasibility condition stating that the grand coalition can achieve x. Now, if $x(N) < v(N)$ holds, then $\beta = v(N) - x(N) > 0$. In such a case, players can still form the grand coalition and each player A_i can receive the better pay-off $\frac{\beta}{n} + x_{A_i}$. Therefore, we must have $x(N) \geq v(N)$. This second inequality demands that the grand coalition cannot achieve more than x. If $x(N) > v(N)$ holds, in total, x allocates more than the maximum value that the grand coalition can create. This is an irrational requirement. Hence, we must have $x(N) = v(N)$. The set of all Pareto efficient pay-off vectors in a game $v \in G^N$ is often referred to as the pre-imputation set of the game, that is, the pre-imputation set of $v \in G^N$ is given by $PI(v) = \{x \in \Re^n \mid x(N) = v(N)\}$. For any two pre-imputations, x and y, $x(N) = v(N)$ and $y(N) = v(N)$ imply that for any real number $0 \leq \lambda \leq 1$, $\lambda x(N) + (1 - \lambda)y(N) = v(N)$, which means that the pre-imputation set is convex. A set is convex if for any two elements of the set, a weighted average of the two elements, where the non-negative weights add up to one, is also an element of the set.

Observation 1: Let the game $v \in G^N$ be arbitrary. Then its pre-imputation set is convex.

Definition 17 Given a game $v \in G^N$, an *imputation* in v is a pay-off vector which is individually and totally rational. We denote the set of all imputations associated with $v \in G^N$ by $I(v)$.

Thus, an imputation is a pay-off vector that assigns each player at least as much as he can earn on his own and assigns all players together the maximum value they can create when they form the grand coalition. Let the game $u \in G^N$ be strategically equivalent to the game $v \in G^N$. Then, it is evident that x is an imputation in v if and only if $qx + \alpha$ is an imputation in u, where q and α are the same as in Definition 9.

For an additive game, $I(v)$ contains exactly one element, namely the vector $(v(\{A_1\}), v(\{A_2\}), \ldots, v(\{A_n\}))$. However, if the game is essential, then $I(v)$ contains infinitely many elements.

Proposition 7 Let the arbitrary game $v \in G^N$ be essential. Then $I(v)$ is an infinite set.

Proof: Given essentiality of $v \in G^N$, $\beta = v(N) - \sum_{A_i \in N} v(\{A_i\}) > 0$. For any non-negative n-coordinated vector $(a_{A_1}, a_{A_2}, \ldots, a_{A_n})$ that satisfies the restriction $\sum_{A_i \in N} a_{A_i} = \beta$, the pay-off vector $y = (y_{A_1}, y_{A_2}, \ldots, y_{A_n})$, where $y_{A_i} = v(\{A_i\}) + a_{A_i}$ for each $A_i \in N$ is an imputation. Since we can choose the vector $(a_{A_1}, a_{A_2}, \ldots, a_{A_n})$ in infinitely many ways, the set of imputations associated with the game $v \in G^N$ is infinite.   □

A problem that may arise with an allocation is that a group of players may be able to do better by working without the others. That is, given a pay-off vector x, if $x(S) < v(S)$ for some non-empty coalition $S \subset N$, then the players in S can improve upon their pay-offs using their own effort. There will be strong opposition to change the pay-off vector on the part of the members of S. This is not the case if the vector x is in the core.

Definition 18   Given a game $v \in G^N$, the *core* of v is the set of all imputations x in $I(v)$ such that $x(S) \geq v(S)$ for all non-empty coalitions $S \subset N$. The core of any game $v \in G^N$ is denoted by $C(v)$.

Thus, the core is based on the notion that a core element must give to each coalition (which may be a single player set) at least as much as it can achieve for itself. This ensures that a core imputation exhibits a strong degree of stability. Also in total, the assigned amount must be equal to the amount that all the players as a whole can earn. This Pareto efficiency condition shows that there is no imputation outside the core where one player can be made better off without making at least one more player worse off. The core, which is a subset of the infinite set $I(v)$ for an essential game, is the first solution concept we wish to study. It can be easily obtained because it is defined in terms of a finite system of linear inequalities. The following observation can be demonstrated quite easily.

Observation 2:   The core of a coalition form game is a convex set.

If we can find any two core allocations, convexity of the core implies that it contains infinitely many allocations.

Example 3   Consider the two-person bargaining game v. A pay-off vector $x = (x_{A_1}, x_{A_2})$ is in the core of the game provided $x_{A_1} \geq 0$, $x_{A_2} \geq 0$ and $x_{A_1} + x_{A_2} = 1$. A pay-off vector satisfying these conditions is an imputation. Thus, for this game, the core and the set of imputations coincide and contain infinitely many pay-off vectors.

Example 4   Let us recall the old car game considered in Chapter 1 (pages 8 and 9). For this game, an imputation $x = (x_A, x_B, x_C)$ is in the core $C(v)$ of the game provided $x_A \geq v(\{A\}) = 0$, $x_B \geq v(\{B\}) = 0$, $x_C \geq$

$v(\{C\}) = 0$, $x_B + x_C \geq v(\{B,C\}) = 0$, $x_A + x_C \geq v(\{A,C\}) = 1050$, $x_A + x_B \geq v(\{A,B\}) = 1000$ and $x_A + x_B + x_C = 1050$. Substituting $x_A = 1050 - x_B - x_C$ in the inequality $x_A + x_C \geq 1050$ and using $x_B \geq 0$, we get $x_B = 0$. Hence, a pay-off vector $x = (x_A, x_B, x_C)$ is in the core if and only if the following constraints are satisfied: $x_A \geq 1000$, $x_B = 0$, $x_C \geq 0$, $x_A + x_C \geq 1050$. Therefore, the core $C(v)$ of the game is given by $C(v) = \{(1050 - d, 0, d) \mid 0 \leq d \leq 50\}$. Clearly, for this game, $C(v)$ is a non-empty proper subset of the set of imputations $I(v)$.

Example 5 In a three-player game v, let player A_1 be a firm that uses an input in its productive activity and each of the other two players A_2 and A_3 is a supplier of this input. Some utility is created if ownership of input is transferred from either or both of A_2 and A_3 to A_1. There will be no utility if this interaction does not take place. Therefore, $v(\{A_1\}) = v(\{A_2\}) = v(\{A_3\}) = v(\{A_2, A_3\}) = 0$. Next, it is assumed that $v(\{A_1, A_2\}) = v(\{A_1, A_3\}) = v(\{A_1, A_2, A_3\}) = 1$. A pay-off vector $x = (x_{A_1}, x_{A_2}, x_{A_3})$ is in the core $C(v)$ provided $x_{A_1} \geq v(\{A_1\}) = 0, x_{A_2} \geq v(\{A_2\}) = 0, x_{A_3} \geq v(\{A_3\}) = 0$, $x_{A_2} + x_{A_3} \geq v(\{A_2, A_3\}) = 0$, $x_{A_1} + x_{A_2} \geq v(\{A_1, A_2\}) = 1$, $x_{A_1} + x_{A_3} \geq v(\{A_1, A_3\}) = 1$ and $x_{A_1} + x_{A_2} + x_{A_3} = 1$. Plugging $x_{A_1} = 1 - x_{A_2} - x_{A_3}$ into $x_{A_1} + x_{A_2} \geq 1$ and using $x_{A_3} \geq 0$, we get $x_{A_3} = 0$. By a similar calculation, we have $x_{A_2} = 0$. Hence, $x_{A_1} = 1$. Thus, $C(v)$ contains exactly one element, namely $(1, 0, 0)$.

3.3 The Core and Dominance Core

A central concept in cooperative game theory is dominance, which refers to the power that a coalition can exert through its ability to go alone.

Definition 19 Consider a game $v \in G^N$; the pay-off vectors x and y and an arbitrary non-empty coalition $S \subseteq N$. We say that x *dominates* y *via the coalition* S, which we write as $x \succ_S y$, if $x_{A_i} > y_{A_i}$ for all $A_i \in S$ and $x(S) \leq v(S)$.

Thus, of two pay-off vectors x and y, x dominates y via the coalition S if x gives more to each of the members of S and x is achievable for S. Given $v \in G^N$, the pay-off vector x, there is no non-empty coalition $S \subseteq N$ such that $x_{A_i} > x_{A_i}$ holds for all $A_i \in S$. Hence, the relation $\succ_S$ is irreflexive, that is, not reflexive. Next, for the pay-off vectors x, y, there is no non-empty coalition $S \subseteq N$ such that $x_{A_i} > y_{A_i}$ for all $A_i \in S$ implies that $y_{A_i} > x_{A_i}$ holds for all $A_i \in S$. Thus, $\succ_S$ is an antisymmetric relation. Finally, for the pay-off vectors x, y, z, if $x_{A_i} > y_{A_i}$ and $y_{A_i} > z_{A_i}$ hold for all $A_i \in S$, then we have $x_{A_i} > z_{A_i}$ for all $A_i \in S$. This means that $\succ_S$ is a transitive relation. Thus, we have the following observation.

Observation 3: The relation $\succ_S$ is irreflexive, antisymmetric and transitive.

> **Definition 20** For the arbitrary game $v \in G^N$, the pay-off vectors x and y, we say that x *dominates* y, which we write as $x \succ_D y$, if $x \succ_S y$ holds for some non-empty coalition $S \subseteq N$.

If x dominates y via $S \subseteq N$, we can as well say that S can improve upon y. It is easy to verify that $\succ_D$ is an irreflexive relation. The following proposition shows that no imputation can dominate another via a single-player coalition.

Proposition 8 Let the game $v \in G^N$ be arbitrary. Then for any $x, y \in I(v)$, neither can dominate the other via a one-player coalition.

Proof: For a game $v \in G^N$, let $x, y \in I(v)$ and let x dominate y via $\{A_i\}$. Then $x_{A_i} > y_{A_i}$. By individual rationality, $x_{A_i}, y_{A_i} \geq v(\{A_i\})$. Dominance also requires that $x_{A_i} \leq v(\{A_i\})$. Hence, we must have $x_{A_i} = v(\{A_i\})$. Given $y_{A_i} \geq v(\{A_i\})$ and $x_{A_i} = v(\{A_i\})$, we cannot have $x_{A_i} > y_{A_i}$. Thus, x cannot dominate y via $\{A_i\}$. □

The dominance relation between two imputations does not hold for the grand coalition.

Proposition 9 Let the game $v \in G^N$ be arbitrary. Then for any $x, y \in I(v)$, neither can dominate the other via the grand coalition.

Proof: For a game $v \in G^N$, let $x, y \in I(v)$ and let x dominate y via the grand coalition N. Since both x and y are Pareto efficient, we have $x(N) = y(N) = v(N)$. However, this contradicts the grand coalitional dominance requirement, $x_{A_i} > y_{A_i}$ for all $A_i \in N$. Hence, x cannot dominate y via the grand coalition N. □

The following proposition characterizes a core element in terms of domination.

Proposition 10 Let the game $v \in G^N$ and $x \in I(v)$ be arbitrary. Then the following conditions are equivalent:

(i) $x \in C(v)$.

(ii) There is no pay-off vector that dominates x.

Proof: We first prove $(i) \Rightarrow (ii)$. If there exists a pay-off vector y such that $y \succ_S x$, then $x(S) < y(S) \leq v(S)$. However, since $x \in C(v)$, we must have

$x(S) \geq v(S)$. This contradicts the above inequality. Consequently, there is no vector y that dominates x.

To prove $(ii) \Rightarrow (i)$, we prove the contrapositive. That is, we prove $not(i) \Rightarrow not(ii)$.[1] Assume that the imputation x is not in $C(v)$. Then there is a coalition S such that $x(S) < v(S)$. Now, define a pay-off vector y as follows:

$$y_{A_i} = \begin{cases} x_{A_i} + \frac{v(S)-x(S)}{|S|}, & \text{if } A_i \in S, \\ 0, & A_i \notin S. \end{cases}$$

Then, $x_{A_i} < y_{A_i}$ for all $A_i \in S$ and $y(S) = x(S) + |S|\frac{v(S)-x(S)}{|S|} = v(S)$. Hence, $y \succ_S x$ holds. Thus, not (i) implies not (ii). Consequently, $(ii) \Rightarrow (i)$. This completes the proof of the proposition. □

Proposition 10 demonstrates that an imputation is in the core if and only if it is not dominated by any pay-off vector.

Another subset of the set of imputations which is also a solution concept for coalition form games is the dominance core. For any $v \in G^N$, let Dom $I(v)$ be the set of all imputations that are dominated by some imputations.

Definition 21 The *dominance core* $DC(v)$ of any game $v \in G^N$ is the set of all undominated elements in $I(v)$, that is, $DC(v) = I(v) \backslash$ Dom $I(v)$.

Clearly, for any $v \in G^N$, $DC(v)$ is also a convex set. The following propositions identify the relationships between the dominance core and the core.

Proposition 11 Let the game $v \in G^N$ be arbitrary. Then, $C(v) \subseteq DC(v)$.

Proof: Assume that $C(v) \subseteq DC(v)$ is false. That is there exists an imputation y such that $y \in C(v)$ and $y \notin DC(v)$. Then there exists $x \in I(v)$ and a non-empty coalition $S \subseteq N$ such that $x \succ_S y$. Therefore, $y(S) < x(S) \leq v(S)$, which implies that $y \notin C(v)$. This is a contradiction to the assumption that $y \in C(v)$. □

---

[1] The *contrapositive* of a statement "if A, then B" is formed by first negating both terms and then by reversing the direction of inference. Thus, the contrapositive of "if A, then B" is "if not B, then not A". A statement and its contrapositive are equivalent, that is, if the statement is true, then its contrapositive is true, and vice versa.

Proposition 12   Let the super-additive game $v \in G^N$ and $x \in I(v)$ be arbitrary. Then the following conditions are equivalent:

(i) $x \in C(v)$.

(ii) $x \in DC(v)$.

Proof: The proof of $(i) \Rightarrow (ii)$ is the same as that of the implication $(i) \Rightarrow (ii)$ of Proposition 10.

To prove $(ii) \Rightarrow (i)$, assume first that x and S are the same as in the proof of the implication $(ii) \Rightarrow (i)$ of Proposition 10. Then define a pay-off vector as follows:

$$
y_{A_i} = \begin{cases} x_{A_i} + \dfrac{v(S)-x(S)}{|S|}, & \text{if } A_i \in S, \\[2mm] v(\{A_i\}) + \dfrac{v(N)-v(S)-\sum_{A_i \in N \setminus S} v(\{A_i\})}{|N \setminus S|}, & \text{if } A_i \notin S. \end{cases}
$$

By super-additivity, $v(N) - v(S) - \sum_{A_i \in N \setminus S} v(\{A_i\}) \geq 0$ and by assumption, $x(S) < v(S)$. Hence, given $x_{A_i} \geq v(\{A_i\})$, it follows that $y_{A_i} \geq v(\{A_i\})$ for all $A_i \in N$. That is, y is individually rational. Next, $y(N) = v(N)$. Therefore, y is an imputation. Note also that $y(S) = v(S)$. Hence, $y \succ_S x$ holds. This shows that under super-additivity, if an imputation is not in the core, then it cannot be an element of the dominance core. That is, not (i) implies not (ii). Hence, $(ii) \Rightarrow (i)$. This completes the proof of the proposition. $\square$

Proposition 11 indicates that the core is a proper subset of the dominance core. On the other hand, Proposition 12 establishes that under super-additivity, a necessary and sufficient condition for an imputation to be in the core is that it is not dominated by any other imputation. In other words, under super-additivity, the two notions of core coincide, that is, for any super-additive game $v \in G^N$, $C(v) = DC(v)$. However, without super-additivity, the result is not true. To see this, consider the following example, which is taken from Aumann (1989).

Example 6   Let the game $v \in G^N$ with the player set $N = \{A_1, A_2, A_3\}$ be defined as $v(\{A_1\}) = 2$, $v(\{A_2\}) = v(\{A_3\}) = 0$, $v(\{A_1, A_2\}) = v(\{A_2, A_3\}) = v(\{A_1, A_3\}) = 3$ and $v(\{A_1, A_2, A_3\}) = 4$. Since we have $v(\{A_1, A_2, A_3\}) < v(\{A_1\}) + v(\{A_2, A_3\})$, the game is not super-additive. The imputation $y = (2, 1, 1)$ is not dominated by any other imputation. Now, a pay-off vector $x = (x_{A_1}, x_{A_2}, x_{A_3})$ is in the core $C(v)$ provided $x_{A_1} \geq v(\{A_1\}) = 2$, $x_{A_2} \geq v(\{A_2\}) = 0$, $x_{A_3} \geq v(\{A_3\}) = 0$, $x_{A_1} + x_{A_2} \geq v(\{A_1, A_2\}) = 3$, $x_{A_2} + x_{A_3} \geq v(\{A_2, A_3\}) = 3$, $x_{A_1} + x_{A_3} \geq$

$v(\{A_1, A_3\}) = 3$ and $x_{A_1} + x_{A_2} + x_{A_3} = 4$. Substituting $x_{A_3} = 4 - x_{A_1} - x_{A_2}$ in $x_{A_2} + x_{A_3} \geq 3$, we get $x_{A_1} \leq 1$. This contradicts the individual rationality condition $x_{A_1} \geq 2$. Hence, the core is empty. Thus, although $y \in DC(v), y \notin C(v)$.

We conclude this section by making some observations on the core of a constant-sum game.

Proposition 13 Let the game $v \in G^N$ be constant-sum and essential. Then $C(v)$ is empty.

Proof: Assume that there exists a constant-sum essential game $v \in G^N$ such that the core $C(v)$ is non-empty and let $x \in C(v)$. Then, from the definition of a core, it follows that for each player $A_i \in N$, $x_{A_i} \geq v(\{A_i\})$ and $\sum_{A_j \in N \setminus \{A_i\}} x_{A_j} \geq v(N \setminus \{A_i\})$. Using $x(N) = x_{A_i} + \sum_{A_j \in N \setminus \{A_i\}} x_{A_j} = v(N)$ and the fact that v is a constant-sum game, we get $\sum_{A_j \in N \setminus \{A_i\}} x_{A_j} \geq v(N \setminus \{A_i\}) \Rightarrow v(N) - x_{A_i} \geq v(N) - v(\{A_i\}) \Rightarrow x_{A_i} \leq v(\{A_i\})$. Hence, for each $A_i \in N$, $x_{A_i} = v(\{A_i\})$. Using essentiality of v and the Pareto efficiency of x, we get $v(N) = \sum_{A_i \in N} x_{A_i} = \sum_{A_i \in N} v(\{A_i\}) < v(N)$. This is a contradiction. Therefore, $C(v)$ is empty. □

For a constant-sum game with non-empty core, essentiality is not possible.

Proposition 14 Let the game $v \in G^N$ with non-empty core be constant-sum. Then it is inessential.

Proof: From the proof of Proposition 13, it easily follows that if a constant-sum game v has a non-empty core and if $x \in C(v)$, then $x_{A_i} = v(\{A_i\})$ for all $A_i \in N$. Using Pareto efficiency of $x \in C(v)$, it follows that $v(N) = x(N) = \sum_{A_i \in N} x_{A_i} = \sum_{A_i \in N} v(\{A_i\})$. Hence, we have $v(N) = \sum_{A_i \in N} v(\{A_i\})$ which gives the inessentiality of v. □

Essentiality is an important feature of coalition form games and the core has a clear merit as a solution concept. In view of Propositions 13 and 14, we will not proceed further with constant-sum games.

3.4 A Condition for the Core to be Non-Empty

From the different examples considered in the earlier section, it follows that the core of a game may be infinite or a finite set. It can as well be an empty set (see Example 8 below). Since the core as a solution concept is quite appealing, it becomes necessary to investigate some conditions under which the core becomes non-empty. For this, we need a concept known as 'balancedness'.

Definition 22 A collection $\Phi = \{S_1, S_2, \ldots, S_k\} \subseteq 2^N$ of coalitions, $\phi \notin \Phi$, is called *balanced* if for any $A_i \in N$, there exists positive numbers δ_{S_j}, $S_j \in \Phi$, such that $\sum_{S_j \in \Phi_{A_i}} \delta_{S_j} = 1$, where $\Phi_{A_i} = \{S_j \in \Phi \mid A_i \in S_j\}$.

Example 7 To illustrate the concept, let $N = \{A_1, A_2, A_3\}$ and consider $\Phi = \{S_1, S_2, S_3\}$, where $S_1 = \{A_2, A_3\}$, $S_2 = \{A_1, A_3\}$ and $S_3 = \{A_1, A_2\}$. Then $\Phi_{A_1} = \{S_2, S_3\}$, $\Phi_{A_2} = \{S_1, S_3\}$ and $\Phi_{A_3} = \{S_1, S_2\}$. For Φ to be balanced, there should exist positive real numbers δ_{S_i} such that $\delta_{S_2} + \delta_{S_3} = 1$, $\delta_{S_1} + \delta_{S_3} = 1$ and $\delta_{S_1} + \delta_{S_2} = 1$. Solving these three equations, we get $\delta_{S_1} = \delta_{S_2} = \delta_{S_3} = 0.5$.

The weights δ_{S_j}, $1 \leq j \leq k$, associated with the balanced collection Φ are called balancing weights. Every partition of N is a balanced collection, where a collection $\{S_1, S_2, \ldots, S_k\}$ is called a partition of N if $S_i \cap S_j = \varnothing$ for all $i \neq j$ and $\cup_{j=1}^{k} S_j = N$. Thus, a balanced collection is a generalized partition. An interpretation of the definition is as follows. Each player A_i is endowed with 1 unit of time and δ_{S_j} is the fraction of time that he devotes to each coalition S_j which contains him in the balanced collection.

Definition 23 A balanced collection is called *minimal balanced* if it does not contain a proper balanced sub-collection.

For a balanced collection to be minimal balanced, it is necessary and sufficient that it has a unique system of balancing weights (Peleg and Sudhölter 2008). Thus, the collection of coalitions we considered in Example 7 is minimal balanced.

The following theorem of Bondareva (1963) and Shapley (1967) provides a necessary and sufficient condition, in terms of balanced collections, for the core of a game to be non-empty.

Theorem 1 Let the game $v \in G^N$ be arbitrary. Then the following conditions are equivalent:

(i) $C(v)$ is non-empty.

(ii) For all balanced collections $\Phi = \{S_1, S_2, \ldots, S_k\}$ and the corresponding balancing weights $(\delta_{S_j})_{S_j \in \Phi}$, the inequality $\sum_{S_j \in \Phi} \delta_{S_j} v(S_j) \leq v(N)$ holds.

Proof: We follow Aumann (1989) in proving the theorem. Without loss of generality, we assume that v is $(0-1)$ normalized.

$(i) \Rightarrow (ii)$. Let $x \in C(v)$. Then $\sum_{A_i \in N} x_{A_i} = v(N)$ and $\sum_{A_i \in S_j} x_{A_i} \geq v(S_j)$ for all $S_j \subset N$. Let $\Phi = \{S_1, \ldots, S_k\}$ be a balanced family with the corresponding balancing weights $\{\delta_{S_j}\}_{S_j \in \Phi}$. Then it follows that for each $S_j \in \Phi, \delta_{S_j} x(S_j) = \delta_{S_j} \sum_{A_i \in S_j} x_{A_i} \geq \delta_{S_j} v(S_j)$. Moreover, $\sum_{S_j \in \Phi} \delta_{S_j} x(S_j) = \sum_{S_j \in \Phi} \delta_{S_j} \sum_{A_i \in S_j} x_{A_i} = \sum_{A_i \in N} \{x_{A_i} (\sum_{S_j \ni A_i} \delta_{S_j})\} = \sum_{A_i \in N} x_{A_i} = v(N)$ since for all $A_i \in N, \sum_{S_j \ni A_i} \delta_{S_j} = 1$. Thus, $v(N) = \sum_{S_j \in \Phi} \delta_{S_j} \sum_{A_i \in S_j} x_{A_i} = \sum_{S_j \in \Phi} \delta_{S_j} x(S_j) \geq \sum_{S_j \in \Phi} \delta_{S_j} v(S_j)$.

$(ii) \Rightarrow (i)$. Assume that $v(N) \geq \sum_{S_j \in \Phi} \delta_{S_j} v(S_j)$ for any balanced family $\Phi = \{S_1, \ldots, S_k\}$ with the corresponding balancing weights $\{\delta_{S_j}\}_{S_j \in \Phi}$. Define a two-person zero-sum game Γ with player set $\{A, B\}$ as follows. Player A chooses a player A_i from N of v. Player B chooses a coalition $S_j \subseteq N$ from v such that $v(S_j) > 0$. The pay-off to player A is

$$h(A_i, S_j) = \begin{cases} \frac{1}{v(S_j)} & \text{if } A_i \in S_j, \\ 0 & \text{otherwise.} \end{cases} \tag{3.1}$$

Claim I: If the mini$-$max value of Γ is at least 1, then $x(S_j) \geq v(S_j)$ for any $S_j \subseteq N$.

Proof of Claim I: As the game v is $(0-1)$-normalized, for any imputation x, we have $x_{A_i} \geq v(\{A_i\}) = 0$ for all $A_i \in N$ and $\sum_{A_i \in N} x_{A_i} = v(N) = 1$. Hence, each imputation can be regarded as a mixed strategy. Now, if the mini$-$max value of Γ is greater than or equal to 1, there is a mixed strategy x (also an imputation) of player A that yields at least 1 irrespective of the strategy chosen by player B. That is, $1 \leq \sum_{A_i \in N} x_{A_i} h(A_i, S_j) = (1/v(S_j)) \sum_{A_i \in S_j} x_{A_i}$ for all $S_j \subseteq N$ with $v(S_j) > 0$. That is, $v(S_j) \leq \sum_{A_i \in S} x_{A_i} = x(S_j)$ for all $S_j \subseteq N$ with $v(S_j) > 0$. If $v(S_j) = 0$, also the inequality holds, since $x_{A_i} \geq v(\{A_i\}) = 0$ for all $A_i \in N$. Hence, $v(S_j) \leq x(S_j)$ for all $S_j \subseteq N$. Moreover, since x is a mixed strategy for player A, $\sum_{A_i \in N} x_{A_i} = v(N) = 1$. This completes the proof of Claim I.

Claim I implies that x is in the core of the game v. Hence, the core is non-empty.

Claim II: The mini$-$max value of the game Γ is at least 1.

Proof of Claim II: Assume to the contrary that the mini$-$max value α of Γ is less than 1, that is, $\alpha < 1$. Note that by choosing $x_{A_i} > 0$ for all $A_i \in N$, player A can guarantee a positive pay-off. Hence, $\alpha > 0$. Since $\min_{S_j \subseteq N}$ $\max_{A_i \in N} h(A_i, S_j) \leq \alpha$, there is a mixed strategy $p = \{p_S\}_{S \subseteq N}$ of player B that gives player A a pay-off of at most α. We define a family of coalitions $\Phi = \{S \subseteq N : p_S > 0, v(S) > 0\}$. Thus, Φ is that family of coalitions that are assigned positive probabilities by player B under the mixed strategy p and that also has a positive worth under v. Then, for each pure strategy $A_i \in N$ of player A, $\alpha \geq \sum_{S \in \Phi} p_S h(A_i; S) = \sum_{S \in \Phi, S \ni A_i} [p_S / v(S)]$, so that $1 \geq \sum_{S \in \Phi, S \ni A_i} [p_S / (\alpha v(S))]$. Now define $\delta_S = [p_S / (\alpha v(S))]$ for each $S \in \Phi$. Then $1 \geq \sum_{S \in \Phi, S \ni A_i} \delta_S$. Let us further define $\delta_{A_i} = 1 - \sum_{S \in \Phi, S \ni A_i} \delta_S$ for all $A_i \in N$ and consider the collection $\mathcal{T} = \{\Phi \cup_{A_i \in N} \{A_i\}\}$. Note that for each $A_i \in N$, $\sum_{S \in \mathcal{T}, S \ni A_i} \delta_S = \sum_{S \in \Phi, S \ni A_i} \delta_S + \delta_{A_i} = 1$ implying that $\mathcal{T}$ is a balanced family of collations with balancing weights $\{\delta_S\}_{S \in \mathcal{T}}$. Using $v(\{A_i\}) = 0$ for all $A_i \in N$ and using our assumption that for any balanced family $\mathcal{F}$, $v(N) \geq \sum_{S_j \in \mathcal{F}} \delta_{S_j} v(S_j)$, we get $\sum_{S \in \mathcal{T}} \delta_S v(S) \leq v(N)$ which implies that $\sum_{S \in \Phi} \delta_S v(S) \leq v(N)$, from which we get $\sum_{S \in \Phi} [p_S / \alpha] \leq v(N) = 1$. Hence, $\sum_{S \in \Phi} p_S \leq \alpha < 1$. However, for p to be a mixed strategy, we require $\sum_{S \in \Phi} p_S = 1$ and hence, we have a contradiction to the fact that p is a mixed strategy of player B. Thus, the mini$-$max value of Γ is at least 1. □

Example 8 To illustrate how this theorem can be used to investigate whether the core of a game is empty, let us take the game considered in Example 6. The collection $\Phi = \{S_1, S_2, S_3\}$, where $S_1 = \{A_2, A_3\}$, $S_2 = \{A_1, A_3\}$ and $S_3 = \{A_1, A_2\}$, is balanced with balancing weights $\delta_{S_1} = \delta_{S_2} = \delta_{S_3} = 0.5$. Then, $\sum_{S_j \in \Phi} \delta_{S_j} v(S_j) = 4.5$ and $v(N) = 4$. This means that there exist a balanced family Φ of coalitions for which the condition $\sum_{S_j \in \Phi} \delta_{S_j} v(S_j) \leq v(N)$ is violated. Hence, the core of the game is empty.

Definition 24 A *game* $v \in G^N$ is called *balanced* if for every balanced family Φ of coalitions with balancing weights $(\delta_{S_j})_{S_j \in \Phi}$, the inequality $\sum\limits_{S_j \in \Phi} \delta_{S_j} v(S_j) \leq v(N)$ holds.

In fact, not all balanced collections are necessary to guarantee that a game is balanced. Bondareva (1963) and Shapley (1967) showed that minimal balanced collections suffice to characterize the class of games with a non-empty core. Unless specified, in this text we will deal with balanced collections. The following proposition shows a direct application of the Bondareva$-$Shapley theorem.

Proposition 15 Let the symmetric game $v \in G^N$ be arbitrary. Then $C(v)$ is non-empty if and only if for any non-empty coalition, $S \subseteq N$, $\frac{v(S)}{|S|} \leq \frac{v(N)}{|N|}$.

Proof: By the Bondareva−Shapley theorem, the core of a game v is non-empty if and only if for any balanced family, $\Phi = \{S_1, S_2, \ldots, S_k\}$ with the corresponding balancing weights $\{\delta_{S_j}\}_{S_j \in \Phi}$, $v(N) \geq \sum_{S_j} \delta_{S_j} v(S_j)$. Now consider any non-empty coalition $S \subseteq N$. Define the family $\mathcal{F} = \{T \subseteq N \mid |T| = |S|\}$. This family is balanced with the balancing weights $\delta_T = 1/\binom{|N|-1}{|T|-1}$ for each $T \in \mathcal{F}$. If the game v is symmetric, then $v(T)$ is the same for all members T of $\mathcal{F}$. Let $v(T) = q$, where $T \in \mathcal{F}$ is arbitrary. For $\mathcal{F}, \sum_{T \in \mathcal{F}} \delta_T(|T|[v(T)/|T|]) = \sum_{T \in \mathcal{F}} \left(1/\binom{|N|-1}{|T|-1}\right)\left(\sum_{A_i \in T}(q/|T|)\right) = \sum_{A_i \in N}\left(\sum_{T \in \mathcal{F}, T \ni A_i}\left(1/\binom{|N|-1}{|T|-1}\right)(q/|T|)\right)$ $= (q/|T|)\sum_{A_i \in N}\left(\sum_{T \in \mathcal{F},\, T \ni A_i}\left(1/\binom{|N|-1}{|T|-1}\right)\right) = (q/|T|)\sum_{A_i \in N}(1) = (v(S)/|S|)|N|$. The last step follows from the fact that $v(T) = v(S) = q$ and from the fact that $|T| = |S|$ for all $T \in \mathcal{F}$. Since the coalition $S \subseteq N$ is arbitrary, the family $\mathcal{F} = \{T \subseteq N \mid |T| = |S|\}$ is arbitrary as well. Therefore, the core is non-empty if and only if $v(N) \geq \sum_{T \in \mathcal{F}} \delta_T (|T| (v(T)/|T|)) = (v(S)/|S|)|N|$, that is, $v(S)/|S| \leq v(N)/|N|$ for any non-empty $S \subseteq N$. □

The quantity $v(S)/|S|$ can be regarded as the average pay-off that a player can expect when he is in the coalition S. Thus, Proposition 16 says that for non-emptiness of the core of a symmetric game, it is necessary and sufficient that the average pay-off a player can receive in any coalition S cannot exceed the corresponding average he can receive in the grand coalition. This, therefore, provides an incentive for formation of the grand coalition in a symmetric game.

3.5 Reasonable Set and Core Cover as Core Catchers

The objective of this section is to present a discussion on two sets related to the core, the reasonable set and the core cover. They are core catchers in the sense that the core of the game is a subset of each of these sets. It is unreasonable that any player in a game will claim more than the maximum marginal contribution he can make to any coalition because this is the maximum threat that he can exert against the coalition. An individually rational pay-off vector that fulfils this condition is called reasonable (Milnor 1952).

Definition 25 A pay-off vector x associated with the game $v \in G^N$ is called *reasonable* if for all A_i,

$$v(\{A_i\}) \leq x_{A_i} \leq \max_{S \subseteq N \setminus \{A_i\}} (v(S \cup \{A_i\}) - v(S)) = b_{\max}^{A_i}(v).$$

Thus, as stated, for reasonableness of a pay-off vector x, in addition to individual rationality $v(\{A_i\}) \leq x_{A_i}$, we also need the boundary condition $x_{A_i} \leq b_{\max}^{A_i}(v)$.

For any arbitrary $v \in G^N$, let $RE(v)$ be the set of all pay-off vectors that are reasonable, that is, $RE(v) = \{x \in \Re^n \mid v(\{A_i\}) \leq x_{A_i} \leq b_{\max}^{A_i}(v)\}$. The following proposition shows that $RE(v)$ is a core catcher.

Proposition 16 For any arbitrary $v \in G^N$, $C(v) \subseteq RE(v)$.

Proof: Consider any game $v \in G^N$ and let $x \in C(v)$. Since $x \in I(v)$, it is an imputation which by definition is individually rational, and hence $x_{A_i} \geq v(\{A_i\})$ for any $A_i \in N$. For x to be in the reasonable set $RE(v)$, we only need to show that $x_{A_i} \leq b_{\max}^{A_i}(v)$ for any $A_i \in N$. Take any $A_i \in N$. Then, using $x(N) = v(N)$ and $x(N \setminus \{A_i\}) \geq v(N \setminus \{A_i\})$, we get $x_{A_i} = x(N) - x(N \setminus \{A_i\}) = v(N) - x(N \setminus \{A_i\}) \leq v(N) - v(N \setminus \{A_i\}) \leq b_{\max}^{A_i}(v)$. Therefore, x is reasonable, that is, $x \in RE(v)$. Since the selection $x \in C(v)$ was arbitrary, it follows that $C(v) \subseteq RE(v)$. □

Example 9 In order to demonstrate that a reasonable pay-off vector need not be a core element, consider the game in Example 5. For this game, the pay-off vector $(x_{A_1}, x_{A_2}, x_{A_3}) = (3, 3, 3)$ is individually rational and satisfies the boundary condition $x_{A_i} \leq b_{\max}^{A_i}(v)$ for all $A_i \in N = \{A_1, A_2, A_3\}$. However, the core of this game being empty does not contain $(3, 3, 3)$ as an element.

For any $A_i \in N$, let $\Delta_{A_i}(N, v) = v(N) - v(N \setminus \{A_i\})$ be the marginal contribution of player A_i to the grand coalition. Implicit under this notion is the given ordering of the players in the grand coalition. This pay-off is the ideally perfect pay-off or Utopian pay-off for A_i because if he demands more, the other players can argue not to include him in the grand coalition on the ground that he is demanding more than his legitimate claim. We write $\Delta(N, v)$ for the n-coordinated vector $[\Delta_{A_1}(N, v), \Delta_{A_2}(N, v), \ldots, \Delta_{A_n}(N, v)]$.

Definition 26 For any arbitrary $v \in G^N$ and any non-empty coalition $S \subseteq N$ containing the player A_i, the *remainder* $R(S, A_i)$ of A_i is defined as $R(S, A_i) = v(S) - \sum_{A_j \in S \setminus \{A_i\}} \Delta_{A_j}(N, v)$.

That is, all players other than A_i in the coalition S receive their Utopian payments and the amount left out in $v(S)$, the worth of the coalition, after these payments is the remainder of A_i in S. The minimum right pay-off $m_{A_i}(v)$ of player A_i is then defined as the maximum value of this remainder, where the maximum is taken over all coalitions of which A_i is a member. Formally,

$$m_{A_i}(v) = \max_{S, S \ni A_i} R(S, A_i). \tag{3.2}$$

Since in the coalition containing A_i, all players other than A_i receive their Utopian pay-offs, A_i can claim at least $m_{A_i}(v)$ in the grand coalition. This amount represents the maximum pay-off that a player can get by forming a coalition and promising each of the other players in the coalition his ideally perfect demand. It provides a justification for the minimum right pay-off. We denote the n-coordinated vector $[m_{A_1}(v), m_{A_2}(v), \ldots, m_{A_n}(v)]$ by $m(v)$.

We now introduce a notation, which we need for the next definition. For any two $n - -$coordinated vectors a and b, $a \leq b$ means that each coordinate of a is not greater than that of b.

Definition 27 For any arbitrary $v \in G^N$, the *core cover* of v, denoted by $CC(V)$, is the set of all imputations associated with v that lie between $m(v)$ and $\Delta(N, v)$, that is, $CC(v) = \{x \in I(v) \mid m(v) \leq x \leq \Delta(N, v)\}$.

Thus, the core cover is one set of imputations that are bounded below by the minimum right pay-off vector and bounded above by the ideally perfect pay-off vector. Each of these two boundary vectors represents a particular notion of value judgement. A pay-off vector in the core cover can be regarded as a compromise between $m(v)$ and $\Delta(N, v)$ (Branzei, Dimitrov and Tijs 2008). The following proposition demonstrates that $CC(v)$ is also a core catcher.

Proposition 17 For any arbitrary $v \in G^N$, $C(v) \subseteq CC(v)$.

Proof: Consider any game $v \in G^N$ and let $x \in C(v)$. Take any $A_i \in N$. Using $x(N) = v(N)$ and $x(N \setminus \{A_i\}) \geq v(N \setminus \{A_i\})$, we get $x_{A_i} = x(N) - x(N \setminus \{A_i\}) = v(N) - x(N \setminus \{A_i\}) \leq v(N) - v(N \setminus \{A_i\}) = \Delta_{A_i}(N, v)$. Hence, $x_{A_i} \leq \Delta_{A_i}(N, v)$ for each $A_i \in N$. Using this inequality, we get the following: for any non-empty $S \subset N$ and each $A_i \in S$, $x(S \setminus \{A_i\}) \leq \sum_{A_j \in S \setminus \{A_i\}} \Delta_{A_j}(N, v)$. Hence, $x_{A_i} = x(S) - x(S \setminus \{A_i\}) \geq v(S) - \sum_{A_j \in S \setminus \{A_i\}} \Delta_{A_j}(N, v) = R(S, A_i)$. Therefore, $x_{A_i} \geq \max_{S:S \ni A_i} R(S, A_i) = m_{A_i}(v)$. Hence, $m(v) \leq x \leq \Delta(N, v)$, implying that $x \in CC(v)$. Since the selection $x \in C(v)$ was arbitrary, it follows that $C(v) \subseteq CC(v)$. □

Proposition 17 indicates that a core element being also an element of the core cover must give each player at least his minimum right pay-off but not more than his ideally perfect demand. Chapter 6 presents further discussion on core catchers.

3.6   Some Variants of the Core

In this section, we analyze some variants of the core that have been suggested in the literature. Each of these variants has its own merits. The first variant we discuss is the ϵ-core, which is a generalization of the core (Shapley and Shubik 1963; 1966). The ϵ-core may be non-empty even if the core is empty.

Definition 28   Let ϵ be a real number. The *ϵ-core* of any arbitrary game $v \in G^N$ is defined as

$$C_\epsilon(v) = \{x \in \Re^n \mid x(N) = v(N) \text{ and } v(S) \leq x(S) + \epsilon \, \forall S \subset N, S \neq \varnothing\}.$$

Clearly, $C_0(v) = C(v)$. The free parameter ϵ is introduced to enlarge the core. $C_\epsilon(v)$ may be interpreted as the set of all Pareto efficient pay-off vectors associated with v that cannot be improved upon by any coalition of players if the coalition formation involves a cost of the magnitude ϵ (bonus of $-\epsilon$ if $\epsilon < 0$). If formation of a coalition $S \subset N$ by leaving the grand coalition entails a cost of $\epsilon > 0$, then the grand coalition can remain stable even if S receives a smaller share than $v(S)$, given that the constraint $v(S) \leq x(S) + \epsilon$ is satisfied. That is, the grand coalition remains stable as long as the coalitional pay-off does not exceed the sum of pay-offs of players in S and the cost of formation of the coalition. Therefore, we can interpret ϵ as a threshold parameter that can block manipulations resulting in instability of the grand coalition. The ϵ-core will be non-empty for large

ϵ and empty for small ϵ. For $\epsilon_1 < \epsilon_2$, $C_{\epsilon_1}(v) \subset C_{\epsilon_2}(v)$. In order to be a substitute for the core, the ϵ-core should be non-empty and ϵ should not be large. The major appeal of the ϵ-core is that it can be used to analyze games whose cores are empty.

Example 10 Let us consider the three-player majority game (see Proposition 6). An allocation $x = \left(x_{A_1}, x_{A_2}, x_{A_3}\right)$ will be in the core $C(v)$ if and only if $x_{A_1} \geq 0, x_{A_2} \geq 0, x_{A_3} \geq 0, x_{A_1} + x_{A_2} \geq 1, x_{A_2} + x_{A_3} \geq 1, x_{A_1} + x_{A_3} \geq 1$ and $x_{A_1} + x_{A_2} + x_{A_3} = 1$. Substituting $x_{A_1} = 1 - x_{A_2} - x_{A_3}$ into $x_{A_1} + x_{A_3} \geq 1$, we get $x_{A_2} \leq 0$. This combined with $x_{A_2} \geq 0$ gives $x_{A_2} = 0$. Similarly, $x_{A_1} = x_{A_3} = 0$. Hence, the core is empty. However, for $\epsilon = 1/3$, the ϵ-core of this game is non-empty and contains the single element $(1/3, 1/3, 1/3)$.

An alternative solution concept whose definition relies on ϵ-core is the least core (Maschler, Peleg and Shapley 1979).

Definition 29 The *least core* of a game $v \in G^N$ is the intersection of all non-empty ϵ-cores of the game.

The least core can alternatively be defined as follows. Let $\hat{\epsilon}$ be the smallest value of ϵ such that $C_\epsilon(v)$ is non-empty. Then, $C_{\hat{\epsilon}}(v)$ is the least core of the game $v \in G^N$. Thus, the least core is a core-type non-empty solution concept.

Equal division of value is often an interesting issue of investigation, particularly in a symmetric game. An imputation is said to be in the equal division core of a game if no coalition can divide its value equally among its members and in the process assigns more to each member than what they can receive under the imputation. Formally,

---

Definition 30 The *equal division core* of a game $v \in G^N$ is the set

$$EDC(v) = \left\{ x \in I(v) \mid \nexists\, S \text{ such that } S \neq \emptyset \text{ and } \frac{v(S)}{|S|} > x_{A_i} \text{ for all } A_i \in S \right\}.$$

It is evident that the core of a game is contained in its equal division core (for further discussion, refer Bhattacharya 2004).

In order to discuss the next variant, assume that the game $v \in G^N$ is not monotone. In such a case, there may exist non-empty coalitions S and $\hat{S}$ such that $S \subset \hat{S}$ and $v(S) > v(\hat{S})$. This indicates that under an allocation x, if $v(S) > \sum_{A_i \in \hat{S}} x_{A_i} \geq v(\hat{S})$ holds, then it will be disliked by the members of $\hat{S}$ (Drechsel and Kimms 2010). An allocation corresponding to $v \in G^N$ is in the sub-coalition perfect core $SCP(v)$ if the pay-off of a coalition S in the grand coalition is not higher than the pay-off of any super-coalition $\hat{S}$ of S. Formally,

---

Definition 31 The *sub-coalition perfect core* of a game $v \in G^N$ is the set

$$SPC(v) = \{x \in \Re^n \mid x(N) = v(N) \text{ and } v(S) \leq \sum_{A_i \in \hat{S}} x_{A_i} \forall S \subset \hat{S} \subseteq N, S \neq \varnothing\}.$$

The core of a game contains the sub-coalition perfect core and the two sets coincide if the game is monotone.

3.7 Stable Sets

The stable set was introduced by von Neumann and Morgenstern (1944). Suppose in a game $v \in G^N$, a coalition S is currently not satisfied with the division of the grand coalition value $v(N)$. It can credibly object by suggesting a stable division x of $v(N)$ which turns out to be better for all members of S. It can as well take a threat strategy to implement $(x)_{A_i \in S}$, the relevant part of x that correspond to the members of S, on its own. Stability of such an objection ensures that it can leash any process of further objections raised by other coalitions. This is the central idea underlying a stable set. It is a set of stable allocations that satisfies two postulates:

(i) No coalition has a credible objection against any stable allocation.

(ii) Some coalition has a credible objection against any non-stable allocation.

Note that the basic concept here is the set concept, whereas in the case of the core, the properties of a pay-off vector alone determine whether it is in the core. While the core is a single set of imputations, a game may have several stable sets. Thus, in this case, stability is a characteristic of sets, not of single pay-off vectors.

Definition 32 For any game $v \in G^N$, a subset $K(v)$ of the set of imputations $I(v)$ is called a *stable set* if the following conditions are satisfied:

(i) For $x, y \in K(v)$, neither can dominate the other.

(ii) For $z \in I(v) \setminus K(v)$, there is an $x \in K(v)$ such that x dominates z.

The first condition is called *internal stability*. It treats all imputations in $K(v)$ identically in the sense that no imputation in $K(v)$ can dominate another imputation in $K(v)$. The second condition is known as *external stability*. It asserts that an imputation outside $K(v)$ is unlikely to be established because it is dominated by an imputation in $K(v)$. Hence, there will be a tendency to shift to an imputation in $K(v)$.

Example 11 In order to illustrate the concept, let us consider the three-player majority game (see Proposition 6). One stable set of this game is $K_1(v) = \{(1/2,1/2,0), (1/2,0,1/2), (0,1/2,1/2)\}$. Since no imputation can dominate another via the single-player coalition and the grand coalition (Propositions 8 and 9), none of the three vectors in this set dominates each other. Note also that the vector $(1/3,1/3,1/3)$ is an imputation of this game and each imputation in $K_1(v)$ dominates it via a two-player coalition. For instance, $(1/2,1/2,0)$ dominates it via the coalition $\{A_1, A_2\}$. A second stable set of this game is $K_2(v) = \{x \in \Re_+^3 \mid x_{A_1} + x_{A_2} = 1, x_{A_3} = 0\}$, where for any positive integer m, $\Re_+^m$ is the non-negative part of the m-dimensional Euclidean space $\Re^m$.

The next theorem establishes a relationship between the dominance core and stable sets of a game.

Theorem 2 For any game $v \in G^N$, let $K(v)$ be a stable set of v. Then

(i) $DC(v) \subseteq K(v)$.

(ii) If $DC(v)$ is a stable set, then it is the unique stable set of the game.

(iii) If the game possesses two or more stable sets, then none of them can be a proper subset of another.

Proof: (i) Let $y \in I(v) \setminus K(v)$. Then by external stability, there is an imputation $x \in K(v)$ such that x dominates y. The pay-off vectors in $DC(v)$ are undominated. Hence, $y \notin DC(v)$. Therefore, $y \in I(v) \setminus DC(v)$. Since the initial selection $y \in I(v) \setminus K(v)$ was arbitrary, we can say that $I(v) \setminus K(v) \subseteq I(v) \setminus DC(v)$, from which it follows that $DC(v) \subseteq K(v)$.

(ii) Let $DC(v)$ and $K(v)$ be two stable sets of the game v. Assume that $K(v) \setminus DC(v)$ is non-empty and let $y \in K(v) \setminus DC(v)$. By the external stability of $DC(v)$, there exists $x \in DC(v)(\subset K(v))$ such that x dominates y. This contradicts the assumption that $K(v)$ is a stable set. Hence, $K(v) \setminus DC(v)$ is an empty set. This along with the fact that $DC(v) \subseteq K(v)$ shows that $K(v) = DC(v)$.

(iii) Let $K_1(v)$ and $K_2(v)$ be two stable sets of the game v. Assume without loss of generality that $K_1(v) \subset K_2(v)$. Take $y \in K_2(v) \setminus K_1(v)$.

Then using arguments similar to that employed in the proof of part (ii) of the theorem, we can show that this contradicts the assumption that $K_2(v)$ is a stable set. Hence, $K_1(v) \not\subset K_2(v)$. Similarly, $K_2(v) \not\subset K_1(v)$.   □

Part (i) of Theorem 2 combined with Proposition 11 shows that for any game $v \in G^N$, $C(v) \subseteq DC(v) \subseteq K(v)$. Part (ii) of Theorem 2 provides a sufficient condition for uniqueness of the stable set. By Proposition 12 and part (ii) of Theorem 2, it also follows that if the game is super-additive and $D(v)$ is a stable set, then the core, dominance core and stable set of the game coincide. Finally, part (iii) of Theorem 2 indicates that each stable set of a game represents a particular type of behaviour.

3.8   Applications

This section provides some applications of the core as a solution concept of cooperative games to some real-life problems. We subdivide our presentation into three subsections.

3.8.1   The Coase theorem

Often activities of an economic agent affect activities of one or more agents in ways that are not taken into account by the operation of the market. We say that externalities occur in such situations. In other words, the side effects of the economic activities of some individuals on others are externalities. When the production of one firm affects the choice of a consumer or production activities of another firm, we say that production externalities exist.

Suppose two chemical firms F_I and F_{II}, upstream firms, are located on the same river. These firms dump their wastes into the river, while the downstream firm F_L, a laundry, uses river water for washing clothes. That is, the upstream firm imposes a pollution cost on the downstream firm. If the upstream firms increase their outputs (hence wastes), the downstream firm's output suffers. With dirtier water, it needs more labour and more chemicals (and hence more cost) to wash the same number of clothes. This is an example of external diseconomy in production. The upstream firms can pay for the damage caused to the downstream firm or they can refuse to make any payment. Each of these two possibilities can be formulated as a coalition form game using the interactions among the firms. We refer to these two games as the liability and non-liability games respectively.

According to the Coase (1960) theorem, given any imperfection in the market that gives rise to an inefficient state, if transaction costs are negligible, negotiations among the concerned parties will lead to the attainment of an efficient state. Following Benoît and Kornhauser (2002), we construct numerical examples to show that the core of the liability game is non-empty, whereas that of the non-liability game is empty. This, therefore, shows a direct application of the Coase theorem since under cooperation among the firms, there is a solution to the resolution of the externality problem. On the other hand, there is no solution to the problem if the firms do not cooperate.

The example we consider is the following. The downstream firm operating on its own earns a profit of 9. If either of the upstream firm operates, a pollution cost of 2 is imposed on the downstream firm. However, if both of them operate, either independently or jointly, this cost increases to 8. Under independent operation, each of them earns a profit of 1 and if they operate jointly, a profit of 7 is earned. The player set is $N = \{F_I, F_{II}, F_L\}$. Let v be the non-liability game. Then, $v(\{F_I\}) = v(\{F_{II}\}) = 1$ and $v(\{F_L\}) = 9 - 8 = 1$, since in this case F_I and F_{II} are non-liable and they both operate. Next, because of cooperation of F_I and non-cooperation of F_{II}, $v(\{F_I, F_L\}) = 9 - 2 = 7$. Similarly, $v(\{F_{II}, F_L\}) = 7$. $v(\{F_I, F_{II}\}) = 7$. Finally, $v(\{F_I, F_{II}, F_L\}) = 9$, since in this case there is cooperation of F_I and F_{II} with F_L. Now, a pay-off vector $x = (x_{F_I}, x_{F_{II}}, x_{F_L})$ will be in the core if and only if $x_{F_I} \geq 1$, $x_{F_{II}} \geq 1$, $x_{F_L} \geq 1$, $x_{F_I} + x_{F_{II}} \geq 7$, $x_{F_I} + x_{F_L} \geq 7$, $x_{F_{II}} + x_{F_L} \geq 7$ and $x_{F_I} + x_{F_{II}} + x_{F_L} = 9$. Substituting $x_{F_I} = 9 - x_{F_{II}} - x_{F_L}$ into $x_{F_I} + x_{F_L} \geq 7$, we get $x_{F_{II}} \leq 2$. Similarly, $x_{F_I} \leq 2$ and $x_{F_L} \leq 2$. Hence, $x_{F_I} + x_{F_{II}} + x_{F_L} \leq 6$ which contradicts the condition $x_{F_I} + x_{F_{II}} + x_{F_L} = 9$. Therefore, the core of the non-liability game is empty.

Any informal negotiation between the laundry and the polluting firms will not be stable. For instance, suppose F_L decides to offer a bribe of 3.5 to each of the upstream firms for not operating. Such an arrangement is unstable because one of F_I and F_{II} may proceed for a separate agreement between itself and F_L since its return from this separate agreement will be higher than 3.5. This kind of instability leads to disruption of arrangements made through informal negotiation. It is similar to the instability of a cartel or collusive arrangement in an oligopolistic model.

In the liability game u, the court compensates any damage done to the laundry, where the compensation is based on the maximum possible return to any coalition containing the laundry. Consequently, $u(\{F_I\})$

$= u(\{F_{II}\}) = u(\{F_I, F_{II}\}) = 0, u(\{F_L\}) = u(\{F_I, F_L\}) = u(\{F_{II}, F_L\}) = u(\{F_I, F_{II}, F_L\}) = 9$. It can be seen that the unique point of the core of this game is $x = (x_{F_I}, x_{F_{II}}, x_{F_L}) = (0, 0, 9)$.

3.8.2 The market game

Assume that the player set is $N = \{A_1, A_2, \ldots, A_n\}$. Each of the players possesses an initial endowment vector of k goods that can be used as inputs for producing a consumption good. Each player A_i has a non-negative valued production function f_{A_i} defined on $x^{A_i} = \left(x_1^{A_i}, x_2^{A_i}, \ldots, x_k^{A_i}\right)$, that is, $f_{A_i}\left(x_1^{A_i}, x_2^{A_i}, \ldots, x_k^{A_i}\right)$, where $x_r^{A_i} \geq 0$ is the quantity of input r used by player A_i for producing the consumption good. The initial endowment input vector of player A_i is denoted by $\omega^{A_i} = \left(\omega_1^{A_i}, \omega_2^{A_i}, \ldots, \omega_k^{A_i}\right)$, where $\omega_r^{A_i} \geq 0$ for all $r \in \{1, \ldots, k\}$ and all $A_i \in N$. The objective of each coalition S in the game is to produce the maximum amount $v(S)$ of the consumption good using the total amounts of different inputs that the coalition have. Formally, for any non-empty coalition $S \subseteq N$,

$$v(S) = \max\left\{\sum_{A_i \in S} f_{A_i}\left(x_1^{A_i}, x_2^{A_i}, \ldots, x_k^{A_i}\right) \mid \sum_{A_i \in S} x^{A_i} = \sum_{A_i \in S} \omega^{A_i}\right\}. \quad (3.3)$$

The feasibility condition $\sum_{A_i \in S} x^{A_i} = \sum_{A_i \in S} \omega^{A_i}$ ensures that the total amount of any input r used by the coalition S is same as the total amount of the corresponding input that the members of coalition initially possess, where $1 \leq r \leq k$ is arbitrary. The essential idea underlying the definition of the function v in (3.3) is that there may be exchange of inputs among the members of the coalition S so that the total output of S as a whole is maximized. This exchange is an indication of cooperation among the members of S. Following Shapley and Shubik (1966, 1969), we now have:

Definition 33 Assume that f_{A_i} is continuous and concave for all $A_i \in N$. Then the game defined by (3.3) is called a *market game*.

The domain of each f_{A_i} in (3.3) is a compact (closed and bounded) set. A closed set contains its boundaries. The sum $\sum_{A_i \in S} f_{A_i}$ is continuous on the same domain. A continuous function defined on a compact set attains its maximum (Rudin 1976, p.89). Hence for any coalition $S \subseteq N$, $v(S)$ in (3.3) exists.

The following example, which is taken from Shapley and Shubik (1969a), illustrates the market game.

Example 12 Let $N = N_1 \cup N_2$, where $N_1 \cap N_2 = \varnothing$ and N_1 and N_2 are non-empty. Assume that $k = 2$, for any $A_i \in N_1$, $\omega^{A_i} = (1,0)$ and for any $A_j \in N_2$, $\omega^{A_j} = (0,1)$. Finally, for any $A_{i'} \in N$, let $f_{A_{i'}}\left(x_1^{A_{i'}}, x_2^{A_{i'}}\right) = \min\left\{x_1^{A_{i'}}, x_2^{A_{i'}}\right\}$. Then the corresponding market game is given by $v(S) = \min\left\{|S \cap N_1|, |S \cap N_2|\right\}$ for all $S \subseteq N$.

The following theorem of Shapley and Shubik (1969) shows that a market game has a non-empty core.

Theorem 3 The core of a market game is non-empty.

Proof: Let Φ be a balanced family with the corresponding balancing weights $\{\delta_S\}_{S \in \Phi}$ and consider $v(S) = \sum_{A_i \in S} f_{A_i}(x_S^{A_i})$, where $x_S^{A_i}$ is the point of the feasible set $\left\{y^{A_i} \in \Re_+^k \mid \sum_{A_i \in S} y_S^{A_i} = \sum_{A_i \in S} \omega_S^{A_i}\right\}$ at which $\sum_{A_i \in S} f_{A_i}(y^{A_i})$ attains its maximum. Let us define $x^{A_i} = \sum_{S \in \Phi, S \ni A_i} \delta_S x_S^{A_i}$. Then it follows that the sum $\sum_{A_i \in N} x^{A_i} = \sum_{A_i \in N} \left(\sum_{S \in \Phi, S \ni A_i} \delta_S x_S^{A_i}\right)$

$= \sum_{S \in \Phi} \left(\sum_{A_i \in S} \delta_S x_S^{A_i}\right) = \sum_{S \in \Phi} \delta_S \left(\sum_{A_i \in S} x_S^{A_i}\right) = \sum_{S \in \Phi} \delta_S \left(\sum_{A_i \in S} \omega^{A_i}\right)$

$= \sum_{S \in \Phi} \left(\sum_{A_i \in S} \delta_S \omega^{A_i}\right) = \sum_{A_i \in N} \left(\sum_{S \in \Phi, S \ni A_i} \delta_S \omega^{A_i}\right) = \sum_{A_i \in N} \omega^{A_i}$

$\left(\sum_{S \in \Phi, S \ni A_i} \delta_S\right) = \sum_{A_i \in N} \omega^{A_i}$, where $\sum_{A_i \in N} \omega^{A_i} \left(\sum_{S \in \Phi, S \ni A_i} \delta_S\right)$

$= \sum_{A_i \in N} \omega^{A_i}$ follows from the assumption that Φ is balanced, that is from $\sum_{S \in \Phi, S \ni A_i} \delta_S = 1$ for all $A_i \in N$. Further, x_{A_i}s' are non-negative since they are averages of non-negative vectors using positive weights. Consequently, $(x^{A_i})_{A_i \in N}$ is a feasible allocation for N. By the definition of v, we then have $v(N) \geq \sum_{A_i \in N} f_{A_i}(x^{A_i})$.

Since f_{A_i} is a concave function, using Jensen's inequality (Royden 1968, p.110), it follows that $f_{A_i}(x^{A_i}) \geq \sum_{S \in \Phi, S \ni A_i} \delta_S f_{A_i}(x_S^{A_i})$. Therefore, we have $v(N) \geq \sum_{A_i \in N} f_{A_i}(x^{A_i}) \geq \sum_{A_i \in N} \left(\sum_{S \in \Phi, S \ni A_i} \delta_S f_{A_i}(x_S^{A_i})\right) = \sum_{S \in \Phi} \delta_S (\sum_{A_i \in S} f_{A_i}(x_S^{A_i})) = \sum_{S \in \Phi} \delta_S v(S)$.

Therefore, by the Bondareva−Shapley Theorem it follows that the core of the market game is non-empty. $\qquad \square$

3.8.3 The travelling salesman game

Consider a travelling salesman who has to travel through a bunch of cities in order to enlarge the distributional channels of a product keeping at the same time his expenses on travelling minimal. This is a cost minimizing game where the salesman starts and finishes at the same point and visits each city exactly once. It is known as the travelling salesman game. Finding the best possible round-trip in the sense of minimum cost is the issue of investigation. Our presentation of this game follows Curiel (1997).

The origin of the travelling salesman game is the travelling salesman optimization problem in combinatorial analysis. The problem can be stated as follows. Given a directed graph with weights on the arcs, it is necessary to find a cycle that visits each node exactly once and has minimal weight. The weight of a cycle is given by the sum of the weights of its arcs. A directed graph is a set of nodes connected by edges with specific directions associated with the edges. In our case, all vertices except one can be associated with the players (cities) and the weights represent intercity travelling costs. This is a cooperative cost game. Let $N = \{A_1, A_2, \ldots, A_n\}$ be the set of all cities. We denote the vertex that does not correspond to any city by A_0. In this game, for any given set of cities $S \subseteq N$, a coalition, a tour for the salesman has to be designed such that the salesman starts at A_0, visits each members of S exactly once and returns to A_0, and the cost of the tour is minimized. Equivalently, we say that the members of the coalition S desire to find a cost minimizing tour for the travelling salesman on the complete graph whose set of vertices is $S \cup \{A_0\}$. In a complete graph, an edge connects each pair of vertices. Given $S = \{A_1, A_2, \ldots, A_k\}$, a tour on $S \cup \{A_0\}$ can be represented by a permutation of S. We denote this permutation by $f(S)$. That is, the elements of $f(S)$ are simply a reordering of the elements of S. More precisely, starting at A_0, the salesman first visits $f(A_1)$, then he visits $f(A_2)$ and so on. The final city he visits is $f(A_k)$, from where he comes back to A_0. The cost of the tour is $w_{A_0 f(A_1)} + w_{f(A_1)f(A_2)} + \cdots + w_{f(A_{k-1})f(A_k)} + w_{f(A_k)A_0}$, where w_{pq} is the intercity travelling cost when the cities involved are p and q, that is, the cost of travelling from city p to city q. Let $F(S)$ be the set of all permutations of S. Then, cost of the coalition S is given by

$$c(S) = \min_{f \in F(S)} \left\{ w_{A_0 f(A_1)} + w_{f(A_1)f(A_2)} + \cdots + w_{f(A_{k-1})f(A_k)} + w_{f(A_k)A_0} \right\}.$$
(3.4)

Thus, $c(S)$ is the minimum cost with which the salesman can travel all the cities in S and this minimum is achieved over all orderings of the locations of the cities in S. The game described by (3.4) is called a *travelling salesman game*.

Let c be a travelling salesman game with intercity costs w_{pq}. Let a_p and b_q respectively be taxes for leaving city p and entering city q, where $p, q \in N_0 \equiv N \cup \{A_0\}$ and $p \neq q$. Define a travelling salesman game $\bar{c}$ with intercity costs $w_{pq} + a_p + b_q$. Then the following proposition, which is taken from Curiel (1997), can be stated.

Proposition 18 Let c be a travelling salesman game with intercity costs w_{pq}. Then there exists a function $s(w)$ that depends on the intercity costs such that the travelling salesman game $\bar{c}$ is minimal balanced if and only if $a_0 + b_0 \geq s(w)$.

Proof: The game $\bar{c}$ is balanced if and only if $\bar{c}(N) \leq \sum_{S \in \Phi} \delta_S \bar{c}(S)$, where Φ is any balanced collection with unique balancing weights $\{\delta_S\}_{S \in \Phi}$. Now, $\sum_{S \in \Phi} \delta_S \bar{c}(S) - \bar{c}(N) = \sum_{S \in \Phi} \delta_S [c(S) + a(S_0) + b(S_0)] - [c(N) + a(N_0) + b(N_0)] = \sum_{S \in \Phi} \delta_S [c(S) + a_0 + b_0] - [c(N) + a_0 + b_0]$. Hence, $\sum_{S \in \Phi} \delta_S \bar{c}(S) - \bar{c}(N) \geq 0$ if and only if $a_0 + b_0 \geq ([c(N) - \sum_{S \in \Phi} \delta_S c(S)] / [\sum_{S \in \Phi} \delta_S - 1])$. Define $s(w) = \max ([c(N) - \sum_{S \in \Phi} \delta_S c(S)] / [\sum_{S \in \Phi} \delta_S - 1])$, where the maximum is defined over all minimal balanced collections. Since the number of minimally balanced collections is finite, $s(w)$ is well defined. Therefore, the inequality $a_0 + b_0 \geq s(w)$ is necessary and sufficient for balancedness of the game $\bar{c}$. □

Since the core of a balanced game is non-empty, the condition $a_0 + b_0 \geq s(w)$ can be regarded as a necessary and sufficient condition for the core of the game $\bar{c}$ to be non-empty. This theorem says that we can always transform a travelling salesman game into a similar game by adding entry and exit taxes so that the transformed game has a non-empty core. Computational issues related to a travelling salesman game are discussed in Chapter 11.

Exercises

3.1 (a) Show that in a coalition form game $v \in G^N$, an allocation x satisfying the efficiency condition $x(N) = v(N)$ is in the core of v if and only if for every non-empty coalition S, $v(N) - v(N \setminus S) \leq x(S)$.

(b) Interpret the inequality $v(N) - v(N \setminus S) \leq x(S)$ in terms of the marginal contribution $v(N) - v(N \setminus S)$ of coalition S.

3.2 Identify the set of imputations for the building rental game considered in Exercise 2.1 of Chapter 2. What is the core of this game?

3.3 Let $v \in G^N$ be strategically equivalent to $u \in G^N$. How are the cores of the two games related?

3.4 Show that the core of a game $v \in G^N$ contains its sub-coalition perfect core.

3.5 Consider a coalition form game $v \in G^N$, where for any coalition S, $v(S) = |S|$. Develop a necessary and sufficient condition for the core of this game to be non-empty.

3.6 In a three-player game v with the player set $\{A_1, A_2, A_3\}$, $v(\{A_1\}) = v(\{A_2\}) = v(\{A_3\}) = 0$, $v(\{A_1, A_2\}) = v(\{A_1, A_3\}) = v(\{A_2, A_3\}) = \theta$ where $0 < \theta < 1$, and $v(\{A_1, A_2, A_3\}) = 1$. Show that for

   (a) $\theta > 2/3$, the core is empty,

   (b) $\theta = 2/3$, the core contains exactly one element, and

   (c) for $\theta < 2/3$, the core contains infinitely many elements.

3.7 In the game considered in Exercise 3.6, identify a stable set in each of the three cases (a), (b) and (c).

3.8 Let the game $v \in G^N$ be balanced. Show that any game $u \in G^N$ which is strategically equivalent to v is also balanced.

3.9 Determine the core of the left shoe−right shoe game defined in Chapter 2 if (i) $|R| = |L| = 2$ and (ii) $|R| = 2$, $|L| = 3$.

3.10 Let $v \in G^N$ be strategically equivalent to $u \in G^N$. Assume also that v is a market game. Will u be a market game as well?

CHAPTER 4

The Bargaining Set, Kernel and Nucleolus

4.1 Introduction

The bargaining set was introduced by Aumann and Maschler (1964). The central idea underlying this solution concept is that a player may abstain from objecting to a proposed allocation because of the apprehension that the objection might lead to a counter-objection by another player. A player definitely tries to enter a firmly established coalition with the objective that his pay-off will be maximized. An allocation in the current context is regarded as firmly established or stable if all the objections against it can be tackled by counter-objections. Thus, it is not sufficient for a coalition of some players to only improve on a particular allocation to raise objections against it. It is also necessary to guarantee that there does not exist any possibility for members of that coalition to be allured by another coalition that can improve on the allocation proposed by the first coalition as an alternative to the originally proposed allocation.

Davis and Maschler (1965) proposed the kernel as a solution concept to cooperative game theory problems. Essential to the definition of the kernel is the coalitional excess, the difference between the pay-off a coalition can achieve on its own and the sum of the pay-offs of the members of the coalition that the proposed allocation assigns to the members. This excess is a measure of the size of the complaint in the sense that it determines the amount by which the coalition as a group falls short of its potential under the allocation. The kernel can be interpreted with respect to effective objections and counter-objections that are stated in terms of excesses and personal minimums. An individually rational pay-off configuration which is in the kernel is also in the bargaining set. Davis and Maschler (1965) also introduced the pre-kernel as a solution concept. The central idea underlying this notion is that any pair of players is in equilibrium in the sense of equality of maximal excesses of coalitions containing one player but not containing the other. Therefore, corresponding to each pre-kernel element, the surplus vector cannot be made more egalitarian by any transfer of utility between arbitrary pair of players. This in turn gives an egalitarian flavour to the pre-kernel as a solution concept for cooperative games with two-player coalitions only.

Another interesting solution concept for cooperative games is the nucleolus, introduced by David Schmeidler in 1969. It is a unique pay-off vector included in the kernel. In it, the excesses for all coalitions are made as small as possible. It lexicographically minimizes the maximal excess. Loosely speaking, it makes the most dissatisfied coalitions as little dissatisfied as possible, the second most dissatisfied coalitions as little dissatisfied as possible, and so on.

The next section of the chapter analyzes the bargaining set. Section 4.3 is concerned with the kernel and pre-kernel. A discussion on the nucleolus and pre-nucleolus is presented in Section 4.4. In Section 4.5, as an applied example, we analyze the bankruptcy problem which deals with a fair way of dividing a firm's estate among its creditors when it gets liquidated.

4.2   The Bargaining Set

The bargaining set consists of all individually rational pay-off configurations such that no coalition has any complaint against them. The precise meaning of complaint relies on the notions' objections and counter-objections. To define these notions formally, we first define a coalition structure.

Definition 34 Given a player set $N = \{A_1, \ldots, A_n\}$ in a coalition form game $v \in G^N$, a *coalition structure* $\Omega = \{S_1, \ldots, S_k\}$ is a partition of N into coalitions, that is, S_i is non-empty for each i, $S_i \cap S_j = \emptyset$ for $i \neq j$, and $\cup_{i=1}^{k} S_i = N$.

Thus, in a coalition structure, no two players can belong to the same coalition.

A pay-off vector is examined with respect to a particular coalition structure. When associated with a particular coalition structure, it is called a pay-off configuration.

Formally,

Definition 35 Given a coalition form game $v \in G^N$, a *pay-off configuration for a coalition structure* $\Omega = \{S_1, \ldots, S_k\}$ is a pay-off vector $x = (x_{A_1}, \ldots, x_{A_n})$ such that $v(S_l) = x(S_l)$ for all $1 \leq l \leq k$.

That is, a pay-off configuration assigns, in total, each coalition in the coalition structure, exactly the amount that the coalition can earn on its own. Often individual rationality is a natural requirement.

Definition 36 Given a coalition form game $v \in G^N$ and a coalition structure $\Omega = \{S_1, \ldots, S_k\}$, a pay-off configuration x is called *individually rational* if $x_{A_i} \geq v(\{A_i\})$ for all $A_i \in N$.

For a given coalition form game $v \in G^N$ and a coalition structure $\Omega = \{S_1, \ldots, S_k\}$, the sets of all pay-off configurations and individually rational pay-off configurations are denoted respectively by $X^0(\Omega)$ and $X(\Omega)$. If $\Omega = \{N\}$, then $X(\{N\})$ is simply the set of imputations for the game $v \in G^N$.

A player A_i in a coalition can object to a proposed allocation x because he thinks that he is getting too little and another player A_j of the coalition is getting too much under x, and to make his objections convincing, he can demonstrate that he can form a new coalition that will include him but not A_j and each member of this new coalition will get more than what he was getting under x.

Definition 37 Given a coalition form game $x \in G^N$, a coalition structure Ω, an individually rational pay-off configuration $x \in X(\Omega)$, a coalition $S_t \in \Omega$ and two members $A_i, A_j \in S_t$, *an objection of A_i against A_j* is a pair (y, S), where S is a coalition containing A_i but not A_j and $y \in \Re^{|S|}$ is a group rational pay-off vector $(y(S) = v(S))$ such that $y_{A_l} > x_{A_l}$ for all $A_l \in S$.

An objection is an argument of one player against another. For an objection to be valid, both the players should belong to the same coalition of the coalition structure. The objection itself may be regarded as a new coalition structure S and an individually rational pay-off configuration. It is a division y of $v(S)$ that is preferred by all members of S to the allocation x. Since $y_{A_l} - x_{A_l} > 0$ for all $A_l \in S$, in moving from S_t to S, player A_i can protect his interest and also provide incentives to the other players for joining S. The amount $y_{A_l} - x_{A_l} > 0$ can be interpreted as the incentive that player A_l gets for joining S. The inequality restriction $y_{A_l} - x_{A_l} > 0$ for all $A_l \in S \setminus \{A_i\}$ is necessary for A_i to get the active participation of the other members when he is taking his business elsewhere.

An objection can produce an effect only if there is no counter-objection against it.

Definition 38   Given a coalition form game $v \in G^N$, a pair (z, T), where T is a coalition and $z \in \Re^{|T|}$ is a group rational pay-off vector $(z(T) = v(T))$, is a *counter-objection against the objection (y, S) of A_i against A_j if T contains A_j but not A_i, $z_{A_l} \geq y_{A_l}$ for all $A_l \in T \cap S$ and $z_{A_l} \geq x_{A_l}$ for all $A_l \in T \setminus S$.*

When A_j proposes the counter-objection (z, T) to (y, S), he can protect his share by forming T $(z_{A_j} \geq x_{A_j})$ and he does not require the consent of A_i $(A_i \notin T)$. It is a division z of $v(T)$ which ensures that if some members of T were in S so that they were offered some benefits by A_i, A_j can match these benefits $(z_{A_l} \geq y_{A_l}$ for all $A_l \in T \cap S)$. Every other member of T gets at least his original payment $(z_{A_l} \geq x_{A_l}$ for all $A_l \in T \setminus S)$.

A plan is in the bargaining set if every objection against it can be tackled by a counter-objection. Loosely speaking, an allocation is in the bargaining set of a game if when some player of the game can bribe a group of dissidents to join him by accepting a second allocation that makes each of them better off; there will be an alternative group with a third allocation under which the amounts received by those who were needed by the dissidents will get at least as much as they were getting in the second plan. Formally,

---

Definition 39 Let $v \in G^N$ be a coalition form game. For a coalition structure Ω, the bargaining set $M(\Omega)$ is the set of all individually rational pay-off configurations with the characteristic that for every objection raised by any player A_i against another player A_j, there is a counter-objection to A_i's objection by A_j. That is,

$$M(\Omega) = \{x \in X(\Omega) : \text{every objection at } x \text{ can be countered}\}.$$

Given an allocation x in a game, it is often possible that a player A_i claims that he is not getting much in comparison with what another player A_j is getting and therefore, he wants to form a coalition along with some other players that will not include A_j so that now everybody will be better off than in x. In response to this, A_j may put forward the counter logic that he can also form a coalition excluding A_i where everybody's position in x will be at least maintained and for the common member of the two coalitions, A_i's offers will definitely be taken care off. If an allocation x satisfies these two conditions, then it will be an element of the bargaining set of the game. This claim-counter claim process is the source of stability of an outcome.

The bargaining set is concerned with actual coalition formation because its elements are defined in terms of particular partitions of the players into coalitions. The provisions underlying the notions' objections and counter-objections have the aroma of a bargaining process. The players need to negotiate with one another in order to make their attempts successful. In contrast, the interpretation of coalition formation is not so explicit in the case of a stable set. Evidently, an imputation will be in the core if and only if no player can have any objection against another player. Consequently, the core is a subset of the bargaining set relative to the coalition structure $\{N\}$ (refer also Maschler 1976). The following theorem of Peleg (1963; 1967), which was also demonstrated by Maschler and Peleg (1966) and Schmeidler (1969), shows that the bargaining set of a game is non-empty. The proof of the theorem relies on the results presented in the following sections of the chapter.

Theorem 4 The bargaining set of a coalition form game $v \in G^N$ is non-empty.

In order to illustrate the bargaining set of a game, we consider the following example.

Example 13 In the three-player majority game we considered before, the players divide 1 unit of pay-off among themselves (Proposition 6). The core of this game is empty. Let $\Omega = \{\{A_1, A_2\}, \{A_3\}\}$ be the coalition structure. Then the individually rational pay-off configuration $(0.5, 0.5, 0)$ is in the bargaining set of the game. To see this, note that player A_2 can make an objection against player A_1 and propose $(0, 0.5 + c, 0.5 - c)$ using $\{\{A_1\}, \{A_2, A_3\}\}$, where $0 < c \leq 0.5$. To this, player A_1 can make the counter-objection $(0.5, 0, 0.5)$ using $\{\{A_1, A_3\}, \{A_2\}\}$. Any individually rational pay-off configuration consisting of a coalition structure and a pay-off vector in which each of the two players who form a coalition gets 0.5 and the remaining player who constitutes a coalition alone gets zero will be in the bargaining set. Likewise, given $\Omega = \{\{N\}\} = \{\{A_1, A_2, A_3\}\}$, the individually rational pay-off configuration (α, α, β), where $0 < \alpha \leq 0.5, 0 \leq \beta < 1$ and $2\alpha + \beta = 1$, is also in the bargaining set.

4.3   The Kernel and Pre-Kernel

The definition of the kernel relies on an alternative concept of objections and counter-objections that are effective, defined in an unambiguous way, and hence are different from the notions of objections—counter-objections employed in the definition of the bargaining set.

Definition 40 Given a coalition form game $v \in G^N$, the *excess of a coalition S* with respect to an allocation x is $e(S, x) = v(S) - x(S)$.

The non-negative excess is an indicator of the amount of gain a coalition S gets if the members of S do not accept the pay-off vector x when it is implemented. On the other hand, if it is negative, then it gives the amount that coalition S loses over its worth by not accepting the allocation x when it comes into effect. The excess for the grand and the empty coalition is zero.

Definition 41 Given a coalition form game $v \in G^N$ and an imputation x, the *surplus $s_{A_i A_j}(x)$ of A_i against A_j* in x is the maximum excess of any coalition that contains A_i but not A_j, that is, $s_{A_i A_j}(x) = \max_{S} \{e(S, x) \mid S \subset N, A_i \in S, A_j \notin S\}$.

The surplus amount $s_{A_i A_j}(x)$ is the maximal amount that player A_i can gain at the imputation x without the cooperation of A_j. When the maximum is achieved for the coalition S, relative to the imputation x, S is the most profitable coalition that includes A_i but excludes A_j.

Definition 42 Given a coalition form game $v \in G^N$ and a coalition structure Ω, the *kernel $K(\Omega)$ of Ω* is

$$K(\Omega) = \{x \in X(\Omega) \mid either\ s_{A_i A_j}(x) \leq s_{A_j A_i}(x)\ or\ x_{A_j} = v(\{A_j\})\ \forall A_i, A_j \in S \in \Omega, A_i \neq A_j\}.$$

If A_i is in a coalition that does not contain A_j and $x_{A_j} > v(\{A_j\})$ holds, then A_i may object by claiming that the allocation is giving too much to A_j. If player A_j is able to join a coalition T that will not contain A_i and finds that the sacrifice made by members of T is more than that made by members of S ($e(T, x) > e(S, x) > 0$) or as a whole, the gain of T is less than that of S ($0 > e(T, x) > e(S, x)$), then A_j can definitely provide a counter logic to A_i's arguments because A_i, being a member of S, enjoys a comparatively advantageous position in terms of sacrifice or gain.

We make the above notions of objection and counter-objections formal in the next two definitions (refer Osborne and Rubinstein 1994).

Definition 43 Given a coalition form game $v \in G^N$, a coalition structure Ω, and an allocation $x \in X(\Omega)$, *an objection of A_i against A_j* is a coalition S that contains A_i but not A_j and $x_{A_i} > v(\{A_j\})$.

Definition 44 Given a coalition form game $v \in G^N$, a coalition structure Ω, and an allocation $x \in X(\Omega)$, *a counter-objection of A_j against A_i* to the objection S of A_i against A_j is a coalition T that contains A_j but not A_i and $e(T, x) \geq e(S, x)$.

If $x_{A_j} > v(\{A_j\})$ holds, then $s_{A_iA_j}(x) \leq s_{A_jA_i}(x)$, that is, the surplus of A_i is not higher than that derived by A_j. Thus, A_j cannot have a legitimate counter-objection against A_i. That is, in such a case A_i's objection to A_j getting too much is justified and we refer to it as effective. If $x_{A_j} = v(\{A_j\})$, then A_j is at his personal minimum in x. In such a case A_i cannot convincingly argue that A_j's payment should be reduced further. In other words, in this case, A_i cannot have any objection against A_j. Given $x_{A_j} = v(\{A_j\})$, for x to be in the kernel, $s_{A_iA_j}(x) > s_{A_jA_i}(x)$. That is, the surplus of A_i should be higher than that derived by A_j. In this situation, A_j can definitely argue that A_i is in a comparatively advantageous position. These observations clearly indicate that the kernel can be interpreted in terms of objections and counter-objections that are effectual.

The kernel has an attractive feature. It is stated with respect to pairs of players which involves comparisons of the pay-offs of the players. However, no such comparisons are necessary in the definitions of the core and the bargaining set. For instance, Proposition 10 of Chapter 3 claims that an imputation is in the core if and only if it is not dominated by any pay-off vector. In this case, the dominance requires a comparison of the pay-off of each player with the amount the imputation gives to the player. There is no notion of comparison across players. However, the kernel is a solution concept in which the pay-offs of different players are meaningfully compared (refer also Serrano 1997).

Example 14 We identify an element of the kernel of the three-player majority game for the coalition structure $\Omega = \{\{A_1, A_2\}, \{A_3\}\}$. The individually rational pay-off configuration $x = (0.5, 0.5, 0)$ is an element of the kernel of this game for Ω. To demonstrate this, note that $v(\{A_1\}) - x_{A_1} = -0.5$ and $v(\{A_1, A_3\}) - x_{A_1} - x_{A_3} = 0.5$. Hence, $s_{A_1A_2}(x) = \max\{v(S) - x(S) \mid$

$A_1 \in S, A_2 \notin S\} = 0.5$. Similarly, $s_{A_2 A_1}(x) = 0.5$. Thus, $s_{A_1 A_2}(x) = s_{A_2 A_1}(x)$. Moreover, $x_{A_3} = v(\{A_3\}) = 0$. Thus, the pay-off configuration x is in the kernel.

The following theorem of Davis and Maschler (1965) shows the relationship between the bargaining set and the kernel.

Theorem 5   The kernel of a coalition form game is a subset of its bargaining set.

Proof: Let $x \in K(\Omega)$. It is necessary to show that $x \in M(\Omega)$. For A_i, $A_j \in S_t \in \Omega$, let (y, S) be an objection of A_i against A_j. Thus, $v(S) = y(S)$ and $y_{A_l} > x_{A_l}$ for all $A_l \in S$. It is also true that $s_{A_i A_j}(x) \geq v(S) - x(S) > 0$. If $x_{A_j} = v(\{A_j\})$, then (z, A_j), where $z_{A_j} = v(\{A_j\})$, is a counter-objection to (y, S). Next, if $x_{A_j} > v(\{A_j\})$, then, since $x \in K(\Omega)$, it must be the case that $s_{A_j A_i}(x) \geq s_{A_i A_j}(x) \geq v(S) - x(S) = y(S) - x(S)$. Now, suppose $s_{A_j A_i}(x)$ is realized through the coalition T which (by definition) contains A_j but not A_i. That is, $s_{A_j A_i}(x) = v(T) - x(T)$. It then follows that $v(T) - x(T) \geq y(S) - x(S)$, which we rewrite as $v(T) \geq y(S) + x(T) - x(S)$. Now, $S \setminus T$ and $S \cap T$ constitute a partition of S, that is, $(S \setminus T) \cap (S \cap T) = \emptyset$ and $(S \setminus T) \cup (S \cap T) = S$. Therefore, $y(S) = y(S \setminus T) + y(S \cap T)$. Likewise, $x(S) = x(S \setminus T) + x(S \cap T)$ and $x(T) = x(T \setminus S) + x(T \cap S)$. Substituting these breakdowns of $y(S)$, $x(S)$ and $x(T)$ on the right-hand side of the inequality $v(T) \geq y(S) + x(T) - x(S)$, we get $v(T) \geq y(S \setminus T) + y(S \cap T) + x(T \setminus S) - x(S \setminus T)$. From the definition of (y, S), it follows that $y(S \setminus T) > x(S \setminus T)$. Therefore, $v(T) > y(S \cap T) + x(T \setminus S)$. Thus, we can get a division z of $v(T)$ such that $z_{A_l} \geq y_{A_l}$ for all $A_l \in T \cap S$ and $z_{A_l} \geq x_{A_l}$ for all $A_l \in T \setminus S$. Hence, (z, T) is a counter-objection to (y, S). A_j is in a position to counter-object to any objection of A_i. Hence, the point x is in the bargaining set. Since $x \in K(\Omega)$ is arbitrary, it follows that the kernel is a subset of the bargaining set. This completes the proof of the theorem. $\square$

Definition 45   Given a coalition form game $v \in G^N$ and a coalition structure Ω, the pre-kernel $PK(\Omega)$ for Ω is

$$PK(\Omega) = \{x \in X^0(\Omega) \mid s_{A_i A_j}(x) = s_{A_j A_i}(x) \; \forall A_i, A_j \in S \in \Omega, A_i \neq A_j\}.$$

One way of interpreting the pre-kernel 'is to assume that it is imposed on the players by some "big brother" who cares only about money and pays no attention to the utilities of the players towards this money' (Maschler 1992, p. 605). When $s_{A_i A_j}(x) = s_{A_j A_i}(x)$ holds, the highest excess that A_i

can make in the coalition without A_j is same as the highest excess the latter can make without the former in the coalition. This may be regarded as a perfect balancing of minimal losses/maximal gains among the players. That is, the set of all pre-kernel elements is the set of all pay-off configurations that balances the maximum surpluses for each distinct pair of players. We may also say that the pre-kernel consists of all pay-off configurations where each pair of players is symmetric with respect to the claims the players can make against each other in a bargaining situation. This bargaining situation gives rise to a bargaining equilibrium which is an element of the pre-kernel. In this case, none of the players can claim an additional amount from the other player to reduce (increase) his loss (gain).

The pre-kernel is also always non-empty. It is evident that $PK(\Omega) \cap X(\Omega) \subseteq K(\Omega)$. Moreover, if $\Omega = \{N\}$ and the game is super-additive, $PK(\{N\}) = K(\{N\})$ (Curiel 1997). We will illustrate the pre-kernel analytically in Section 4.5.

4.4 The Nucleolus, Pre-Nucleolus and Proportional Nucleolus

Given a coalition form game, we may be interested in knowing how dissatisfied each coalition is with a proposed imputation and try to minimize the maximum dissatisfaction. More precisely, given that $e(S, x)$ measures (un)happiness of coalition S with the allocation x, we try to determine a pay-off vector that minimizes the maximum excess. This is the idea underlying the nucleolus. We will explain the concept using a vector $\theta(x)$ constructed by arranging the excesses of the $2^{|N|} - 1$ non-empty subsets of N in non-increasing order. To define this rigorously, let $S_1, S_2, \ldots S_{2^{|N|}-1}$ be an arrangement of the coalitions for which $e(S_i, x) \geq e(S_{i+1}, x)$ for $i = 1, \ldots, 2^{|N|} - 2$. Then, $\theta(x)$ is the vector of $\theta_i(x)$ values defined by $\theta_i(x) = e(S_i, x)$, where $i = 1, \ldots, 2^{|N|} - 1$. For any two non-identical vectors $\theta(x)$ and $\theta(y)$, we say that $\theta(x)$ is lexicographically larger than $\theta(y)$, $\theta(x) \succ_l \theta(y)$ for short, if for

$$i = \min\{j \in \{1, \ldots, 2^{|N|} - 1\}, \theta_j(x) \neq \theta_j(y)\}, \theta_i(x) > \theta_i(y). \qquad (4.1)$$

In words, $\theta(x)$ assigns a higher value than $\theta(y)$ to the first coordinate on which they are different. If $\theta_i(x) = \theta_i(y)$ for all $i = 1, \ldots, 2^{|N|} - 1$, then we say that $\theta(x)$ is lexicographically identical to $\theta(y)$ and we denote this by $\theta(x) =_l \theta(y)$. The notation $\theta(x) \succeq_l \theta(y)$ is used to denote either $\theta(x) =_l$

$\theta(y)$ or $\theta(x) \succ_l \theta(y)$. To illustrate this, consider $v \in G^N$ with $|N| = 3$; let $\theta(x) = (100, 90, 80, 72, 3, 1, 0)$ and $\theta(y) = (100, 90, 80, 70, 30, 10, 8)$. Then $\theta(x) \succ_l \theta(y)$.

Definition 46 Given a coalition form game $v \in G^N$, *the nucleolus* $\mathbf{N}(v)$ *of the game is defined as*

$$\mathbf{N}(v) = \{y \in I(v) \mid \theta(x) \succeq_l \theta(y) \text{ for all } x \in I(v)\}.$$

Thus, the nucleolus of the game is the set of all imputations having the lexicographically smallest excesses. The nucleolus can be motivated as follows. On the argument that the one who yells loudest gets attention first, where loudness is directly proportional to the extent of dissatisfaction, we look at those coalitions with highest excesses for a fixed imputation. Then we adjust the imputation, if possible, to make this highest excess smaller. After making the highest excess as small as possible, we look at the next highest excess and adjust the imputation to make it as low as possible. This is done sequentially in the decreasing order of excesses. For defining the nucleolus, we have implicitly assumed that the coalition structure is $\{N\}$ (refer Maschler 1992). The following theorem of Schmeidler (1969) establishes a relationship between the kernel and the nucleolus.

Theorem 6 The nucleolus of a coalition form game $v \in G^N$ is a subset of its kernel defined for the coalition structure $\{N\}$.

Proof: Let x be an imputation of the game $v \in G^N$ and assume that x is not an element of $K(\{N\})$, the kernel of the game for the coalition structure $\{N\}$. It is necessary to show that x is not in $\mathbf{N}(v)$, the nucleolus of the game. Since $x \notin K(\{N\})$, there are players A_i and A_j such that $x_{A_j} > v(\{A_j\})$ and $s_{A_i A_j}(x) > s_{A_j A_i}(x)$. Let p and q be the smallest integers such that $s_{A_i A_j}(x) = v(S_p) - x(S_p) > s_{A_j A_i}(x) = v(S_q) - x(S_q)$, where $(A_i \in S_p, A_j \notin S_p$, and $A_j \in S_q, A_i \notin S_q)$. Given that $x_{A_j} > v(\{A_j\})$, we can get $0 < \epsilon \le x_{A_j} - v(\{A_j\})$ such that $y = (x_{A_1}, \ldots, x_{A_{i-1}}, x_{A_i} + \epsilon, x_{A_{i+1}}, \ldots, x_{A_{j-1}}, x_{A_j} - \epsilon, x_{A_{j+1}}, \ldots, x_{A_{|N|}})$ is an imputation. For $r < p$, either $A_i, A_j \in S_r$ or $A_i, A_j \notin S_r$, otherwise the condition $s_{A_i A_j}(x) = v(S_p) - x(S_p)$ is violated. Consequently, we have $x(S_r) = y(S_r)$, which in turn implies that $\theta_r(x) = \theta_r(y)$. For $r = p$, we have $v(S_p) - y(S_p) = v(S_p) - x(S_p) - \epsilon$. Hence, for sufficiently small $\epsilon > 0$, it follows that $\theta_p(x) > \theta_p(y)$, from which it follows that there exists an imputation y such that $\theta(x) \succeq_l$

$\theta(y)$. This shows that x is not an element of $\mathbf{N}(v)$ and hence completes the proof of the theorem.   □

The next theorem of Schmeidler (1969) shows that the nucleolus is non-empty.

Theorem 7 For any coalition form game $v \in G^N$ with $I(v) \neq \varnothing$, the nucleolus is non-empty.

Proof: First observe that all the excess functions are continuous. Now, the minimum and maximum of a finite number of continuous functions are continuous (Royden 1968, p.47). Each θ_k being first defined as the minimum of finitely many continuous functions and then as the maximum of a finite number of continuous functions, is continuous on the set of imputations.

Since the set of all imputations of a coalition form game is defined in terms of a finite number of weak inequalities involving real numbers, it is compact. Let $\rho_1 = \min\{\theta_1(x) : x \in I(v)\}$ and $X_1(v) = \{x \in I(v) \mid \theta_1(x) = \rho_1\}$. Since $I(v)$ is a closed set and θ_1 is continuous, ρ_1 exists (Apostol 1974, p.95) and $X_1(v)$ is non-empty and compact (a closed subset of a compact set is compact (Rudin 1976, p.37)). Next, θ_2 is continuous and letting $\rho_2 = \min\{\theta_2(x) : x \in I(v)\}$ and $X_2(v) = \{x \in X_1(v) \mid \theta_2(x) = \rho_2\}$, we note that $X_2(v)$ is non-empty and compact.

The proof now proceeds by induction. Suppose that $X_{i-1}(v)$ is non-empty and compact. Given continuity of θ_i, let $\rho_i = \min\{\theta_i(x) : x \in I(v)\}$ and $X_i(v) = \{x \in X_{i-1}(v) \mid \theta_i(x) = \rho_i\}$. Then, $X_i(v) \subset X_{i-1}(v)$ is non-empty and compact. Thus, by the method of induction, $X_i(v)$ is non-empty and compact for all $i = 1, \ldots, 2^{|N|} - 1$. Since $X_{2^{|N|}-1}(v)$ is the nucleolus, the proof is complete.   □

Schmeidler (1969) also showed that the nucleolus is a singleton.

Theorem 8 For any coalition form game $v \in G^N$ with $I(v) \neq \varnothing$, the nucleolus consists of a single point.

Proof: Let $x, y \in \mathbf{N}(v)$. For $0 \le \alpha \le 1$, let $S_1, \ldots, S_{2^{|N|}-1}$ be an arrangement of the coalitions such that

$$\theta(\alpha x + (1 - \alpha)y) = (e(S_1, \alpha x + (1 - \alpha)y), \ldots, e(S_{2^{|N|}-1}, \alpha x + (1 - \alpha)y)).$$
$$(4.2)$$

The right-hand side of Eq.(4.2) can be rewritten as $(e(S_1, \alpha x), \ldots,$ $e(S_{2^{|N|}-1}, \alpha x)) + (e(S_1, (1 - \alpha)y), \ldots, e(S_{2^{|N|}-1}, (1 - \alpha)y)) = \alpha(e(S_1, x), \ldots,$

$e(S_{2|N|-1}, x)) + (1 - \alpha)(e(S_1, y), \ldots, e(S_{2|N|-1}, y)) = \alpha a + (1 - \alpha)b$, where $a = (e(S_1, x), \ldots, e(S_{2|N|-1}, x))$ is a permutation of the elements in the vector $\theta(x)$ and $b = (e(S_1, y), \ldots, e(S_{2|N|-1}, y))$ is a permutation of the elements of the vector $\theta(y)$. Since $\theta(x) \succeq_l a$ and $\theta(y) \succeq_l b$, it follows that $\alpha\theta(x) \succeq_l \alpha a$ and $(1 - \alpha)\theta(y) \succeq_l (1 - \alpha)b$ from which we get

$$\alpha\theta(x) + (1 - \alpha)\theta(y) \succeq_l \alpha a + (1 - \alpha)b = \theta(\alpha x + (1 - \alpha)y). \tag{4.3}$$

Now, since $x, y \in N(v)$, $\theta(x) = \theta(y)$. Hence from the definition of nucleolus, it follows that

$$\theta(\alpha x + (1 - \alpha)y) \succeq_l \theta(x) = \theta(y) = \alpha\theta(x) + (1 - \alpha)\theta(y). \tag{4.4}$$

From (4.3) and (4.4), we get

$$\theta(\alpha x + (1 - \alpha)y) = \alpha\theta(x) + (1 - \alpha)\theta(y) = \theta(x) = \theta(y) = \alpha a + (1 - \alpha)b. \tag{4.5}$$

Condition (4.5) is true for all $0 < \alpha < 1$. Differentiating all sides of the equation $\theta(x) = \theta(y) = \alpha a + (1 - \alpha)b$ with respect to α, we get $a = b$, which in turn gives $a = b = \theta(x) = \theta(y)$. Therefore, in a, b, $\theta(x)$ and $\theta(y)$, the coalitions are ordered in the same way. Hence, all excesses in x and y are equal, which shows that $x = y$. □

Now, given that the kernel is a superset of the nucleolus, the bargaining set is a superset of the kernel and the nucleolus is non-empty (for any coalition form game with non-empty imputation), we can state the following corollary to Theorem 8.

Corollary 1 For any coalition form game $v \in G^N$ with $I(v) \neq \emptyset$, the bargaining set and kernel are non-empty.

Example 15 Following Friedman (1986), we consider the coalition form game $v \in G^N$, where $N = \{A_1, A_2, A_3\}$ and $v(\{A_1\}) = v(\{A_2\}) = v(\{A_3\}) = 0$. Next, $v(\{A_1, A_2\}) = 4$, $v(\{A_1, A_3\}) = 2$, $v(\{A_2, A_3\}) = 3$ and $v(\{A_1, A_2, A_3\}) = 6$. The allocation $x = (2, 3, 1)$ is the unique element of the nucleolus. To demonstrate this, note that $e(\{A_1\}, x) = -2$, $e(\{A_2\}, x) = -3$, $e(\{A_3\}, x) = -1$, $e(S, x) = -0.5$ for any two-person coalition S, and $e(N, x) = 0$. This gives $\theta(x) = (0, -0.5, -0.5, -0.5, -1, -2, -3)$. For any alternative imputation $\hat{x}$, the excesses of each of the three two-person coalitions will sum up to -1.5, but at least one of the coalitions would have an excess larger than -0.5. Hence, $\theta(\hat{x}) \succ_l \theta(x)$ for any imputation $\hat{x}$. Consequently, x is the lexicographically minimum element.

Definition 47   Given a coalition form game $v \in G^N$, *the pre-nucleolus* $\mathbf{PN}(v)$ *of the game is defined as*

$$\mathbf{PN}(v) = \{y \in PI(v) \mid \theta(x) \succeq_l \theta(y) \text{ for all } x \in PI(v)\}.$$

The pre-nucleolus of a game is the set of all pre-imputations having the lexicographically smallest excesses (Sobolev 1975). Thus, while the nucleolus is a minimization problem on the set of imputations of a coalition form game, the pre-nucleolus is the same minimization problem on the set of pre-imputations. For any coalition form game $v \in G^N$, the pre-nucleolus is always a singleton. If a coalition form game $v \in G^N$ either has a non-empty core or if it is super-additive, then the pre-nucleolus and the nucleolus coincide (Peleg and Sudhölter 2003).

The proportional nucleolus (Young et al. 1982) differs from the nucleolus (pre-nucleolus) with respect to the definition of the excesses of the coalitions. For the proportional nucleolus, excesses are defined by the formula $[v(S) - x(S)]/v(S)$. Thus, while in the case of nucleolus (pre-nucleolus) we consider absolute excesses, for the proportional nucleolus, we consider proportional excesses. Using these excesses, we can now define the proportional nucleolus the way nucleolus (pre-nucleolus) has been defined. The proportional nucleolus of a positive valued game is non-empty and a singleton. This solution concept has an interesting application to cost allocation problems which occur when cooperation among several departments of an organization gives rise to economies of scale.

4.5   Applications

Often we come across a bankruptcy situation where there are claims against an estate and the sum of the claims exceeds the estate's worth. In such a situation, it is natural to investigate what would be a 'fair' way of dividing the estate among the claimants.

Let $N = \{A_1, \ldots, A_n\}$ be the set of creditors/claimants. A *bankruptcy problem* is an ordered pair (E, d), where $E > 0$ represents the size of the estate, $d = (d_{A_1}, \ldots, d_{A_n}) \in \tilde{\Re}_+^{|N|}$ is the non-negative vector of debts to the members of the set of creditors/claimants N such that $\sum_{A_i \in N} d_{A_i} \geq E > 0$.[1] We can think of a bankrupt organization with an estate of size E which has to be divided among N creditors of the organization, where d_{A_i} is the claim made by creditor $A_i \in N$. The inequality $\sum_{A_i \in N} d_{A_i} \geq E > 0$ indicates that the estate may be insufficient to meet the total amount of the debts. The difference $(\sum_{A_i \in N} d_{A_i} - E)$ specifies the amounts of debts that cannot be repaid by the organization. If $\sum_{A_i \in N} d_{A_i} - E > 0$, the problem arises when we consider the allocation of E among the n creditors. An allocation for a bankruptcy problem (E, d) is a vector $x = (x_{A_1}, \ldots, x_{A_n}) \in \Re_+^{|N|}$ satisfying the efficiency condition $\sum_{A_i \in N} x_{A_i} = E$, where x_{A_i} is the amount given to creditor A_i. A solution for bankruptcy problems is a function ξ that associates each bankruptcy problem (E, d) with an allocation.

Alternatively, the bankruptcy problem can be treated as a tax collection problem. Here, d_{A_i} is the maximum revenue that can be collected from taxpayer A_i and E is the size of the revenue the government desires to collect. (O'Neill 1982; Aumann and Maschler 1985; Herrero and Villar 2001; Thomson 2003 and Aumann 2010.)

Definition 48 A *bankruptcy game* $v_{E,d} : 2^{|N|} \rightarrow \Re$ associated with a general bankruptcy problem (E, d) is defined by

$$v_{E,d}(S) = \max \left\{ 0, E - \sum_{A_i \in N \setminus S} d_{A_i} \right\} \qquad (4.6)$$

---

for all non-empty $S \subseteq N$.

Aumann and Maschler (1985) showed that the bankruptcy game is convex and gave a detailed formula for its nucleolus. (See Chapter 6 for a treatment of convex games.) The worth of a coalition is positive if the total claim of the complement of the coalition is less than the estate, otherwise it is zero. That is, the coalition has a positive worth only if its complement as a whole does not demand the entire estate. A significant characteristic of the bankruptcy game is that it provided a convincing explanation of the solution found in the ancient (more than 2000 years ago) Babolyian Talmud.

Aumann and Maschler (1965) also showed that the unique consistent solution of a bankruptcy problem is the nucleolus of the corresponding

---

[1] Here $\Re_+^{|N|}$ is the non-negative orthant of the $|N|$- dimensional Euclidean space with the origin deleted.

bankruptcy game. A solution is consistent if any two creditors use the contested garment principle to divide the total amount allotted to them by the solution. The contested garment principle can be described as follows. 'Two hold a garment; one claims it all, the other claims half. Then, one is awarded 3/4 and the other 1/4.' The division rule goes as follows. The person who has a lower claim concedes fifty per cent of the garment to the other. Therefore, the remaining fifty per cent is the issue of dispute here and it is divided equally between the claimants. Analytically, suppose a person claims that his share in an estate is r and another person claims that his share is s, where $0 < r,s \leq 1, r+s > 1$. Then, the contested garment solution to this bankruptcy problem is the following: the first person will receive $(1-s) + [(r+s-1)/2]$ and the second person will receive $(1-r) + [(r+s-1)/2]$. This is because the second person agrees that the first person's share should be $(1-s)$ and the balance $1 - [(1-s)+(1-r)] = r+s-1$ is divided equally between them so that the first person gets $(1-s) + [(r+s-1)/2]$. By a parallel argument, the second person gets $(1-r) + [(r+s-1)/2]$.

The contested garment solution is, in fact, the two-claimant version of the Talmudic solution—an alternative solution that solves the bankruptcy problem uniquely (Thomson 2003 and Maschler, Solan and Zamir 2013). Let $N = \{A_1, A_2\}$ be the two creditors (claimants). If $E \leq d_{A_1}, d_{A_2}$, then each creditor can claim that he should have the entire estate. In such a case, equal sharing is a fair rule of division of the estate. If $d_{A_1} \leq E \leq d_{A_2}$, then A_1 agrees that A_2 should get $E - d_{A_1}$. The remainder is $E - (E - d_{A_1}) = d_{A_1}$, which should be equally divided between the claimants so that A_2 gets $(E - d_{A_1}) + (d_{A_1}/2) = E - (d_{A_1}/2)$ and A_1 gets $d_{A_1}/2$. Likewise, for $d_{A_2} \leq E \leq d_{A_1}$, A_1 gets $E - (d_{A_2}/2)$ and A_2 gets $d_{A_2}/2$. If $d_{A_1}, d_{A_2} < E$, then A_1 agrees that A_2 should get $E - d_{A_1}$ and A_2 agrees that A_1 should get $E - d_{A_2}$. The balance $E - [(E - d_{A_1}) + (E - d_{A_2})] = d_{A_1} + d_{A_2} - E$ should be equally divided between the claimants so that A_1 gets $(E - d_{A_2}) + (d_{A_1} + d_{A_2} - E)/2 = (E + d_{A_1} - d_{A_2})/2$. Similarly, A_2 gets $(E + d_{A_2} - d_{A_1})/2$. We write this in a more compact form as follows:

$$(y_{A_1}, y_{A_2}) = \xi(E; d_{A_1}, d_{A_2}) = \begin{cases} \left(\frac{E}{2}, \frac{E}{2}\right) & \text{if } E \leq d_{A_1}, d_{A_2}, \\ \left(\frac{d_{A_1}}{2}, E - \frac{d_{A_1}}{2}\right) & \text{if } d_{A_1} \leq E \leq d_{A_2}, \\ \left(E - \frac{d_{A_2}}{2}, \frac{d_{A_2}}{2}\right) & \text{if } d_{A_2} \leq E \leq d_{A_1}, \\ \left(\frac{E + d_{A_1} - d_{A_2}}{2}, \frac{E + d_{A_2} - d_{A_1}}{2}\right) & \text{if } d_{A_1}, d_{A_2} \leq E. \end{cases}$$

$$(4.7)$$

Here y_{A_1} is the amount received by the first creditor and the second creditor receives y_{A_2}. It is evident that in all the cases considered in (4.7), $y_{A_1} + y_{A_2} = E$. The function ξ is continuous in its arguments. Given (d_{A_1}, d_{A_2}), ξ is increasing in E.

If the number of claimants N is more than two and if $(1/2) \sum_{A_i \in N} d_{A_i} \geq E$ (that is, half the sum of the debts is not less than the estate), then the Talmudic solution is $y = (y_{A_1}, \ldots, y_{A_n})$, where $y_{A_i} = \min\{c, (1/2)d_{A_i}\}$ for each $A_i \in N$ and c is chosen such that $\sum_{A_i \in N} \min\{c, (1/2)d_{A_i}\} = E$. Thus, in this case, the Talmudic criterion does not give each claimant more than half his claim, which means that $y_{A_i} \leq (1/2)d_{A_i}$. On the other hand, if $(1/2) \sum_{A_i \in N} d_{A_i} \leq E$, then $y_{A_i} = d_{A_i} - \min\{c, (1/2)d_{A_i}\}$ for each $A_i \in N$, where c is chosen such that $\sum_{A_i \in N}[d_{A_i} - \min\{c, (1/2)d_{A_i}\}] = E$ (Thomson 2003).

The unique Talmudic solution of the bankruptcy problem coincides with the unique pre-kernel solution of the (convex) bankruptcy game.

Exercises

4.1 Demonstrate rigorously that the core of a coalition form game is a subset of its bargaining set.

4.2 Consider the coalition form game $v \in G^N$, where $N = \{A_1, A_2, A_3\}$, $v(\{A_1\}) = v(\{A_2\}) = v(\{A_3\}) = 0$, $v(\{A_2, A_3\}) = 5$ and $v(N) = v(\{A_1, A_2\}) = v(\{A_1, A_3\}) = 10$. Determine one element of the bargaining set of this game if the coalition structure is $\{N\}$. Can there be more than one element of this bargaining set? Justify your answer rigorously.

4.3 Do you agree with the statement that the individually rational pay-off vector $(1/3, 1/3, 1/3)$ is not an element of the kernel of the three-player majority game with respect to the coalition structure $\{N\}$? Demonstrate your claim.

4.4 Show that for a coalition form game $v \in G^N$, $x \in C(v)$ if and only if $e(S, x) \leq 0$ for all $S \subset N$ and $e(N, x) = 0$.

4.5 Does the individually rational pay-off configuration $(0, 0.5 + c, 0.5 - c)$, where $0 < c < 0.5$, belong to the bargaining set of the three-player majority game given that the coalition structure is $\{\{A_1, A_2\}, \{A_3\}\}$?

4.6 Consider any coalition form game $v \in G^N$ where $N = \{A_1, A_2\}$. Show that the pre-imputation $(v(\{A_1\}) + [v(\{A_1, A_2\}) - v(\{A_2\})]/2, v(\{A_2\}) + [v(\{A_1, A_2\}) - v(\{A_1\})]/2)$ is the pre-nucleolus.

[*Hint:* First try to show that for a pre-imputation $x = (x_{A_1}, x_{A_2})$ to be a member of the pre-nucleolus, it is necessary that $e(\{A_1\}, x) = e(\{A_2\}, x)$. Then, use $x_{A_1} + x_{A_2} = v(\{A_1, A_2\})$ to get the result.]

4.7 Consider a bankruptcy problem where $N = \{A_1, A_2, A_3\}$, the debt vector is $d = (60, 80, 120)$ and the estate value is 150. Determine its Talmudic solution and show that this coincides with the pre-kernel of the corresponding bankruptcy game.

4.8 Consider the coalition form game $v \in G^N$ with the player set $N = \{A_1, A_2, A_3\}$, where $v(\{A_1\}) = v(\{A_2\}) = v(\{A_3\}) = v(\{A_1, A_2\}) = 0$ and $v(N) = v(\{A_2, A_3\}) = v(\{A_1, A_3\}) = 1$. Compute the excesses with respect to the allocations $(1/3, 1/3, 1/3)$ and $(1/6, 1/3, 1/2)$ and rank them lexicographically.

CHAPTER 5

The Shapley Value

5.1 Introduction

As a solution concept to cooperative games, the core consists of a set of imputations without distinguishing one element of the set from another. It is a useful indicator of stability. However, the core may be quite large or even empty. A more comprehensive solution to cooperative games is the stable set or the von Neumann–Morgenstern solution. However, here also no single point solution exists so that we can associate a single point vector to a coalition form game. These solution concepts cannot predict a unique expected pay-off corresponding to a given game. If an arbiter's objective is the assignment of a unique outcome, which may be decided by the arbiter in a fair and impartial manner, then these solution concepts are inappropriate.

In an axiomatic approach, Shapley (1953) characterized a unique solution using a set of intuitively reasonable axioms. Shapley's solution is popularly known as the Shapley value. The central idea underlying the Shapley value is that each player should be given his marginal contribution to a coalition, if we consider all possible permutations for forming the grand coalition. Therefore, in a sense, the player is paid out his fair share of the value from the coalition for having joined the coalition. The Shapley value of a player is the expected value of the marginal contributions of the player over all possible orderings.

In the next section of the chapter, the Shapley value is defined by an axiomatic approach. The characterization theorem is explained in Section 5.3. Section 5.4 presents a discussion on Young's (1985; 1988) alternative characterization of the Shapley value using an axiom involving monotonicity of the marginal contributions. This section also analyzes the Shapley value using the potential function introduced by Hart and Mas-Colell (1989). Finally, some applications of the Shapley value are discussed in Section 5.5.

5.2 The Formal Framework: Definitions and Axioms

In different orders of grand coalition formation, a player's marginal contributions are likely to vary. These marginal contributions indicate how important the player in the overall cooperation is. A natural question here is what pay-off can a player reasonably expect from his cooperation. The Shapley value provides an answer to this.

In order to present the Shapley value formally, we need some preliminaries, stated in terms of the set of players $N = \{A_1, \ldots, A_n\}$ and G^N, the set of all games with the player set N.

Definition 49 For any coalition form game $v \in G^N$, players A_i and A_j are called *substitutes* in v if for any $S \subseteq N \setminus \{A_i, A_j\}$, $v(S \cup \{A_i\}) = v(S \cup \{A_j\})$.

Given that the coalition S does not contain the players A_i and A_j, and the pay-off of the coalitions when they join S separately are equal, it is reasonable to regard A_i and A_j as substitutes. Equivalently, if in each coalition containing either player A_i or player A_j, we replace A_i by A_j or vice-versa, the coalition worth will remain unchanged. Since we can rewrite $v(S \cup \{A_i\}) = v(S \cup \{A_j\})$ as $v(S \cup \{A_i\}) - v(S) = v(S \cup \{A_j\}) - v(S)$, players A_i and A_j are substitutes if and only if their marginal contributions to the expanded coalitions $S \cup \{A_i\}$ and $S \cup \{A_j\}$ are equal.

In order to illustrate the idea, let us consider the following example, which is taken from Gura and Maschler (2008).

Example 16 Consider the coalitional form game $v \in G^N$ with the player set $N = \{A_1, A_2, A_3, A_4\}$, where $v(\{A_1\}) = v(\{A_2\}) = v(\{A_3\}) = v(\{A_4\}) = 0$, $v(\{A_1, A_2\}) = 8$, $v(\{A_1, A_3\}) = v(\{A_2, A_3\}) = 9$, $v(\{A_1, A_4\}) = v(\{A_2, A_4\}) = 15$, $v(\{A_3, A_4\}) = 5$, $v(\{A_1, A_2, A_3\}) = 20$, $v(\{A_1, A_2, A_4\}) = 30$, $v(\{A_1, A_3, A_4\}) = v(\{A_2, A_3, A_4\}) = 50$, and $v(\{A_1, A_2,$

$A_3, A_4\}) = 60$. Since the worth of a coalition that includes A_1 as the additional player is the same as that when A_2 is included as the additional player, players A_1 and A_2 are substitutes in this game.

> **Definition 50** For any coalition form game $v \in G^N$, player $A_i \in N$ is called a *null player* if for any coalition $S \subseteq N \setminus \{A_i\}$, $v(S \cup \{A_i\}) = v(S)$.

Since player A_i is not able to change the worth of any coalition by joining it, quite logically, we can regard him as a null player.

Example 17 Consider a coalition form game $v \in G^N$ with the player set $N = \{A_1, A_2, A_3, A_4\}$, where $v(\{A_1\}) = v(\{A_2\}) = v(\{A_3\}) = v(\{A_4\}) = 0$, $v(\{A_1, A_2\}) = v(\{A_1, A_3\}) = v(\{A_1, A_4\}) = 0$ and $v(\{A_2, A_3\}) = v(\{A_2, A_4\}) = v(\{A_3, A_4\}) = 1$ and $v(S) = 1$ for all S such that $|S| \in \{3, 4\}$. Since the inclusion of player A_1 to any coalition that does not contain him does not change the worth of the coalition, A_1 is a null player. Equivalently, A_1 is a null player because removing him from any coalition containing him leaves the worth of the resulting coalition unaltered.

> **Definition 51** The game $v \in G^N$ is called the sum of two games $u, w \in G^N$ if for every coalition $S \subseteq N$, $v(S) = u(S) + w(S)$. We can as well say that given any $v \in G^N$, we can split it into two games $u, w \in G^N$ whose sum is the original game $v \in G^N$.

Example 18 Consider the coalitional form game $v \in G^N$ with the player set $N = \{A_1, A_2, A_3\}$, where $v(\{A_1\}) = 1, v(\{A_2\}) = 4, v(\{A_3\}) = 5, v(\{A_1, A_2\}) = 8$, $v(\{A_1, A_3\}) = v(\{A_2, A_3\}) = 9$ and $v(\{A_1, A_2, A_3\}) = 20$. Observe that this game is the sum of two games $u, w \in G^N$, where for the coalition form game u, $u(\{A_1\}) = 0, u(\{A_2\}) = 4, u(\{A_3\}) = 1, u(\{A_1, A_2\}) = 5, u(\{A_1, A_3\}) = 7, u(\{A_2, A_3\}) = 5, u(\{A_1, A_2, A_3\}) = 9$, and for the coalition form game w, $w(\{A_1\}) = 1, w(\{A_2\}) = 0, w(\{A_3\}) = 4$, $w(\{A_1, A_2\}) = 3, w(\{A_1, A_3\}) = 2, w(\{A_2, A_3\}) = 4, w(\{A_1, A_2, A_3\}) = 11$.

> **Definition 52** Given a coalition form game $v \in G^N$, a value function Φ is an operator that assigns a vector of pay-offs $\Phi(v) = (\Phi_{A_1}(v), \dots, \Phi_{A_n}(v)) \in \Re^{|N|}$, where $N = \{A_1, \dots, A_n\}$ and $\Re^{|N|}$ is the n-dimensional Euclidean space. Formally, a value function $\Phi : G^N \to \Re^{|N|}$.

For any $v \in G^N$ and any player $A_i \in N$, the component $\Phi_{A_i}(v)$ in the vector $\Phi(v) = (\Phi_{A_1}(v), \dots, \Phi_{A_n}(v))$ represents player A_i's pay-off from his participation in the game v. It is also known as v's value for player A_i. Besides which, it is often referred to as the power of player A_i in the game v.

The definition of the Shapley value relies on Shapley's axioms. They are stated below in terms of an arbitrary value function $\Phi : G^N \to \Re^{|N|}$.

- **Symmetry (SYM):** If players A_i and A_j are substitutes in any $v \in G^N$, then $\Phi_{A_i}(v) = \Phi_{A_j}(v)$.

- **Null player condition (NPC):** If A_i is a null player in any $v \in G^N$, then $\Phi_{A_i}(v) = 0$.

- **Efficiency (EFF):** For all $v \in G^N$, $\sum\limits_{A_i \in N} \Phi_{A_i}(v) = v(N)$.

- **Additivity (ADD):** For any $v, w \in G^N$ and any $A_i \in N$, $\Phi_{A_i}(v + w) = \Phi_{A_i}(v) + \Phi_{A_i}(w)$.

SYM does not discriminate between a player and his substitute. Since the two players' marginal contributions to each coalition are the same, they should get the same pay-off. Thus, the pay-off of a player depends on the role he plays in the game, not on other characteristics like names of the players. A null player is unable to contribute anything to a coalition he decides to join. Therefore, a null player's pay-off should be zero. EFF demands that the sum of the values for all players should be equal to the amount the coalition consisting of all the players can guarantee to itself. If $\sum_{A_i \in N} \Phi_{A_i}(v) < v(N)$, then the part $v(N) - \sum_{A_i \in N} \Phi_{A_i}(v) > 0$ will be wasted in the process of division. The inequality $\sum_{A_i \in N} \Phi_{A_i}(v) > v(N)$ is ruled out because the players cannot ask for more than the total amount available to them. In a situation where the set of players plays two different games independently, we may regard the sum of two games as a single game. ADD says that each player ultimately gets the sum of pay-offs that he gets in individual games. It can be interpreted as follows. Suppose that any coalition S of players can obtain its worth $v(S)$ in two installments. Thus, there exists v_1 and v_2 such that $v(S) = v_1(S) + v_2(S)$ for all $S \subseteq N$. Then ADD means that $\phi_{A_i}(v) = \phi_{A_i}(v_1) + \phi_{A_i}(v_2)$ for all $A_i \in N$. That is, for each player, the value will simply be the sum of his values from the installments.

Definition 53 A value function $\Phi : G^N \to \Re^{|N|}$ is called a Shapley value if it satisfies the axioms SYM, NPC, EFF and ADD.

5.3 Characterization of the Shapley Value

The objective of this section is to present the axiomatic characterization of the Shapley value and analyze its properties.

Theorem 9 (Shapley 1953) A Shapley value is unique, that is, there exists a unique value function satisfying the Shapley axioms (SYM, NPC, EFF and ADD). It is given by the formula

$$\Phi^{Sh}_{A_i}(v) = \sum_{S \subseteq N \setminus \{A_i\}} \left(\frac{|S|!(|N|-|S|-1)!}{|N|!} \right) [v(S \cup \{A_i\}) - v(S)] \qquad (5.1)$$

where $A_i \in N$ and for any coalition S, $|S|!$ is the number of possible orderings of the players in S.

Before we demonstrate the theorem, we interpret the formula (5.1) and illustrate it using an example. The last term on the right-hand side of Eq.(5.1) is the amount by which the pay-off of the coalition S increases when A_i joins it. This is the marginal contribution of player A_i to the coalition S. There are $|N|!$ orderings of the formation of the grand coalition and all orderings are equally likely. Now, out of $|N|!$ possible orderings of the players in N, there are $|S|!$ different orderings in which the first $|S|$ players can precede A_i and $(|N|-|S|-1)!$ different orderings in which the remaining $N \setminus S \cup \{A_i\}$ players follow A_i. Consequently, there is a total of $|S|!(|N|-|S|-1)!$ permutations in which the players in S precede A_i. Given that all permutations of the players for formation of the grand coalition are equi-probable, $[|S|!(|N|-|S|-1)!]/|N|!$ is the probability that A_i joins the coalition S that does not contain him. Note that here all coalitions of size $|S|$ are equally likely for A_i, that is, his chance of joining any coalition of size S is the same. Evidently, $\sum_{S \subseteq N \setminus \{A_i\}} [|S|!(|N|-|S|-1)!]/|N|! = 1$. Therefore, the Shapley value is a mathematical expectation, given a model of random coalition formation. It is a weighted average of the marginal contributions that the player makes to each coalition when he joins it, where the positive weights depend on the number of players in the game and the number of members in each coalition. It allocates higher pay-offs to players who make larger marginal contributions. Since in the computation of the Shapley value, all players enter the grand coalition one by one, each of them receiving the entire additional benefit he brings to the coalition formed just before his entrance, we can regard it as a fair way of distributing the worth of the set of all players among different players.

We may now illustrate the Shapley value using an example.

Example 19 Recall the firm−input supplier game $v \in G^N$ considered in Example 5, where $N = \{A_1, A_2, A_3\}$, $v(\{A_1\}) = v(\{A_2\}) = v(\{A_3\}) = v(\{A_2, A_3\}) = 0$ and $v(\{A_1, A_2\}) = v(\{A_1, A_3\}) = v(N) = 1$. The number of possible orderings of the player set $N = \{A_1, A_2, A_3\}$ is $3! = 6$. These orderings are: (A_1, A_2, A_3); (A_1, A_3, A_2); (A_2, A_1, A_3); (A_2, A_3, A_1); (A_3, A_1, A_2); and (A_3, A_2, A_1). If the grand coalition is formed as (A_2, A_1, A_3), then the coalition $S = \{A_1, A_2\}$ earns a worth of one and its worth is zero without player A_1. Thus, the marginal contribution of player A_1 here is $v(\{A_1, A_2\}) - v(\{A_2\}) = 1$. Likewise, A_1's marginal contribution in each of the orderings (A_2, A_3, A_1); (A_3, A_1, A_2); and (A_3, A_2, A_1) is 1, and the coefficient of each of them is $1/6$. Hence, the Shapley value for player A_1 is $\Phi_{A_1}^{Sh}(v) = 4/6$. Note that players A_2 and A_3 are substitutes in this game, which implies that their Shapley values are equal. Consequently, in view of EFF and SYM, the Shapley value of each of A_2 and A_3 is $\Phi_{A_2}^{Sh}(v) = \Phi_{A_3}^{Sh}(v) = (1 - \Phi_{A_1}^{Sh}(v))/2 = 1/6$. Recall that the only core element of this game is $(1, 0, 0)$, which is different from the Shapley value.

Proof of Theorem 9: The idea of the proof is taken from Aumann (1989). It is done in two steps. The first step is to show that if a value satisfying the Shapley axioms exists, then it has to be unique. The next step is to show that the value given by (5.1) satisfies the Shapley axioms and hence, guarantees the existence of such a value.

Uniqueness: Let Φ be a value function on G^N. Define for each coalition $T \subseteq N$, where T is non-empty, a game v_T as follows:

$$v_T(S) = \begin{cases} 1 & \text{if } T \subseteq S, \\ 0 & \text{otherwise.} \end{cases} \tag{5.2}$$

Note that for any real k, kv_T is also a game. Choose any $A_i \in N \setminus T$. If $T \not\subset S$, then $T \not\subset S \cup \{A_i\}$ since $A_i \notin T$. This implies that $kv_T(S) = kv_T(S \cup \{A_i\}) = k.0 = 0$. Next, if $T \subseteq S$, then $T \subset S \cup \{A_i\}$. Hence, $kv_T(S) = kv_T(S \cup \{A_i\}) = k.1 = k$. Since, $A_i \in N \setminus T$ is arbitrary, it follows that members of $N \setminus T$ are null players in kv_T. Hence by NPC, $\Phi_{A_i}(kv_T) = 0$ for all $A_i \in N \setminus T$.

Now, choose $A_i, A_j \in T$ but $A_i, A_j \notin S$. Therefore, $T \not\subset S$, which shows that $T \not\subset S \cup \{A_i\}$ and $T \not\subset S \cup \{A_j\}$ so that $kv_T(S \cup \{A_i\}) = kv_T(S \cup \{A_j\}) = k.0 = 0$. Given that $A_i, A_j \in T$ are arbitrary, it follows that members of T are substitutes in kv_T. Consequently, by SYM, $\Phi_{A_i}(kv_T) = \Phi_{A_j}(kv_T)$ for all $A_i, A_j \in T$. Therefore, $\sum_{A_i \in T} \Phi_{A_i}(kv_T) = |T|\Phi_{A_i}(kv_T)$ for any $A_i \in T$.

Since any $T \subseteq N$, by EFF, it follows that $\sum_{A_i \in N} \Phi_{A_i}(kv_T) = kv_T(N) = k.1 = k$. Now, $\sum_{A_i \in N} \Phi_{A_i}(kv_T) = \sum_{A_i \in T} \Phi_{A_i}(kv_T) + \sum_{A_i \in N \setminus T} \Phi_{A_i}(kv_T)$, which gives $k = \sum_{A_i \in T} \Phi_{A_i}(kv_T) = |T| \Phi_{A_i}(kv_T)$. Thus,

$$\Phi_{A_i}(kv_T) = \begin{cases} \dfrac{k}{|T|} & \text{if } A_i \in T, \\ 0 & \text{otherwise.} \end{cases} \tag{5.3}$$

Observe that G^N is an Euclidean space of dimension $2^{|N|} - 1$ and corresponding to each non-empty coalition T there is a v_T game. Since there are $2^{|N|} - 1$ non-empty coalitions, there are $2^{|N|} - 1$ games of the type v_T. We know the vector $\Phi(kv_T)$ for all non-empty coalitions T and real numbers k; hence by ADD, we know $\Phi(\sum_{r=1}^{q} k_r v_{T_r})$ for all linear combinations $\sum_{r=1}^{q} k_r v_{T_r}$ of v_Ts and real numbers k_rs. If v_{T_r}s are linearly independent, then the linear combination $\sum_{r=1}^{q} k_r v_{T_r}$ is unique. Any game in G^N is expressed uniquely as a linear combination of games of the type v_{T_r}s, given that v_{T_r}s are linearly independent.   Therefore, if we demonstrate that v_{T_r}s are linearly independent, then the uniqueness of the Shapley value follows.

Assume to the contrary that v_{T_r}s are linearly dependent. Arrange the non-empty coalitions T_r such that $|T_1| \geq |T_2| \geq \ldots \geq |T_m|$, where $m = 2^{|N|} - 1$ and all T_rs are different from each other. Since v_{T_r}s are linearly dependent, there exists T_p such that

$$v_{T_p}(S) = \sum_{r=1}^{p-1} b_r v_{T_r}(S) \tag{5.4}$$

for all coalitions $S \subseteq N$, where b_rs are constants and not all b_rs are zero. If we take $S = T_p$ in (5.4), then (5.4) reduces to $v_{T_p}(T_p) = \sum_{r=1}^{p-1} b_r v_{T_r}(T_p)$ and, using the definition of v_{T_r}, we get $1 = \sum_{r=1}^{p-1} b_r.0$, which is a contradiction. Therefore, v_{T_r}s are linearly independent. This completes the uniqueness part of the proof.

Existence: To prove the existence part, all we have to show is that the value function Φ^{Sh} given by the formula (5.1) satisfies NPC, SYM, EFF and ADD.

Consider $v \in G^N$ and let $A_i \in N$ be a null player. Then for player A_i, $\Phi_{A_i}^{Sh}(v) = \sum_{S \subseteq N \setminus \{A_i\}} \{[|S|!(|N| - |S| - 1)!]/|N|!\}.0 = 0$ implying NPC.

If players A_i and A_j are substitutes in $v \in G^N$, then $v(S \cup \{A_i\}) = v(S \cup \{A_j\})$ for all $S \subseteq N \setminus \{A_i, A_j\}$. Therefore, for all $S \subseteq N \setminus \{A_i, A_j\}$, we have the following:

$$v(S \cup \{A_i\}) - v(S) = v(S \cup \{A_j\}) - v(S), \text{and} \tag{S1}$$

$$v(S \cup \{A_i, A_j\}) - v(S \cup \{A_j\}) = v(S \cup \{A_i, A_j\}) - v(S \cup \{A_i\}). \tag{S2}$$

Using formula (5.1) and the implications of substitutability given by (S1) and (S2), we get

$$\Phi_{A_i}^{Sh}(v) = \sum_{S \subseteq N \setminus \{A_i\}} \left(\frac{|S|!(|N| - |S| - 1)!}{|N|!} \right) [v(S \cup \{A_i\}) - v(S)]$$

$$= \sum_{S \subseteq N \setminus \{A_i, A_j\}} \left(\frac{|S|!(|N| - |S| - 1)!}{|N|!} \right) [v(S \cup \{A_i\}) - v(S)]$$

$$+ \sum_{S \subseteq N \setminus \{A_i, A_j\}} \left(\frac{|S \cup \{A_j\}|!(|N| - |S \cup \{A_j\}| - 1)!}{|N|!} \right) [v(S \cup \{A_i, A_j\}) - v(S \cup \{A_j\})]$$

$$= \sum_{S \subseteq N \setminus \{A_i, A_j\}} \left(\frac{|S|!(|N| - |S| - 1)!}{|N|!} \right) [v(S \cup \{A_j\}) - v(S)]$$

$$+ \sum_{S \subseteq N \setminus \{A_i, A_j\}} \left(\frac{|S \cup \{A_i\}|!(|N| - |S \cup \{A_i\}| - 1)!}{|N|!} \right) [v(S \cup \{A_i, A_j\}) - v(S \cup \{A_i\})]$$

$$= \sum_{S \subseteq N \setminus \{A_j\}} \left(\frac{|S|!(|N| - |S| - 1)!}{|N|!} \right) [v(S \cup \{A_j\}) - v(S)]$$

$$= \Phi_{A_j}^{Sh}(v).$$

Therefore, if in a coalitional game $v \in G^N$, players A_i and A_j are substitutes, then $\Phi_{A_i}^{Sh}(v) = \Phi_{A_j}^{Sh}(v)$. Hence, we have SYM.

Consider any $v \in G^N$ and the value function given by the formula (5.1). For EFF, observe that using formula (5.1), we obtain

$$\sum_{A_i \in N} \Phi_{A_i}^{Sh}(v) = \sum_{A_i \in N} \sum_{S \subseteq N \setminus \{A_i\}} \left(\frac{|S|!(|N| - |S| - 1)!}{|N|!} \right) [v(S \cup \{A_i\}) - v(S)]. \tag{5.5}$$

Consider the double sum on the right-hand side of condition (5.5) and take any coalition $S \subseteq N$ and the coefficients associated with $v(S)$. Note that if $A_i \in S$, then the coefficient of $v(S)$ is $([|S \setminus \{A_i\}|!(|N| - |S|)!]/|N|!)$ and if $A_j \notin S$, then it is $(-1).([|S|!(|N| - |S \cup \{A_j\}|)!]/|N|!)$. Therefore, using condition (5.5), we get

$$\sum_{A_i \in N} \Phi_{A_i}^{Sh}(v) \qquad\qquad =$$
$$\sum_{A_i \in N} \sum_{S \subseteq N \setminus \{A_i\}} \left(\frac{|S|!(|N| - |S| - 1)!}{|N|!} \right) [v(S \cup \{A_i\}) - v(S)]$$

$$=$$
$$\sum_{S \subseteq N} \left\{ \sum_{A_i \in S} \left(\frac{|S \setminus \{A_i\}|!(|N| - |S|)!}{|N|!} \right) v(S) - \sum_{A_j \in N \setminus S} \left(\frac{|S|!(|N| - |S \cup \{A_j\}|)!}{|N|!} \right) v(S) \right\}$$

$$=$$
$$v(N) + \sum_{S \subset N, S \neq \emptyset} \left\{ \left(\frac{|S|!(|N| - |S|)!}{|N|!} \right) v(S) - \left(\frac{|S|!(|N| - |S|)!}{|N|!} \right) v(S) \right\} - v(\emptyset)$$

$$= v(N).$$

Thus, for any $v \in G^N$, $\sum_{A_i \in N} \Phi_{A_i}^{Sh}(v) = v(N)$ and we have EFF.

Consider any $v, w \in G^N$ and the resulting $v + w \in G^N$. Then for any $A_i \in N$,

$$\Phi_{A_i}^{Sh}(v + w) = \sum_{S \subseteq N \setminus \{A_i\}} \left(\frac{|S|!(|N| - |S| - 1)!}{|N|!} \right) [(v + w)(S \cup \{A_i\}) - (v + w)(S)]$$

$$= \sum_{S \subseteq N \setminus \{A_i\}} \left(\frac{|S|!(|N| - |S| - 1)!}{|N|!} \right) [v(S \cup \{A_i\}) - v(S)]$$

$$+ \sum_{S \subseteq N \setminus \{A_i\}} \left(\frac{|S|!(|N| - |S| - 1)!}{|N|!} \right) [w(S \cup \{A_i\}) - w(S)]$$

$$= \Phi_{A_i}^{Sh}(v) + \Phi_{A_i}^{Sh}(w).$$

Since the selection of $v, w \in G^N$ and $A_i \in N$ were all arbitrary, it follows that the value function given by formula (5.1) satisfies ADD. □

In the uniqueness part of the proof of the theorem, we have made use of the fact that any game $v \in G^N$ can be expressed as a linear combination of the set of all coalition form games $\{\{v_T\}_{T \subseteq N}\}$ defined in (5.2). More specifically, one can show that for any coalition form game $v \in G^N$,

$$v(S) = \sum_{T \subseteq N} \alpha_T v_T(S) \text{ for all } S \subseteq N, \text{ where } \alpha_T = \sum_{Q \subseteq T} (-1)^{|T| - |Q|} v(Q).$$

To illustrate this, we use an example from Roth (1988). Consider the game $v \in G^N$ with the player set $N = \{A_1, A_2, A_3\}$, where the coalition pay-offs are as follows: $v(\{A_1\}) = 10, v(\{A_2\}) = v(\{A_3\}) = v(\{A_2, A_3\}) = 0, v(\{A_1, A_2\}) = 20$ and $v(\{A_1, A_3\}) = v(N) = 30$. Observe that $\alpha_{\{A_1\}} = v(\{A_1\}) = 10, \alpha_{\{A_2\}} = \alpha_{\{A_3\}} = 0, \alpha_{\{A_1, A_2\}} = v(\{A_1, A_2\}) - v(\{A_1\}) - v(\{A_2\}) = 20 - 10 = 10, \alpha_{\{A_1, A_3\}} = v(\{A_1, A_3\}) - v(\{A_1\}) - v(\{A_3\}) = 30 - 10 = 20$ and $\alpha_{\{A_2, A_3\}} = 0$. Finally, $\alpha_N = v(N) - v(\{A_1, A_2\}) - v(\{A_1, A_3\}) - v(\{A_2, A_3\}) + v(\{A_1\}) + v(\{A_2\}) + v(\{A_3\}) = 30 - 20 - 30 - 0 + 10 + 0 + 0 = -10$. Therefore, the worth $v(S)$ of any coalition S of this game can be determined from the following linear combination $10v_{\{A_1\}}(S) + 10v_{\{A_1, A_2\}}(S) + 20v_{\{A_1, A_3\}}(S) - 10v_{\{A_1, A_2, A_3\}}(S)$. For example, if the coalition is $S = \{A_1, A_3\}$, then $v(\{A_1, A_3\}) = 10v_{\{A_1\}}(\{A_1, A_3\}) + 10v_{\{A_1, A_2\}}(\{A_1, A_3\}) + 20v_{\{A_1, A_3\}}(\{A_1, A_3\}) - 10v_{\{A_1, A_2, A_3\}}(\{A_1, A_3\}) = 10.1 + 10.0 + 20.1 - 10.0 = 30$.

The Shapley value can be regarded as a remarkable contribution to the well-known marginalist principle in economic theory; each individual should be paid on the basis of his marginal contribution. It is a reasonable proposal for uniquely dividing the total amount that the players of the game as a whole can earn. On the other hand, the core consists of a set of stable pay-off vectors. While there is a unique Shapley value for each game, the core of a game may be empty. The core elements as well as the Shapley value satisfy the efficiency property. There is no general relationship between the two solution concepts. They are different and each has got its own appealing features. The Shapley value need not be an element of the core if it is non-empty. Even if the core is a single element set, it may not coincide with the core element. However, for a convex game, it is an element of the core (see Chapter 6). The Shapley value also does not clearly say anything about the bargaining process. While for the bargaining set the coalition structure has a status quo, no such notion exists in the case of the Shapley value. However, it must also be noted that there are certain similarities between the Shapley value and the pre-nucleolus. For any coalitional game $v \in G^N$, both the Shapley value and the pre-nucleolus exist and are unique. For two-player and symmetric games, the Shapley value and the pre-nucleolus are identical (Peleg and Suthölter). There is another class of games called PS games for which the pre-nucleolus coincides with the Shapley value. For a PS game, $[v(S \cup \{A_i\}) - v(S)] + [v(N \setminus S) - v(N \setminus [S \cup \{A_i\}])] = c_{A_i}$ for each $S \subset N$, each $A_i \in N$ and $c_{A_i} \in \Re$, where c_{A_i} is a player specific constant (Kar, Mitra and Mutuswami 2009). Like the Shapley value, the pre-nucleolus satisfies SYM, NPC and EFF. Unlike the Shapley value, the pre-nucleolus fails to satisfy ADD.

5.4   A Discussion on Some Alternative Characterizations

It is evident that among the Shapley axioms, ADD does not have much normative content. It is quite convenient, mathematically, but difficult to motivate. The behaviour of the sum game $v + w$ may not be related to that of the component v or w, where $v, w \in G^N$. Young (1985; 1988) dropped ADD, and instead, employed a principle known as monotonicity of marginal contributions to develop an alternative characterization of the Shapley value. According to this principle, for any two games $v, w \in G^N$, if a player's marginal contribution to any coalition in v is at least as large as that in w, then the player's pay-off under w cannot be higher than that under v. Formally,

---

Definition 54   Monotonicity of marginal contributions (MMC)
For any $v, w \in G^N$, if for all $S \subseteq N$, $v(S \cup \{A_i\}) - v(S) \geq w(S \cup \{A_i\}) - w(S)$, then $\Phi_{A_i}(v) \geq \Phi_{A_i}(w)$.

Since the Shapley value of a player is the weighted average of his marginal contributions to all possible coalitions, it is obvious that it satisfies this principle. The following theorem of Young (1985; 1988) shows that the axiom MMC plays an important role in an alternative characterization of the Shapley value.

Theorem 10 The Shapley value is the only value function that satisfies SYM, EFF and MMC.

Thus, Young's (1985; 1988) theorem provides a counterpart to Theorem 9 (Shapley 1953). He dropped ADD as well as NPC, and instead, used MMC. One implication of MMC is marginality. *Marginality* means that the solution should pay the same to a player in two games if his marginal contributions to coalitions is the same in both games. The idea of marginality has a strong tradition in economic theory.

What is surprising about Theorem 9 (Shapley 1953) is that nothing in the axioms (with the possible exception of NPC) hints at the idea of marginal contributions, so marginality is a consequence of SYM, NPC, EFF and ADD taken together. Theorem 10 (Young 1985) on the other hand assumes marginality to derive the Shapley value which is additive. Thus, ADD is a consequence of MMC, SYM and EFF taken together.

Hart and Mas-Colell (1989) provided further characterization of the Shapley value using the concept of potential. The essential idea underlying this is that each $v \in G^N$ can be associated with a single number

$P(N,v)$ and player A_i's marginal contribution with respect to $v \in G^N$ is $P(N,v) - P(N \setminus \{A_i\}, v)$, where $(N \setminus \{A_i\}, v)$ is the restriction of $v \in G^N$ to the player set $N \setminus \{A_i\}$. Thus, this procedure avoids the tedious way of looking at all the coalitions A_i can join and the marginal contributions made by A_i to each coalition. The function $P : G^N \to \Re$ with $P(\emptyset, v) = 0$ is said to be a potential function if $\sum_{A_i \in N} [P(N,v) - P(N \setminus \{A_i\}), v)] = v(N)$. That is, P qualifies as a potential function if the marginal contributions add up to the worth of the grand coalition.

Theorem 11 There exists a unique potential function P. For every $v \in G^N$, the resulting pay-off vector $(P(N,v) - P(N \setminus \{A_1\}, v), \ldots, P(N,v) - P(N \setminus \{A_n\}, v))$ of marginal contributions coincides with the Shapley value of the game. Moreover, the potential of a game $v \in G^N$ is uniquely determined by the condition $\sum_{A_i \in N} [P(N,v) - P((N \setminus \{A_i\}), v)] = v(N)$ applied only to the game and its sub-games (that is, to all (S, v) for all $S \subseteq N$).

Theorem 11 identifies the Shapley value as the unique efficient solution that possesses a potential. That is, there is a unique potential with respect to which each player's marginal contribution becomes his Shapley value.

Myerson (1977) used ideas from graph theory to provide a framework within which one can discuss a broad class of partial cooperation structures and study the question of how the outcome of a game should depend on which players cooperate with each other. In this context, Myerson (1977) provides a new derivation of the Shapley value. This result is discussed in detail in the appendix of this chapter.

5.5 Applications

Allocation of joint costs of a common service among customers is an important issue in many real-life problems. Basically, the development of a project serving a large number of customers is dependent on the formulation of a pricing policy that motivates the individual customers to cooperate. For instance, two doctors who share an office, share joint costs. Suppose five nearby municipalities are considering construction of a new airport jointly because a single landing strip will be sufficient to accommodate their needs. However, they need to decide on the allocation of construction and maintenance costs. A multi-product firm distributes overhead costs among its various products and divisions. Some farms are connected to each other and to a national highway by a not so well-built road. Each farm will benefit from being connected to the highway by a paved road. The farms need to distribute the costs of paving the road among themselves.

The above examples clearly indicate that a cost allocation problem bears some similarity with the determination of the value of cooperative games. Therefore, following the developments in cooperative games, new cost allocation methods have been suggested [refer Young (1994) for an elegant discussion.]. In particular, a large part of the literature has been devoted to the application of the Shapley value because of its nice axiomatic structure. Littlechild and Owen (1973) and Roth and Venechaia (1979) suggested the use of the Shapley value to allocate costs in the situations like airport landing and firm accounting problems.

To present the problem analytically, let us consider the problem of allocating costs for providing some service among the set of customers $N = \{A_1, \ldots, A_n\}$ (see Chapter 2). As before, for any $S \subset N$, $c(S)$ is the least cost of providing the service to the members of S. An allocation is a vector $x = (x_{A_1}, \ldots, x_{A_n})$ such that $\sum_{A_i \in N} x_{A_i} = c(N)$, where x_{A_i} is the part of the total cost $c(N)$ assigned to player A_i. The equality $\sum_{A_i \in N} x_{A_i} = c(N)$ may be regarded as a cost recovery condition. A cost allocation method is a function $\Phi : G^N \to \Re^{|N|}$, where G^N now represents the set of all cost-sharing games, given that the set of service users is N. That is, for every cost-sharing game $c \in G^N$, there corresponds a unique allocation.

We can interpret the Shapley axioms in the current context as follows. NPC may be treated as the condition that those who do not use the service should not be charged for it. SYM may be interpreted as the requirement that everyone who uses the service should be charged equally for it. Finally, to understand ADD, assume that the total costs can be broken down into two different components—say operating costs c^1 and capital costs c^2. Then, ADD means that for any coalition $S \subseteq N$, the sum of the operating and the capital cost is simply the coalition S's total cost of using the service.

The unique cost allocation rule that satisfies NPC, SYM and ADD is the Shapley value and the unique cost assigned to player $A_i \in N$ is given by Eq.(5.1) with v being replaced by the cost-sharing game c. For a concave cost-sharing game, its core contains the Shapley value (see Chapter 6). Chapter 6 provides an interpretation of the Shapley value as the random arrival rule for solving a bankruptcy problem. In Chapter 7, we will show that the Shapley value has a very important application in modelling the power of members of a voting body.

5.6   Appendix

5.6.1   Graphs, cooperation and the Shapley value

Let $N = \{A_1, \ldots, A_n\}$ denote the non-empty finite set of players. A *graph* on N is a set of *unordered pairs of distinct numbers* of N referred to as *links* and is denoted by $A_i : A_j$. Observe that $A_i : A_j = A_j : A_i$ since a link is an unordered pair. Let $g^N = \{A_i : A_j \mid A_i, A_j \in N, A_i \neq A_j\}$ be the complete graph of all links. Then, let $GR = \{g \mid g \subseteq g^N\}$ be the set of all possible graphs on N. The basic idea is that players may cooperate in a game by forming a series of bilateral agreements among themselves. These bilateral cooperative agreements can be represented by links between the agreeing players—any cooperation structure can be represented by a set of agreement links. In this way, one can identify the set of all possible cooperation structures with GR, the set of all graphs on the set of players.

5.6.2   Coalitions and connectedness

Consider a non-empty coalition $S \subseteq N$. Suppose $g \in GR$ and $A_i, A_j \in S$ are given. Then, we say that A_i and A_j are *connected* in S by g if and only if *there is a path in g which goes from A_i to A_j and stays within S*. That is, A_i and A_j are connected in S by g if $A_i = A_j$ or if there is some $k \geq 1$ and a sequence $(A^0, A^1, \ldots, A^k)$ such that $A^0 = A_i$, $A^k = A_j$ and, for all $r \in \{1, \ldots, k\}$, $A^{r-1} : A^r \in g$ and $A^r \in S$. Given $g \in GR$ and $S \subseteq N$, there is a unique partition of S which groups players together if and only if they are connected in S by g. We will denote this partition by S/g ("S divided by g"), so

$$S \backslash g = \{\{A_i \mid A_i \text{ and } A_j \text{ are connected in } S \text{ by } g\} \mid A_j \in S\}.$$

We can interpret S/g as the collection of smaller coalitions into which S would break up, if players could only coordinate along the links in g. For example, if $N = \{A_1, \ldots, A_5\}$ and $g = \{A_1 : A_2, A_1 : A_4, A_2 : A_4, A_3 : A_4\}$, then $\{A_1, A_2, A_3\}/g = \{\{A_1, A_2\}, \{A_3\}\}$ and $N/g = \{\{A_1, A_2, A_3, A_4\}, \{A_5\}\}$. When we speak of *connectedness* without any reference to any specific coalition, we always mean *connectedness in N*. Given a cooperative graph g, the connectedness–partition N/g is the natural coalition structure associated with the graph g. The idea is that even if two players do not have a direct agreement link between themselves, they may still effectively cooperate if they both have an agreement with the same mutual friend or if they are otherwise connected by the cooperative graph.

5.6.3   Allocation rule

Let $v \in G^N$ and let GR be the set of all possible cooperation structures for the game v. The outcomes of v can be represented by pay-off allocation vectors in $\Re^{|N|}$.

Definition 55 An *allocation rule* for $v \in G^N$ is a function $Y : GR \to \Re^{|N|}$ such that
$$\forall g \in GR, \ \forall S \in N/g, \ \sum_{A_i \in S} Y_{A_i}(g) = v(S). \tag{5.6}$$

Condition (5.6) asserts that if S is a connected component of g, then the members of S ought to allocate to themselves the total wealth $v(S)$ available to them. Notice that the allocation within a connected coalition S still depends on the actual graph g. For example, an allocation might give higher pay-off to player A_1 in $g_1 = \{A_1 : A_2, A_1 : A_3, A_1 : A_4\}$ than in $g_2 = \{A_1 : A_2, A_2 : A_3, A_3 : A_4\}$ though condition (5.6) requires that $\sum_{A_i \in \{A_1, A_2, A_3, A_4\}} Y_{A_i}(g_1) = v(\{A_1, A_2, A_3, A_4\}) = \sum_{A_i \in \{A_1, A_2, A_3, A_4\}} Y_{A_i}(g_2)$.

Definition 56 An allocation rule $Y : GR \to \Re^{|N|}$ is *stable* if and only if:

$\forall g \in GR, \forall A_i : A_j \in g, Y_{A_i}(g) \geq Y_{A_i}(g \setminus (A_i : A_j))$ and
$Y_{A_j}(g) \geq Y_{A_j}(g \setminus (A_i : A_j)). \tag{5.7}$

A stable allocation rule has the property that two players always benefit from a bilateral agreement. Hence, if the allocation rule was stable, then all players would want to be linked to as many others as possible and we could expect the complete cooperation graph g^N to be the cooperation structure of the game. To narrow the range of allocation rules, we may apply the equal gains principle—two players should gain equally from their bilateral agreement.

Definition 57 An allocation rule $Y : GR \to \Re^{|N|}$ is *fair* if and only if:

$\forall g \in GR, \forall A_i : A_j \in g, Y_{A_i}(g) - Y_{A_i}(g \setminus (A_i : A_j)) = Y_{A_j}(g) - Y_{A_j}(g \setminus (A_i : A_j)). \tag{5.8}$

Consider the 'divide the dollar' game $v \in G^N$, where $N = \{A_1, A_2\}$, $v(\{A_1\}) = v(\{A_2\}) = 0$ and $v(\{A_1, A_2\}) = 1$. To be an allocation rule for v, it is necessary that Y must satisfy $Y_{A_1}(\emptyset) = Y_{A_2}(\emptyset) = 0$, $Y_{A_1}(\{A_1 : A_2\}) + Y_{A_2}(\{A_1 : A_2\}) = 1$ (where $\emptyset$ is the empty graph with no links). Stability requires that $Y_{A_1}(\{A_1 : A_2\}) \geq Y_{A_1}(\emptyset) = 0$ and $Y_{A_2}(\{A_1 : A_2\}) \geq Y_{A_2}(\emptyset) = 0$. The only fair allocation rule has Y_{A_1}

$(\{A_1 : A_2\}) = Y_{A_2}(\{A_1 : A_2\}) = 0.5$, which is also the Shapley value of the divide the dollar game.

Definition 58 Given a coalition form game $v \in G^N$ and a graph $g \in GR$, define v/g to be a characteristic function game such that

$$\forall S \subseteq N, \ (v/g)(S) = \sum_{T \in S/g} v(T). \tag{5.9}$$

One may interpret v/g as *the coalition form game which would result if we alter the situation represented by v, requiring that players can only communicate along links in g.*

5.6.4   The theorem

Theorem 12 Given a coalition form game $v \in G^N$, there is a unique fair allocation rule $Y : GR \rightarrow \Re^{|N|}$ [satisfying conditions (5.6) and (5.8)]. This fair allocation rule also satisfies $Y(g) = \Phi^{Sh}(v/g)$ for all $g \in GR$, where $\Phi^{Sh}(.)$ is the Shapley value operator. Furthermore, if v is super-additive, then the fair allocation rule is stable.

Since $v/g^N = v$, we get $Y(g^N) = \Phi^{Sh}(v)$ for the fair allocation rule Y. Thus, this notion of cooperation graphs and fair allocation rules provide a new derivation of the Shapley value.

Proof of Theorem 12:   This proof is taken from Myerson (1977). We first show that there is at most one fair allocation rule for a given game v. Suppose both $Y^1 : GR \rightarrow \Re^{|N|}$ and $Y^2 : GR \rightarrow \Re^{|N|}$ satisfy conditions (5.6) and (5.8) and are different. Let g be a graph with a minimum number of links such that $Y^1(g) \neq Y^2(g)$. Let $y^1 = Y^1(g)$ and $y^2 = Y^2(g)$. By minimality of g, if $A_i : A_j$ is any link of g, then $Y^1(g \setminus A_i : A_j) = Y^2(g \setminus A_i : A_j)$. Hence, condition (5.8) implies that $y^1_{A_i} - y^1_{A_j} = Y^1_{A_i}(g \setminus A_i : A_j) - Y^1_{A_j}(g \setminus A_i : A_j) = Y^2_{A_i}(g \setminus A_i : A_j) - Y^2_{A_j}(g \setminus A_i : A_j) = y^2_{A_i} - y^2_{A_j}$. Therefore, $y^1_{A_i} - y^2_{A_i} = y^1_{A_j} - y^2_{A_j}$ whenever A_i and A_j are linked and also when they are in the same connected component S of g. Thus, we can write $y^1_{A_i} - y^2_{A_i} = d_S(g)$, where $d_S(g)$ depends on S and g only, but not on A_i. However, by condition (5.6), $\sum_{A_i \in S} y^1_{A_i} = \sum_{A_i \in S} y^2_{A_i}$. Hence, $0 = \sum_{A_i \in S}(y^1_{A_i} - y^2_{A_i}) = |S| d_S(g)$, and therefore, $d_S(g) = 0$ implying that $y^1 = y^2$ and we have a contradiction. Thus, there can be at most one fair allocation rule.

It now remains to show that $Y(g) = \Phi^{Sh}(v/g)$ implies that conditions (5.6) and (5.8) are satisfied, along with condition (5.7), if v is super-additive.

We will show condition (5.6) first. Select $g \in GR$. For each $S \in N/g$, define w^S to be a coalition form game such that $w^S(T) = \sum_{R \in (T \cap S)/g} v(R)$, for all $T \subseteq N$. Since any two players connected in T by g are also connected in N by g, we get $T/g = \cup_{S \in N/g} (T \cap S)/g$. Therefore, $v/g = \sum_{S \in N/g} w^S$ since for each $T \subseteq N$, $(v/g)(T) = \sum_{Q \in T/g} v(Q) = \sum_{S \in N/g} \{\sum_{Q \in (T \cap S)/g} v(Q)\} = \sum_{S \in N/g} w^S(T)$. Moreover, for $S \in N/g$, $w^S(T) = w^S(T \cap S)$. Therefore, for any $S, T \in N/g$,

$$\sum_{A_i \in S} \Phi_{A_i}^{Sh}(w^T) = \begin{cases} w^S(N) & \text{if } T = S \\ 0 & \text{if } T \cap S = \emptyset. \end{cases}$$

Thus, by additivity of Φ^{Sh}, if $S \in N/g$, then it follows that $\sum_{A_i \in S} \Phi_{A_i}^{Sh}(v/g) = \sum_{T \in N/g} \sum_{A_i \in S} \Phi_{A_i}^{Sh}(w^T) = w^S(N) = \sum_{R \in S/g} v(R) = v(S)$ and condition (5.6) is satisfied.

To show that condition (5.8) holds, select any $g \in GR$ and any $A_i : A_j \in g$. Define the coalition form game $W = v/g - v/(g \setminus (A_i : A_j))$. Observe that $S/g = S/(g \setminus (A_i : A_j))$ if $\{A_i, A_j\} \not\subseteq S$. Hence, if $A_i \notin S$ or $A_j \notin S$, we get $W(S) = \sum_{T \in S/g} v(T) - \sum_{T \in S/(g \setminus (A_i : A_j))} v(T) = 0$. Therefore, the only coalitions with non-zero wealth in W are coalitions containing both A_i and A_j. Consequently, by the symmetry axiom of Shapley (1953), it follows that $\Phi_{A_i}^{Sh}(W) = \Phi_{A_j}^{Sh}(W)$. By additivity of Φ^{Sh}, $\Phi_{A_i}^{Sh}(v/g) - \Phi_{A_i}^{Sh}(v/(g \setminus (A_i : A_j))) = \Phi_{A_i}^{Sh}(W) = \Phi_{A_j}^{Sh}(W) = \Phi_{A_j}^{Sh}(v/g) - \Phi_{A_j}^{Sh}(v/(g \setminus (A_i : A_j)))$.

Finally, we will show condition (5.7). Observe that $S/(g \setminus (A_i : A_j))$ always refines S/g, and if $A_i \notin S$, then $S/(g \setminus (A_i : A_j)) = S/g$. Hence, if v is super-additive, then $(v/g)(S) = \sum_{T \in S/g} v(T) \geq \sum_{T \in S/(g \setminus (A_i : A_j))} v(T) = (v/(g \setminus (A_i : A_j)))(S)$ and the inequality becomes equality if $A_i \notin S$. Thus, if $W = v/g - v/(g \setminus (A_i : A_j))$, then $W(S) \geq 0$ for all S and $w(S) = 0$ if $A_i \notin S$. Hence, $W(S \cup \{A_i\}) \geq W(S)$ for all $S \in N \setminus \{A_i\}$ and $\Phi_{A_i}^{Sh}(W) \geq 0$ since the Shapley value is the expected marginal contribution of a player. Therefore, $\Phi_{A_i}^{Sh}(v/g) - \Phi_{A_i}^{Sh}(v/(g \setminus (A_i : A_j))) = \Phi_{A_i}^{Sh}(W) \geq 0$, which proves stability.   □

Exercises

5.1 Determine the Shapley value of the two-person bargaining game analyzed in Chapter 3 using the axioms of symmetry and efficiency. Show that it is an element of the core of the game. Can you identify the reason for inclusion of the Shapley value in the core?

5.2 Consider a game v with the player set $N = \{A_1, A_2, A_3\}$ and whose coalition pay-offs are as follows: $v(\{A_1\}) = 1$, $v(\{A_2\}) = 2$, $v(\{A_3\}) = 3$, $v(\{A_2, A_3\}) = 5$, $v(\{A_1, A_2\}) = 4$, $v(\{A_1, A_3\}) = 6$, $v(N) = 9$. Determine the Shapley value of this game.

5.3 Determine the Shapley value of the non-liability game considered in Chapter 3.

5.4 Give an example of a three-person game in which any two players are substitutes.

5.5 What is the Shapley value of each player in an additive game?

5.6 Let the coalition pay-offs of a game $v \in G^N$ be defined as $v(S) = \sum_{A_i \in S} r_{A_i}$, where $r \in \Re_{+}^{|N|}$ is a vector, S is any non-empty coalition and $\Re_{+}^{|N|}$ is the non-negative orthant of the $|N|$-dimensional Euclidean space $\Re^{|N|}$. Determine the Shapley value of this game. Under what necessary and sufficient condition can a player in this game be a null player? Examine the implication of the symmetry axiom on the vector.

5.7 Prove or disprove the following statement: The Shapley value of a game coincides with that of its dual game.

5.8 Consider two values $\Phi_1, \Phi_1 : G^N \to \Re^{|N|}$ that satisfy the axioms of null player condition, symmetry and efficiency. Then show that any convex mix $\lambda\Phi_1 + (1 - \lambda)\Phi_2$, where $0 \leq \lambda \leq 1$ is a constant, also satisfies these axioms.

5.9 Formulate: (i) a four-person game in which two persons are null players and the remaining two persons are substitutes, (ii) a four-person game in which there are no substitute players, (iii) a four-person game in which any two of three persons are substitutes for each other but the remaining person is not a substitute of any other person.

5.10 Determine the Shapley value of the landowner–peasants game considered in Chapter 1 and in Chapter 2.

5.11 For a five-person game v, let $v(S) = \left(\sum_{A_i \in S} r_{A_i}\right)^2$, where S is any non-empty coalition and $r = (1, 3, 2, 5, 3)$. Determine the Shapley value of this game.

5.12 Consider a three-person game v, where $v(\{A_i\}) = 0$ for all $A_i \in \{A_1, A_2, A_3\}$, $v(\{A_1, A_2\}) = 30$, $v(\{A_1, A_3\}) = 40$, $v(\{A_2, A_3\}) = 50$ and $v(\{A_1, A_2, A_3\}) = 120$. Show that its kernel consists of only one element. Does this coincide with the Shapley value of the game?

CHAPTER 6

The Core, Shapley Value and Weber Set

6.1 Introduction

Given a particular way of forming the grand coalition in a coalition form game, the marginal contribution of a player to the grand coalition is the amount by which the worth of the coalition increases when he joins the coalition of players that precede him. For instance, the marginal contribution of each share holder in a joint profit-making business is the additional amount of profit that he can guarantee to the coalition of players who have joined the business before him. The Weber set is the smallest convex set containing the set of marginal contribution vectors of the players.

In the next section of this chapter, we will introduce the Weber set of a game and show that it contains the core of the game (Weber 1988). In Section 6.3, we will study the properties of convex coalition form games. Convexity of a coalition form game may be interpreted as the condition where there are higher incentives for joining a coalition as the size of the coalition increases (Shapley 1971). This section also shows that for a convex game, the core is non-empty. It is then shown that the Weber set and the core of a game coincide if and only if the game is convex. It is also demonstrated that the bankruptcy game is an example of a convex game. Next, we show that the Shapley value for a convex game is an element of the core, which in turn demonstrates that the core of a convex game is non-empty. In Section 6.4, we will analyze random order values and their relations with the Weber set and the Shapley value. It is explicitly proven that O'Neill's (1982) random arrival rule, a solution to the bankruptcy problem, coincides with the Shapley value of the corresponding bankruptcy game.

6.2 The Weber Set and Core

Recall that given a particular arrangement or permutation of players in the grand coalition of a game, the corresponding marginal contribution vector gives each player his marginal contribution to the coalition formed by his entrance according to the specific permutation. Note that the set of all marginal contribution vectors in a game is a closed set.

We begin this section with the following property of a marginal contribution vector.

Observation 1: Assume that the players $N = \{A_1, \ldots, A_n\}$ in the game $v \in G^N$ are arranged in the order $(A_1, \ldots, A_n)$. Then, the corresponding marginal contribution vector $x = (x_{A_1}, \ldots, x_{A_n})$, where $x_{A_1} = v(\{A_1\})$, $x_{A_2} = v(\{A_1, A_2\}) - v(\{A_1\}), \ldots, x_{A_n} = v(N) - v(\{A_1, \ldots, A_{n-1}\})$ is a pre-imputation.

To verify Observation 1, note that $\sum_{A_i \in N} x_{A_i} = v(\{A_1\}) + v(\{A_1, A_2\}) - v(\{A_1\}) + \ldots + v(N) - v(\{A_1, \ldots, A_{n-1}\}) = v(N)$. Thus, x is a Pareto efficient pay-off vector, which means that x is a pre-imputation. Although, it uses a particular ordering of the players, this observation is quite general in the sense that if we consider an alternative ordering of the players, then the corresponding marginal contribution vector also becomes a pre-imputation.

Let $M(v)$ be the set of the vectors of all marginal contributions in the game $v \in G^N$. Consider the game $v \in G^N$, where $N = \{A_1, A_2, A_3\}$. Then, $M(v)$ is the largest obtainable set from the collection $\{M^{\sigma^k}(N, v)\}_{k=1}^6$ given in the right column of Table 6.1. Here σ^k represents a generic permutation of the player set $N = \{A_1, A_2, A_3\}$ and, in particular, $\sum_{A_i \in N} M_{A_i}^{\sigma^k}(N, v) = v(N)$ for $k = 1, 2, \ldots, 6$.

We can look for the smallest convex set containing all the marginal contributions vectors. This is precisely the Weber set, a core catcher of the game. The intersection of all closed convex sets containing $M(v)$, the set of vectors of all marginal contributions in the game $v \in G^N$, is a closed convex set which contains $M(v)$ and which is contained in every closed

Table 6.1 Potential elements for $M(v)$ obtainable from $\{M^{\sigma^k}(N,v)\}_{k=1}^{6}$

Ordering	$M^{\sigma}(N,v) = (M^{\sigma}_{A_1}(N,v), M^{\sigma}_{A_2}(N,v), M^{\sigma}_{A_3}(N,v))$
$\sigma^1 = (A_1, A_2, A_3)$	$M^{\sigma^1}(N,v) = (v(\{A_1\}), v(\{A_1,A_2\}) - v(\{A_1\}), v(N) - v(\{A_1,A_2\}))$
$\sigma^2 = (A_1, A_3, A_2)$	$M^{\sigma^2}(N,v) = (v(\{A_1\}), v(N) - v(\{A_1,A_3\}), v(\{A_1,A_3\}) - v(\{A_1\}))$
$\sigma^3 = (A_2, A_1, A_3)$	$M^{\sigma^3}(N,v) = (v(\{A_1,A_2\}) - v(\{A_2\}), v(\{A_2\}), v(N) - v(\{A_1,A_2\}))$
$\sigma^4 = (A_2, A_3, A_1)$	$M^{\sigma^4}(N,v) = (v(N) - v(\{A_2,A_3\}), v(\{A_2\}), v(\{A_2,A_3\}) - v(\{A_2\}))$
$\sigma^5 = (A_3, A_1, A_2)$	$M^{\sigma^5}(N,v) = (v(\{A_1,A_3\}) - v(\{A_3\}), v(N) - v(\{A_1,A_3\}), v(\{A_3\}))$
$\sigma^6 = (A_3, A_2, A_1)$	$M^{\sigma^6}(N,v) = (v(N) - v(\{A_2,A_3\}), v(\{A_2,A_3\}) - v(\{A_3\}), v(\{A_3\}))$

convex set that contains $M(v)$. This set, which we denote by $Co(M(v))$, is called the *convex hull* of $M(v)$ (Royden 1968, p. 207). That is, the convex hull of $M(v)$ is the unique minimal closed convex set containing $M(v)$. Equivalently, the convex hull $Co(M(v))$ of $M(v)$ is the set of all convex combinations of the elements in $M(v)$. Formally,

$$Co(M(v)) = \{\sum_{k=1}^{m} \lambda_k x^k \mid x^1, \ldots, x^m \in M(v), \lambda_k \geq 0, k = 1, \ldots, m, \sum_{k=1}^{m} \lambda_k = 1\}.$$

> **Definition 59** The *Weber set* $WE(v)$ of a coalition form game $v \in G^N$ is the convex hull of the set containing the $|N|!$ marginal vectors corresponding to the $|N|!$ permutations of the players in N.

The following theorem of Weber (1988), whose proof is taken from Derks (1992), shows that the core of a game is always a subset of its Weber set.

Theorem 13 The core $C(v)$ of a game $v \in G^N$ is a subset of its Weber set $WE(v)$, that is, $C(v) \subseteq WE(v)$.

Proof: Assume that there is an allocation $x \in C(v)$ such that $x \notin WE(v)$. We now use a separating hyperplane theorem, which states that for every closed and convex set in the $|N|$-dimensional Euclidean space $\Re^{|N|}$ and every point that is not in the set, there exists a hyperplane that separates the point and the set. By the convexity and closedness of $WE(v)$, there exists a vector $y \in \Re^{|N|}$ such that for each $z \in WE(v)$, the inner product $z.y$ exceeds $x.y$. Let us denote the set of all permutations of the players in N by $\Sigma(N)$. Then in particular,

$$M^{\sigma}(N,v).y > x.y \tag{6.1}$$

where $\sigma \in \Sigma(N)$ is arbitrary and $M^{\sigma}(N,v)$ is the marginal contribution vector corresponding to the ordering generated by the permutation σ.

Let $(\hat{A}_1, \ldots, \hat{A}_n)$ be that permutation of the players such that $y_{\hat{A}_1} \geq \ldots \geq y_{\hat{A}_n}$. The corresponding marginal contribution vector is denoted by $\hat{M}(N, v)$. That is, $\hat{M}(N, v) = (v(\hat{A}_1), \ldots, v(\hat{A}_1, \ldots, \hat{A}_n) - v(\hat{A}_1, \ldots, \hat{A}_{n-1}))$. Since $x \in C(v)$,

$$\hat{M}(N, v).y = \sum_{i=1}^{n} y_{\hat{A}_i} [v(\{\hat{A}_1, \hat{A}_2, \ldots, \hat{A}_i\}) - v(\{\hat{A}_1, \hat{A}_2, \ldots, \hat{A}_{i-1}\})]$$

$$= \left(y_{\hat{A}_n} v(N) - y_{\hat{A}_1} v(\varnothing)\right) + \sum_{i=1}^{n-1} \left(y_{\hat{A}_i} - y_{\hat{A}_{i+1}}\right) v(\{\hat{A}_1, \hat{A}_2, \ldots, \hat{A}_i\})$$

$$\leq y_{\hat{A}_n} \left(\sum_{j=1}^{n} x_{\hat{A}_j}\right) + \sum_{i=1}^{n-1} \left\{\left(y_{\hat{A}_i} - y_{\hat{A}_{i+1}}\right) \left(\sum_{j=1}^{i} x_{\hat{A}_j}\right)\right\}$$

$$= \sum_{i=1}^{n} \left\{y_{\hat{A}_i} \left(\sum_{j=1}^{i} x_{\hat{A}_j}\right)\right\} - \sum_{i=2}^{n} \left\{y_{\hat{A}_i} \left(\sum_{j=1}^{i-1} x_{\hat{A}_j}\right)\right\}$$

$$= \sum_{i=1}^{n} y_{\hat{A}_i} x_{\hat{A}_i} = x.y.$$

From the above steps, it follows that $\hat{M}(N, v).y \leq x.y$ which contradicts condition (6.1).   □

Thus, the Weber set is built on the idea that players can enter the cooperative game in any order and receive their marginal contributions upon entering. Arbitrary convex combinations of such marginal contribution vectors represent players' entry into the game and collection of their pay-offs under arbitrary probability distributions. The Weber set, the convex hull of the set of marginal contribution vectors, is the set of all these expected pay-offs. It has the sub-additivity property, that is, $WE(v + w) \subseteq WE(v) + WE(w)$.

6.3   Some Properties of a Convex Game

As we will see later, the following possible property of a game often plays an important role.

Definition 60 A game $v \in G^N$ is called *convex* if $v(S \cup T) + v(S \cap T) \geq v(S) + v(T)$ for all $S, T \subseteq N$.

Convexity of a game implies its super-additivity: if $S \cap T = \emptyset$, then Definition 60 reduces to the definition of super-additivity of a game. The intuition underlying convexity will be apparent from the following condition:

For all $A_i \in N$ and $S \subseteq T \subseteq N \setminus \{A_i\}$; $v(S \cup \{A_i\}) - v(S) \leq v(T \cup \{A_i\}) - v(T)$. (6.2)

This condition means that the incentive for joining a coalition increases if the coalition grows. That is, a player's marginal contribution to a coalition is larger than what he could have contributed to a sub-coalition. Thus, it can be interpreted as the requirement that marginal contribution is non-decreasing in terms of set-theoretic inclusion.

The following theorem establishes equivalence between convexity and condition (6.2).

Proposition 19 Let the game $v \in G^N$ be arbitrary. Then the following statements are equivalent:

(i) v is convex.

(ii) v satisfies condition (6.2).

Proof: $(i) \Rightarrow (ii)$. Consider any $A_i \in N$ and any $S \subseteq T \subseteq N \setminus \{A_i\}$. Then, $v(S \cup \{A_i\}) + v(T) \leq v([S \cup \{A_i\}] \cup T) + v([S \cup \{A_i\}] \cap T) = v(T \cup \{A_i\}) + v(S)$. This gives $v(S \cup \{A_i\}) - v(S) \leq v(T \cup \{A_i\}) - v(T)$.

$(ii) \Rightarrow (i)$. Consider any non-empty $S, T \subseteq N$ and let $T \setminus S = \{A_{(1)}, \ldots, A_{(t-1)}, A_{(t)}\}$. Then, $v(T) - v(S \cap T) = [v([S \cap T] \cup \{A_{(1)}\}) - v(S \cap T)] + \sum_{k=2}^{t} [v([S \cap T] \cup_{r=1}^{k} \{A_{(r)}\}) - v([S \cap T] \cup_{r=1}^{k-1} \{A_{(r)}\})]$. Applying condition (6.2) to each of the third bracketed terms on the right-hand side of the above equality, we get $v(T) - v(S \cap T) \leq [v(S \cup \{A_{(1)}\}) - v(S)] + \sum_{k=2}^{t} [v(S \cup_{r=1}^{k} \{A_{(r)}\}) - v(S \cup_{r=1}^{k-1} \{A_{(r)}\})] = v(S \cup T) - v(S)$. From the last condition, we get $v(S) + v(T) \leq v(S \cup T) + v(S \cap T)$ which is convexity. $\square$

Proposition 19 shows that in a convex game, it is preferable to join a coalition as the number of players in the coalition increases.

A game $c \in G^N$ is *concave* if $-c$ is convex. A sufficient condition for sub-additivity of a game is its concavity, that is, a concave game satisfies sub-additivity. If in condition (6.2), we write $-c$ for v, then the inequality gets reversed, that is, for all $A_i \in N$ and $S \subseteq T \subseteq N \setminus \{A_i\}$; $c(S \cup \{A_i\}) - c(S) \geq c(T \cup \{A_i\}) - c(T)$. This inequality says that by joining a coalition with more players, a player causes a smaller increase in total costs. In view of Proposition 19, it can be claimed that this inequality for cost games holds if and only if the game is concave.

The next proposition shows that the core of a convex game is non-empty. The proof relies on identifying a pay-off vector x which satisfies Pareto efficiency and the stability condition $x(S) \geq v(S)$ for all non-empty coalitions $S \subset N$. The latter condition coincides with individual rationality when S is a single-player coalition.

Proposition 20 Let $v \in G^N$ be convex. Assume that the players are arranged in the order $(A_1, A_2, \ldots, A_n)$. Then the corresponding marginal contribution vector $x = (x_{A_1}, x_{A_2}, \ldots, x_{A_n})$, where $x_{A_1} = v(\{A_1\})$, $x_{A_2} = v(\{A_1, A_2\}) - v(\{A_1\})$, $\ldots$, $x_{A_n} = v(N) - v(N \setminus \{A_n\})$ is an element of the core $C(v)$ of the game v.

Proof: We have already shown that x is a Pareto efficient pay-off vector (see Observation 1). Now it is necessary to show that $x(S) \geq v(S)$ for all non-empty coalitions $S \subset N$. Observe first that $x_{A_1} = v(\{A_1\})$ and $x_{A_i} = v(\{A_1, \ldots, A_i\}) - v(\{A_1, \ldots, A_{i-1}\}) \geq v(\{A_i\})$ for all $i = 2, \ldots, n$ (by Proposition 6.2). Hence, x is an imputation. Let $S \subset N$ be an arbitrary coalition with $|S| \geq 2$, say $S = \{A_{(1)}, A_{(2)}, \ldots, A_{(s)}\}$ such that $(1) < (2) < \ldots < (s)$. Then for $1 \leq k \leq s$, by applying Proposition 19, we get the following.

(1). If $A_{(1)} \neq A_1$, then $v(\{A_{(1)}\}) \leq v(\{A_1, \ldots, A_{(1)}\}) - v(\{A_1, \ldots, A_{(1)-1}\}) = x_{A_{(1)}}$ and, if $A_{(1)} = A_1$, then $v(\{A_{(1)}\}) = v(\{A_1\}) = x_{A_{(1)}}$.

(2). For each $k \in \{2, \ldots, s\}$, $v(\{A_{(i)}, \ldots, A_{(k)}\}) - v(\{A_{(i)}, \ldots, A_{(k-1)}\}) \leq v(\{A_1, \ldots, A_{(k)}\}) - v(\{A_1, \ldots, A_{(k)-1}\}) = x_{A_{(k)}}$.

Summing the inequalities (in (1) and (2)) from $k = 1$ to $k = s$, we get

$$v(\{A_{(1)}\}) + \sum_{k=2}^{s} [v(\{A_{(1)}, \ldots, A_{(k)}\}) - v(\{A_{(1)}, \ldots, A_{(k-1)}\})]$$
$$\leq \sum_{k=1}^{s} x_{A_{(k)}}. \tag{6.3}$$

Observe that the left-hand side of (6.3) equals $v(\{A_{(1)}, A_{(2)}, \ldots, A_{(s)}\}) = v(S)$ and the right-hand side is equal to $\sum_{A_i \in S} x_{A_i} = x(S)$. Hence from inequality (6.3), it follows that $v(S) \leq x(S)$ for all $S \subset N$ with $|S| \geq 2$.

This inequality along with the fact that x is an imputation ensures that $x \in C(v)$. □

In the proof of Proposition 20, we have established that the given imputation $(v(\{A_1\}), v(\{A_1, A_2\}) - v(\{A_1\}), \ldots, v(N) - v(N \setminus \{A_n\}))$ is in the core $C(v)$ of the coalition form game $v \in G^N$. In this case, the players have been arranged in the order $(A_1, A_2, \ldots, A_n)$. The same result will be obtained if we change the ordering of the players. In other words, given any permutation $(\hat{A}_1, \hat{A}_2, \ldots, \hat{A}_n)$ of the players of the game $v \in G^N$, the vector $(v(\{\hat{A}_1\}), v(\{\hat{A}_1, \hat{A}_2\}) - v(\{\hat{A}_1\}), \ldots, v(N) - v(N \setminus \{\hat{A}_n\}))$, is also in the core $C(v)$ of the game v.

For an imputation x to be an element of the core $C(v)$ of a game $v \in G^n$, it is necessary that the stability condition $x(S) \geq v(S)$ holds for all non-empty coalitions $S \subset N$. However, it may be the case that a core element x does not satisfy the coalitional or group rationality condition $x(S) = v(S)$ for all non-empty coalitions $S \subset N$. The following proposition shows that convexity of the game is a sufficient condition to ensure the existence of a desired type of imputation (Maschler, Solan and Zamir 2013).

Proposition 21 Let the game $v \in G^N$ be convex. Then for each non-empty coalition $S \subset N$, there exists an imputation x that satisfies the equality $x(S) = v(S)$.

Proof: Let us order the players such that players of S appear first. Let us denote this permutation of the players by $(\hat{A}_1, \hat{A}_2, \ldots, \hat{A}_n)$ so that the set of players in coalition S is given by $S = \{\hat{A}_1, \ldots, \hat{A}_s\}$. The corresponding marginal contribution vector is given by $\hat{M}(N, v) = (v(\{\hat{A}_1\}), v(\{\hat{A}_1, \hat{A}_2\}) - v(\{\hat{A}_1\}), \ldots, v(N) - v(N \setminus \{\hat{A}_n\}))$. It is easy to verify that for this imputation, we have $x(S) = \sum_{i=1}^{s} x_{\hat{A}_i} = v(\{\hat{A}_1\}) + [v(\{\hat{A}_1, \hat{A}_2\}) - v(\{\hat{A}_1\})] + \ldots + [v(S) - v(S \setminus \{\hat{A}_s\})] = v(\{\hat{A}_1, \ldots, \hat{A}_s\}) = v(S)$. □

Theorem 13 shows that the core of a game is a subset of the Weber set. The converse is true if the game is convex. The following theorem shows that the core of a game coincides with its Weber set if and only if the game is convex (Shapley 1971 and Ichiishi 1981).

Theorem 14 Let the game $v \in G^N$ be arbitrary. Then the following statements are equivalent:

(i) v is convex.

(ii) $WE(v) = C(v)$.

Proof: $(i) \Rightarrow (ii)$. Given convexity of v, in view of Theorem 13, it is sufficient to prove that each marginal vector of v is a core element. This is already demonstrated by Proposition 20. See also the discussion after the proof of Proposition 20.

$(ii) \Rightarrow (i)$. Assume that all marginal vectors of v are core elements. Let $S, T \subseteq N$ be arbitrary. Consider the ordering of players such that players in $S \cap T$ appear first, the players in $T \setminus S$ and $S \setminus T$ appear at the second and third stages, respectively and the remaining players appear finally. Let us denote this permutation of the players by $(A'_1, A'_2, \ldots, A'_n)$. We can write these four sets as $S \cap T = \{A'_1, \ldots, A'_k\}$, $T \setminus S = \{A'_{k+1}, \ldots, A'_q\}$, $S \setminus T = \{A'_{q+1}, \ldots, A'_r\}$ and $N \setminus [S \cup T] = \{A'_{r+1}, \ldots, A'_n\}$. Denote the corresponding marginal vector by $M'(N, v)$. Since $M'(N, v) \in C(v)$,

$$v(S) \leq \sum_{A'_i \in S} M_{A'_i}(N, v)$$

$$= \sum_{i=1}^{k} M_{A'_i}(N, v) + \sum_{i=q+1}^{r} M_{A'_i}(N, v)$$

$$= v(\{A'_1, \ldots, A'_k\}) + [v(\{A'_1, \ldots, A'_{q+1}\}) - v(\{A'_1, \ldots, A'_q\})]$$

$$+ [v(\{A'_1, \ldots, A'_{q+2}\}) - v(\{A'_1, \ldots, A'_{q+1}\})]$$

$$+ \ldots + [v(\{A'_1, \ldots, A'_r\}) - v(\{A'_1, \ldots, A'_{r-1}\})]$$

$$= v(\{A'_1, \ldots, A'_k\}) - v(\{A'_1, \ldots, A'_q\}) + v(\{A'_1, \ldots, A'_r\})$$

$$= v(S \cap T) - v(T) + v(S \cup T).$$

From the above inequality, we get $v(S) \leq v(S \cap T) - v(T) + v(S \cup T)$ from which it follows that $v(S) + v(T) \leq v(S \cup T) + v(S \cap T)$. Hence, the game v is convex. $\qquad \square$

Proposition 22 Let $v \in G^N$ be convex. Then the Shapley value of the game v belongs to the core, that is $\Phi^{Sh}(v) \in C(v)$.

Proof: Given that $\Sigma(N)$ is the set of all permutations of the players in N, the Shapley value $\Phi^{Sh}_{A_i}(v)$ for player A_i is $\Phi^{Sh}_{A_i}(v) = \sum_{\sigma \in \Sigma(N)} (1/|N|!) M^{\sigma}_{A_i}(N, v)$, where $M^{\sigma}_{A_i}(N, v)$ is the marginal contribution of player A_i when the grand coalition is formed in the order specified by the permutation σ, that is, $M_{A_i}^{\sigma}(N,v) = v(\{A_1^{\sigma}, \ldots, A_i^{\sigma}\}) - v(\{A_1^{\sigma}, \ldots, A_{i-1}^{\sigma}\})$. Now $1/|N|! > 0$ and $\sum_{\sigma \in \Sigma(N)} (1/|N|!) = 1$. Therefore, $\Phi_{A_i}^{Sh}(v)$ is simply a convex combination of player A_i's marginal contributions over all possible orders $\Sigma(N)$ of the players in N. Hence, the vector of Shapley values $\Phi_{A_i}^{Sh}(v) = \sum_{\sigma \in \Sigma(N)} (1/|N|!) M_{A_i}^{\sigma}(N,v)$ of player A_is in the game v is an element of the Weber set $W(v)$. Since for a convex game $WE(v) = C(v)$ (Theorem 14), $\Phi^{Sh}(v) \in C(v)$. $\qquad\square$

Remark 1 We have noted in Chapter 3 that the core of a game may be empty. In view of Proposition 22, we can conclude that the core of a convex game is non-empty and contains the Shapley value. It also follows that the core of a concave cost-sharing game is non-empty and contains the Shapley value.

6.3.1 The bankruptcy game

Let us recall the bankruptcy game considered in Chapter 4, where $v_{E,d}(S) = \max\left\{0, E - \sum_{A_j \in N\setminus S} d_{A_j}\right\}$, where $S \subseteq N$. That is, the amount due to the players in S is the left over from the estate after the creditors who are not in S receive their claims fully, if the left over is positive. Otherwise, they do not receive anything. In other words, the amount that the creditors in S can guarantee to themselves is either zero or a positive leftover.

We now show that a bankruptcy game is convex. The proof of this result relies on the following proposition.

Proposition 23   A bankruptcy game is monotonic.

Proof: For $S, T \subseteq N$, we have $v_{E,d}(S) = \max\left\{0, E - \sum_{A_j \in N\setminus S} d_{A_j}\right\}$ and $v_{E,d}(T) = \max\left\{0, E - \sum_{A_j \in N\setminus T} d_{A_j}\right\}$. If $S \subseteq T \subseteq N$, then $\sum_{A_j \in N\setminus T} d_{A_j} \leq \sum_{A_j \in N\setminus S} d_{A_j}$, which implies that $E - \sum_{A_j \in N\setminus T} d_{A_j} \geq E - \sum_{A_j \in N\setminus S} d_{A_j}$. Therefore, if $v_{E,d}(S) > 0$, then $v_{E,d}(S) = \max\left\{0, E - \sum_{A_j \in N\setminus S} d_{A_j}\right\} \leq \max\left\{0, E - \sum_{A_j \in N\setminus T} d_{A_j}\right\} = v_{E,d}(T)$. If $v_{E,d}(S) = 0$, then we have $v_{E,d}(S) \leq \max\left\{0, E - \sum_{A_j \in N\setminus T} d_{A_j}\right\} = v_{E,d}(T)$. Thus, in each case, we have $v_{E,d}(S) \leq v_{E,d}(T)$. $\qquad\square$

Theorem 15 A bankruptcy game is convex.

Proof: Consider $S \subseteq T \subseteq N \setminus \{A_i\}$. Assume that $v_{E,d}(S) > 0$ so that $E - \sum_{A_j \in N \setminus S} d_{A_j} > 0$. Given that $S \subset S \cup \{A_i\}$ and $S \subseteq T \subset T \cup \{A_i\}$, by Proposition 23, $v_{E,d}(S \cup \{A_i\}) \geq v_{E,d}(S) > 0$ and $v_{E,d}(T \cup \{A_i\}) \geq v_{E,d}(T) \geq v_{E,d}(S) > 0$. From the definition of the bankruptcy game, it follows that $v_{E,d}(S \cup \{A_i\}) = \max\{0, E - \sum_{A_j \in N \setminus [S \cup \{A_i\}]} d_{A_j}\}$, which implies that $v_{E,d}(S \cup \{A_i\}) - v_{E,d}(S) = d_{A_i}$. Likewise, $v_{E,d}(T \cup \{A_i\}) - v_{E,d}(T) = d_{A_i}$. Hence, $v_{E,d}(S \cup \{A_i\}) - v_{E,d}(S) = v_{E,d}(T \cup \{A_i\}) - v_{E,d}(T)$.

Let $v_{E,d}(S) = 0$. Then $v_{E,d}(S) = E - \sum_{A_j \in N \setminus S} d_{A_j} = E - \sum_{A_j \in N \setminus [S \cup \{A_i\}]} d_{A_j} - d_{A_i} \leq 0$, which implies that $E - \sum_{A_j \in N \setminus [S \cup \{A_i\}]} d_{A_j} \leq d_{A_i}$. Hence, $v_{E,d}(S \cup \{A_i\}) \leq d_{A_i}$, where d_{A_i} may be zero or positive. If $v_{E,d}(T) = 0$, then given that $v_{E,d}(S) = 0$, the inequality $v_{E,d}(S \cup \{A_i\}) - v_{E,d}(S) \leq v_{E,d}(T \cup \{A_i\}) - v_{E,d}(T)$ is same as $v_{E,d}(S \cup \{A_i\}) \leq v_{E,d}(T \cup \{A_i\})$, which is true in view of Proposition 23. If $v_{E,d}(T) > 0$, then $E - \sum_{A_j \in N \setminus T} d_{A_j} > 0$ and $v_{E,d}(T \cup \{A_i\}) > 0$ (by Proposition 23). Further, $v_{E,d}(T \cup \{A_i\}) - v_{E,d}(T) = d_{A_i}$. Thus, given $v_{E,d}(S) = 0$, $v_{E,d}(T \cup \{A_i\}) - v_{E,d}(T) = d_{A_i}$ and $v_{E,d}(S \cup \{A_i\}) \leq d_{A_i}$, we get $v_{E,d}(S \cup \{A_i\}) - v_{E,d}(S) \leq v_{E,d}(T \cup \{A_i\}) - v_{E,d}(T)$. This demonstrates that the bankruptcy game is convex.

$\square$

Remark 2 From Proposition 20 and Theorem 15, it follows that *the core of a bankruptcy game is non-empty.*

Example 20 Recall the old car game considered in Chapter 1, Section 1.2. The marginal contribution vectors (M_A, M_B, M_C) corresponding to the 6 permutations of the players are $(0, 1000, 50)$, $(0, 0, 1050)$, $(1000, 0, 50)$, $(1050, 0, 0)$, $(1050, 0, 0)$ and $(1050, 0, 0)$ (see Table 6.2). The Weber set is the convex hull of these marginal contribution vectors. On the other hand, the core is the set of all convex combinations of the points $(0, 1000, 50)$, $(0, 0, 1050)$, $(1000, 0, 50)$ and $(1050, 0, 0)$.

Table 6.2 Marginal contributions of the players in the old car game

Ordering	M_A	M_B	M_C
(A, B, C)	0	1000	50
(A, C, B)	0	0	1050
(B, A, C)	1000	0	50
(B, C, A)	1050	0	0
(C, A, B)	1050	0	0
(C, B, A)	1050	0	0

6.4 Random Order Values and the Random Arrival Rule

According to the random order value, a player in a game is assigned the average of his marginal contributions over all the coalitions which he may join. Formally, let $\{p_\sigma : \sigma \in \Sigma(N)\}$ be a probability distribution over the set of permutations $\Sigma(N)$ of the n players in N, where $n = |N|$. A random order value $(\xi_{A_1}, \xi_{A_2}, \ldots, \xi_{A_n})$ on G^N is defined as

$$\xi_{A_i}(v) = \sum_{\sigma \in \Sigma(N)} p_\sigma M^\sigma_{A_i}(N, v) \tag{6.4}$$

for all $A_i \in N$ and $v \in G^N$, where $M^\sigma_{A_i}(N, v)$ stands for the marginal contribution of player A_i, given that the formation of the grand coalition takes place in the order defined by the permutation σ. Implicit under the definition of a random order value are the assumptions that coalition formation takes place sequentially and the perception $\{p_\sigma : \sigma \in \Sigma(N)\}$ of the likelihood of various orderings is the same across players. A player's component of the random order value is precisely his expected marginal contribution.

A random order value possesses several interesting properties, which are summarized in the following observations.

Observation 2: A sufficient condition for non-negativity of a random order value is that the underlying game is monotonic.

To see why Observation 2 is true, note that under monotonicity of the game $v \in G^N$, $M^\sigma_{A_i}(N, v) \geq 0$ for any $\sigma \in \Sigma(N)$. Further, $p_\sigma \geq 0$ for all $\sigma \in \Sigma(N)$ and $\sum_{\sigma \in \Sigma(N)} p_\sigma = 1$. Hence, $\xi_{A_i}(v) \geq 0$. Thus, monotonicity of the game ensures that a player's expected marginal contribution is never negative.

Observation 3: For any $v \in G^N$, $(\xi_{A_1}(v), \ldots, \xi_{A_n}(v))$ is a pre-imputation.

It is quite easy to see that $\sum_{A_i \in N} \xi_{A_i}(v) = \sum_{A_i \in N} \{\sum_{\sigma \in \Sigma(N)} p_\sigma M^\sigma_{A_i}(N, v)\} = \sum_{\sigma \in \Sigma(N)} p_\sigma \{\sum_{A_i \in N} M^\sigma_{A_i}(N, v)\} = \sum_{\sigma \in \Sigma(N)} p_\sigma v(N) = v(N)$. Hence, we have Observation 3. Therefore, a random order value is one way of dividing the worth of the grand coalition in a probabilistic way.

Observation 4: For each coalition $S \subseteq N$, any $v, w \in G^N$ and $\alpha, \beta \in \Re$, define $(\alpha v + \beta w)(S) = \alpha v(S) + \beta w(S)$. Then, $\xi_{A_i}(\alpha v + \beta w) = \alpha \xi_{A_i}(v) + \beta \xi_{A_i}(w)$ for all $A_i \in N$.

This observation, which we refer to as *linearity* and whose proof is quite easy, strengthens the additivity condition introduced in the previous chapter. Linearity also shows that a random order value is homogenous of degree one, that is, for any given $\alpha > 0$, $\xi_{A_i}(\alpha v) = \alpha \xi_{A_i}(v)$ for all $A_i \in N$.

If $p_\sigma = (1/|N|!)$ for every $\sigma \in \Sigma(N)$, then $\xi_{A_i}(v)$ in (6.4) coincides with the Shapley value for each $A_i \in N$. This shows that the Shapley value can be interpreted as a random order value. The Weber set 'is the set of all imputations associated with v by some random order value' (Weber 1988, p. 116). That is, the Weber set of $v \in G^N$ is the set $\{x \in \Re^n \mid x = (\xi_{A_1}(v), \ldots, \xi_{A_n}(v)) \, for \, some \, p_\sigma\}$.

6.4.1 The bankruptcy problem

The random arrival rule is a division rule in the bankruptcy problem (O'Neill 1982). Assume that the claimants arrive one at a time. On arrival, a claimant receives the minimum between his claim and the fraction of the estate left. The vector of awards resulting from the division depends on the order in which the claimants arrive. To make the division fair, the rule assumes that all the orders of arrival are equally likely and then takes the expectation. Formally,

---

Definition 61 Let (E, d) be a bankruptcy problem. The random arrival rule γ^{RA} assigns to each claimant $A_i \in N$

$$\gamma_{A_i}^{RA}(E, d) = \frac{1}{|N|!} \sum_{\sigma \in \Sigma(N)} \min\left\{ d_{A_i}, \max\left\{ 0, E - \sum_{A_j \in P^\sigma(A_i)} d_{A_j} \right\} \right\}, \quad (6.5)$$

---

where $P^\sigma(A_i)$ denotes the set of preceding players of A_i under the permutation σ.

Thus, the random arriving rule says that each creditor computes all he can get according to the order of his arrival, over all possible orders. In order to rewrite the formula in a more compact form, define

$$b_{A_i} = \begin{cases} d_{A_i} & \text{if } E - \sum_{A_j \in P^\sigma(A_i)} d_{A_j} > d_{A_i}, \\ E - \sum_{A_j \in P^\sigma(A_i)} d_{A_j} & \text{if } d_{A_i} \geq E - \sum_{A_j \in P^\sigma(A_i)} d_{A_j} \geq 0, \\ 0 & \text{if } 0 \geq E - \sum_{A_j \in P^\sigma(A_i)} d_{A_j}. \end{cases} \quad (6.6)$$

Now, for any coalition $S \subseteq N \setminus \{A_i\}$, the number of possible orderings in which S can arise is $|S|!(|N| - |S| - 1)!$. This is because the players in S, which does not contain A_i, can be arranged in $|S|!$ ways and the remaining players $N \setminus [S \cup \{A_i\}]$ who follow A_i can be arranged in $(|N| - |S| - 1)!$ ways. Hence, the total number of possible orderings for which we can have $P^\sigma(A_i) = S$ is $|S|!(|N| - |S| - 1)!$. Given that all the orderings are equally likely, out of $|N|!$ orderings of the players in N, this situation arises in the fraction $[|S|!(|N| - |S| - 1)!]/|N|!$ of the total number of orderings. Consequently,

$$\gamma_{A_i}^{RA}(E, d) = \sum_{S \subseteq N \setminus \{A_i\}} \left(\frac{|S|!(|N| - |S| - 1)!}{|N|!} \right) b_{A_i}. \tag{6.7}$$

If in the formula (5.1) for the Shapley value for a general game, we write

$$v(S \cup \{A_i\}) - v(S) = \begin{cases} d_{A_i} & \text{if } E - \sum_{A_j \in P^\sigma(A_i)} d_{A_j} > d_{A_i}, \\ E - \sum_{A_j \in P^\sigma(A_i)} d_{A_j} & \text{if } d_{A_i} \geq E - \sum_{A_j \in P^\sigma(A_i)} d_{A_j} \geq 0, \\ 0 & \text{if } 0 \geq E - \sum_{A_j \in P^\sigma(A_i)} d_{A_j}, \end{cases} \tag{6.8}$$

then it becomes the Shapley value of player A_i for the bankruptcy game considered above. This shows that *the random arrival rule as a resolution to the bankruptcy problem coincides with the Shapley value of the associated bankruptcy game.*

We conclude this section by giving a numerical illustration of the random arrival rule. Consider a joint enterprize consisting of a garage, a gas station and a restaurant. The joint venture was started by all the partners simultaneously. After a couple of years, the partners decided to sell everything because of differences in opinion and dissolve the partnership. An arbiter was employed by the court to sell the property and distribute the proceeds among the partners.

The sum of the claims made by the partners against the estate exceeded its worth. The claims were respectively 100, 200 and 300 units of money and the estate worth was 250 units of money. In such a case, the arbiter can suggest the random arrival rule as a resolution to the problem. Alternatively, the Shapley value of the corresponding bankruptcy game can be as well a solution. As we have observed in the earlier section, these two solutions to the problem coincide. The common solution is given by $(125/3, 275/3, 350/3)$.

Exercises

6.1 Consider a bankruptcy problem in which the estate is 600 units and the claims are 150, 200 and 350 units, respectively. Translate the problem into a bankruptcy game and resolve the problem using the random arrival rule. Show that the random arrival rule coincides with the Shapley value.

6.2 Consider the three-player game v with $v(\{A_1\}) = v(\{A_2\}) = v(\{A_3\}) = v(\{A_2, A_3\}) = 0$, $v(\{A_1, A_2\}) = v(\{A_1, A_3\}) = v(\{A_1, A_2, A_3\}) = 1$. The core of this game consists of the single element $(1, 0, 0)$. Identify the Weber set of this game. Clearly demonstrate that the core element is in the Weber set.

6.3 Consider a market in which the only two buyers of a good are A_2 and A_3. A_1 is the single seller of the good. The reservation prices of the seller and the buyers are respectively 5, 7 and 9. Formulate the game in characteristic function form. Determine the core and the Shapley value of the game. Is the Shapley value an element of the core? What is the Weber set of this game?

6.4 Show that the two-person $(0 - 1)$ normalized game is convex. Demonstrate that the Weber set of the game coincides with its core.

6.5 Consider the three-player game v with $v(\{A_1\}) = v(\{A_2\}) = v(\{A_3\}) = 0$, $v(\{A_1, A_2\}) = 90$, $v(\{A_1, A_3\}) = 80$, $v(\{A_2, A_3\}) = 70$ and $v(\{A_1, A_2, A_3\}) = 120$. Construct an element of the Weber set of this game which is different from its marginal contribution vectors.

6.6 Show that an additive game is convex.

6.7 Let $v \in G^N$ be strategically equivalent to $w \in G^N$. Show that if v is convex, then w is convex as well.

6.8 Show that the horse game defined in Chapter 2 is not convex.

CHAPTER 7

Voting Games

7.1 Introduction

The measurement of voting power is a very important topic in social sciences. It is concerned with the power of a member of a voting body or a board that makes yes-or-no decisions on a proposed resolution (or bill) by votes according to some unambiguous criterion. Examples of such decision-making bodies are the United Nations Security Council, the International Monetary Fund, the Council of Ministers in the European Union and the governing body of any corporate house etc.

The voting process of any collective decision-making body is governed by its own constitution, which prescribes the decision-making rule for the body. The individual votes are aggregated using the decision rule to determine the decision of the body as whole. Generally, when a proposal is presented before a voting body, its members are asked to vote either for the proposal ('yes') or against it ('no'). (The more general case when abstention is allowed is discussed later in Section 7.6.) The individual votes are then transformed into a collective decision of the body using the laid down rules.

By voting power of an individual voter, we mean his capability to alter the outcome of the voting procedure by changing his position on the proposed bill. It is an indicator of the extent to which a voter has control over the decision of the voting body. It should rely on the voter's importance in casting the deciding vote. To illustrate this, consider a voting situation where there are three voters, namely a, b and c. These three voters are distinguished by the characteristic that the numbers of votes they have are respectively 9, 4 and 2. Also suppose that the decision rule imposes the condition that at least 12 votes are necessary for any resolution to get through. Now, we may be tempted to conclude that since the number of votes of a is more than two times that of b, the power of a must be greater than that of b. Also since c has a positive number of votes, c should have some positive power. However, after a careful examination, it follows that both a and b must vote 'yes' jointly for the passage of the resolution. Even if both a and c support the resolution by voting 'yes', it will not be passed unless b votes for it as well. Likewise, when both b and c vote 'yes' and a votes 'no', the resolution will not be passed. The position taken by c becomes immaterial. That is, it does not matter whether c votes for or against the resolution. Thus, c has no control over the collective action of the body and has no power even though he has a positive number of votes. Moreover, the claim that the power of voter a is higher than that of b is not true. This is because the passage of the resolution cannot be cleared without a 'yes' vote from each of them. Consequently, both of them enjoy equal voting power. What emerges from this example is that a proper scientific analysis is required to construct any measure of individual voting power. More generally, it is necessary to model decision-making in collectives containing several decision makers formally.

The most well-known measures of voting power are the Shapley–Shubik (1954) and the Banzhaf (1965) measures. The former is defined as the fraction of orderings for which a voter is the swing or pivotal. For a particular ordering of voters, its swing voter is the person whose deletion from the winning coalition of voters of which he is the last member in the given order, will make the resulting contracting coalition, a losing one (A coalition of voters is called winning if 'yes' votes from exactly the voters in that coalition can guarantee the passage of a resolution. Non-winning coalitions are called losing.). In fact, the Shapley–Shubik measure is an application of the well-known Shapley value (Shapley 1953) to a voting game, which is a formulation of a voting system in a coalitional form game. The Banzhaf measure of a voter's power relies on the number of coalitions in which the voter is pivotal. Alternatives and variations of these two measures were suggested, among others, by Rae (1969), Coleman (1971), Deegan and Packel (1978), Holler (1982) and Johnston (1978).

We can provide additional reasons to justify the evaluation of a decision rule of a collective body. Suppose in a voting body, unanimous consent of all the members is necessary to pass a resolution, that is, every member has to support the passage of the resolution, more precisely, every members has to vote 'yes' to pass it. Clearly, the power of the collective body to act is very small here. In fact, in an extreme situation where only one member votes 'no', and the remaining members vote 'yes', the body is unable to transform the position taken by the majority of the members into an actual collective action. Hence, it might sometimes be important to evaluate the power of the entire voting body itself rather than that of a particular member of the body. Here we are concerned with the propensity of the voting body to vote in a specific unambiguous way regarding a proposed resolution. An indicator in such a case will quantify the extent to which the collective body is able to control the outcome of a division of it. It is a quantification of the extent of collective decision-making power of a voting body.

After presenting the background material in Section 7.2; in Section 7.3, we formally define an individual voting power measure, and discuss some well-known measures.[1] Some extensions of our analysis, particularly, alternative approaches to voting power, are also analyzed in this section. Then in Section 7.4, we present some reasonable postulates for an individual power measure. In Section 7.5, we discuss some characterizations and interpretations of well-known power measures. In Section 7.6, modifications of power measures when voters have more than two alternatives to choose from are reported. Some characteristics of the voting body as a whole are presented in Section 7.7. Finally, Section 7.8 lists some applications where these measures have been used.

7.2   Background

We can model a voting situation with a voter set of $N = \{A_1, \ldots, A_n\}$ as a coalition form game $v \in G^N$. A voting situation is framed in terms of a monotonic game, the range of whose characteristic function is the set $\{0, 1\}$. We assign the value 1 to any coalition that can pass a resolution and 0 to any coalition that cannot. Here a voter is a player in the game. A coalition S is called winning or losing if it can or cannot pass a resolution. Such a game is often referred to as a simple game. Formally,

---

[1]For recent discussions on alternative voting power measures, see, among others Felsenthal and Machover (1998), Roy (2005) and Laruelle and Valenciano (2008). A brief discussion on several measures is also available in Peleg and Sudhölter (2007).

Definition 62 Given a set of voters N, a game $v \in G^N$ is called a *voting game* (or, a *simple game*) if $v : 2^N \to \{0, 1\}$ satisfies the following conditions:

  (i) $v(\emptyset) = 0$,
  (ii) $v(N) = 1$ and,
  (iii) for $S \subseteq T \subseteq N$, $v(S) \le v(T)$.

Definition 62 formalizes the idea of a collective body where decisions are taken by voting. The decision-making rule is concretized by the characteristic function v. If all the voters unanimously vote against a proposed bill, the committee rejects it, which means that an empty coalition is losing [condition (i)]. If all the voters unanimously vote for the bill, the committee recommends its passage, that is, the grand coalition is winning [condition (ii)]. Condition (iii) is a monotonicity principle. A voting game satisfying this condition is called a *monotonic* voting game. One implication of this condition is that if a coalition S can pass a bill, then any superset T of S can pass it as well. It also does not rule out the possibility that if S is a losing coalition, then any superset T of S can be winning. The set of all voting games will be denoted by SG. Obviously, $SG \supset SG^N$, the set of all voting games in N. It is also true that $SG^N \subset G^N$.

The following observation is a simple implication of the above definition.

Observation 5: A voting game need not be super-additive.

Consider the voting game $v \in SG^N$ with $N = \{A_1, A_2\}$ and $v(\{A_1\}) = v(\{A_2\}) = v(\{A_1, A_2\}) = 1$. Then $v(\{A_1, A_2\}) = 1 < v(\{A_1\}) + v(\{A_2\}) = 2$, which is a violation of super-additivity.

Definition 63 A voting game $v \in SG^N$ is called *proper* if $v(S) = v(T) = 1$ implies that $S \cap T \ne \emptyset$.

This condition implies that two winning coalitions in a voting game are non-disjoint. Hence, in a proper voting game, incompatible bills cannot be accepted. $v \in SG^N$ is *improper* if it has at least two disjoint winning coalitions. Since improper voting games do not correspond to any coherent decision rules, they are quite out of place (Felsenthal and Machover 1995), and hence we will not discuss them further.

For any $v \in SG^N$, we denote the set of all winning (losing) coalitions in v by $W(v)(L(v))$. Consequently, for any $S \subseteq N$, $v(S) = 1(0)$ is equivalent to the condition that $S \in W(v)(L(v))$. Clearly, any $v \in SG^N$ is fully portrayed by the corresponding $W(v)$. Evidently, for any $v \in SG^N$, $|W(v)|$

$+|L(v)| = 2^{|N|}$. For any $v \in SG^N$, we denote the set of all winning (losing) coalitions of which A_i is a member by $W_{A_i}(v)$ $(L_{A_i}(v))$.

Definition 64 Given $v_1 \in SG^{N_1}$, $v_2 \in SG^{N_2}$, we define the *union game* $v_1 \vee v_2 \in SG^{N_1 \cup N_2}$ as the game with the voter set $N_1 \cup N_2$, where a coalition $S \subseteq N_1 \cup N_2$ is winning if and only if either $v_1(S \cap N_1) = 1$ or $v_2(S \cap N_2) = 1$.

That is, for a coalition S to be winning in the union game $v_1 \vee v_2 \in SG^{N_1 \cup N_2}$, S must be winning in either v_1 or in v_2 [Also refer Holler and Packel (1983) for an allied concept of 'mergeability of games'].

Definition 65 Given $v_1 \in SG^{N_1}$, $v_2 \in SG^{N_2}$, we define the *intersection game* $v_1 \wedge v_2 \in SG^{N_1 \cup N_2}$ as the game with the voter set $N_1 \cup N_2$, where a coalition $S \subseteq N_1 \cup N_2$ is winning if and only if $v_1(S \cap N_1) = 1$ and $v_2(S \cap N_2) = 1$.

That is, for a coalition to be winning in the intersection game $v_1 \wedge v_2 \in SG^{N_1 \cup N_2}$, it has to win in each of the component games v_1 and v_2.

Definition 66 A game $v \in SG^N$ is called *decisive* if for all $S \subseteq N$, $v(S) + v(N \setminus S) = 1$

For a decisive game, if a coalition is winning, then its complement must be losing. A coalition as well as its complement cannot be winning or losing simultaneously. Obviously, a constant-sum game becomes a decisive game in the context of simple games.

Definition 67 Let $v \in SG^N$ be arbitrary.

  (i) For any $S \subseteq N$, $A_i \in N$ is called *swing* in S if $v(S) = 1$ but $v(S \setminus \{A_i\}) = 0$.

  (ii) For any $S \subseteq N$, $A_i \in N$ is called *swing outside* S if $v(S) = 0$ but $v(S \cup \{A_i\}) = 1$.

  (iii) Any $S \subseteq N$, is called *minimal winning* if $v(S) = 1$ but there does not exist $T \subset S$ such that $v(T) = 1$.

Thus, A_i is swing, also called pivotal, key or critical, in the winning coalition S if his exclusion from S makes the resulting coalition $S \setminus \{A_i\}$ losing. Similarly, A_i is swing outside the losing coalition S if his inclusion in S makes the resulting coalition $S \cup \{A_i\}$ winning. For any A_i, the number of winning coalitions in which A_i is swing is the same as the number of losing coalitions outside which he is swing (Burgin and Shapley 2001, Corollary 4.1). For any $v \in SG^N$ and $A_i \in N$, we denote this common number by $m_{A_i}(v)$. Equivalently, $m_{A_i}(v)$ stands for the number of coalitions for which $A_i \in N$ is swing in v. Often we say that $m_{A_i}(v)$ is the number of swings of A_i. The set of minimal winning coalitions in the game $v \in SG^N$ is denoted by $MW(v)$.

Definition 68 Let $v \in SG^N$ be arbitrary. Then, $A_i \in N$ is called a *dictator* in v if $\{A_i\}$ is the only minimal winning coalition of v.

Clearly, from the definition, it follows that if $\{A_i\}$ is the sole minimal winning coalition, then $A_i \in S$ whenever S is a winning coalition. If a game has a dictator, then he is the only swing voter in it.

Definition 69 Let $v \in SG^N$ be arbitrary. (i) A coalition S is called a *blocking coalition* in v if its complement is losing, that is, $S \subset N$ is blocking if $N \setminus S \in L(v)$. (ii) A voter $A_i \in N$ is called a *blocker* or *veto voter* if $\{A_i\}$ is a blocking coalition.

A blocker has the power to prevent any decision by leaving a winning coalition, that is, by leaving a winning coalition, he makes it losing. We can characterize a blocker A_i as a member of every minimal winning coalition of v. Evidently, a dictator is a blocker, but a blocker is not necessarily a dictator. In fact, a dictator in a game is the only blocker in the game. However, the converse is not true, that is, a game may have several blockers. If there are two or more blockers in a game, then it cannot have a dictator. In a decisive game, the notions 'winning' and 'blocking' are equivalent. Since the grand coalition N is always winning, that is, $v(N) = 1$, a blocker A_i can as well be characterized as a voter such that $v(N \setminus \{A_i\}) = 0$. If A_i is not a blocker, then $v(N \setminus \{A_i\}) = 1$.

Definition 70 For any arbitrary $v \in SG^N$, a voter $A_i \in N$ is called

    (i) a *dummy voter* in v if $v(S \cup \{A_i\}) = v(S) + v(\{A_i\})$ for all $S \subseteq N \setminus \{A_i\}$,

    (ii) a *null voter* in v if $v(S \cup \{A_i\}) = v(S)$ for all $S \subseteq N \setminus \{A_i\}$.

In any situation, a dummy contributes precisely $v(\{A_i\})$, the worth of the coalition consisting only of him. Consequently, he has no strategic role to play in the context of voting. If $v(\{A_i\}) = 0$, then the dummy voter A_i is called a null player. Thus, a null voter is one who contributes nothing to the game. That is, a null player A_i in a game v is defined as a voter who is never swing in v.[2] A null player A_i is unable to transform a winning

---

[2]However, many authors call a player who is never swing in a simple game, a dummy player. Refer for example, Owen (1978; 1982) and Dubey and Shapley (1979) and Felsenthal and Machover (1995; 1998). However, here we make a distinction between the two.

(losing) coalition into a losing (winning) by leaving (joining) it. In other words, he does not have any influence in bringing about the passage or defeat of some bill. More generally, we say that the marginal contribution of the player A_i to the expanded coalition $S \cup \{A_i\}$ is zero (see Chapter 5). A voter $A_i \in N$ is called a *non-null* in v if he is not null in v.

An extremely important voting game is a weighted majority game.

Definition 71 For a set of voters $N = \{A_1, \ldots, A_n\}$, a *weighted majority game* is a pair $v = (w; q)$, where $w = (w_{A_1}, \ldots, w_{A_n})$ is the vector of non-negative weights of the voters in N, q is a positive real number quota such that $\sum_{A_i \in N} w_{A_i} \geq q$ and

$$v(S) = \begin{cases} 1 & \text{if } \sum_{A_i \in S} w_{A_i} \geq q, \\ 0 & \text{otherwise.} \end{cases} \tag{7.1}$$

That is, voter A_i exercises his voting right by casting w_{A_i} votes and q is the quota of votes needed to pass a bill. Since by definition, the grand coalition is winning, there is at least one winning coalition in the game. A weighted voting game will be proper if $\sum_{A_i \in N} (w_{A_i}/2) < q$. The games $v = (w; q)$ and $v_a = (aw; aq)$, where $a > 0$, are equivalent in the sense that any $S \subseteq N$ in v is winning if and only if it is winning in v_a, that is, $\sum_{A_i \in S} w_{A_i} \geq q$ if and only if $\sum_{A_i \in S} aw_{A_i} \geq aq$. Likewise, the games $v = (w; q)$ and $u = (w + c.1^{|N|}; q + c)$ are equivalent, where $1^{|N|}$ is the $|N|$ coordinated vector of ones and c is a scalar such that each of the weights in the weight vector $w + c.1^{|N|}$ is non-negative and $q + c > 0$.

Real-life examples of weighted majority voting bodies are the United Nations Security Council, Council of Ministers in the European Union, the United States Electoral College (with the states as voters) and the New York State county boards. However, not all voting games are weighted majority games. For instance, in the United States legislative system, a winning coalition has to contain the President and a majority of both the Senate and the House of Representatives or two-thirds of both the Senate and the House.

Often the games specified in the following definition become necessary for axiomatic characterization of power indices.

Definition 72 For any $S \subseteq N$, the *unanimity game* is the game $U_S \in SG^N$ whose only winning coalitions are S and all supersets of S.

Evidently, in $U_N \in SG^N$, the only winning coalition is the grand coalition.[3]

---

[3]Observe that, although not explicitly stated, unanimity games were used earlier in the

The following proposition specifies the properties of a core element in a voting game.

Proposition 24 Let $v \in SG^N$ be a voting game. The core of v, $C(v)$, is given by the set $\{x \in \Re^{|N|} \mid x_{A_i} = 0 \text{ if } A_i \text{ is not a blocker and } x \in I(v)\}$.

Proof: Let $x \in C(v)$. Then since $x \in I(v)$, $x_{A_i} \geq 0$ for all $A_i \in N$ and $x(N) = v(N) = 1$. For any A_i who is not a blocker, $v(N \setminus \{A_i\}) = 1$. Then using group rationality, $x(N \setminus \{A_i\}) \geq v(N \setminus \{A_i\}) = 1 = x(N) = x(N \setminus \{A_i\}) + x_{A_i}$ which implies that $x_{A_i} \leq 0$. Therefore, if A_i is not a blocker, then $x_{A_i} = 0$.

Let x be an imputation and $x_{A_i} = 0$ for each voter A_i who is not a blocker. Given that $v(N) = x(N) = 1$ and $x_{A_i} = 0$ for each non-blocker voter A_i, the set B of blockers is non-empty and $x(B) = 1$. If $S \subseteq N$ is winning, then $B \subseteq S$ since a blocker is a member of every winning coalition. Hence, $x(S) = x(B) = 1$. Consequently, $x(S) = v(S)$, since for a winning coalition S, $v(S) = 1$. If $S \subset N$ is losing, then $v(S) = 0$ and $S \cap B \neq B$. Since $x \in I(v)$, $x(S) \geq 0 = v(S)$. Consequently, in both cases, $x(S) \geq v(S)$. This in turn shows that x satisfies the group rationality condition for inclusion as a core element. This completes the proof of the proposition. □

The next proposition shows that the core of a voting game is non-empty if and only if there is at least one blocker in the game.

Proposition 25 Let the game $v \in SG^N$ be arbitrary. Then the following conditions are equivalent:

(i) $C(v)$ is non-empty.

(ii) There is at least one blocker in the game.

Proof: $(i) \Rightarrow (ii)$. Given that the core is non-empty, let $x \in C(v)$ so that $x(N) = v(N) = 1$. Therefore, there must exist a voter A_i such that $x_{A_i} = \delta > 0$. Then by group rationality, $1 > 1 - \delta = x(N \setminus \{A_i\}) \geq v(N \setminus \{A_i\})$ implying that $v(N \setminus \{A_i\}) = 0$ (since $v(S) \in \{0,1\}$ for all $S \subseteq N$). This implies that $N \setminus \{A_i\}$ is a losing coalition. This is same as the condition that A_i is a blocker.

characterization of the Shapley value (see Theorem 5.1). For further discussion on these definitions, refer Shapley (1962), Dubey and Shapley (1979), Owen (1978), Felsenthal and Machover (1995; 1998), Dubey, Einy and Haimanko (2005), Barua, Chakravarty and Roy (2005; 2006) and Laruelle and Valenciano (2008).

$(ii) \Rightarrow (i)$. Let B be the set of all blockers in v. Define the pay-off vector $x \in \Re^{|N|}$ as follows

$$
x_{A_i} = \begin{cases} \frac{1}{|B|} & \text{if } A_i \text{ is a blocker,} \\ 0 & \text{if } A_i \text{ is not a blocker.} \end{cases} \tag{7.2}
$$

Then, x is an imputation in $v \in SG^N$ with the additional restriction that $x_{A_i} = 0$ if A_i is not a blocker. Hence, by Proposition 24, x is a core element. □

7.3 Measures of Individual Voting Power

Power is a very important concept in political science. While power is a many-faceted phenomenon, our objective here is to analyze the notion of power as it is reflected in a formal voting system. Most of the measures existing in the literature measure a-priori voting power of individual voters. The information necessary for analyzing an individual power measure in a game is contained completely in the set $W(v)$. Consequently, the notion of power that these measures quantify is solely characterized by the decision rule itself in an environment of a-priori ignorance about real-life issues, like the nature of the bills tabled for voting, the voters' actual interests, mutual affinities and non-affinities etc. Any possibility of including information exogenous to the rule for calculating such a measure is ruled out. There have been criticisms of a-priori measures because of their reliance on incomplete information. However, in view of their easy implementation through offering only an 'yes' or 'no' alternative and intuitive interpretation, several a-priori voting power measures have established themselves as important analytical tools for studying actual voting power through their long usage [Refer Felsenthal and Machover (1998) and Braham and Holler (2005)]. Initially, we assume that a voter has the option of voting 'yes' or 'no' only. Since in real-life situations there are other options available to the voter, we will discuss the case of more than two alternatives in a later section.

Definition 73 Given a set of voters N, a voting power measure of voter $A_i \in N$ is a mapping $\varphi_{A_i} : SG^N \to \Re_+$, that is, a non-negative real-valued function defined on SG^N.

It is an indicator of the influence of voter A_i over the outcome of the voting procedure. For any $v \in SG^N$, $\varphi_{A_i}(v)$ indicates the power A_i possesses in v for the passage or defeat of a resolution.

Following Felsenthal and Machover (1998), we propose the following three postulates as the minimal set of conditions which a reasonable individual voting power measure should fulfill.

(i) **Iso-invariance (INV):** Let $v \in SG^N$ and $\hat{v} \in SG^{\hat{N}}$ be isomorphic, that is, there exists a bijection h of N onto $\hat{N}$ such that for all $S \subseteq N$, $v(S) = 1$ if and only if $\hat{v}(h(S)) = 1$, where $h(S) = \{h(x) : x \in S\}$. Then, $\varphi_{A_i}(v) = \varphi_{h(A_i)}(\hat{v})$.

(ii) **Ignoring null voters (IGN):** For any $v \in SG^N$ and for any null voter $A_d \in N$, $\varphi_{A_i}(v) = \varphi_{A_i}(v_{-A_d})$ for all $A_i \in N \setminus \{A_d\}$, where v_{-A_d} is the game obtained from v by excluding A_d, that is, v_{-A_d} is the restriction of v on the voter set $N \setminus \{A_d\}$, which means that v_{-A_d} is the game v with the domain $2^{N \setminus \{A_d\}}$. Similarly, $\varphi_{A_i}(v) = \varphi_{A_i}(v_{+A_d})$, where v_{+A_d} is obtained from v by including $A_d \notin N$ as a null voter.

(iii) **Vanishing just for null voter (VJN):** For any $v \in SG^N$, $\varphi_{A_i}(v) = 0$ if and only if $A_i \in N$ is null.

According to INV, the permutation of the voters does not change the power of a voter. Consequently, any characteristic other than the information contained in the game, for example, the names and sexes of voters, are irrelevant to the measurement of voting power. It is an anonymity condition. When other characteristics are required to play a role, INV will not be satisfied.

As we have noted from the definition of a null voter, his marginal contribution to any coalition he is joining is zero—hence he cannot affect the voting outcome by his inclusion in the game. This shows that his inclusion cannot have any impact on the powers of other voters. Likewise, his exclusion from a coalition should not affect the powers of other voters. This is what IGN demands.

A null voter has no influence over the conclusive outcome of the voting process. He has no ability to change the voting outcome by changing his vote; he cannot cast the deciding vote. Since essential to the notion of power of a voter is the capability of becoming critical, his power should be minimal (zero) if he is null (refer Dubey 1975; Dubey and Shapley 1979; Taylor 1995 and Burgin and Shapley 2001). A similar argument can be provided from the reverse direction. Therefore, VJN can be regarded as a minimality property for power measures.

While IGN specifies that the absolute power of a voter remains unaltered under exclusion (inclusion) of a null voter from (in) the game, it does not say how the power of one voter relative to that of another gets affected in this scenario. The following postulate, which was introduced by Barua, Chakravarty and Roy (2005; 2006), may be regarded as a relative counterpart to IGN:

Relative null voter ignoring principle (RNP): Let v and v_{-A_d} be the games as given in IGN. Then, for any two players $A_i, A_j \in N \setminus \{A_d\}, \varphi_{A_i}(v_{-A_d})/\varphi_{A_j}(v_{-A_d}) = \varphi_{A_i}(v)/\varphi_{A_j}(v)$, where φ_{A_i}s are assumed to be positive.

RNP says that the power of a voter $A_i \in N$ relative to that of another voter $A_j \in N$ remains unaffected if a null voter is excluded from the game. An analogous version of RNP can be formulated if a null voter is included in the game. Evidently, IGN implies RNP but the converse is not necessarily true. For instance, $m_{A_i}(v)$ satisfies RNP but not IGN.[4]

The conditions IGN, INV and VGN are concerned with absolute measures of power. However, often, we may be interested in knowing how the control over the collective action of a voting body is shared by all the voters. A normalization postulate can take care of this requirement (Felsenthal and Machover 1995).

(iv) **Normalization (NOM):** For any $v \in SG^N$, $\sum_{A_i \in N} \varphi_{A_i}(v) = 1$.

Felsenthal and Machover (1998) referred to a power measure satisfying NOM as a power index. We will maintain this terminological difference in the remainder of this chapter. The relevance of NOM has been questioned by some authors. Laruelle and Valenciano (2001; 2008) questioned the interpretation of NOM as an a-priori requirement for a power measure. In a simple super-additive game, the requirement that the individual power measures' components sum up to 1 cannot be considered as a simple normalization. In fact, the efficiency condition ($\sum_{A_i \in N} \varphi_{A_i}(v) = v(N)$) should be taken as the required criterion. In the case of different games, NOM requires that the sum of the power measures in all the games is the same. 'It is as if percentages of cakes of different sizes were compared' (Laruelle and Valenciano 2008, p.64). This is a highly restricted condition. Further, NOM is not a necessary postulate to study the power of a voter relative to that of another in a game.

In the remainder of this section, we will discuss some well-known power measures.[5] Before we formally discuss the measures, it may be worthwhile to mention an early expression of the main intuition involved

---

[4]For relevance of INV, IGN and VJN in characterizations of power measures, see Section 7.5.

[5]A discussion on common behaviour of power measures has been provided by Gambarelli (1983).

in power measures, that is, the intuition that in weighted voting games, a voter's chance to win differs from the weight. This idea occurred to Luther Martin, a delegate from Maryland in the Constitutional Convention held in Philadelphia in 1777. Actually, Martin had in mind what has later been formalized as the Banzhaf measure (refer Riker 1986 and Gambarelli and Owen 2004).

The first systematic and scientific approach to the measurement of voting power was suggested by Penrose (1946). The central idea underlying the Penrose measure is that the power of a voter is increasingly related to the way he casts his vote, that is, the more often the outcome of the voting procedure goes the way he votes. However, his contribution did not receive much attention in the literature until it was independently rediscovered by Banzhaf (1965). Two other contributors who rediscovered this again later were Rae (1969) and Coleman (1971). However, mainstream literature regards the paper by Shapley and Shubik (1954) as the seminal work on this issue.

Shapley–Shubik index:

The Shapley–Shubik index is the restriction of the Shapley value (Shapley 1953) to voting games, that is, when the Shapley value of player A_i is applied to voting games, we get the Shapley–Shubik index of the power of voter A_i. Formally, the *Shapley–Shubik index* of power of voter A_i is defined as $SS_{A_i} : SG^N \to \Re$, where

$$SS_{A_i}(v) = \sum_{\substack{S \subseteq N \setminus \{A_i\}, S \cup \{A_i\} \text{ is winning and } S \text{ is losing in } v}} \frac{|S|!(|N| - |S| - 1)!}{|N|!}$$

$$= \frac{\text{Number of orderings in which } A_i \text{ is pivotal}}{\text{Total number of orderings of the voters}}, \tag{7.3}$$

with $v \in SG^N$ being arbitrary.

The SS index focuses on permutation of the entire set of voters and relies on the orders in which the winning coalitions are formed. It is concerned with a voter who is the last person to join a losing coalition and transform it into a winning one. To understand the ideas underlying the index, suppose that a resolution is tabled for voting. The voters form a queue to vote for the resolution, with the first voter in the queue being the most enthusiastic supporter of the resolution and the last voter opposing it to the maximum possible extent. The remaining voters line up in the queue in decreasing order of support. All the voters have a common knowledge about the proposed resolution in the sense that they are exposed to the same information for and against the proposal. As soon as a minimal winning coalition has voted in favour of it, the resolution is declared passed. Given an ordering of voters, there is exactly one voter such that the coalition of all voters before him constitutes a losing coalition and his joining the coalition converts it into a winning coalition. He is the pivotal or swing voter in this ordering. Equivalently, we say that the swing voter for this ordering is the person whose deletion from the winning coalition of voters, of which he is the last member in the given order, turns the contracting coalition from a winning to a losing one. It is assumed that all the orderings of the formation of the grand coalition are equally probable. SS_{A_i} is simply the proportion of the orderings in which A_i is the swing or critical voter.

Banzhaf measure:

While the Shapley−Shubik index is based on the order of formation of a winning coalition, the Banzhaf (1965) measure relies on the critical position of a voter in any winning coalition, irrespective of the order in which it may be formed. It deals with alternative combinations of voters in which a voter is pivotal. This measure is not concerned with the 'chronological order' in which the winning coalitions are formed. Following Owen (1978), Dubey and Shapley (1979) and Burgin and Shapley (2001), we define the crude or raw Banzhaf power measure BR_{A_i} of voter A_i in a game $v \in SG^N$ as, $m_{A_i}(v)$, the number of swings of A_i in v. Formally, the *raw Banzhaf measure* $BR_{A_i} : SG^N \to \Re_+$ is defined as

$$BR_{A_i}(v) = m_{A_i}(v), \tag{7.4}$$

where $v \in SG^N$ is arbitrary. Banzhaf actually defined and used this raw measure for measuring the power of the voter A_i. This measure is also referred to as the Banzhaf score of voter A_i. By definition, BR_{A_i} is bounded between 0 and $2^{|N|-1}$, where the lower bound is achieved if A_i is a null voter. In contrast, the measure takes on its maximal value $2^{|N|-1}$ when A_i is a dictator.

The *non-normalized Banzhaf power measure* $BZN_{A_i}(v)$ is obtained by normalizing $BR_{A_i}(v)$ over the interval $[0, 1]$—this is done by dividing $BR_{A_i}(v)$ with $2^{|N|-1}$, the maximal value that $m_{A_i}(v)$ can achieve. More precisely,

$$BZN_{A_i}(v) = \frac{m_{A_i}(v)}{2^{|N|-1}}.$$ (7.5)

If in a voting model, each voter A_i's probability of voting 'yes' or 'no' on a bill is chosen independently from the uniform distribution $[0,1]$, then the probability that the outcome will be affected by A_i's vote is estimated by BZN_{A_i} (Straffin 1977, 1988, 1994). If this probability is the same across the voters, then the probability that voter A_i's vote affects the outcome is estimated by his Shapley–Shubik power SS_{A_i}. More generally, consider a situation in which each voter's voting in favour of or against a bill is randomly drawn independently from a distribution with expectation $1/2$. Then, $m_{A_i}(v)/2^{|N|-1}$ is the probability p_{A_i} that other voters will vote such that a proposed bill will be accepted or rejected depending on whether A_i votes for or against it (Leech 1990). Since BZN_{A_i} does not involve the numbers of coalitions in which voters other than A_i are swing, Felsenthal and Machover (1995) regarded it as an absolute measure of voter A_i's power.

The *Banzhaf normalized index* BZ_{A_i} of voter A_i is the ratio between his power, as measured by the non-normalized Banzhaf measure (or the Banzhaf score), and the sum of such measures for all the voters. Formally,

$$BZ_{A_i}(v) = \frac{m_{A_i}(v)}{\sum_{A_j \in N} m_{A_j}(v)}.$$ (7.6)

The concept of the Banzhaf measure has also been extended to the space of all coalition form games G^N. The corresponding formula for Banzhaf measure is given by $(1/2^{|N|-1}) \sum_{S \subseteq N \setminus \{A_i\}} [v(S \cup \{A_i\}) - v(S)]$. This is referred to as the *Banzhaf value for player* A_i (Owen 1975 and Dubey and Shapley 1979).

Rae measure:

The central idea underlying the Rae (1969) measure is to determine the total number of ways in which a voter agrees with the outcome of the voting process. A measure of *agreement for voter* A_i in a game $v \in SG^N$ can be defined as

$$\rho_{A_i}(v) = |\{S : A_i \in S \in W(v)\} \text{ or } \{S : A_i \notin S \notin W(v)\}|.$$ (7.7)

The identity $\rho_{A_i}(v) = m_{A_i}(v) + 2^{|N|-1}$ was proved by Dubey and Shapley (1979), who also remarked that the close connection between $BNZ_{A_i}(v)$

and $\rho_{A_i}(v)$ arising through this identity was not noticed for quite some time after 1969.

It is natural to argue that a suitable normalization of $\rho_{A_i}(v)$ can be regarded as a measure of the power of voter A_i in $v \in SG^N$. One such normalization is $\rho_{A_i}(v)/2^{|N|}$, which equals $(1 + BNZ_{A_i}(v))/2$. This is the probability that A_i agrees with the voting outcome (Penrose 1946). It is bounded between $1/2$ and 1, where the lower bound is achieved if A_i is a null voter. An alternative normalization that will meet VGN is $((1 + BNZ_{A_i}(v))/2) - (1/2)$ which equals $(BNZ_{A_i}(v))/2$. This alternative measure, which is also known as the Penrose (1946) measure, takes on the (maximal) value $1/2$ when A_i is a dictator (Felsenthal and Machover 1998). In view of the close relationship between these measures and BNZ, we will not discuss them further.

Coleman measures:

According to Coleman (1971), the power of an individual member of a collective body, when power is interpreted as 'influence' over the outcome of the collective decision process, can be invoked in two ways: the member can initiate an action or can prevent an action from being taken. This becomes evident from the role played by a blocker. A blocker's 'yes' vote is necessary for the passage of a resolution but a blocker alone cannot clear the passage of a resolution. That is, while the blocker can prevent the passage of a bill by his own action (ignoring how others vote), he cannot pass a bill with his own voting capacity. To capture these two aspects of power, Coleman (1971) suggested two measures for individual power that indicate an individual voter's power to prevent action and initiate action respectively.

(I) Preventive measure: Given $v \in SG^N$, *Coleman's preventive power measure* $CP_{A_i}(v)$ is a measure of the ability of voter A_i to prevent a decision being taken. More precisely, it is defined as the proportion of winning coalitions in the game in which A_i's defection is critical, that is,

$$CP_{A_i}(v) = \frac{m_{A_i}(v)}{|W(v)|}. \tag{7.8}$$

Like the Banzhaf measures, this measure also avoids the extraneous notion of orderings involved in the Shapley–Shubik index. $CP_{A_i}(v)$ can be interpreted as A_i's probability to block a bill. This is because $|W(v)|$ is the number of situations which lead to the passage of a bill and out of these

$|W(v)|$ cases, A_i's 'yes' vote is critical in $m_{A_i}(v)$ cases. Consequently, the probability that A_i can block the passage of a bill is $m_{A_i}(v)/|W(v)|$. It indicates voter A_i's probability of being critical, conditional to the proposal being accepted under the assumption that all coalitions are equiprobable, that is, the voters make yes−no decision independently with probability $1/2$ for each (Laruelle and Valenciano 2005). This measure is bounded between 0 and 1, where the lower and upper bounds are achieved in the extreme cases in which A_i is a null voter and a blocker respectively.

The following relationship exists between $CP_{A_i}(v)$ and the non-normalized Banzhaf power measure $BZN_{A_i}(v)$

$$m_{A_i}(v) = 2^{|N|-1} BZN_{A_i}(v) = |W(v)| CP_{A_i}(v). \tag{7.9}$$

Since $m_{A_i}(v) = 2|W_{A_i}(v)| - |W(v)|$ (Dubey and Shapley 1979), $CP_{A_i}(v)$ can alternatively be written as

$$CP_{A_i}(v) = 2\frac{|W_{A_i}(v)|}{|W(v)|} - 1. \tag{7.10}$$

That is, $CP_{A_i}(v) = 2(|W_{A_i}(v)|/|W(v)|) - 1$ is the number by which two times the ratio between the number of winning coalitions containing A_i and the number of winning coalitions in the game exceeds unity.

Barua, Chakravarty and Sarkar (2012) suggested the following variant of CP as a measure of power:

$$BC_{A_i}(v) = \frac{m_{A_i}(v)}{|W_{A_i}(v)|}. \tag{7.11}$$

where $v \in SG^N$ is arbitrary. Clearly, BC is an attainable upper bound of CP in the sense that for any $v \in SG^N$ and $A_i \in N$, $CP_{A_i}(v) \le BC_{A_i}(v)$. BC is also not an index in the sense that the sum of the powers of individual players is not equal to one. Inverse of this measure, when multiplied with the CP, gives us the König−Brauninger (1998) measure of voter A_i's inclusiveness. More precisely, the König−Brauninger measure is given by $KB_{A_i}(v) = |W_{A_i}(v)|/|W(v)|$. This measure is positively linearly related to CP as follows: $KB_{A_i}(v) = (1 + CP_{A_i}(v))/2$. Hence, it is a violator of VGN. However, it will rank two voting games in terms of the powers of individual voters in the same way as CP.

(II) Initiative measure: Given $v \in SG^N$, *Coleman's initiative power measure* $CI_{A_i}(v)$ for voter A_i is complementary to his power to initiate an action—it is a measure of his ability to turn an otherwise losing coalition into a wining one. Formally, it is defined as the number of situations in which A_i is critical as a proportion of the number of losing coalitions $L(v)$, the total number of divisions that do not produce clearance of a resolution. Formally,

$$CI_{A_i}(v) = \frac{m_{A_i}(v)}{|L(v)|} = \frac{m_{A_i}(v)}{2^{|N|} - |W(v)|} = \frac{CP_{A_i}(v)}{\frac{2^{|N|}}{|W(v)|} - 1}. \qquad (7.12)$$

The measure $CI_{A_i}(v)$ represents the probability that A_i can initiate an action. This measure can be interpreted in terms of the probability of A_i's vote being critical, conditional to the proposal being rejected. Coleman's measures can be used to decompose the Banzhaf non-normalized measure into two different components of the power of a member of a collective body. Let $H = |W(v)|/2^{|N|}$ be the proportion of winning coalitions in the game. This is the probability that the voting body acts. Then

$$BZN_{A_i}(v) = 2CP_{A_i}(v)H = 2CI_{A_i}(v)(1 - H). \qquad (7.13)$$

Thus, the probability that a voter is swing, $BZN_{A_i}(v)/2$, is simply the product of the conditional probability of a swing given that the voting body acts $(CP_{A_i}(v))$ and the probability of action of the voting body (H). This is also the product of the conditional probability of a swing given that the voting body does not act $(CI_{A_i}(v))$ and the probability of no action of the voting body $(1 - H)$.

Dubey and Shapley (1979) showed that the non-normalized Banzhaf measure $BZN_{A_i}(v)$ is the harmonic mean of the two Coleman measures (refer also Brams and Affuso 1976). More precisely,

$$\frac{1}{BZN_{A_i}(v)} = \frac{1}{2}\left(\frac{1}{CP_{A_i}(v)} + \frac{1}{CI_{A_i}(v)}\right). \qquad (7.14)$$

In a proper game, an individual's power to initiate action does not exceed his power to prevent action. Often the two Coleman measures are clubbed with Banzhaf non-normalized measure and jointly called the *Banzhaf–Coleman measure* (Owen 1978).

In order to illustrate the behaviour of the Coleman measures, following Felsenthal and Machover (1998, p.50−51), we consider the following weighted majority games. One game is $u = (w_{A_1}, w_{A_2}, w_{A_3}, w_{A_4}; q) = (3, 2, 1, 1; 4)$ and the other game is $v = (w_{A_1}, w_{A_2}, w_{A_3}, w_{A_4}; q) = (3, 2, 1, 1; 5)$. That is, v is obtained from u through an increase of the quota. It is easy to verify that $BZN_{A_1}(u) = 3/4$, $BZN_{A_2}(u) = BZN_{A_3}(u) = BZN_{A_4}(u) = 1/4$ and $BZN_{A_1}(v) = 5/8$, $BZN_{A_2}(v) = 3/8$ and $BZN_{A_3}(v) = BZN_{A_4}(v) = 1/8$. Note that voter A_1 is a blocker in v but not in u. One can check that $CP_{A_1}(u) = 3/4$, $CI_{A_1}(u) = 3/4$ but $CP_{A_1}(v) = 1$ and $CI_{A_1}(v) = 5/11$. In going from u to v, voter A_1 gains power to prevent action by more than 33% and loses power to initiate action by more than 39%, whereas his loss of Banzhaf power is less than 17%. This small loss of Banzhaf power is a consequence of two opposite directional changes, substantial increase in power to prevent action and a very high amount of loss in power to initiate action. A similar illustration can be provided using the normalized Banzhaf measure. Therefore, as Felsenthal and Machover (1998, p.51) pointed out, the two Coleman measures 'can give you information that you cannot get by looking at' the non-normalized Banzhaf measure. A relation that exists among the normalized Banzhaf index, normalized versions of the two Coleman and the Banzhaf measures is as follows:

$$BZ_{A_i}(v) = \frac{CP_{A_i}(v)}{\sum_{A_j \in N} CP_{A_j}(v)} = \frac{BZN_{A_i}(v)}{\sum_{A_j \in N} BZN_{A_j}(v)} = \frac{BR_{A_i}(v)}{\sum_{A_j \in N} BR_{A_j}(v)}$$

$$= \frac{CI_{A_i}(v)}{\sum_{A_j \in N} CI_{A_j}(v)}. \tag{7.15}$$

Deegan−Packel index:

Deegan and Packel (1978) argued that only minimal winning coalitions should be the point of issue in determining a voter's power. They suggested an index under the assumptions that all minimal winning coalitions are equally likely and that players in such a coalition, which is winning by definition, will equally share the prize of victory available to the winning camp. This in turn implies that any two voters belonging to the same minimal winning coalitions will possess the same power. Given $v \in SG^N$, the *Deegan−Packel index* for voter A_i is defined as,

$$DP_{A_i}(v) = \frac{1}{|MW(v)|} \sum_{S \in MW_{A_i}(v)} \frac{1}{|S|}. \tag{7.16}$$

where $MW_{A_i}(v)$ is the set of minimal winning coalitions in v containing A_i.

Johnston index:

Laver (1978) criticized the Banzhaf measure on the ground that it assigns one point to a voter if he can destroy a coalition, regardless of the total number of the other voters who are capable of doing this. Johnston (1978) proposed an index that takes care of this criticism. It relies on the pre-supposition that instead of voter A_i being assigned one point from each coalition S in which A_i is pivotal, A_i should be assigned only $(1/piv(S))$th of a point, where $piv(S)$ is the number of voters who are pivotal in S. Given $v \in SG^N$, the *Johnston score* of A_i in v is defined as $\Xi_{A_i}(v) = \sum\{piv(S)^{-1} : S \in W(v), S \setminus \{A_i\} \notin W(v)\}$. Then the *Johnston power index* of voter A_i is defined as,

$$JN_{A_i}(v) = \frac{\Xi_{A_i}(v)}{\sum_{A_j \in N} \Xi_{A_j}(v)}. \tag{7.17}$$

It can be treated as a hybrid of the Banzhalf and Deegan$-$Packel indices.

Holler index:

Another measure that is based on minimal winning coalitions is the Holler index (Holler 1982; Holler and Packel 1983), though the argument for considering minimal winning coalitions is different from that of the Deegan$-$Packel index. This index is alternatively known as the public good index. It relies on the essential characteristic of a public good: non-rivalry in consumption and non-excludability in access. If the outcome of a voting game is to provide a public good, each member of the winning coalition will enjoy a common benefit from the undivided value of the coalition. Only minimal winning coalitions are considered because when it comes to the supply of a public good, winning coalitions with additional players will form by sheer 'luck' due to the potential for free riding. Given $v \in SG^N$, and assuming that the chances of forming all minimal winning coalitions are equal, the *public good index for voter A_i* is given by

$$PGI_{A_i}(v) = \frac{|MW_{A_i}(v)|}{\sum_{A_j \in N} |MW_{A_j}(v)|}. \tag{7.18}$$

The absolute public good measure, the non-normalized version of PGI_{A_i} is given by

$$PGI'_{A_i}(v) = \frac{|MW_{A_i}(v)|}{|MW(v)|}. \tag{7.19}$$

All the power measures and indices listed above, except KB, satisfy INV, IGN and VJN. In our discussion, SS, BZ, DP, JN and PGI have been referred to as indices in the sense that they also satisfy NOM. However, BZN, CP, BC and CI, being non-normalized, were referred to as measures.

It will now be worthwhile to analyze a distinction that is made in the literature among the measures discussed above. According to Coleman (1971, p. 272), the problem of decision-making in collectivities is not about bargaining for 'division of the spoils among the winners, but rather the problem of controlling the action of the collectivity'. These actions lead to their own consequences and distribution of spoils. There can be no subdivisions of the spoils among the members of the winning coalition (refer also Leech 2002).

Coleman (1971) also pointed out one characteristic of the Shapley—Shubik index. This property says that the idea behind voting power measured by the Shapley—Shubik index is not the power to influence the outcome of the collective decision body in the usual sense, that is, whether the passage of a resolution is to be cleared or not. Rather, it is the power of the voter to claim a share in the fixed prize that goes only to the victorious camp. This is because the Shapley—Shubik index is an application of the Shapley value for simple games. One feature of the Shapley value for a simple game is that the total value of the game is 1, and a winning coalition receives the value of the game. Thus, implicit under this index is the idea that power in a collectivity involves a division of a fixed utility (which is normalized at 1) among the members of the winning coalition.

In view of Coleman's observations, Felsenthal and Machover (1998) suggested two interpretations of a voter's capability of controlling the outcome of a division. The first interpretation is in terms of a policy-seeking behaviour—a person's voting power is interpreted as the capacity to change the end result of the voting process by changing his attitude towards the bill. Decisions are on actions to be taken by the collective body, for instance, the provision of a public good or the enactment of a law of which the consequences are given exogenously to every member of the voting body and cannot be bargained over. A voter generally takes a decision regarding his stand on the bill by comparing his expected pay-off from the passage of the resolution with that arising from its failure. For any voter and any bill, these exogenously given pay-offs are independent of the decision rule governing the voting body. They refer to this notion of power as 'I-power' of voting (I stands for influence).

The second concept of power, which is quantified in terms of voters' expected pay-off, was termed 'P-power' by them (P stands for power). In this case, under a positive outcome of the voting game, the winning coalition receives some amount of transferable utility, the 'prize of power', which the members of the coalition can freely divide among themselves without any efficiency loss. The pay-off to members of the losing coalition is zero. A voter's P-power is represented by his expected pay-off. That is, P-power indicates the power of a voter to claim a share in the fixed prize of success, available only to the winning group of voters. Given that the size of the prize is normalized at unity, NOM is an appropriate property for indices of P-power. However, if the concern of voting is a collective action, rather than the problem of division of purses, NOM becomes irrelevant. From the viewpoint of I-power, the notion of absolute power is the meaningful concept. Consequently, in measuring I-power, NOM is not a relevant postulate. However, for both the notions of power, IGN, VJN and INV are sensible (for further discussion, refer Barua, Chakravarty and Sarkar 2012).

In view of the above discussion, we can argue that SS, BZ, DP, JN and PGI, which demonstrate relative power, are indices of P-power. In contrast, BZN, CP, BC and CI, which indicate absolute power, are measures of I-power. Since the idea underlying the Holler index is the notion of a public good, the concept of splitting of purses is inappropriate here.

7.4 Postulates for a Measure of Voting Power

This section discusses some postulates for a measure of voting power. They enable us to understand the power measures in greater detail. In fact, they also become helpful to distinguish between I-power and P-power measures. These postulates were suggested in rigorous form by Felsenthal and Machover (1995; 1998).[6] We first present and discuss them formally and later on classify them in terms of their appropriateness for measures of I-power and P-power.

The first postulate we consider states that the value of the power measure of a non-null voter is positive.

Non-null voter postulate (NNP): For any power measure $\varphi : SG^N \to \Re_+$, if A_i is a non-null voter in $v \in SG^N$, then $\varphi_{A_i}(v) > 0$.

A voter is either null or non-null. By definition, a power measure is non-negative. Therefore, an implication of VJN is that the power measure of a voter takes on its minimum value, zero, if and only if the voter is null. This shows that a power measure satisfying VJN will verify NNP.

The next postulate we consider is dominance. In order to state this formally, we first define the following:

Definition 74 For $v \in SG^N$, $A_j \in N$ is said to *dominate* $A_i \in N$, what we write $A_j \succeq A_i$, if and only if $S \cup \{A_i\} \in W(v) \Rightarrow S \cup \{A_j\} \in W(v)$ for all $S \subseteq N \setminus \{A_i, A_j\}$. If $A_j \succeq A_i$ but not $A_i \succeq A_j$, then A_j is said to *strictly dominate* A_i ($A_j \succ A_i$, for short).

The dominance relation $\succeq$, which satisfies transitivity and reflexivity, says that any winning coalition that contains A_i must remain a winning coalition if A_j replaces A_i. It may be noted that the strict relation $\succ$ is transitive but not reflexive. The relation $\succeq$ satisfies completeness as well if $v \in SG^N$ is a weighted majority game.

Dominance postulate (DOM): A power measure $\varphi : SG^N \to \Re_+$ respects the *dominance postulate* if $A_j \succeq A_i$ for $v \in SG^N$ implies that $\varphi_{A_j}(v) \geq \varphi_{A_i}(v)$.

This postulate demands that given $A_j \succeq A_i$, A_j's contribution to the victory of a coalition cannot not be lower than that of A_i. This supports the view that A_j must be at least as powerful as A_i. A special case of DOM is monotonicity, which requires that in a weighted majority game, if the voting weight of A_j is at least as much as that of A_i, then A_i cannot have more power than A_j.

---

[6]Direct and indirect discussions on these postulates and related issues were made, among others, by Shapley (1973), Brams (1975), Dreyer and Schotter (1980), Peleg (1981),Schotter (1982), Freixas and Gambarelli (1997), Turnovec (1997), Felsenthal and Machover (1998a, 2002), Felsenthal, Machover and Zwicker (1998), Laruelle and Valenciano (2008), Barua, Chakravarty and Roy (2006) and Barua, Chakravarty and Sarkar (2012). For statements which show that the Coleman measures satisfy the different postulates, we follow Barua, Chakravarty and Roy (2006) and Barua, Chakravarty and Sarkar (2012), and for similar statements for other measures, we follow Felsenthal and Machover (1995; 1998).

Monotonicity postulate (MON): A power measure φ satisfies *monotonicity* if for the weighted majority game $v \in SG^N$, and for any two voters A_i and A_j, $w_{A_j} \geq w_{A_i}$ implies that $\varphi_{A_j}(v) \geq \varphi_{A_i}(v)$.

While SS, BR, BZN, BZ, JN, CP, BC, CI and JN satisfy DOM, and hence MON; DP does not even fulfill MON (Deegan and Packel 1982 and Felsenthal and Machover 1995; 1998). PGI is also a violator of MON. However, when the weight of each voter is positive and the sum of the weights is normalized at unity, PGI satisfies MON if the quota $q = 1/2$ and the number of null voters equals $(|N| - g)$, where $g \leq 4$ (Holler, Ono and Steffen 2001).

Freixas and Gambarelli (1997) and Felsenthal and Machover (1998) argued that DOM (MON) should be regarded as an intuitively appealing postulate for a measure of voting power, whether I-power or P-power. However, Deegan and Packel (1978; 1982), Brams and Fishburn (1995), Holler (1997; 1998), Braham and Steffen (2002) questioned the unambiguous relevance of DOM (MON), as a postulate for a power measure. If characteristics like ideological affinities are taken into account in the measurement of a voter's influence on the voting outcome, then notions like dominance are not broadly defined (refer Braham and Steffen 2002 and Holler and Napel 2004). In such a case, INV may not hold. Inappropriateness of DOM has been observed in the Owen−Shapley (1989) spatial power measure, which modifies SS and takes into account the ideological proximity among voters (Holler and Napel 2004). The same reasoning applies to PGI, which relies on the assumption that coalitional values are public goods.

In order to state the next postulate, let us consider the following:

Definition 75 $u,v \in SG^N$ and let $A_i, A_j \in N$ be such that the following four conditions are satisfied:

  (i) If $S \subseteq N$ is such that either both $A_i \in S$ and $A_j \in S$, or, both $A_i \notin S$ and $A_j \notin S$, then $S \in W(u)$ if and only if $S \in W(v)$.

  (ii) If $S \subseteq N$ is such that $A_i \in S$ but $A_j \notin S$ and $S \in L(u)$, then $S \in L(v)$.

  (iii) If $S \subseteq N$ is such that $A_i \notin S$ but $A_j \in S$ and $S \in W(u)$, then $S \in W(v)$.

  (iv) $W(u) \neq W(v)$.

    Then we will say that the relation $TR(u, A_i; v, A_j)$ holds.

Condition (i) says that a coalition $S \subseteq N$, which is symmetric in terms of belongingness of voters A_i and A_j, will have the same outcome in u and v, that is, either winning or losing. According to condition (ii), a losing coalition in u containing A_i but not A_j cannot become winning in v.

Condition (iii) means that a winning coalition in u containing A_j but not A_i is winning in v. Finally, the set of winning coalitions in u is different from that in v.

Transfer postulate (TRP): Let $u, v \in SG^N$ and let $A_i, A_j \in N$ be such that $TR(u, A_i; v, A_j)$ holds. Then, $\varphi_{A_i}(v) \geq \varphi_{A_i}(u)$.

To understand this, suppose in going from game $u \in SG^N$ to another game $v \in SG^N$, voter A_i gains some new pivotal roles and voter A_j loses some pivotal roles [conditions (i)−(iii) in Definition 75]. Thus, we can say that the game v is obtained from u through a transfer of voting right of A_j to A_i. Consequently, A_i's power in v cannot be less than that in u. A similar argument establishes that A_j's power in u must be at least as much as that in v.

In the case of weighted majority games, TRP means that a voter A_i cannot lose power if he receives some weight from another voter A_j. Formally, let $u = (w; q)$ and $v = (\hat{w}; q)$ be two weighted majority games over the same set of voters N, where $w = (w_{A_1}, \ldots, w_{A_n})$, $\hat{w} = (\hat{w}_{A_1}, \ldots, \hat{w}_{A_n})$, $\hat{w}_{A_i} = w_{A_i} + c$, $\hat{w}_{A_j} = w_{A_j} - c$, $\hat{w}_{A_k} = w_{A_k}$ for all $A_k \in N \setminus \{A_i, A_j\}$, $c > 0$, $w_{A_j} - c \geq 0$ and $|N| = n$. Thus, A_j transfers a part or whole of his voting weight to A_i. Hence, TRP requires that $\varphi_{A_i}(v) \geq \varphi_{A_i}(u)$.

Certainly, if A_i is null and continues to remain null with additional weight, then A_i's power should not decrease. However, with additional weight, if A_i becomes non-null from null or if he was originally non-null before receiving the additional weight, then also A_i's power should not reduce after the transfer. This shows that several possibilities regarding change of statuses of power of A_i and A_j may arise while going from u to v.

The measures BR, BZN, CP, BC, CI and the SS index satisfy TRP. However, the indices BZ, DP and JN are violators of TRP. It may be worthwhile to note that a power measure satisfying INV and TRP will satisfy DOM. However, even if INV is given, an indicator satisfying DOM may not satisfy TRP. For instance, both BZ and JN satisfy INV and DOM but not TRP.

A relative version of TRP was suggested by Barua, Chakravarty and Roy (2006). While TRP is stated in terms of power of either the donor or the recipient of the transfer, this relative counterpart to TRP involves both the donor and the recipient.

Relative transfers principle (RTP): If u and v are two games as given in TRP, then

$$\frac{\varphi_{A_j}(v)}{\varphi_{A_i}(v)} \leq \frac{\varphi_{A_j}(u)}{\varphi_{A_i}(u)} \tag{7.20}$$

where φ_{A_j}s and φ_{A_i}s are positive.

Clearly, TRP implies RTP. However, the converse is not true. For instance, BZ verifies RTP but not TRP.

The statement of the next postulate relies on the following definition.

> **Definition 76** Given $u \in SG^N$, assume that the voters $A_i, A_j \in N$ are merged into one voter A_{ij}. Then the post-merger voting game is $v \in SG^{\hat{N}}$, where $\hat{N} = N \setminus \{A_i, A_j\} \cup \{A_{ij}\}$, $v(S) = u(S)$ if $S \subseteq \hat{N} \setminus \{A_{ij}\}$, and $v(S) = u(S \setminus \{A_{ij}\} \cup \{A_i, A_j\})$ if $A_{ij} \in S$.

That is, the set $\{A_i, A_j\}$ of two voters $A_i, A_j \in N$ in the game forms a bloc and works as a single voter. Evidently, this produces a new voting game, which is obtained by replacing the two voters by the new voter representing the bloc. In a bloc, separate identities of the constituents of the bloc do not exist as voters, whereas in a coalition, separate identities of members exist as voters.

Bloc postulate (BOP): Given $u \in SG^N$, assume that the voters $A_i, A_j \in N$ are amalgamated into one voter A_{ij}. The bloc postulate requires that for any voter $A_k \in \{A_i, A_j\}$, $\varphi_{A_{ij}}(v) \geq \varphi_{A_k}(u)$ provided that $A_l \in \{A_i, A_j\} \setminus A_k$ is non-null.

BOP demands that when a voter A_k swallows the voting power of a non-null voter A_l, then the voting power of A_k cannot be larger than that of the bloc consisting of these two voters. In other words, A_k, who may be null or non-null, does not lose power by acquiring the power of a non-null voter A_l. This is supported by the logical reasoning that a person will not join a bloc if the voting right of the bloc is lower than his own voting power. The postulate BOP is similar in nature to super-additivity and additivity. In fact, BOP drops out as an implication of TRP, INV and VGN. The power functions SS, BR, BZN, CP, BC and CI satisfy BOP but the indices BZ, DP and JN are its violators.

In the following proposition, we demonstrate an implication of Definition 76 with respect to the number of swings of a bloc.[7]

Proposition 26   Given any $u \in SG^N$, for any two voters $A_i, A_j \in N$, the sum of their number of swings $m_{A_i} + m_{A_j}$ is a non-negative even integer.

---

[7]Felsenthal and Machover (1995, Theorem 11.1) implicitly demonstrated this proposition while determining the value of the Banzhaf–Coleman measures for a bloc voter. However, the proof presented below, which is taken from Barua, Chakravarty and Roy (2005), is different from their proof.

Moreover, if the voters $A_i, A_j \in N$ are merged into one voter A_{ij}, then the number of swings of the bloc voter A_{ij} in the post-merger game $v \in SG^{\hat{N}}$ is $(m_{A_i} + m_{A_j})/2$.

Proof: $m_{A_i} + m_{A_j} = \sum_{S \subseteq N \setminus \{A_i\}} [u(S \cup \{A_i\}) - u(S)] + \sum_{S \subseteq N \setminus \{A_j\}} [u(S \cup \{A_j\}) - u(S)]$

$$= \sum_{S \subseteq N \setminus \{A_i, A_j\}} [u(S \cup \{A_i\}) - u(S)] + \sum_{S \subseteq N \setminus \{A_i, A_j\}} [u(S \cup \{A_i, A_j\}) - u(S \cup \{A_j\})]$$

$$+ \sum_{S \subseteq N \setminus \{A_i, A_j\}} [u(S \cup \{A_j\}) - u(S)] + \sum_{S \subseteq N \setminus \{A_i, A_j\}} [u(S \cup \{A_i, A_j\}) - u(S \cup \{A_i\})]$$

$$= 2 \sum_{S \subseteq N \setminus \{A_i, A_j\}} [u(S \cup \{A_i, A_j\}) - u(S)] =$$

$$2 \sum_{S \subseteq N \setminus \{A_i, A_j\}} [v(S \cup \{A_i, A_j\}) - v(S)],$$

$$= 2m_{A_i A_j},$$

where $m_{A_i A_j}$ is the number of swings of the merged voter A_{ij} in the game v. Since $m_{A_i A_j} \geq 0$ is an integer, it follows that $m_{A_i} + m_{A_j}$ is an even integer. It also follows that $m_{A_i A_j}$ equals $(m_{A_i} + m_{A_j})/2$. □

The next two postulates, which display two different roles of a blocker, were suggested for a P-power measure.

Blockers share postulate (BSP): For any $v \in SG^N$, if $A_b \in N$ is a blocker and $S \in W(v)$, then $\varphi_{A_b}(v) \geq (1/|S|)$.

Added blockers postulate (ABP): Given $u \in SG^N$, suppose that $v \in SG^{\hat{N}}$ is obtained from u by adding $A_b \notin N$ as a blocker in v, so that $\hat{N} = N \cup \{A_b\}$. Then for any two non-null voters $A_i, A_j \in N$,

$$\frac{\varphi_{A_i}(u)}{\varphi_{A_j}(u)} = \frac{\varphi_{A_i}(v)}{\varphi_{A_j}(v)}. \tag{7.21}$$

Like RGN and RTP, BSP and ABP also introduce relativity into voting-power measurement since they are specified involving two or more different voters. Since a blocker A_b's departure from any winning coalition S will transform it into a losing one, he is an indispensable partner of S, given that the winning coalition S has been formed. Consequently, A_b's claim for purse cannot be lower than that of any member of S. Thus, if S

is formed with A_b as a member, then A_b's demand will be at least $(1/|S|)$ of the purse. In other words, in relative terms, A_b will demand at least $(1/|S|)$. Now, any other winning coalition T must contain A_b and he will join T if he is offered at least $(1/|S|)$ in relative terms. Hence, A_b's unconditional relative demand or expected pay-off turns out to be at least $(1/|S|)$.

Given that game v is obtained from u by adding a blocker A_b, who is not a voter of u, the winning coalitions of v are simply those of u, with the additional constraint that the blocker must be a member of every winning coalition of u. However, the blocker's inclusion in any losing coalition of u cannot convert it into a winning coalition in v. Consequently, we can argue that the power of a non-null voter A_i relative to that of another non-null voter A_j is the same in both u and v. This is what ABP demands. The postulate follows from a stronger postulate, which says that the power of a non-null voter remains unchanged if a blocker is added to the game. We refer to this stronger postulate as the 'absolute added blocker's postulate'.

From our discussion in the section, it follows that while an I-power measure should satisfy VJN, INV, IGN, DOM, TRP and BOP, a P-power measure should verify VJN, INV, IGN, NOM, BOP, DOM, TRP, BSP and ABP.

In Table 7.1, which is a variant of a table provided in Barua, Chakravarty and Sarkar (2012), we present a brief summary of our discussion concerning how different postulates were satisfied by some of the voting power measures that have been proposed in literature. A '$\sqrt{}$' means that the postulate is satisfied by the concerned measure, whereas an 'X' indicates violation.

Table 7.1 A comparative summary of different power measures and their behaviour vis-a-vis the postulates

Measure	IGN	INV	VJN	BSP	TRP	ABP	NOR	DOM	BOP
SS	$\sqrt{}$	$\sqrt{}$	$\sqrt{}$	$\sqrt{}$	$\sqrt{}$	X	$\sqrt{}$	$\sqrt{}$	$\sqrt{}$
BR	X	$\sqrt{}$	$\sqrt{}$	$\sqrt{}$	$\sqrt{}$	$\sqrt{}$	X	$\sqrt{}$	$\sqrt{}$
BZ	$\sqrt{}$	$\sqrt{}$	$\sqrt{}$	X	X	$\sqrt{}$	$\sqrt{}$	$\sqrt{}$	X
BZN	$\sqrt{}$	$\sqrt{}$	$\sqrt{}$	X	$\sqrt{}$	$\sqrt{}$	X	$\sqrt{}$	$\sqrt{}$
CI	$\sqrt{}$	$\sqrt{}$	$\sqrt{}$	X	$\sqrt{}$	$\sqrt{}$	X	$\sqrt{}$	$\sqrt{}$
DP	$\sqrt{}$	$\sqrt{}$	$\sqrt{}$	X	X	X	$\sqrt{}$	X	X
JN	$\sqrt{}$	$\sqrt{}$	$\sqrt{}$	X	X	X	$\sqrt{}$	$\sqrt{}$	X
CP	$\sqrt{}$	$\sqrt{}$	$\sqrt{}$	$\sqrt{}$	$\sqrt{}$	$\sqrt{}$	X	$\sqrt{}$	$\sqrt{}$
BC	$\sqrt{}$	$\sqrt{}$	$\sqrt{}$	$\sqrt{}$	$\sqrt{}$	$\sqrt{}$	X	$\sqrt{}$	$\sqrt{}$

From Table 7.1, it follows that except SS, CP and BC, all other indicators are violators of more than one postulate. While the performance of BNZ, SS, CI, CP and BC are satisfactory as measures of I-power, acceptability of SS or CP or BC as a P-power measure is dependent on how seriously we consider the violation of ABP or NOR by the corresponding measure. Since CP and BC are not normalized, they cannot be interpreted as probability distributions. An easy upper bound of $\sum_{A_i \in N} CP_{A_i}(v)$ is $|N|$, which is attained when all the voters are blockers, that is, the game is the unanimity game where the only winning coalition is the grand coalition. Also, zero is a lower bound of $\sum_{A_i \in N} CP_{A_i}(v)$. For a game with at least one non-null voter, this sum is positive. On the other hand, for a game with at least one blocker, it is at least one (Barua, Chakravarty and Sarkar 2012). It has been demonstrated by Barua, Chakravarty, Roy and Sarkar (2004) that

$$\frac{2^{|N|} - |W(v)|}{2^{|N|-1}} \le \sum_{A_i \in N} CP_{A_i}(v) \le \frac{|N|.(2^{|N|} - |W(v)|)}{2^{|N|-1}}. \tag{7.22}$$

Consequently, for $2^{|N|-1} > |W(v)|$, $\sum_{A_i \in N} CP_{A_i}(v) > 1$ and for $|W(v)| \ge 2^{|N|-1}(2 - (1/|N|))$, $\sum_{A_i \in N} CP_{A_i}(v) \le 1$. Since a P- power index of a voter can be treated as the part of his claim in the purse that the winning camp receives, in case we decide to measure P-power by CP, $1 - \sum_{A_i \in N} CP_{A_i}(v)$ can be regarded as the size of efficiency loss if $1 - \sum_{A_i \in N} CP_{A_i}(v) > 0$.

In a recent contribution, Freixas and Marciniak (2013) noted a common property, the egalitarian property, of SS, BZN and the Johnston score. A power measure satisfying this property becomes more scattered across voters in a game with a given level of consensus, the quota in a weighted majority game in which all voters have only one vote and only the grand coalition is winning, than in a game with higher level of consensus. Thus, for P-power measures, this property means that with higher level of consensus, the difference of pay-offs between two voters decrease. Freixas, Marciniak and Pons (2012) identified games in which SS, BZ and the Johnston score are ordinally equivalent in the sense that they rank voters in the same way (refer also Diffo and Moulen 2002). An assessment of inequality in the distribution of voting power was made in an earlier contribution by Laurealle and Valenciano (2004).

Some additional attempts have been made to measure the power of individual voters. Some authors have extended some of the power measures discussed above. Standard power indices are often criticized on the ground that they do not take into account voter's preferences and are policy blind. They treat all coalitions as equally probable or all vote sequences as being equally likely. There is anonymity among the voters. However, in the case of division of voters over an ideological spectrum (say from left to right), the problem is one of modelling this situation in a realistic way. Perlinger (2000) considered a class of spectrum voting games in which formation of only connected coalitions (that is, there is no ideological gap between members belonging to a coalition) are allowable.[8] He then suggested the use of Markov–Polya measure as a parametric family of power measures. Bilal, Albuquerque and Hosli (2001) developed spatial voting power measures that rely on the policy preferences of various players. This framework combines the spatial theory of voting (in which voters are assumed to be distributed along a policy scale) with voting power analysis. Hoede and Bakker (1982) suggested a measure by taking into account the preferences of the voter and the social structure in which the voters may be able to influence each other. Rusinowska and Swart (2007) showed that when all the players are independent, this measure reduces to BZN. While the measures discussed above assign real numbers to the voters as indicators of their influence in a voting situation, Taylor and Zwicker (1997) suggested interval measures of power that associate intervals of real numbers with the voters.

One implicit assumption in the definition of BZN is that the influence of a swing voter on a coalition is independent of other swing voters in that coalition. However, in real-life, it becomes important to verify whether with this characteristic, he is the only voter or not. With this objective in mind, the following modification of BZN, which is referred to as the *enhanced Banzhaf power measure*, EBP, was suggested by Burgin and Shapley (2001):

$$EBP_{A_i}(v) = \sum_{S \subseteq N} c_S(A_i), \qquad (7.23)$$

where

$$= \begin{cases} 0 & \text{if } A_i \text{ is not swing,} \\ \frac{1}{k} & \text{if } S \text{ contains } k \text{ swing voters including } A_i. \end{cases} \qquad (7.24)$$

Napel and Widgrn (2001) considered a strengthened version of VJN, using the notion of inferior voters. A voter A_i is *inferior* if and only if there exists

---

[8]However, Brams, Jones and Kilgour (2002) argued that there are no a-priori reasons to believe that only connected coalitions will form.

another voter A_j who is critical in all coalitions in which A_i is critical but who can himself form a coalition in which he is critical without A_i being critical. The strengthened version of VJN is called the *inferior player axiom*, which says that if A_i is inferior in $v \in SG^N$, then $\varphi_{A_i}(v) = 0$. Using the notion of inferior players, Napel and Widgrén suggested a modification of BZN as a strict power measure, which is defined as

$$SPI_{A_i}(v) = \frac{\eta_{A_i}(v)}{2^{|N|-1}},\tag{7.25}$$

where

$$\eta_{A_i}(v) = \begin{cases} m_{A_i}(v) & \text{if } A_i \text{ is inferior,} \\ 0 & \text{otherwise.} \end{cases}\tag{7.26}$$

A modification of the Shapley value in the context of simple games with an a-priori system of unions represented by coalition structures was considered by Owen (1995). A similar modification of the Banzhaf measure was suggested by Owen (1982). Alonso-Meijide and Fiestras-Janeiro (2002) adopted an intermediate solution between the two (refer also Albizuri 2001 and Amer, Carreras and Gimnez 2002).

Mercik (2000) introduced a power measure for a cabinet, which is nominated by a legislature, consisting of many disjoint and cohesive subgroups. The Shapley–Shubik or the Banzhaf approach to the evaluation of power, when employed in the Marcik framework, yields trivial results—1 for majority cabinets and 0 for minority cabinets. Mercik's measure of the power of a cabinet is a function of the sizes and cohesiveness of supporting subgroups, where the cohesiveness of a subgroup is represented by the probability that a member votes the same way as the leader of the subgroup.

7.5 Characterizations and Interpretations

Different measures may rank voters differently in terms of their power (Saari and Sieberg 2000). It, therefore, becomes important to isolate situations in which a particular measure becomes the best suited. Equivalently, it becomes important to specify a set of axioms that are necessary and sufficient to characterize a particular measure. An axiomatic characterization enables us to understand the particular measure in a specific way through the axioms employed in the characterization exercise. At least one of the axioms provides a new insight into the characterized power measure. However, it has also been argued that the axiomatic approach may be insufficient to settle the dispute of choosing a power measure. Discussion of the axioms from the perspective of trying to get more empirical content into the analysis is definitely an important question. Since this is a separate issue, we will not go for any further discussion along this line. In this section, we provide a brief discussion on alternative characterizations of some power measures or their value counterparts.

The major contribution to this area concerns SS and BZN. Different sets of axioms have been employed by different authors to characterize them. However, among some of the common axioms that have been used in a majority of the exercises are NPC, INV and EFF.[9] Dubey (1975) characterized SS, whereas Dubey and Shapley (1979) used a similar set of axioms to characterize BR. The axioms that were employed in both the characterizations were NPC, INV, and a sum principle, which is referred to in literature as the 'transfer axiom'[10]. It is defined is follows:

Transfer axiom (TRA): Given $u, v \in SG^N$, a power measure φ satisfies the transfer principle if $\varphi(u \vee v) + \varphi(u \wedge v) = \varphi(u) + \varphi(v)$, where $u \vee v$ and $u \wedge v$ are the same as the ones defined in Section 7.2.

The name of this principle is motivated by the following observation: The game $u \wedge v$ is obtained from $u \in SG^N$ when all those coalitions that win only in u are made losing. In contrast, $u \vee v$ arises from $v \in SG^N$ when these same coalitions are made winning. Hence, $u \wedge v$ and $u \vee v$ arise from u and v when winning coalitions are 'transferred' from one game to the other (Weber 1988). This axiom parallels the condition characterizing additive measures (in the sense of measure theory), such as probabilities. If B_1 and B_2 are two events in a probability space and $\vee$ and $\wedge$ denote the conjunction and disjunction operations respectively, then it is known that $P(B_1 \vee B_2) + P(B_1 \wedge B_2) = P(B_1) + P(B_2)$, where P stands for probability.

The fourth axiom, which makes a clear distinction between SS and BZN, is that of efficiency. While efficiency has been used in the characterization of SS, the axiom of Banzhaf total power was employed in characterizing BR. Banzhaf total power axiom, which is a modified

---

[9]NPC and EFF were specified in Chapter 5 in terms of values for general games. However, it is trivial to reformulate them on the domain of simple games.

[10]Note that in spite of the similarity in their names, the transfer principle is different from TRP.

version of the efficiency criterion, is given by $\sum_{A_i \in N} \varphi_{A_i}(v) = \sum_{A_i \in N} m_{A_i}(v)$.

The characterization theorems of Dubey (1975) and Dubey and Shapley (1979) may now be stated.

Theorem 16 (Dubey 1975): Given a set of voters N, for any voter $A_i \in N$, the only power measure $\varphi_{A_i} : SG^N \to \Re_+$ that satisfies EFF, NPC, INV and TRA is SS_{A_i}, the Shapley$-$Shubik power index for voter A_i.

Theorem 17 (Dubey and Shapley 1979): Given a set of voters N, for any voter $A_i \in N$, the only power measure $\varphi_{A_i} : SG^N \to \Re_+$ that satisfies the Banzhaf total power axiom, NPC, INV and TRA is BR_{A_i}, the raw Banzhaf power measure for voter A_i.

Though TRA has been subsequently used by many authors, it has also been criticized for lacking clarity to some extent (refer Roth 1977; Straffin 1982; Felsenthal and Machover 1995 and Laruelle and Valenciano 2001). Dubey, Einy and Haimanko (2005) provided an equivalent form of this axiom, which makes its meaning clearer. It says that change in power essentially depends on change in the voting game only, that is, $\varphi(u) - \varphi(v) = \varphi(\hat{u}) - \varphi(\hat{v})$, where $u, v, \hat{u}, \hat{v} \in SG^N$ such that $W(u) - W(v) = W(\hat{u}) - W(\hat{v})$ (refer also Feltkamp 1995). Laruelle and Valenciano (2001) revised the axioms of Dubey and Shapley (1979) to characterize SS and BZN on the set of proper simple games. Einy and Haimanko (2011) replaced the efficiency axiom by a weaker axiom, the gain$-$loss axiom to characterize the Shapley$-$Shubik power index. According to the gain$-$loss axiom, the gain in power of a player must be a loss in the power of another player. It does not require the specification of the extent of gain or loss.

For any $v \in SG^N$, Owen (1972; 1975) defined its multilinear extension (MLE) as a function of n real variables:

$$f(r_{A_1}, \ldots, r_{A_n}) = \sum_{S \subseteq N} \left[\left\{ \prod_{A_i \in S} r_{A_i} \prod_{A_j \notin S} (1 - r_{A_j}) \right\} v(S) \right], \qquad (7.27)$$

where $n = |N|$. For the purpose at hand, it is assumed that the domain of f is the n-dimensional unit cube $[0,1]^n$. Here, r_{A_j} can be regarded as the probability that player A_j will join a (random) coalition S. MLE of v can be interpreted as the probability that a winning coalition will form. As Owen

(1975; 1988) demonstrated, integration of the gradient of MLE along the main diagonal of the cube gives SS, whereas evaluation of the gradient at the fixed point $(1/2, 1/2, \ldots, 1/2)$ gives BZN.

Owen (1978) used a composition principle to develop a characterization of the Banzhaf value on the space of all constant sum games. According to the composition principle, the power of voter A_j in the two-tier compound game is equal to A_j's power in the first tier game multiplied by the power of A_j's delegate in the second tier game. (Refer also Dubey, Einy and Haimanko 2005, for a more recent characterization of BZN using the composition principle. For related discussions, refer Muto 1999 and Albizuri and Ruiz 2001.)

Deegan and Packel (1978) characterized DP using an axiom which parallels TRA. This axiom, which has been referred to as the mergeability property, demands that, given $u, v \in SG^N$, the power in $u \vee v$ is a weighted mean of the powers of the component games, where the weights are the numbers of minimal winning coalitions in the respective games. Holler and Packel (1983) used a similar axiom to characterize PGI.

The contribution of Lorenzo-Friere, Alonso-Meijide, Casas-Mndez and Fiestras-Janeiro (2007) was the development of the first characterization of the Johnston measure using a critical mergeabilty axiom, which says that the power of a voter is a weighted mean of the power of unanimity games of critical coalitions, where for any $S \subseteq N$, the critical coalition associated with S is the set of swing players in S. These authors also provided a new characterization of the Deegan–Packel measure using a minimal monotonicity postulate which says that if the set of minimal winning coalitions containing a voter in a game is a subset of the set of minimal winning coalitions containing this player in another game, then the power of the voter in the latter game is not less than that in the former.

Myerson (1980) suggested the balanced contributions axiom, which says that given any coalition and a pair of players in it, one player's gain or loss because of the other player's withdrawal from the coalition should be the same for each player. Both the Shapley and the Banzhaf values satisfy this axiom. Myerson (1980) proved that this axiom and efficiency characterize the Shapley value (refer also Sanchez 1997).

Lehrer's (1988) characterization of the Banzhaf value uses the equal treatment axiom and the dummy player property. The former is Shapley's (1953) symmetry axiom (refer also Malawski 2002). On the other hand, the dummy player property demands that the value assigned to a dummy player is simply his worth in the game. The equal treatment axiom, adapted in the context of power, has also been used by Barua, Chakravarty and Roy (2005a) to characterize BZN. Nowak's (1997) characterization of the Banzhaf value provides an interesting application of Young's (1985) marginal contributions axiom (see Chapter 5).[11]

Most of the characterizations of a power measure or of a value, discussed above, uses at least three axioms. In a more recent paper, Barua, Chakravarty and Sarkar (2009) developed a two (hence minimal) axiom characterization of the Banzhaf measure, the two Coleman measures and the Shapley–Shubik index. These characterizations rely on the following axioms or some variants of them.

Sum principle (SUP): For $u, v \in SG^N$ and for any $A_i \in N$,

$$\varphi_{A_i}(u \vee v) = h^u_{A_i} \varphi_{A_i}(u) + h^v_{A_i} \varphi_{A_i}(v) - h^{u \wedge v}_{A_i} \varphi_{A_i}(u \wedge v) \qquad (7.28)$$

where $h^u_{A_i} = |W_{A_i}(u)|/|W(u \vee v)|, h^v_{A_i} = |W_{A_i}(v)|/|W(u \vee v)|$ and

$$h^{u \wedge v}_{A_i} = |W(u \vee v)|/|W(u \vee v)|.$$

Power in unanimity games (PUG): For any unanimity game $U_S \in SG^N$,

$$\varphi_{A_i}(U_S) = \begin{cases} 1 & \text{if } A_i \in S, \\ 0 & \text{otherwise.} \end{cases}$$

The sum principle is a weighted version of Dubey's (1975) transfer axiom, where the weight assigned to the power measure of $A_i \in N$ in any game is the number of winning coalitions of the game that contains A_i, expressed as a proportion of the number of winning coalitions in the union game $(u \vee v)$. To understand this in the context of Coleman's preventive power measure, suppose voter A_i has high preventive power in u but the number of winning coalitions in u is small in comparison with that in the union game $(u \vee v)$. This means that A_i's preventive power is high in situations where winning itself is relatively rare. This should be appropriately reflected in A_i's preventive power in the union game. One way of capturing this is to multiply the power in u by the weight $h^u_{A_i}$ so that in the transformed power measure, $h^u_{A_i} \varphi_{A_i}(u)$ moderates the value of $\varphi_{A_i}(u)$ by taking into account the relative importance of u with respect to $u \vee v$. A similar explanation holds for the

---

[11]See Haller (1994) and Brink and Laan (1998) for additional characterizations of the Banzhaf and Shapley values.

transformation $h^v_{A_i} \varphi_{A_i}(v)$. If there are some winning coalitions that are both in u and v, then $h^u_{A_i} \varphi_{A_i}(u) + h^v_{A_i} \varphi_{A_i}(v)$ overestimates A_i's preventive power. This is because some preventive power assigned to A_i in both u and v have already been incorporated in the respective games. Then, moderation of $\varphi_{A_i}(u \wedge v)$ by $h^{u \wedge v}_{A_i} = |W(u \wedge v)| / |W(u \vee v)|$, which indicates the relative importance of the intersection with respect to the union game, eliminates the double effect. Combining the above expressions, we get SUP.

To understand the second axiom, note that in the context of preventive power, it is natural to assume that the power of a null voter is the minimum and that of a blocker is the maximum. In the unanimity game, each voter of the coalition S is a blocker. Therefore, PUG is a natural specification of powers of a blocker and a null voter. These two axioms are independent in the sense that none of them implies or is implied by the other.

Barua, Chakravarty and Sarkar (2009) showed that an individual power measure satisfies SUP and PUG if and only if it is the Coleman preventive power measure. Let us now modify SUP by altering the weights as follows: $h^u_{A_i} = |L_{A_i}(u)| / |L(u \vee v)|$, $h^v_{A_i} = |L_{A_i}(v)| / |L(u \vee v)|$ and $h^{u \wedge v}_{A_i} = |L_{A_i}(u \wedge v)| / |L(u \vee v)|$. Also consider the following axiom that specifies the power of voter A_i in a pseudo dictatorial game D_S, a game in which each minimal winning coalition consists of only one voter:

$$\varphi_{A_i}(D_S) = \begin{cases} 1 & \text{if } A_i \in S, \\ 0 & \text{otherwise,} \end{cases}$$

where $D_S \in SG^N$. These two axioms provide a characterization of the Coleman initiative power index.

Next, if we change PUG to PUG', which says that the power of voter A_i in a unanimity game U_S is given by

$$\varphi_{A_i}(U_S) = \begin{cases} \frac{1}{|S|} & \text{if } A_i \in S, \\ 0 & \text{otherwise,} \end{cases}$$

then PUG' along with Dubey's TRA provides a characterization of the Shapley–Shubik index SS. Finally, suppose the power of voter A_i in a unanimity game U_S is measured as follows:

$$\varphi_{A_i}(U_S) = \begin{cases} \frac{1}{2^{|S|-1}} & \text{if } A_i \in S, \\ 0 & \text{otherwise.} \end{cases}$$

The non-normalized Banzhaf measure BZN is characterized by this axiom and TRA. If the above axiom is modified by replacing U_S by D_S, then the modified axiom along with Dubey's TRA characterizes BZN.

In the Shapley value (hence in the SS index), all the players are treated symmetrically in the sense that they all get the same weight. However, if one player's effort to the success of a project is greater than that of another player, then these two players should not be treated symmetrically in the allocation of the worth. Likewise, one player may represent a large constituency with many individuals and another player's constituency is rather small, then their symmetric treatment is not appropriate. Weighted Shapley value for an exogenously given family of weights was introduced by Shapley (1953a). Axiomatic characterizations of the weighted Shapley value have been provided by Shapley (1981), Hart and Mas-Collel (1989), Kalai and Samet (1987), Weber (1988) and Nowak and Radzik (1995). Radzik, Nowak and Driessen (1997) identified a set of axioms that uniquely determines the weighted Banzhaf value for an exogenously given system of weights. A characterization of the weighted BZN was developed by Barua Chakravarty and Roy (2005).

7.6 Voting Power with More than Two Alternatives

Our analysis has so far been confined to voting game models in which abstention was not taken into consideration. However, in real-life voting situations, abstention is different from voting 'no'. For instance, in the United Nations Security Council, if a permanent member votes 'no', a tabled proposal is rejected because of its veto power, no matter how the other members vote. However, if a permanent member abstains from voting, the proposal may be accepted, provided the other conditions stipulated in the decision-making rule are satisfied. Consequently, the study of the voting power of individual members when they are required to choose one of r ($r \geq 2$) alternatives is a worthwhile exercise. Bolger (1993) uniquely extended the Shapley value to games with r alternatives. This value gives a-priori evaluation for each player relative to each alternative. A similar characterization for BZN was provided by Bolger (2002).[12]

---

[12] A closely related r-game was introduced by Amer, Carreras and *Magaña* (1998). They also defined the Shapley–Shubik measure for it. An extensive study of ternary voting rules, where the voters have the choice of abstaining, apart from voting 'yes' and 'no', was made by Felsenthal and Machover (1997; 1998). They extended some measures to the ternary

We conclude this section with a brief analytical discussion. Abstention has been modelled by a game where each player faces one of three options $0, -1, 1$. The game itself can still take two values 0 and 1. Abstention by voter A_i is formulated as A_i taking on the value -1. The definition of a game $v \in SG^N$ is extended in the following way. Given that N is the set of voters, $v : \{0, 1, -1\}^{|N|} \to \{0, 1\}$. For any $S \in \{0, 1, -1\}$, we write S_{A_i} for the option that A_i exercises in the coalition S.

In this framework, the number of swings for voter A_i and the set of winning coalitions containing him has been defined in literature as follows:

For any $S \in \{0, 1, -1\}^{|N|}$, let us denote an element of $S \in \{0, 1, -1\}^{|N|}$ by $T = \zeta_{A_i}(S)$, where $T_{A_i} = 0$ and $T_{A_j} = S_{A_j}$ if $A_j \neq A_i$, $W_{A_i} = \{S \in \{0, 1, -1\}^{|N|} : v(S) = 1, S_{A_i} = 1\}$ and $m_{A_i} = \{S \in \{0, 1, -1\}^{|N|} : v(S) = 1, S_{A_i} = 1, v(\zeta_{A_i}(S)) = 0\}$.

As before, voter A_i is a null voter if $m_{A_i} = 0$ and a blocker if $S_{A_i} = 1$ for all coalitions $S \in W(v)$, the set of winning coalitions in the game. Note that now a voter A_i is critical not only if he can change the outcome of voting by changing his vote from 'yes' to 'abstain', but also from 'abstain' to 'no'. Therefore, the meaning of m_{A_i} is slightly different from that in simple voting games. The transfer postulate now in addition to satisfying conditions (i)−(iv) should satisfy the following two conditions:

(v) If $S_{A_i} = -1$, then $S \in W(u)$ if and only if $S \in W(v)$.

(vi) If $S_{A_j} = -1$, then $S \in W(u)$ if and only if $S \in W(v)$.

The remaining postulates remain unaltered. With the above definitions, the Coleman measure for voter A_i's preventive power, extended to the ternary voting situation, becomes $m_{A_i}(v)/W(v)$. Felsenthal and Machover (1997; 1998) showed that the extension of voter A_i's power, as measured by the non-normalized Banzhaf measure, to ternary voting situations is given by $m_{A_i}(v)/3^{|N|-1}$.

7.7 Measures of Power of Collectivity

In this section, we will provide a discussion on some measures of power of a voting body as a whole.

framework. See also Ono (2000), Lindler (2002), Freixas and Zwicker (2003), Freixas (2005), Tehantcho, Lambo, Pongou and Engoulou (2008) and Parker (2012), for discussion on related issues.

7.7.1 Decisiveness measure

Coleman (1971) suggested a probabilistic measure of what he referred to as 'the power of a collectivity to act'. Given the set of decision-making rules governing the collectivity, this indicator, which is known in the literature as a decisiveness measure, represents the degree of ease with which individual members' interests in the collective action can be transformed into a collective action. Thus, it is a characteristic of the collective body itself, rather than of any particular member of the body.

Carreras (2005) developed a probabilistic model of voting that leads to the definition of the decisiveness measure in a natural way. If for any voter A_i, the independent probability that he will vote in favour of a proposed resolution is $1/2$, then the probability that the resolution will get the passage of the voting body is Coleman's measure of the power of a collectivity to act. That is why in the remainder of the section, we refer to this as the Carreras–Coleman decisiveness measure. Carreras also studied several properties of this measure.

Given $v \in SG^N$, the *Carreras–Coleman measure of the power of a collectivity to act* is given by,

$$CC(v) = \frac{\sum_{S \subseteq N} v(S)}{2^{|N|}}. \tag{7.29}$$

This measure shows the propensity of the voting body to vote for or against a proposed resolution in an unambiguous way. It can be treated as the extent of deference of the concerned voting body to the clearance of a resolution. In other words, it represents the inclination of the voting body towards the passage of the proposed bill. Since $v(S) = 1$ or 0 depending on whether S is a winning or a losing coalition, we can rewrite $CC(v)$ as

$$CC(v) = \frac{|W(v)|}{2^{|N|}}. \tag{7.30}$$

Given that $|W(v)|$ is the total number of winning coalitions and $2^{|N|}$ is the total number of coalitions in $v \in SG^N$, $CC(v)$ represents the probability of accepting a resolution by the voting body. It can as well be interpreted as the probability of a random coalition to be winning when each voter's probability of being included in the coalition is $1/2$. It is 'intended to measure the possibilities that some winning coalition forms in this game' (Carreras 2005, p. 374).

If $u \in G^N$ is the dual of $v \in G^N$, then $CC(u) + CC(v) = 1$. That is, the value of the decisiveness measure for a game can be obtained by taking the complement of the value of its dual game from unity. It is iso-invariant in the sense that if $u \in G^N$ is isomorphic to $v \in G^N$, then $CC(u) = CC(v)$. It is easy to see that

$$\frac{1}{2}BZN_{A_i}(v) = CC(v) - CC(v_{-A_i}), \tag{7.31}$$

where v_{-A_i} is the game obtained by deleting voter A_i from the game v. The loss of the decisive power of collectivity $CC(v) - CC(v_{-A_i})$ is half the Banzhaf non-normalized measure of voter A_i. Equivalently, we say that it is a measure of the marginal contribution of voter A_i to the power of collectivity when he joins the grand coalition $N \setminus \{A_i\}$ (Carreras 2005 and Dragan 1996).

Since the grand coalition is always winning, the measure always takes on a positive value. It achieves its lower bound $1/2^{|N|}$ if there is only one winning coalition. If there is a dictator in the game, then he is a member of $2^{|N|-1}$ winning coalitions. Consequently, when there is a dictator in the game, the measure takes on the value $1/2$. Thus, in this case, the value of the decisiveness measure is simply half the value of the dictator's non-normalized Banzhaf measure. This condition along with the non-decreasing condition of decisive power under merger of two or more voters turns out to be equivalent to the decisive power in a unanimity game. (refer Barua, Chakravarty and Roy 2009, for discussion on this and several related issues).

A generalization of the CC measure was suggested by Laruelle and Valenciano (2005) using a probabilistic model. For any $v \in SG^N$, they consider a probability distribution over the set of *voting configurations*, p : $2^{|N|} \rightarrow \Re_+$, $0 \leq p \leq 1$ for any $S \subseteq N$ and $\sum_{S \subseteq N} p(S) = 1$, where $p(S)$ is the probability that the voters in S vote in favour of the resolution and the voters outside S vote not supporting the resolution. The *Laruelle–Valenciano generalized measure* is given by

$$\text{Prob}\{\text{the resolution is accepted}\} = \sum_{S:S \in W(v)} p(S). \tag{7.32}$$

CC becomes a particular case of this measure when p assigns the same probability to all voting configurations.

7.7.2   Sensitivity measure

A second important characteristic of a voting game is sensitivity. Dubey and Shapley (1979) argued that $\sum_{A_i \in N} m_{A_i}(v)$ 'reflects *volatility* or degree of *suspense* in the decision rule' (op cit., p. 106). It can be regarded as a measure of 'democratic participation' indicating the decision rule's responses to the wishes of the average voter. Sensitivity is a device for measuring the chances of a close decision. It gives the number of situations in which different voters are in the pivotal positions of being able to alter the outcome of voting by changing their votes. It is an indicator of the degree of naturalness with which a decision rule responds to the fluctuations in the desires of voters.   Holler and Li (1995) restricted attention to minimal winning coalitions and defined the sum of the swingers of all minimal winning coalitions as an indicator of the total power in the system.

Felsenthal and Machover (1998) suggested the use of the following transformed version of Dubey and Shapley's (1979) measure as a sensitivity measure:

$$DS(v) = \frac{\sum_{A_i \in N} m_{A_i}(v)}{2^{|N|-1}}. \tag{7.33}$$

DS is the sum of the non-normalized Banzhaf measures of power of different voters in the game. Barua, Chakravarty, Roy and Sarkar (2004), who characterized it by a set of independent axioms and investigated its properties in detail referred to it as the Banzhaf$-$Coleman$-$Dubey$-$Shapley sensitivity measure.   [In the historical sketch of their book, Felsenthal and Machover (1998), pointed out that this index was originally suggested by Penrose (1946).]

Since non-normalized Banzhaf measures can be interpreted in terms of probability; DS can as well be interpreted similarly. It is simply the sum of the marginal contributions of different voters to the power of collectivity. DS is increasing in swings of voters, that is, for any two voting games $u, v \in SG^N$, if $m_{A_i}(u) \geq m_{A_i}(v)$ for all $A_i \in N$, with strict inequality for some A_i, then $DS(u) > DS(v)$. This iso-invariant measure remains unaltered under addition or deletion of a null voter. Its value for any $v \in SG^N$ coincides with the dual of $v \in SG^N$ [refer Dubey and Shapley (1979) and Barua, Chakravarty, Roy and Sarkar (2004)].

Under certain assumptions, Dubey and Shapley (1979) demonstrated that for a decisive game $v \in SG^N$, $\sum_{A_i \in N} m_{A_i}(v) \geq 2^{|N|-1}$. DS achieves its maximal value $\left(r.\binom{|N|}{r}\right)/2^{|N|-1}$ if and only if all the coalitions containing more than $[|N|/2]$ voters are winning and less than $[|N|/2]$ voters are losing, where $r = [|N|/2] + 1$ and $[x]$ means the integral part of x (Dubey and Shapley 1979).

It has often been found that simple voting games with similar sensitivity differ greatly with respect to their propensities to pass a resolution. In view of this, Felsenthal and Machover (1998) also introduced a resistance coefficient with the objective of measuring the opposite of complaisance in a voting situation. They defined the resistance coefficient as

$$R(v) = \frac{2^{|N|-1} - |W(v)|}{2^{|N|-1} - 1}. \tag{7.34}$$

Clearly, under ceteris paribus assumptions, an increase in $R(v)$ is equivalent to a reduction in $CC(v)$.

7.8   Applications

In this section, we apply the measures analyzed in the earlier sections to some real-life problems to demonstrate their usefulness. Our discussion is subdivided into two subsections.

7.8.1   Voting in the United Nations Security Council

The United Nations Security Council, one of the most important bodies in international politics, has fifteen members: five permanent members with veto powers (United States, Russia, France, England and China) and ten non-permanent members elected by the General Assembly for a two-year term. Each member has one vote. At least nine votes are required to take a decision on any matter. Acceptance of a resolution requires 'yes' votes of at least four non-permanent members in addition to the concurrence of all five permanent members. Generally, an abstention of a permanent member is not regarded as a veto.

Let us denote the set of non-permanent members by NPM and write PM for the set of permanent members. Note that any pair of members in NPM is symmetric, which is true as well for any pair of members in PM. For each $A_i \in NPM$, we first calculate the number of coalitions S that are not winning but $S \cup \{A_i\}$ are, that is, for which A_i is swing from outside. In any ordering of the members, a member in NPM becomes a swing voter from outside if and only if seven members of NPM, including the swing voter, come last in the ordering. Given $A_i \in NPM$, there are $\binom{9}{3} = 9!/(3!6!)$ coalitions S for which A_i is swing from outside. This is because given $A_i \in NPM$, in addition to five members in PM, such a coalition must include three out of nine members in NPM who are different from A_i. Now, there are eight members who precede A_i in the ordering. Therefore, the Shapley−Shubik power of a member in NPM is $(9!8!6!)/(3!6!15!) = 0.00186$ [refer equation (7.3)]. Since each pair of members in NPM is symmetric, the total Shapley−Shubik power for all non-permanent members is $10 \times (0.00186) = 0.0186$. Since the Shapley−Shubik index is normalized, the total power of five permanent members is $(1 − 0.0186) = 0.9814$ and hence, the power of any permanent member is $(0.9814)/5 = 0.1963$ (approx.). Thus, while the members of NPM as a whole enjoy 1.86% of total power, the power enjoyed by the members of PM is 98.14%.

7.8.2 Voting in the Council of Ministers of the European union

Another application is the measurement of voting power in the Council of Ministers of the European union (EU). Six core members (France, Germany, Italy, Belgium, Netherlands and Luxembourg) of EU founded its predecessor, the European economic community (EEC), in 1958. It was expanded in 1973 to include Denmark, Ireland and England as new members. Each country had a voting weight and there was a quota for the acceptance of a resolution. Hence, voting system in the EEC Council was a simple weighted majority voting criterion. For instance, in the 1973 form of EEC, 41 votes out of a total 58 votes assigned to different members were necessary to enact a bill. Calculation of the Shapley− Shubik indices for member countries of EEC for its 1958 and 1973 councils can be found in Straffin (1994).

In the Nice Treaty, signed in 2001, a voting system assigning each country a number of votes and fixing a rule, known as qualified majority, for approval of a proposal was given. These rules for qualified majority voting were changed in the Treaty of Lisbon, signed in 2007. A double majority was recommended for an act to be adopted—there must be the support of at least 55% of the EU member states and at least 65% of the population of the EU. Several authors have investigated the properties of the voting system in the EU council. Approaches based on standard power measures have been used. The interested reader may refer to Leech (2002a), Felsenthal and Machover (2004) and Latuelle and Valenciano (2008).

Exercises

7.1 Each of the following statements is either true or false.   If the statement is true, prove it. If it is false, give a counter-example or justify your answer by logical reasoning.

    (a) If S is a winning coalition, then any subset of S is definitely not winning.

    (b) If S is a winning coalition and if S is partitioned into two sets S' and S'', then exactly one of S' and S'' will be winning.

    (c) If S and S' are winning coalitions, then the set of all common voters in S and S' is a winning coalition.

    (d) The United Nations Security Council is a weighted majority voting body.

    (e) Let $u, v \in SG^N$ be arbitrary. Then, $SS_{A_i}(u \vee v) \geq SS_{A_i}(u)$.

7.2 Give an example of a game in which the non-normalized Banzhaf power of a bloc consisting of two voters will be equal to the sum powers of the constituents.

7.3 In an organization, a bill is approved if stockholders with at least 51 per cent of the shares in total support the bill.   Calculate the normalized Banzhaf measure and the Shapley–Shubik index for a large stockholder with 30 per cent of the shares when the remaining shares are split equally among

    (a) five other stockholders;

    (b) seven other stockholders.

Why is the major stockholder less powerful in (b) than in (a)?

7.4 A committee consists of a chairman with four votes, one senior member with two votes and three junior members with one vote each.   Five votes are necessary to carry a motion.   Calculate the distribution of power using the Shapley–Shubik index and the non-normalized Banzhaf measure.

7.5 Give an example of a game in which

    (a) the Coleman and non-normalized Banzhaf measures differ,

    (b) the Sahapley–Shubik index and the non-normalized Banzhaf measure differ,

    (c) the Coleman measures and the Shapley–Shubik index differ.

7.6 Consider the following pairs of weighted majority games:

(a) $(2,1,1;3)$ and $(3,2,2;4)$,

(b) $(2,1,1;3)$ and $(4,2,2;6)$.

Are the games in each pair equivalent in the sense that they have the same winning coalitions?

7.7 Consider a set of four voters, each with one vote. One of the voters is a blocker. At least three votes are necessary to pass a bill. Calculate the numbers of swings of the voters.

7.8 Determine a necessary and sufficient condition for a weighted majority game to be proper.

7.9 Identify a game in which the power of any voter is the same for both the Shapley–Shubik and the normalized Banzhaf indices.

7.10 Show that if a weighted majority game is altered by assigning veto power to one of the voters, then the new voting body is also a weighted majority game.

7.11 Prove that for a proper voting game, a voter's power to prevent action is never less than his power to initiate action.

7.12 Show that if a voting game has at least one blocker, then it is balanced.

CHAPTER 8

Mathematical Matching

8.1 Introduction

This chapter is devoted to the analysis of a two-sided matching market that consists of two sets of non-overlapping agents. The major objective here is to discuss the possibility of matching a set of agents with another set of agents. For instance, in a marriage problem, a set of men and a set of women need to be matched in pairs.

Such a market differs from a standard commodity market in which market price determines whether a person is a buyer or a seller. For example, a person may be a buyer of a good at some price and a seller of another good at some other price—the market is not two-sided. Additional examples of matching problems include: firms have to be matched with workers, hospitals have to be matched with interns, colleges have to admit students and football players require matching with clubs. 'The term matching refers to the bilateral nature of exchange in these markets—for example, if I work for some firm, then that firm employs me' (Roth and Sotomayor 1990, p.1). These markets are definitely different from markets for goods in which a person may be buyer of one good (say, potato) and a seller of another good (say, rice).

The matching theory is a leading area in economic theory because of its importance and also because of the difficulties involved in the allocation of indivisible resources. The appropriate tools for analysis are linear programming and combinatorics. In recent years, it has become quite popular because of applications game theory to study matching problems.

One very important problem in the analysis of matching problems is stability. The problem is to find a stable matching between two sets of agents given a set of preferences for each agent. An allocation where no person will make any gain from a further exchange is called stable. In their pioneering contribution, Gale and Shapley (1962) defined a matching problem and the concept of stable matching. They also showed that stable matchings always exist and suggested an algorithm for computing stable matchings. Alvin Roth related the Gale–Shapley framework to the algorithms used for matching residents and hospitals in the United States of America. Roth and Sotomayor (1990) is a classic reference that systematically analyzes the different problems in the area.[1]

In the next section of this chapter, we present the Gale–Shapley (1962) basic model of matching 'men to women', analyze the concept of stable matching and the core of a marriage market. The Gale–Shapley algorithm 'deferred acceptance procedure' is presented in Section 8.3. Section 8.4 discusses many-to-one matchings, where there are institutions in one side of the market and individuals on the other. Finally, Section 8.5 analyzes matchings in which one side of the market does not have any preference.

It may be worthwhile to note that problems of matching arise in many other situations. For instance, an absent-minded secretary prepares n letters and n envelopes but then randomly inserts the letters into the envelopes. A match occurs if a letter is inserted into the proper envelope. Several persons come to the office with umbrellas on a rainy day and keep the umbrellas in the same place. A match occurs if a person collects his umbrella while leaving the office.

8.2 The Marriage Model

The basic problem is that given a set of women and a set of men, it is necessary to form couples from among them. More formally, the problem is one of pair-wise matching that investigates how men and women can be paired up when their views regarding the best matches are different. In other words, every member of a particular sex is to rank members of the opposite sex using his/her preferences for a marriage partner.

---

[1]Elegant discussions on some of the issues are also available in Maschler, Solan and Zamir (2013), Osborne (2004), Peters (2008) and Serrano (2013). Parts of our discussion in this chapter are based on these five contributions.

8.2.1   The basic formulation

We have a set $W = \{w_1, \ldots, w_n\}$ of n women and a set $M = \{m_1, \ldots, m_n\}$ of n men. Each woman $w_i \in W$ has a preference relation, that is, a complete and transitive binary relation, over $M \cup \{w_i\}$ so that staying single is an option for each woman. Completeness of a binary relation shows that any two distinct alternatives can be compared. Assume that every person's preference relation is strict—there is no indifference between any two partners. Likewise, each man m_j has a preference relation over $W \cup \{m_j\}$, which allows the possibility that a man prefers to remain single. We denote the preference relations of w_i and m_j by $\succ_{w_i}$ and $\succ_{m_j}$ respectively. Thus, $m_k \succ_{w_i} m_l$ is used to indicate that w_i prefers m_k to m_l as a marriage partner. The preferences of each person can be represented by an ordered list. For instance, if $W = \{w_1, w_2, w_3\}$ and $M = \{m_1, m_2, m_3\}$, then $P(m_1) = w_2 \succ_{m_1} w_1 \succ_{m_1} m_1$ means that as a marriage partner, w_2 tops in m_1's preference profile. His second preference is w_1 and he prefers staying single rather than marrying w_3. We write $W \cup M$ to denote the set of woman and man. A marriage market consists of the sets W, M and the set of preference lists of the individuals in these two sets. We can write a marriage market in a more compact form as (W, M, P), where $P = \{P(w_1), \ldots, P(w_n); P(m_1), \ldots, P(m_n)\}$ is the set of preference lists.

Definition 77 A *marriage matching* μ is a function associating each man $m \in M$ with an element of the set $W \cup \{m\}$ and each woman $w \in W$ with an element of $M \cup \{w\}$ such that if a man m is matched to a woman w, then the woman w is matched to the man m.

Thus, a matching μ of the set of persons $W \cup M$ is a function defined on $W \cup M$ that splits the set into pairs, each consisting of one woman and one man, and single persons. If w_i and m_j are matched so that $\mu(w_i) = m_j$, then $\mu(m_j) = w_i$ and we write (w_i, m_j) to denote this. We say that w_i and m_j are *partners* or *mates* of each other under the matching μ. If a person a, man or woman, prefers to *remain single*, then $\mu(a) = a$. A matching simply generates an allocation of the set of persons $W \cup M$. Each man (woman) cares only about his (her) partner, not about anyone else's partner. When a pair (w_i, m_j) has been formed by a matching μ, we say that $w_i(m_j)$ has been assigned to $m_j(w_i)$ under μ. A woman (man) $w_i(m_j)$ is *acceptable* to a man (woman) $m_j(w_i)$ if $m_j(w_i)$ prefers $w_i(m_j)$ to being unmatched.

The situation has the structure of a coalition form game because we may treat $W \cup M$ as the set of players. For any coalition S, the set of all matchings of the members S is the set of actions/worths of the coalition and each individual prefers one outcome to another by considering the mate he or she is assigned.

In order to illustrate the idea, we will consider the following example (refer Roth and Sotomayor 1990).

Example 21 The set of women is $W = \{w_1, w_2, , w_3\}$ and the set of men is $M = \{m_1, m_2, m_3\}$. In Table 8.1, the first three columns indicate the preferences of three women and the last three columns represent the preferences of three men.

The first column of the table shows that as a marriage partner w_1's most preferred choice is m_1, m_3 is her second choice of man and m_2 is her third choice. The other columns of the table can be explained similarly. Moreover, the preferences are such that each person $a \in W \cup M$ prefers to get matched than staying single.

Table 8.1 A man–woman matching problem

$P(w_1)$	$P(w_2)$	$P(w_3)$	$P(m_1)$	$P(m_2)$	$P(m_3)$
m_1	m_3	m_1	w_2	w_1	w_1
m_3	m_1	m_3	w_1	w_3	w_2
m_2	m_2	m_2	w_3	w_2	w_3

8.2.2 Stability

As in other coalition games, a key concept in matching problems is stability. In order to analyze stability in matching problems, we first consider the blocking problem induced by unhappy persons.

> **Definition 78** A marriage matching μ' is said to be *blocked* by a woman w_i if she is matched to a man m_j such that $w_i \succ_{w_i} \mu'(w_i)$ holds, that is, she would prefer to be single rather than being matched to the man m_j under μ'.

We say that the matching μ' is blocked by the unhappy woman w_i. Equivalently, we say that the woman w_i objects to the matching μ'. Thus, μ' matches a pair (w_i, m_j), where the individuals are not mutually acceptable. Likewise, a man m_j blocks or objects to a matching μ' if he is matched to a woman w_i such that $m_j \succ_{m_j} \mu'(m_j)$ holds.

> **Definition 79** A marriage matching μ is called *individually rational* if it is *not blocked* by any individual.

A marriage matching which is blocked by an individual is called individually irrational. The reasoning behind this terminology is the following. Given that remaining single is in the set of possible choices of w_i and w_i prefers remaining single to getting paired with a man m_j, a matching μ' under which she is coupled with m_j is unacceptable. Therefore, an individually irrational μ' can be improved upon by an individual because staying single is an option for a person.

Definition 80 A *pair* (w_i, m_j) is said to *block* or object to a marriage matching $\bar{\mu}$ if w_i and m_j are not matched by $\bar{\mu}$ but prefer each other to their partners assigned under $\bar{\mu}$, that is, $m_j \succ_{w_i} \bar{\mu}(w_i)$ and $w_i \succ_{m_j} \bar{\mu}(m_j)$ hold.

Equivalently, a marriage matching $\bar{\mu}$ *can be improved upon* by some pair (w_i, m_j) for which $m_j \succ_{w_i} \bar{\mu}(w_i)$ and $w_i \succ_{m_j} \bar{\mu}(m_j)$ hold.

Definition 81 A marriage matching μ is *stable* if it cannot be blocked by any individual or any pair of individuals. Equivalently, a stable marriage matching μ is a matching that cannot be improved upon by any individual or any pair of individuals.

Therefore, under a stable marriage matching, no man, no woman and no pair of a man and a woman will benefit by deviating from the matching.

Consider the preferences given in Table 8.1 of Example 21. Let us consider the matching $\bar{\mu}$ representing the allocation (w_1, m_1), (w_2, m_2) and (w_3, m_3). This is not a stable matching because under the preferences represented in Table 8.1, we have $m_1 \succ_{w_2} \bar{\mu}(w_2)$ and $w_2 \succ_{m_1} \bar{\mu}(m_1)$. That is, (w_2, m_1) is a blocking pair for $\bar{\mu}$. In contrast, the matching generating the allocation (w_1, m_1), (w_2, m_3) and (w_3, m_2) is stable because no blocking pair exists in this case.

A natural question here is: how can stable matchings be computed? A convenient procedure is the deferred acceptance procedure suggested by Gale and Shapley (1962). A discussion on this is relegated to the next section.

8.2.3   The core

Since the core as a solution concept of a coalition form game is highly fascinating with many interesting characteristics, we will now investigate properties of the core of a marriage market. In view of Proposition 10, we can define the core of such a market by domination. As a first step, we have the following.

Definition 82 In a marriage market (W, M, P), a matching μ' *dominates* another matching $\hat{\mu}$ if there exists a coalition A, which is contained in $W \cup M$ such that for all men m and women w in A, $\mu'(m) \in A$, $\mu'(w) \in A$, $\mu'(m) \succ_m \hat{\mu}(m)$ and $\mu'(w) \succ_w \hat{\mu}(w)$.

That is, all the individuals in A have been matched using μ' and all matched persons are in A. Further, every individual in A prefers μ' to $\hat{\mu}$. A matching is called undominated if it not dominated by any other matching.

Definition 83 The core $C(W, M, P)$ of a marriage market (W, M, P) is the set of all undominated matchings.

The core of a matching game has the characteristic that by any rearrangement, no group of individuals will be able to produce a matching that will make all the individuals in the group better off.

The definition of the core relies on any coalition of individuals, whereas the definition of stability is based on singletons and pairs. The following theorem, which is taken from Roth and Sotomayor (1990), establishes the relation between stable and core matchings.

Theorem 18 Let μ be any matching in a marriage market (W, M, P). Then the following conditions are equivalent:

(i) μ is stable.

(ii) $\mu \in C(W, M, P)$.

Proof: $(i) \Rightarrow (ii)$. If $\mu \notin C(W, M, P)$, then μ is dominated by some matching μ' via some coalition A. Then, every member of A prefers μ' to μ. If A consists of a single individual, then individual rationality is violated. Otherwise, for $w_i \in A$, let $m_j = \mu'(w_i)$ so that $w_i = \mu'(m_j)$. Then, w_i prefers m_j to $\mu(w_i)$ and m_j prefers w_i to $\mu(m_j)$. This means that μ is blocked by (w_i, m_j). Thus, not (ii) implies not (i). Hence, $(i) \Rightarrow (ii)$.

$(ii) \Rightarrow (i)$. Suppose μ is not stable. If μ is individually irrational, then it is dominated via a single person coalition. If it can be improved upon by some pair (w_i, m_j) so that $m_j \succ_{w_i} \mu(w_i)$ and $w_i \succ_{m_j} \mu(m_j)$ hold, then it is dominated via the coalition $\{w_i, m_j\}$ by any matching $\hat{\mu}$ for which $\hat{\mu}(w_i) = m_j$. Hence, $\mu \notin C(W, M, P)$. Thus, not (i) implies not (ii). Therefore, $(ii) \Rightarrow (i)$. □

Theorem 18 shows that the core of a marriage game coincides with the set of all stable matchings.

8.2.4   Two variants

Instead of assuming that staying single is an option for each woman and man, we can make the preference structure more restricted by ruling out this possibility so that every woman has a strict preference relation on the set of men M and every man has a strict preference relation on the set of women W. The set $W \times M$ denotes the set of all ordered pairs of the form (w_i, m_j), where $i, j = 1, 2, \ldots, n$. A marriage matching μ is now defined as a one-to-one correspondence from W to M.

By definition, every woman can be paired with exactly one man and vice versa. Alternatively, we can say that a matching is a set of ordered pairs from $W \times M$ such that each woman in W and each man in M appear in at most one pair. Evidently, a matching is a collection of n pairs of the following form $\{(w_1, m_1), (w_2, m_2), \ldots, (w_n, m_n)\}$. It may be noted that for the particular matching $\{(w_1, m_1), (w_2, m_2), \ldots, (w_n, m_n)\}$, the n pairs can be written in terms of μ as $(w_i, \mu(w_i) = m_i), i = 1, 2, \ldots, n$.

In order to define stability, we need to consider pairwise objections or blockings. A matching is stable if it does not have any blocking pair. Stable means that no pair of a man and a woman can break the matching by choosing a different partner.

A second variant of the marriage problem considered in Subsection 8.2.1 is that the number of men does not equal the number of women. Let the numbers of men and women be respectively l and k, that is, $W = \{w_1, \ldots, w_k\}$ and $M = \{m_1, \ldots, m_l\}$. Assume that $l > k$, so that each of $l - k$ men cannot be matched to a women (The analysis of the case where $l < k$ is similar).

Definition 84 A marriage matching μ is a function associating each man m with an element of the set $W \cup \{m\}$ such that under this function every woman is associated with one man.

The following definition relies on the assumption that staying single is ranked the worst in a man m's preference relation defined on $W \cup \{m\}$.

Definition 85 Given a marriage matching, a man m and a woman w object to the matching if m is single or is matched with a woman $\bar{w}$ and he prefers w to $\bar{w}$; and w prefers m to $\bar{m}$ with whom she is matched under the matching.

A matching is called stable if it is not blocked by any pair of man and woman.

8.3   The Gale–Shapley Algorithm

Gale and Shapley (1962) introduced the deferred acceptance procedure, an algorithm that induces a stable matching, for example, for the marriage market or college admissions. It shows that irrespective of preference orderings, one can always find a stable matching. In this section, we only present a verbal discussion of the procedure.   An analytical discussion along with illustrations using numerical examples is available in Chapter 13.

The procedure operates in a series of rounds. The members of one gender, say W, become the proposers and the members of the other gender, M, accept or reject proposals. Each woman proposes to her highest ranked choice. Each man who receives more than one proposal will either prefer to stay single by rejecting all of them or picks his highest preference from the set of proposals received and rejects the remaining proposals. A proposal that is not rejected makes a provisional match between the corresponding woman and man. If all the proposals are accepted, the procedure terminates and the provisional matches become final. Otherwise, in the second round, all women who were rejected in the first round propose to their second-ranked men. Each man now picks his best mate from the set of women who proposed to him at the second round and the partner with whom he was matched provisionally at the first round and rejects others and so on. The algorithm will terminate at the round at which no man will reject any proposal so that all proposals are accepted and a matching materializes.

Since there are finitely many men and women in the market, for any preferences, the deferred acceptance algorithm terminates after a finite number of rounds. The algorithm also terminates with a stable matching system. This is because if some pair (w_i, m_j) is not matched, then either w_i never proposed to m_j or a proposal has indeed been made but was rejected because m_j had a better alternative. This means that the matching cannot be improved upon by such a pair. Further, no single person can improve upon the matching because no woman will propose to an unacceptable man and each man rejects an unacceptable woman.

By the same arguments, the deferred acceptance procedure in which proposals are made by men generates a stable matching. Given the preferences, the matching produced when the set of proposers is M may or may not be the same as that when W was the set of proposers. A change in the order in which proposals are made by the women (or men) does not change the stable matching induced by the Gale–Shapley algorithm.

A stable matching is called optimal for a man if no other stable matching makes him better off. Likewise, a stable matching is optimal for a woman if no other stable matching makes her better off. Given any preference structure, the stable matching generated by the deferred acceptance procedure is optimal for the women if the women propose. For each man, this also yields his least preferred partner from among the women. Similarly, when the men propose, the stable matching obtained using the deferred acceptance procedure is optimal for the men and worst off for the women.

In view of Theorem 18 and the discussion made in this section, it is true that a marriage game has a non-empty core which contains the stable matching produced by each deferred acceptance procedure. There can be stable matchings other than those produced by the deferred acceptance procedure with the men or women being the proposers. It may be worthwhile to mention that the Gale–Shapley algorithm is applicable to the variants we have discussed in Subsection 8.2.4. Variations of this algorithm are used in hospital assignment problems in the USA, where recently graduated doctors submit individual preferences over hospitals, and hospitals have their own preferences over graduates. We analyze a problem of this type in the next section.

8.4   Many-to-One Matchings

It is possible to think of variations of the men–women matching problem in different settings. In this section, we will discuss many-to-one matching problems such as between students and colleges and workers and firms. In many countries of the world, a large number of students apply for admission to a small number of medical colleges. Since the number of applicants is usually much greater than the total number of admission quotas of different colleges, many students seek admission in several medical colleges. Each student has preferences over the set of colleges and each college has its own ranking of the students. Likewise, in a firm–worker matching model, a worker has preferences over the set of firms in which he is willing to work and each firm has preferences over the subset of workers it is willing to employ. For concreteness, we restrict our discussion to the firm–worker model. However, the analysis applies equally well to the college–student matching problem, where the firms

can be treated as colleges and workers as students. One important difference from the marriage model is that each firm may not be able to
employ all the workers; it may offer employment only to a certain
number of workers using its preferences. This number is the firm's employment quota.

Let $F = \{F_1, \ldots, F_n\}$ be the set of n firms and $A = \{w_1, \ldots, w_m\}$ be
the set of m workers. The complete transitive relation of firm F_i on A is
denoted by $\succ_{F_i}$ and $\succ_{w_j}$ stands for the complete transitive relation of the
worker w_j on F. For instance, $P(w_j) : F_2 \succ_{w_j} F_3 \succ_{w_j} w_j \succ_{w_j} \ldots$ means that
the only firms the worker w_j will accept as his employers are F_2 and F_3, in
that order.

Definition 86 A firm–worker matching is a function μ from $F \cup W$ to $F \cup W$ such
that for all F_i and w_j:

(i) $\mu(w_j) \in F \cup \{w_j\}$
(ii) $w_j \in \mu(F_i)$ if and only if $\mu(w_j) = F_i$,
(iii) $\mu(F_i) \subseteq A$ and $|\mu(F_i)| \leq q_i$, where $q_i \geq 1$ is firm F_i's employment quota.

In (i), $\mu(w_j) \in F$ means that w_j is employed in a firm in F, whereas $\mu(w_j) \in \{w_j\}$ means that w_j is unemployed. Thus, w_j is either employed in a firm
or unemployed. In either case, $|\mu(w_j)| = 1$. Condition (ii) says that F_i
employs w_j if and only if w_j is employed in F_i. According to condition (iii),
F_i may employ some of or all the workers and its employment level does
not exceed its quota. We say that F_i is matched to the set of workers $\mu(F_i)$
and w_j is matched to the firm $\mu(w_j)$. Thus, if a firm F_i has an employment
quota of 3, then $\mu(F_i) = (w_1, w_2)$ means that F_i employs only two workers
w_1 and w_2, and keeps one position unfilled. We will say that a firm F_i is
acceptable to a worker w_j if w_j prefers F_i to being unmatched, that is, being
employed by F_i rather than remaining unemployed. Similarly, a worker is
acceptable to a firm if it prefers recruiting him to being without having
him as an employee.

A matching μ with $\mu(w_j) = F_i$ is blocked by an individual if either
the firm is unacceptable to the worker or the worker is unacceptable to
the firm. A matching $\hat{\mu}$ is blocked by a pair (w_j, F_i) if each partner of the
pair prefers each other to their assignments under the matching, that is,
$w_j \succ_{F_i} \bar{\mu}(F_i)$ and $F_i \succ_{w_j} \bar{\mu}(w_j)$ hold. A matching is (pairwise) stable if it is
not blocked by any individual or any pair.

We now wish to look at the existence of stable matchings in this
environment. However, the above notion of stability does not rule out all

possible blocking situations.   For instance, we may need to consider coalitions consisting of several firms and workers. For this purpose, we restrict our attention to responsive preferences, which are defined below.

Definition 87 (Responsive preferences): For all $S \subseteq A$ with $|S| < q_i$, and $w_k, w_l \in A \setminus S$, $S \cup \{w_k\} \succ_{F_i} S \cup \{w_l\}$ if and only if $w_k \succ_{F_i} w_l$ and $S \cup \{w_k\} \succ_{F_i} S$ if and only if w_k is acceptable to F_i.

According to responsive preferences, if a firm F_i has a set of employees S and its employment quota is not yet full, then out of two new workers w_k and w_l who are seeking employment in F_i, F_i will include w_k in its existing set of employees if and only if it prefers w_k to w_l. Further, F_i will prefer to get its set of employees extended by including w_k so that the expanded set becomes preferable to the existing set if and only if w_k is acceptable to F_i. The framework in which firms (colleges) can have preferences over groups of workers (students) was considered first in Roth (1985).

Definition 88 A matching $\bar{\mu}$ is blocked by a coalition $S \subseteq F \cup A$ if there exists another matching μ such that for all $w_j \in S \cap A$ and all $F_i \in S \cap F$:

   (i) $\mu(w_j) \in S$,

   (ii) $\mu(w_j) \succ_{w_j} \bar{\mu}(w_j)$,

   (iii) $w_k \in \mu(F_i)$ implies that $w_k \in S \cup \bar{\mu}(F_i)$, and

   (iv) $\mu(F_i) \succ_{F_i} \bar{\mu}(F_i)$.

According to condition (i) of Definition 88, every worker in S is matched to a firm in S. Condition (ii) says that every worker in S prefers the new matching to the old one. Condition (iii) demands that under μ every firm F_i in S is matched to new workers only from S although it may remain to be matched to some of its old workers from $\bar{\mu}(F_i)$. Finally, condition (iv) requires that every firm prefers its new set of workers to the old set.

Definition 89 A firm–worker matching is called *group stable* if it not blocked by a coalition of any size.

As noted in Roth and Sotomayor (1990), under responsiveness of preferences, this notion of group stability is equivalent to pairwise stability.

Theorem 19 Let the preferences be responsive and μ be a matching. Then the following conditions are equivalent.

(i) μ is pairwise stable.

(ii) μ is group stable.

Proof: $(i) \Rightarrow (ii)$. Suppose μ is blocked by a coalition S and a matching μ'. Then there must exist a worker w_j and a firm F_i such that $w_j \in \mu'(F_i)$ but $w_j \notin \mu(F_i)$ such that w_j and F_i block μ (otherwise, it cannot be the case that $\mu'(F_i) \succ_{F_i} \mu(F_i)$, since F_i has responsive preferences). Thus, coalition blocking implies pairwise blocking, that is, not (ii) implies not (i). Hence, $(i) \Rightarrow (ii)$.

$(ii) \Rightarrow (i)$. Pairwise instability clearly implies group instability, that is, not (i) implies not (ii). Thus, $(ii) \Rightarrow (i)$. $\qquad\qquad\square$

Example 22 Consider a set $F = \{F_1, F_2\}$ of two firms and consider a set $A = \{w_1, w_2, w_3\}$ of three workers. The preferences of the workers and the firms are represented in Table 8.2.

Table 8.2 A many-to-one matching

$P(w_1)$	$P(w_2)$	$P(w_3)$	$P(F_1)$	$P(F_2)$
F_1	F_1	F_1	w_1	w_2
F_2	F_2	F_2	w_2	w_1
$-$	$-$	$-$	w_3	w_3

From Table 8.2, it follows that the preference profile of firm F_1 is $P(F_1)$: $w_1 \succ_{F_1} w_2 \succ_{F_1} w_3$. The identical preferences of the three workers are given in the first three columns. There are no entries in the third row for these three columns because the number of firms is two. Suppose the quotas of the two firms F_1 and F_2 be 1 and 2 respectively. Then, the unique stable matching assigns w_1 to F_1 and w_2, w_3 to F_3.

8.5 Matchings when One Side Does not have Preferences

We will now discuss two situations in which one of the two sides does not have any preferences. The roommate assignment problem is a situation of this type. Suppose an even number of students, say $2n$, where n is any positive integer, are to be allotted to n double-bed rooms. Let $T = \{s_1, s_2, \ldots, s_{2n}\}$ be the set of students. Each student s ranks all the remaining $2n - 1$ students as his/her roommate. This roommate problem differs from the marriage problem in the sense that all the participants belong to a single pool instead of being identified as members of two different pools such as M and W. In the roommate problem, we can pair any two members of the same set, whereas in the marriage problem we cannot pair any two members of the set $W \cup M$, that is, we cannot pair any two men or any two women.

Definition 90 A roommate matching μ is a function that associates each student s with an element of the set $T \setminus \{s\}$.

We say that a pair of students (s_i, s_j), where $i, j = 1, \ldots, 2n$, $i \neq j$, blocks a matching $\bar{\mu}$ if they are not roommates but prefer each other to their actual roommates assigned under the matching $\bar{\mu}$, that is, $s_j \succ_{s_i} \bar{\mu}(s_i)$ and $s_i \succ_{s_j} \bar{\mu}(s_j)$ hold. A matching is stable if it is not blocked by any pair of students.

Gale and Shapley (1962) observed that a stable matching may not exist for this matching problem. To see this formally, we consider the following example, which is taken from Gura and Maschler (2008).

Example 23 Let $T = \{s_1, s_2, s_3, s_4\}$ be the set of four students who are to be allotted to two different rooms in a dorm. Four columns of Table 8.3 indicate the preferences of the students.

Table 8.3 A roommate matching problem

$P(s_1)$	$P(s_2)$	$P(s_3)$	$P(s_4)$
—	s_3	s_1	s_1
s_2	—	s_2	s_2
s_3	s_1	—	s_3
s_4	s_4	s_4	—

Thus, for example, s_3's most preferred choice as roommate is s_1, s_2 is her second choice and s_4 is her least preferred choice. Since s_i cannot choose herself as her roommate, there is no entry in the table corresponding to the row–column combination (i, i), $i = 1, 2, 3, 4$. The possible allotments of the four students as roommates are as follows: (a) (s_1, s_2), (s_3, s_4), (b) (s_1, s_3), (s_2, s_4), and (c) (s_1, s_4), (s_2, s_3). For allotment (a), (s_2, s_3) is a blocking pair because each student prefers each other to her respective roommate assigned under the allotment. Likewise, (s_1, s_2) and (s_1, s_3) are blocking pairs for allotments (b) and (c), respectively. Here s_4 is the least preferred choice of all the other students and s_4's assigned roommate will get a partner whom she prefers to s_4 and who will like her as her most preferred roommate. This gives rise to the blocking problem.

A second assignment game in which there are no preferences in one of the two sides is a house exchange game. There is a set of n house owners $h = \{h_1, \ldots, h_n\}$ and each owner has a strict preference over the set of houses $H = \{H_1, \ldots, H_n\}$, where H_i is the house possessed by owner h_i. The objective is to make the house owners better off through an exchange of houses. Each person cares only about the house he gets. Thus, in this exchange economy model, the number of indivisible goods is the same as the number of market participants. We denote a house exchange market by (h, H, P), where P is the set of preference lists of the house owners.

Definition 91   A house matching μ is a one-to-one correspondence from h to H.

Each individual is allotted one house and no house is assigned to more than one individual. One option for house owner h_i is to keep his own favourite house, that is, $\mu(h_i) = H_i$.

Since there is a finite number of house owners, there is at least one cycle. To understand this, let $h = \{h_1, h_2\}$ and $H = \{H_1, H_2\}$. When two persons exchange their houses, that is, if $\mu(h_1) = H_2$ and $\mu(h_2) = H_1$, we say that h_1h_2 is a cycle of order 2. On the other hand, $\mu(h_i) = H_i$ for $i = 1, 2$, corresponds to a cycle of order 1. If $h = \{h_1, h_2, h_3\}$ and $H = \{H_1, H_2, H_3\}$, then $\mu(h_1) = H_2$, $\mu(h_2) = H_3$ and $\mu(h_3) = H_1$ represents a cycle $h_1h_2h_3$ of order 3.

Shapley and Scraff (1974) proposed an algorithm, the top trading cycle, suggested to them by David Gale, which solves the exchange problem. A sequence $h_{(1)}, h_{(2)}, \ldots, h_{(l)}$ of house owners, $l \geq 1$, such that the favourite house of $h_{(i)}$ is $H_{(i+1)}$, where $1 \leq i \leq l - 1$ and the favourite house of $h_{(l)}$ is $H_{(1)}$ represents a top trading cycle of order l. If $l = 1$, then person $h_{(1)}$ already possesses his favourite house. The top trading cycle procedure goes as follows. First we identify the cycles among the houses at the top of the owners' preferences and each owner in each cycle is assigned his favourite house. Such house owners along with their assignments are then removed from the market. If there is at least one remaining house, proceed to the next step. At the next step, we first look for the cycles at the top of the remaining owners' preferences and each owner in each cycle is assigned his favourite house among the remaining houses. This procedure continues until all the houses are assigned among the owners. Given that the preferences are strict, the algorithm gives a unique allocation (Roth and Postlewaite 1977).

We may illustrate the procedure by an example.

Example 24 Let $h = \{h_1, h_2, h_3, h_4\}$ be a set of four house owners whose preferences for the set of houses $H = \{H_1, H_2, H_3, H_4\}$ are given in Table 8.4.

Table 8.4 A house matching problem

$P(h_1)$	$P(h_2)$	$P(h_3)$	$P(h_4)$
H_3	H_1	H_1	H_2
H_2	H_4	H_4	H_3
H_1	H_2	H_2	H_1
H_4	H_3	H_3	H_4

For example, owner h_1 prefers the house of owner h_3 over the house of owner h_2 over his own house, which is preferred to the house of owner h_4. For the first round of the top trading cycle, $h_1 h_3$ constitutes a cycle of order 2. Consequently, they are assigned their favourite houses, that is, H_1 is assigned to h_3 and h_1 gets H_3. Now, the houses H_1, H_3, and the owners h_1, h_2 are removed from the scene. We then note that H_4 is h_2's favourite choice and h_4 desires H_2 so that now $h_2 h_4$ becomes a cycle of order 2. Therefore, the houses H_2 is assigned to h_4 and H_4 is assigned to h_2. This completes the process. Now, suppose the preference structure of h_2 changes to $P(h_2) : H_1 \succ_{h_2} H_2 \succ_{h_2} H_4 \succ_{h_2} H_3$. Then at the second round, h_2 will be a cycle of order 1 and will be assigned his own house H_2. After eliminating h_2 and H_2 from the scene, at the third round, h_4 will be assigned the house H_4.

> **Definition 92** An assignment of houses to owners is in the *core* of the house exchange market if there does not exist a coalition S of house owners that can redistribute the houses they own such that they all prefer the houses resulting from the reallocation to the houses they are getting under the assignment.

Shapley and Scarf (1974) demonstrated that the core of a house matching problem is non-empty. If everybody owns his favourite house, then the assignment that enables him to retain his own favourite house is in the core.

Proposition 27   The assignment of houses brought about by the top trading cycle procedure is in the core of the house exchange market.

Proof: In the first round of the top trading cycle, each house owner receives his favourite house so that no subgroup of these owners can make all its members better off than what they have received in the first round of the cycle by any redistribution of houses among themselves. Now, consider a subgroup of owners who were assigned houses in the second round but no owners who were assigned houses in the first round. Members of this coalition do not possess houses that were eliminated after completion of the first round and they are assigned favourite houses from among the houses the coalition owns. Such a coalition cannot make its members better off by redistribution of houses among themselves. A similar argument applies to coalitions with house owners who were assigned houses in the later rounds of the top trading cycle procedure. This in turn demonstrates that assignment of houses actuated by the top trading cycle procedure is in the core of the house exchange market.   □

We define the strong core of a game as one that consists of all allocations on which no coalition could make all its members at least as good as and at least one member better off. If the preferences of the house owners are strict, then the strong core of a house exchange market consists of the unique assignment affected by the top trading cycle procedure.

Exercises

8.1 Consider a matching problem with 3 men and 3 women. Their preferences are represented in the following table. Construct one stable matching and one unstable matching for these preferences.

$P(w_1)$	$P(w_2)$	$P(w_3)$	$P(m_1)$	$P(m_2)$	$P(m_3)$
m_1	m_1	m_1	w_1	w_1	w_1
m_2	m_2	m_2	w_2	w_2	w_2
m_3	m_3	m_3	w_3	w_3	w_3

8.2 Four students are to be allotted to two different rooms in pairs. Their preferences are indicated below. Is there any stable matching of these students in pairs?

$P(s_1)$	$P(s_2)$	$P(s_3)$	$P(s_4)$
—	s_1	s_4	s_1
s_4	—	s_2	s_2
s_2	s_4	—	s_3
s_3	s_3	s_1	—

8.3 In the man–woman matching problem where preferences are represented in the following table, identify a stable matching induced by the Gale–Shapley algorithm when the men propose.

$P(w_1)$	$P(w_2)$	$P(w_3)$	$P(w_4)$	$P(m_1)$	$P(m_2)$	$P(m_3)$	$P(m_4)$
m_1	m_3	m_3	m_2	w_3	w_2	w_2	w_3
m_2	m_1	m_2	m_1	w_2	w_1	w_4	w_1
m_3	m_4	m_4	m_3	w_4	w_3	w_1	w_4
m_4	m_2	m_1	m_4	w_1	w_4	w_3	w_2

8.4 Consider a house exchange problem among 4 persons whose preferences are shown in the following table. Identify one top trading cycle.

$P(h_1)$	$P(h_2)$	$P(h_3)$	$P(h_4)$
H_3	H_1	H_1	H_2
H_2	H_2	H_4	H_3
H_1	H_3	H_2	H_1
H_4	H_4	H_3	H_4

8.5 Show that there is no stable division of the students whose preferences are shown in the following table. Can you explain the reason for an unstable matching?

$P(s_1)$	$P(s_2)$	$P(s_3)$	$P(s_4)$
–	s_3	s_4	s_1
s_3	–	s_1	s_3
s_4	s_1	–	s_2
s_2	s_4	s_2	–

8.6 Use the Gale–Shapley algorithm to identify a stable matching when women propose and the preferences of men and women are specified in the following table.

$P(w_1)$	$P(w_2)$	$P(w_3)$	$P(m_1)$	$P(m_2)$	$P(m_3)$
m_3	m_3	m_2	w_1	w_1	w_2
m_2	m_1	m_3	w_2	w_2	w_1
m_1	m_2	m_1	w_3	w_3	w_3

CHAPTER 9

Non-Transferable Utility Cooperative Games

9.1 Introduction

The coalition games we have analyzed in the earlier chapters are transferable utility (TU) games. In such games, each coalition is assigned a pay-off (utility) represented by a real number with the interpretation that the members of the coalition can divide this pay-off in an unambiguous manner. In contrast, for non-transferable utility (NTU) games, the pay-offs for each coalition are represented by a set of pay-off (utility) vectors indexed by the members of the coalition. Transferability of utility is a simplifying assumption which makes the analysis quite convenient. However, the transferability assumption may be undesirable in many applications. To illustrate this, consider a bilateral monopoly, a market situation in which a single seller confronts a single buyer. For concreteness, assume that a monopsonistic supplier of a rare metal, which is needed to produce an alloy, faces a monopolistic buyer, the only producer of the alloy. That is, a monopoly supplier of an input faces a monopoly demander of the input. It is known that in such a situation, the market outcome is indeterminate and the outcome must be settled through bargaining. If the producer ceases production, the supplier will not be able to sell the metal. On the other hand, if the supplier refuses to sell the metal, there will be no production of the alloy. In either case, no positive pay-off will be created for each of them. On the other hand, if the two parties decide to cooperate and come to a settlement, some positive pay-off will be created for each of them. However, the settlement does not involve any transfer of pay-off between the two parties. The settlement between the parties is the outcome of an NTU cooperative game. A unique solution to this bargaining problem emerges if the Nash (1950) bargaining model is adopted.

Extensive studies on NTU games were started only in the 1960s and the literature is not very voluminous. A large part of the literature is devoted to the analysis of bargaining games in which only the individual players and the grand coalition play a role. Therefore, an analysis on the Nash (1950) bargaining model will be presented in Section 9.3. A systematic comparison of this with a different approach to bargaining that draws techniques and concepts from non-cooperative game theory is also made in the section. Section 9.4 presents the exchange economy model as an alternative application of NTU games. However, to begin, in Section 9.2, we present the definition of the characteristic function of an NTU game and illustrate it with an example. We also define the core of an NTU game in this section.

9.2   The Basic Model

As in the earlier chapters, we assume that $N = \{A_1, \ldots, A_n\}$ is the finite set of players, $2^{|N|}$ denotes the collection of all coalitions of N, where $|N| = n \geq 2$ is a positive integer. There is no standard definition of NTU games in literature and many results are sensitive to the details specified in the definition. The general definition of NTU games we present below follows McLean (2002).

Definition 93 Given the player set $N = \{A_1, \ldots, A_n\}$, a *cooperative game v with non-transferable utility* (NTU) is a correspondence that assigns for each non-empty coalition $S \subseteq N$, a non-empty subset $v(S)$ of $\Re^{|S|}$ and $v(\emptyset) = 0$.

The above definition is fairly broad. Often it is assumed that $v(S)$ is proper, closed, convex and comprehensive. Closedness of $v(S)$ means that it contains its boundaries. As stated earlier, convexity of $v(S)$ says that for any two elements of $v(S)$, a weighted average of the two elements is also an element of $v(S)$, where the sum of the non-negative weights equals 1. According to comprehensiveness of $v(S)$, if $x \in v(S)$, then for any $y \leq x$, $y \in v(S)$, where $y \leq x$ means that $y_{A_i} \leq x_{A_i}$ for all $A_i \in S$ (refer McLean 2002 and Hart 2004). Since transferability is given up, we can no longer claim that the worth of a coalition can be divided among its members. Instead, each coalition will have a set of pay-off vectors, where the dimension of the vectors is given by the number of players in the coalition. The interpretation of v is that $v(S)$ is the set of all $|S|$-dimensional vectors of pay-offs which the coalition S can guarantee to itself without seeking cooperation from the players in $N \setminus S$. If $x \in v(S)$, the utility of A_i when S breaks down as a coalition is x_{A_i}. An NTU game v with the player set N is denoted by the pair $(N; v)$. A transferable utility game $\bar{v} \in G^N$ can be transformed into a non-transferable utility game $(N; v)$ by setting $v(S) = \{x \in \Re^{|S|} \mid \sum_{A_i \in S} x_{A_i} \leq \bar{v}(S)\}$ for all non-empty coalitions $S \subseteq N$.

Example 25 For a game $(N; v)$ with the player set $N = \{A_1, A_2, A_3\}$, let $v(\{A_i\}) = \{x_{A_i} \mid x_{A_i} \leq c\}$, $A_i \in N$, $v(\{A_i, A_j\}) = \{(x_{A_i}, x_{A_j}) \mid x_{A_i} \leq 1, x_{A_j} \leq 1\}$ for all $A_i, A_j \in N$, $A_i \neq A_j$ and, finally let $v(\{A_1, A_2, A_3\}) = \{(x_{A_1}, x_{A_2}, x_{A_3}) \mid x_{A_1} + x_{A_2} + x_{A_3} \leq 2 + c\}$, where $0 \leq c < 1$ is a constant. This is an NTU game because for each $S \subseteq N$, $v(S)$ is a set and the dimension of any element of $v(S)$ is $|S|$.

Let $(N; v)$ be an NTU game. A pay-off vector is an element of $\Re^{|N|}$. For $y \in v(N)$, a non-empty coalition $S \subset N$ can improve upon y if there exists $x \in v(S)$ such that $x_{A_i} > y^S_{A_i}$ for all $A_i \in S$, where y^S is the projection of y on $\Re^{|S|}$, that is, y^S is the sub-vector of y corresponding to the players in S. Equivalently, we say that the outcome x for $S(x \in v(S))$, where $S \subset N$ is non-empty and x dominates $y \in v(N)$.

Definition 94 The *core* $C(N; v)$ of an NTU game $(N; v)$ is defined as

$$C(N; v) = \{x \mid x \in v(N) \text{ and there is no } S \subset N \text{ that can improve upon } x\}.$$

Definition 94 states that no coalition of players can improve upon a pay-off vector in the core of an NTU game. In other words, the core of an NTU game is defined as the set of all undominated pay-off vectors in $v(N)$. The central idea underlying the core for games with both transferable and non-transferable utility is essentially the same. In both cases, the core is based on undomination of pay-off vectors. The core of the game considered in Example 25 is the set $\{(1, 1, c), (1, c, 1), (c, 1, 1)\}$.

For discussions on other solution concepts for NTU games, for example, the bargaining set, the kernel, the nucleolus and the Shapley value, the reader is referred to Friedman (1986), McLean (2002), Hart (2004), and Peleg and Sudhölter (2007). Scarf (1967), Billera (1970) and Shapley (1973a) discuss the non-emptiness of the core of an NTU game.

9.3   Cooperative Bargaining Games

In the cooperative game theoretic approach to bargaining, all the actions of the players are controlled by some binding agreements between them. The process of bargaining and negotiations by which agreements are reached are ignored. The approach is concerned only with the content of the agreement. Further, it does not say anything about why bargaining may not be successful always—that is, there may not be an agreement.

In order to motivate the formal presentation of a cooperative bargaining model, let us consider an illustrative example, where T units of a perfectly divisible good is to be distributed among the persons in the set $N = \{A_1, \ldots, A_n\}$. Each person $A_i \in N$ is characterized by a von Neumann−Morgenstern utility function $U_{A_i} : [0, T] \to \Re$. If the persons are able to reach a unanimous agreement on some division of the good, then the corresponding $|N|$-tuple of utilities is the outcome of the game. In contrast, if there is any disagreement among players, then each player ends up with the utility $U_{A_i}(0)$, which means that he does not receive anything.

The formulation of the associated NTU game is as follows:

$$v(N) = \{x \in \Re^{|N|} \mid \exists \omega_{A_i} \geq 0, A_i \in N, \sum_{A_i \in N} \omega_{A_i} = T; x_{A_i} \leq U_{A_i}(\omega_{A_i}), A_i \in N\}$$

and for any $S \subset N$,

$$v(S) = \{x \in \Re^{|S|} \mid x_{A_i} \leq U_{A_i}(0)\}. \tag{9.1}$$

Therefore, the grand coalition will benefit from cooperation. The assumption $\sum_{A_i \in N} \omega_{A_i} = T$ ensures that the division does not involve any wastage. The set of possible divisions of the good is given by $\{\omega \in \Re^{|N|} \mid \omega_{A_i} \geq 0, A_i \in N, \sum_{A_i \in N} \omega_{A_i} = T\}$. The disagreement outcome, the outcome that emerges when the players fail to reach a unanimous agreement, is the vector $0.1^{|N|}$, where $1^{|N|}$ is the $|N|$-coordinated vector of ones. By definition, this outcome is not an element of the set of possible divisions. The set of utility profiles corresponding to the set of possible agreements is $\{y \in \Re^{|N|} \mid y_{A_i} = U_{A_i}(\omega_{A_i}), A_i \in N, (\omega_{A_1}, \omega_{A_2}, \ldots, \omega_{A_n}) \neq 0.1^{|N|}\}$. The utility vector corresponding to the disagreement outcome is $(U_{A_1}(0), U_{A_2}(0), \ldots, U_{A_n}(0))$. It may be important to note that in the above formulation of the NTU game, there is no notion of interpersonal comparisons of utilities. There is, however, intra-personal comparison;

each person compares what he will get if there is cooperation among the players with what he will get if there is no unanimous agreement.

To analyze Nash's (1950) model of bargaining, for simplicity of exposition, we will assume that there are only two players, an assumption that will be retained in the remainder of the section. However, our discussion applies equally well to an $|N|$-person situation, where $|N| > 2$ is arbitrary but finite. We also maintain the issue that the two players face the problem of dividing a perfectly divisible good of T units. Let M denote the feasible set, the set of possible pairs of utilities and the utility vector $(U_{A_1}(0), U_{A_2}(0))$ corresponding to the disagreement outcome is denoted by $d = (d_{A_1}, d_{A_2})$, that is, $(U_{A_1}(0), U_{A_2}(0)) = (d_{A_1}, d_{A_2})$. Often d is referred to as the threat point.

From now on, we will restrict our attention to the pair (M, d). This in turn implies that we are ignoring all non-utility features at the outset. The attitudes of the bargainers are completely reflected in their utilities.

Definition 95 A *two-person bargaining problem* or a *cooperative bargaining game* is a pair (M, d), where M is a set of pairs of utility vectors (the set of pairs of utilities on agreement outcomes) and d is the disagreement utility vector satisfying the following conditions:

(i) M is compact (closed and bounded) and convex,

(ii) $d \in M$,

(iii) there is an element $v = (v_{A_1}, v_{A_2}) \in M$ such that $v_{A_1} > d_{A_1}$ and $v_{A_2} > d_{A_2}$.

Boundedness of M requires that it should be a proper subset of $\Re^2$, where the coordinates of boundary points are finite, that is, it is a subset of a large disc. An example of a compact and convex subset of $\Re^2$ is $[0, 1] \times [0, 2]$. Since players may agree to disagree, the disagreement utility pair should be an element of M. This is ensured by condition (*ii*). The players should also have incentives for arriving at an agreement, that is, if there is an agreement on some outcome, then the utility of each player from the corresponding outcome should be higher than his disagreement utility. Condition (*iii*) is such an incentive providing assumption. Let B denote the set of all two-person bargaining games.

A bargaining solution is a rule that assigns a unique point in M for each bargaining problem. Formally,

---

Definition 96 A bargaining solution is function $f : B \rightarrow \Re^2$ such that for any $(M, d) \in B$, $f(M, d) \in M$.

Definition 96, which is taken from Nash (1950), says that given the bargaining game (M, d), $f(M, d)$, the solution of the game, is a 2-tuple utility vector that belongs to M.

Given that $d \in M$, the possibility of d emerging as the solution of the bargaining game is not ruled out, that is, it can as well be the case that $f(M, d) = d$. There can be many more solutions. Nash (1950) argued that a bargaining solution should satisfy four intuitively reasonable axioms. The Nash bargaining solution is a solution for cooperative bargaining games that fulfil these four axioms.

Weak Pareto efficiency (WPE): For any bargaining game (M, d), if $x, y \in M$ are such that $x > y$, then $f(M, d) \neq y$, where $x > y$ means that $x_{A_1} > y_{A_1}$ and $x_{A_2} > y_{A_2}$.

According to WPE, the two players should behave collectively in a rational manner. That is, if one utility vector assigns higher utility to each person than another vector, then the latter cannot be a solution to the bargaining game. In other words, one agreement generating lower utilities than another agreement cannot be acceptable to the players.

Affine coinvariance (AFC): Consider the bargaining game (M, d). Let $(\hat{M}, \hat{d})$ be the bargaining game obtained from (M, d) by taking independent affine transformations of the utilities of the two players. That is, for any arbitrary $v = (v_{A_1}, v_{A_2}) \in M$ and for real numbers $\alpha_{A_1} > 0$, $\alpha_{A_2} > 0$, β_{A_1} and β_{A_2}, $\hat{M}$ is the set of all pairs $(\alpha_{A_1} v_{A_1} + \beta_{A_1}, \alpha_{A_2} v_{A_2} + \beta_{A_2})$ and $\hat{d} = (\alpha_{A_1} d_{A_1} + \beta_{A_1}, \alpha_{A_2} d_{A_2} + \beta_{A_2})$. Then, $f(\hat{M}, \hat{d}) = (\alpha_{A_1} f_{A_1}(M, d) + \beta_{A_1}, \alpha_{A_2} f_{A_2}(M, d) + \beta_{A_2})$.

In the formulation of the bargaining game, utility is a concept as real as money. Preferences of a person are represented by a von Neumann–Morgenstern utility function. This means that representations of preferences are unique up to an affine transformation, a linear transformation with a positive slope. The information conveyed by such a utility function remains invariant under an affine transformation. For instance, the level of temperature C measured on the Celsius scale can be converted into the Fahrenheit temperature F using the affine transformation $F = (9C/5) + 32$—no information is lost with the transformation. An important characteristic here is that we can talk about differences in the measurement scale. AFC requires that the solution should not be affected by the numerical representation of individual preferences if the underlying preferences remain unchanged. Note that generality is maintained in taking the transformations, in the sense that different transformations are applied to different persons' utilities. Convexity and compactness of the set of utility pairs are retained under affine transformations of the utility values.

Symmetry (SYM): Let (M, d) be a bargaining game where $d_{A_1} = d_{A_2}$. Further, if $(v_{A_1}, v_{A_2}) \in M$, then $(v_{A_2}, v_{A_1}) \in M$. Then, $f_{A_1}(M, d) = f_{A_2}(M, d)$.

If the disagreement utility levels are the same and the set M is symmetric in the sense that a reordering of the two arguments of any element in M is also an element of M, then the outcome of the bargaining problem should assign the same utility to each player. That is, SYM demands that if the two bargainers have identical preferences and are in the same circumstances, then the solution should give them the same pay-off. If (M, d) is a bargaining game, we do not have any information by which one player can be distinguished from the other. In other words, under SYM, all characteristics other the information contained in the model, for example, the names of the bargainers, are irrelevant to the solution of the bargaining problem.

Independence of irrelevant alternatives (IIA): Let (M, d) and $(\hat{M}, \hat{d})$ be two bargaining games such that $M \subseteq \hat{M}$, $d = \hat{d}$ and $f(\hat{M}, \hat{d}) \in M$. Then, $f(M, d) = f(\hat{M}, \hat{d})$.

IIA means that if the solution of a larger set is an element of a smaller set, then this is the solution of the smaller set as well. That is, if the set of possible utility vectors shrinks to a smaller set containing the original solution outcome of the bargaining problem, then the solution outcome should not change. Therefore, under IIA, the bargaining outcome remains unchanged if the agreements that the bargainers do not make do not remain feasible any longer. Equivalently, the process of bargaining can be shortened by narrowing down the original set of utility vectors to a smaller set without changing the outcome of the original bargaining problem.

Definition 97 For any $(M, d) \in B$, the *Nash bargaining solution* $f^N : B \rightarrow \Re^2$ is defined as

$$f^N(M, d) = \max_{(v_{A_1}, v_{A_2})} (v_{A_1} - d_{A_1})(v_{A_2} - d_{A_2}), \tag{9.2}$$

where $(v_{A_1}, v_{A_2}) \in M$ such that $v_{A_1} \geq d_{A_1}, v_{A_2} \geq d_{A_2}$.

That is, the Nash solution maximizes the product of individual utility gains over the disagreement points. The objective function in (9.2) is known as the Nash product.

The following theorem of Nash (1950) can now be stated.

Theorem 20 Let $f : B \to \Re^2$ be a bargaining solution. Then the following statements are equivalent.

(i) $f = f^N$.

(ii) f satisfies WPE, AFC, SYM, and IIA.

Proof: $(i) \Rightarrow (ii)$. We first show that the solution defined in (9.2) exists and is unique. The Nash product $(v_{A_1} - d_{A_1})(v_{A_2} - d_{A_2})$ is a continuous function on M. A continuous function achieves its maximum on a compact set (Rudin 1976, p.89). Since M is compact, a solution to $\max_{(v_{A_1}, v_{A_2})}(v_{A_1} - d_{A_1})(v_{A_2} - d_{A_2})$ exists. This maximum is also achieved at a unique point. To prove this, note that the Nash product is a strictly quasi-concave function.[1] Now, suppose the two points (v'_{A_1}, v'_{A_2}) and (v''_{A_1}, v''_{A_2}) maximize the Nash product. Then for any $0 < c < 1$, the convex combination $(cv'_{A_1} + (1 - c)v''_{A_1}, cv'_{A_2} + (1 - c)v''_{A_2})$, which is an element of M because of its convexity, generates a higher value of the Nash product than that achieved at (v'_{A_1}, v'_{A_2}) and (v''_{A_1}, v''_{A_2}). This is a contradiction to the assumption that (v'_{A_1}, v'_{A_2}) and (v''_{A_1}, v''_{A_2}) maximize the Nash product. Therefore, the Nash solution is well-defined and unique.

We now need to verify that f^N satisfies the four Nash axioms. The contours of the Nash product are rectangular hyperbolas that are asymptotic to the axes and the origin is at the disagreement utility point. The contour passing through f^N touches the upper right boundary of M at f^N itself. Thus, f^N satisfies WPE (See Fig. 9.1.). Next, let us take the bargaining game $(\hat{M}, \hat{d})$ considered in AFC. If $f^N(M, d) = (\bar{v}_{A_1} - d_{A_1})(\bar{v}_{A_2} - d_{A_2})$ for some $(\bar{v}_{A_1}, \bar{v}_{A_2}) \in M$, then $f^N(\hat{M}, \hat{d}) = \theta(\bar{v}_{A_1} - d_{A_1})(\bar{v}_{A_2} - d_{A_2})$, where $\theta = \alpha_{A_1}\alpha_{A_2} > 0$. That is, the Nash solution of $f^N(\hat{M}, \hat{d})$ is simply a positive multiple of its solution of (M, d). The positive constant θ does not affect the point at which the Nash product is maximized. Thus, $f^N(\hat{M}, \hat{d}) = (\alpha_{A_1}f^N_{A_1}(M, d) + \beta_{A_1}, \alpha_{A_2}f^N_{A_2}(M, d) + \beta_{A_2})$. Hence, the Nash solution satisfies AFC.

---

[1] A real-valued function g defined on a subset D of the n-dimensional Euclidean space $\Re^n$ is called *strictly quasi-concave* if for $x, y \in D$, $g(cx + (1 - c)y) > min\{g(x), g(y)\}$, where $0 < c < 1$.

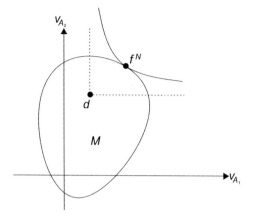

Figure 9.1

To check whether SYM is satisfied, note that if $d_{A_1} = d_{A_2}$, the contours of the Nash product will be symmetric around the 45° line. If M is symmetric around the line, then f^N will also be on the line and hence, SYM is satisfied (see Fig. 9.2). IIA is obviously satisfied by f^N since the maximum that a function can achieve on a set is at least as large as that it can achieve on a subset.

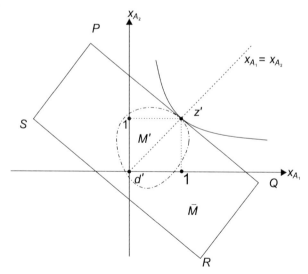

Figure 9.2

$(ii) \Rightarrow (i)$. Assume that a solution f satisfies WPE, AFC, SYM and IIA. We need to demonstrate that $f = f^N$. More precisely, for arbitrary $(M, d) \in$

B, if $z = f(M,d)$, then we have to show that $z = (z_{A_1}, z_{A_2}) = f^N(M,d)$. Derive (M',d') from $f(M,d)$ by taking the affine transformations $\alpha_{A_1} v_{A_1} + \beta_{A_1}$ and $\alpha_{A_2} v_{A_2} + \beta_{A_2}$ of arbitrary utility values v_{A_1} and v_{A_2} of the two persons, where $\alpha_{A_i} = (1/(z_{A_i} - d_{A_i})) > 0$, $\beta_{A_i} = (-d_{A_i}/(z_{A_i} - d_{A_i})) < 0$ for $i = 1, 2$. Then, z and d gets transformed into $z' = (1,1)$ and $d' = (0,0)$ respectively. By AFC, we have $z = f(M,d)$ if and only if $z' = f(M',d')$. Also by AFC, $z' = (1,1) = f(M',d')$. Hence, proving $f(M,d) = f^N(M,d)$ when f satisfies WPE, AFC, SYM and IIA is equivalent to proving that $f(M',d') = f^N(M',d')$ when f satisfies WPE, SYM and IIA.

The Nash product of the transformed game (M',d') is $x_{A_1} x_{A_2}$, where $x = (x_{A_1}, x_{A_2}) \in M'$. The line PQ is tangent to the contour of the Nash product $x_{A_1} x_{A_2}$ at the Nash solution $(1,1)$ of the transformed game (M',d'). Since the Nash product is maximized at $z' = (1,1)$ over the convex set M', all elements of M' except z' must lie below the line PQ. The slope of the contour of the Nash product $x_{A_1} x_{A_2}$ at the Nash solution is $(dx_{A_2}/dx_{A_1}) = -1$, which in turn implies that the slope of the line PQ is also -1. Let us now construct another bargaining game $(\bar{M},d')$, where $\bar{M}$ is the rectangle $PQRS$, which is symmetric around the 45° line, so that M' is contained in $PQRS$. This is possible by the boundedness of M' (See Fig. 9.2.).

We will now consider the solution outcome $f(\bar{M},d')$. Since f satisfies WPE, $f(\bar{M},d')$ must be on PQ, the upper boundary of $\bar{M}$. Since f also satisfies SYM, the solution outcome must be on the 45° line. Thus, WPE and SYM imply that $f(\bar{M},d') = (1,1)$. However, M' is a subset of $\bar{M}$ with the same disagreement utility vector $d' = (0,0)$ and contains the solution outcome $f(\bar{M},d')$. Consequently, by IIA, $f(M',d') = f(\bar{M},d') = (1,1) = f^N(M',d')$. This completes the proof of the implication $(ii) \Rightarrow (i)$. □

The following example, which is taken from Friedman (1968), shows an application of the Nash bargaining model.

Example 26 Consider a firm which is a monopolist in the output market and a monopsonist in the labour market. A labour union has a monopoly position in the labour market and its utility function is given by $u = \sqrt{wL}$, where w is the wage rate and L is the level of employment. The inverse demand function the firm faces is given by $p = 100 - q$, where p and q are respectively the price and output of the firm. Its production function is $q = L$. Hence, the firm's profit function is given by $\pi = L(100 - L) - wL$. Since the firm values profit; this is also the utility function of the firm. The disagreement utility point is $(0,0)$. The Pareto efficient curve can be obtained by maximizing $F(w,L) = c[L(100 - L) - wL] +$

$(1-c)\sqrt{wL}$, where $0 < c < 1$. The two first order conditions are $\frac{\partial F(w,L)}{\partial L} =$
$c(100 - 2L - w) + 0.5(1 - c)w\sqrt{(wL)^{-1}} = 0$ and $\frac{\partial F(w,L)}{\partial w} = -c + 0.5(1 - c)L\sqrt{(wL)^{-1}} = 0$. These two equations can be solved for c. Equating the two expressions for c, we get $\pi = 2500 - u^2$. This is the Pareto efficient curve. The Nash solution can be found by maximizing $\pi u = 2500u - u^2$ with respect to u. The solution outcome is $(u, \pi) = (16.67\sqrt{3}, 1666.67)$.

Several alternatives to the Nash solution have been proposed in literature. One equally appealing alternative model that has been studied extensively is the Raiffa model, analyzed by Luce and Raiffa (1957, Fig. 10, p. 136). Kalai and Smorodinsky (1975) characterized the Raiffa model axiomatically. The central idea is that each player desires to have the maximum possible utility in M. Let $\bar{m}_{A_1}$ and $\bar{m}_{A_2}$ respectively be the maximum possible utilities that players A_1 and A_2 can get in M. It may be worthwhile to note that $(\bar{m}_{A_1}, \bar{m}_{A_2})$ may not be an element of M. The point $(\bar{m}_{A_1}, \bar{m}_{A_2})$, which is referred to as the ideal utility point in the game (M, d), reflects the bargaining strength of the players, in the sense that an increase in $\bar{m}_{A_i}$ may make player A_i unwilling to accept a suggested agreement. The Raiffa−Kalai−Smorodinsky solution $f^R(M, d)$ to the bargaining game (M, d) is the point of intersection of the upper right boundary of M with the straight line joining the disagreement utility point and the ideal utility point. This solution satisfies WPE, SYM and AFC. However, there is no reason why it should coincide with the Nash solution (See Fig. 9.3).

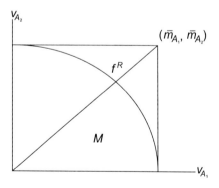

Figure 9.3

The egalitarian solution $f^E(M, d)$ is the maximal point of M with equal coordinates: $f^E_{A_1}(M, d) - d_{A_1} = f^E_{A_2}(M, d) - d_{A_2}$ (Kalai, 1977 and Myerson, 1977a). The essential idea underlying $f^E(M, d)$ is that gains should be equal across bargainers (See Fig. 9.4). Assuming that $d = (0,0)$, $f^E(M,0)$ is the only solution that satisfies SYM, WPE and monotonicity. A solution f satisfies *monotonicity* if $f(M,d) \leq f(M',d)$, where $M \subseteq M'$ that is, each coordinate of $f(M,d)$ is not greater than that of $f(M',d)$ (see Thomson, 1992).

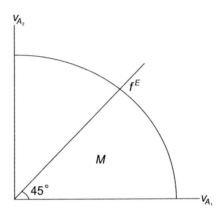

Figure 9.4

We now briefly discuss the non-cooperative bargaining model of Rubinstein (1982) in which bargaining is regarded as a strategic process. In contrast to the cooperative models discussed earlier, in this model, the bargaining strategies, which do not involve any binding agreements, specify the offers and counter-offers of the players. It becomes possible to look for an equilibrium pair of strategies and analyze the agreement generated by the equilibrium strategies.

In the Rubinstein model, the two individuals, A and B, bargain for the division of a perfectly divisible object of size 1. The object is assumed to produce utility. Bargaining takes place over time, at time points $t = 0, 1, 2, \ldots$. At even time points, A makes a proposal and B accepts or rejects it. At odd time points, B makes a proposal and A accepts or rejects it. The game continues with the players making offers sequentially until one of them accepts a proposal. The game terminates as soon as a proposal is accepted and if the proposal (x_A, x_B) is made and accepted at time t, the pay-offs or utilities of the players are $(\delta^t x_A, \delta^t x_B)$, where $x_A + x_B = 1$ and $0 < \delta < 1$ is a discount factor. Both players know the discount factor. The same amount of the object received at a later date is less valuable than that received at an earlier date. It is a game of complete information in the sense that at each time point, each player knows the complete history of the game (the proposals made and rejected). If no proposal is ever accepted, the game terminates with the disagreement utility point $(0,0)$.

Suppose A has the proposal (y_A, y_B) in mind and B has a proposal (z_A, z_B) in mind. If B does not accept (y_A, y_B), then he expects to get z_B in the next period. His expectation is guided by the motivation that $\delta z_B > y_B$. Given that (z_A, z_B) is B's proposal, there is definitely no need to offer more than δz_B to B. This gives rise to the equation $y_B = \delta z_B$. By a similar argument, we find that $z_A = \delta y_A$. This is the result of the Rubinstein bargaining approach which says that player A starts with the proposal (y_A, y_B) and player B accepts it so that the game terminates with the utility vector (y_A, y_B). This informal analysis can be made more formal using the sequential non-cooperative game concept and the underlying sub-game perfect equilibria result in (y_A, y_B) (or (z_A, z_B) if player B makes the first proposal. One feature of this non-cooperative solution is that $z_A z_B = y_A y_B$, so that there is a structural similarity between the Nash solution and the Rubinstein non-cooperative solution. If $\delta = 1$, then the vectors (y_A, y_B) and (z_A, z_B) coincide and this identical solution also becomes the Nash solution where $(0,0)$ is the disagreement utility vector.[2]

9.4 Exchange Economy

In an exchange economy, each economic agent has an initial endowment of goods and a preference relation represented by some utility function over the bundle of goods. Agents exchange endowments of goods among themselves with the objective of increasing their utilities. The set of possible equilibria in this pure trade economy consists of bundles that will not give each agent a lower utility than what he would get by consuming his own initial endowment and no subset of agents can do better on its own.

Definition 98 An *exchange economy* is a tuple $(N, k, (a^{A_i})_{A_i \in N}, (U_{A_i})_{A_i \in N})$, where N is the finite set of agents, the positive integer k is the number of goods, a^{A_i} is the initial endowment vector of k goods of agent A_i such that each component of the k coordinated vector $\sum_{A_i \in N} a^{A_i}$ is positive and for each agent A_i, there is a continuous, increasing and strictly quasi-concave utility function U_{A_i} defined on the set of bundle of goods $\Re^k$.

---

[2]Part of our discussion on non-cooperative bargaining is based on Peters (2008). For formal treatments, refer Rubinstein (1982) and Sutton (1986). Refer also Binmore, Rubinstein and Wolinsky (1986).

The assumption that $\sum_{A_i \in N} a^{A_i}$ is positive ensures that there is a positive quantity of each good in the economy. In this economy, the agents exchange goods among themselves to increase their utilities. However, there is no pay-off that is transferable among the agents.

Definition   99 Given an exchange economy $(N, k, (a^{A_i})_{A_i \in N}, (U_{A_i})_{A_i \in N})$, we define the corresponding *exchange economy game* as the NTU game $(N, X, v, (U_{A_i})_{A_i \in N})$, where $X = \{x = (x^{A_1}, \ldots, x^{A_n}) \mid x^{A_i} \in \Re^k_+ \text{ for all } A_i \in N\}$ is the set of outcomes (the vector x^{A_i} gives the quantities of different goods possessed by agent $A_i \in N$ in the outcome x). The utility function for agent $A_i \in N$ is defined as follows: for any two outcomes x and y, $x \succeq y$ if and only if $U_{A_i}(x^{A_i}) \geq U_{A_i}(y^{A_i})$ and the value sets $v(S)$ are defined as follows: $v(S) = \{x \in X \mid \sum_{A_i \in S} x^{A_i} = \sum_{A_i \in S} a^{A_i} \text{ and } x^{A_j} = a^{A_j} \text{ for all } A_j \in N \setminus S\}$, where $S \subseteq N$.

The definition of the utility function indicates that each agent is concerned only with his own consumption. We define $v(S)$ such that agents outside the coalition S do not participate in the trading activities and decide to hold on their initial endowments. Recall that in a market game, the agents can transfer pay-offs among themselves, whereas in the current context, only goods are transferred.

Definition 100 The *core of an exchange economy game* $(N, X, v, (U_{A_i})_{A_i \in N})$ is the set of all outcomes $x \in v(N)$ such that there does not exist any non-empty coalition $S \subseteq N$ and $y \in v(S)$ satisfying $\sum_{A_i \in S} y^{A_i} = \sum_{A_i \in S} a^{A_i}$ and $U_{A_j}(y^{A_j}) > U_{A_j}(x^{A_j})$ for all $A_j \in S$.

That is, the core of an exchange economy game is the set of all outcomes with the characteristic that no coalition of agents will be able to do better by rejecting them and trading among themselves. Equivalently, we say that a core outcome cannot be improved upon by any coalition of agents.

Let us now assume that it is possible to define a price for each good, which each agent treats as being given. Let us denote the price of good j by p_j and the vector of prices of k goods by p. The total cost of the bundle x^{A_i} of agent A_i is $p.x^{A_i} = \sum_{j=1}^{k} p_j x_j^{A_i}$, where $x_j^{A_i}$ is the quantity of good j possessed by agent A_i in the bundle x^{A_i}. The value of the initial endowment of the agent is $p.a^{A_i} = \sum_{j=1}^{k} p_j a_j^{A_i}$, where $a_j^{A_i}$ is the initial endowment of good j of agent A_i. The quantity $p.a^{A_i}$ is the amount of money that the agent has at his disposal. Agent A_i can afford to get a bundle y^{A_i} such that $p.y^{A_i} \leq p.a^{A_i}$. This is the budget constraint of the agent.

Definition 101 The *competitive equilibrium* of an exchange economy $(N, k, (a^{A_i})_{A_i \in N}, (U_{A_i})_{A_i \in N})$ is a pair $(\hat{p}, \hat{x})$, where $\hat{p} \in \Re_+^k$ is a positive price vector and $\hat{x}$ is an allocation $(\sum_{A_i \in N} a^{A_i} = \sum_{A_i \in N} x^{A_i})$ such that for each agent A_i, we have $\hat{p}.\hat{x}^{A_i} \leq \hat{p}.a^{A_i}$ and $U_{A_i}(\hat{x}^{A_i}) > U_{A_i}(x^{A_i})$ for any x^{A_i} for which $\hat{p}.x^{A_i} \leq \hat{p}.a^{A_i}$.

The equality $\sum_{A_i \in N} a^{A_i} = \sum_{A_i \in N} x^{A_i}$ stipulates that an allocation results from trading. On the other hand, the condition $U_{A_i}(\hat{x}^{A_i}) > U_{A_i}(x^{A_i})$ for any x^{A_i} for which $\hat{p}.x^{A_i} \leq \hat{p}.a^{A_i}$, means that among all the allocations that an agent can afford, he will choose one of his most preferred outcomes.

In a competitive equilibrium, in this price-governed exchange economy model introduced by Walras, each agent will possess the utility maximizing bundle and all choices are consistent in the sense that equality will hold between the total demand and total supply for each good. After the agents have traded to a competitive equilibrium, they will not desire to carry out any further trade. This is because a competitive equilibrium is a core allocation. The following theorem, whose proof is taken from Osborne and Rubinstein (1994), states this formally.

Theorem 21 Let $(\hat{p}, \hat{x})$ be a competitive equilibrium of the exchange economy $(N, k, (a^{A_i})_{A_i \in N}, (U_{A_i})_{A_i \in N})$. Then, $(\hat{p}, \hat{x})$ belongs to the core of the exchange economy game $(N, X, v, (U_{A_i})_{A_i \in N})$.

Proof: Suppose $\hat{x}$ is not a core allocation. Then, there exists a non-empty coalition S and $y \in v(S)$ satisfying $\sum_{A_i \in S} y^{A_i} = \sum_{A_i \in S} a^{A_i}$ and $U_{A_i}(y^{A_i}) > U_{A_i}(\hat{x}^{A_i})$ for all $A_i \in S$. By definition of the competitive equilibrium, we have $\hat{p}.y^{A_i} > \hat{p}.a^{A_i}$ for all $A_i \in S$. Summing over the agents in S, we get $\hat{p}.\sum_{A_i \in S} y^{A_i} > \hat{p}.\sum_{A_i \in S} a^{A_i}$. Since the prices are positive, it follows that $\sum_{A_i \in S} y^{A_i} > \sum_{A_i \in S} a^{A_i}$, which contradicts the condition $\sum_{A_i \in S} y^{A_i} = \sum_{A_i \in S} a^{A_i}$. $\qquad\square$

The core of a two-agent economy with two goods can be identified graphically using the Edgeworth box. Let the two agents be A and B. The length of the horizontal side of the rectangular box is the total endowment of one good and the length of the vertical side of the box represents the total endowment of the other good. One corner of the box gives the origin for one agent and its diametrically opposite corner will be the origin for the other agent. The locus of all points of tangencies of the indifference curves of the two agents in this box is called the contract curve. The contract curve will pass through the origins of the agents. An allocation on the contract curve is Pareto efficient. An allocation of fixed quantities of the two goods in this exchange economy is said to be Pareto efficient if through a reallocation, one agent cannot be made better off without making the other worse off.

In Fig. 9.5, O_A and O_B are the origins of A and B respectively. The indifference curve of agent A through the endowment point (a^A, a^B) will intersect the contract curve at the point b. On the other hand, the point c is the point of intersection of the indifference of agent B through (a^A, a^B) and the contract curve. The core consists of all allocations on the contract curve enclosed between b and c.

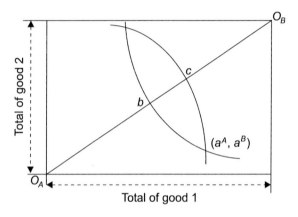

Figure 9.5

Exercises

9.1 Consider a cooperative bargaining game whose solution is the disagreement utility point. Which of the Nash axioms are violated/ satisfied by this solution? Demonstrate rigorously.

9.2 Show that for any cooperative bargaining game $(M, d) \in B$, the Nash product function $g(v_{A_1}, v_{A_2}) = (v_{A_1} - d_{A_1})(v_{A_2} - d_{A_2})$ is strictly quasi-concave.

9.3 Identify the core of the two-person (A and B) and two-good (1 and 2) exchange economy in which the utility functions and the endowments are as follows: $U_A(x_1^A, x_2^A) = x_1^A x_2^A$, $a^A = (1/2, 1/2)$ and $U_B(x_1^B, x_2^B) = x_1^A x_2^A$, $a^B = (1/2, 1/2)$.

9.4 Consider an NTU game v with the player set $N = \{A_1, A_2.A_3\}$, such that $v(\{A_1, A_2, A_3\}) = \{(x_{A_1}, x_{A_2}, x_{A_3}) \mid x_{A_1} + x_{A_2} + 2x_{A_3} \leq 15,$ $x_{A_1} \leq 15, x_{A_2} \leq 15, x_{A_3} \leq 7.5\}$, $v(\{A_1, A_2\}) = \{(x_{A_1}, x_{A_2}) \mid x_{A_1} +$

$x_{A_2} \leq 5$, $x_{A_1} \leq 5$, $x_{A_2} \leq 5\}$, $v(\{A_1, A_3\}) = \{(x_{A_1}, x_{A_3}) \mid x_{A_1} + 2x_{A_3} \leq 10$, $x_{A_1} \leq 10$, $x_{A_3} \leq 5\}$, $v(\{A_2, A_3\}) = \{(x_{A_2}, x_{A_3}) \mid x_{A_2} + 2x_{A_3} \leq 5$, $x_{A_2} \leq 5$, $x_{A_3} \leq 2.5\}$, $v(\{A_2\}) = \{x_{A_2} \mid x_{A_2} \leq 5\}$ and $v(\{A_j\}) = \{x_{A_j} \mid x_{A_j} \leq 0\}$ for $j = 1,3$. Determine the core of this game.

9.5 Give an example to illustrate the Nash axiom 'independence of irrelevant alternatives'.

9.6 Make a systematic comparison between a market game and an exchange economy game.

9.7 Graphically illustrate the Nash axioms 'independence of irrelevant alternatives', 'symmetry' and 'affine coinvariance'.

CHAPTER 10

Linear Programming

One of the most important practical optimization problems prevalent in practically all walks of life is the linear programming (LP) problem. It crops up in various engineering, operations research, scheduling and many other different scenarios. Due to its important, the problem has been extensively studied since the middle of the previous century. As a result, a deep literature has developed around the problem and connections have been established to other sciences.

Our reason for considering LP in this book is its connection to several aspects of cooperative game theory. The problem of determining whether the core of a game is empty can be formulated as an LP problem. Similar formulations can be made for the nucleolus. In this chapter, we provide a brief introduction to LP and describe the connections to the core and the nucleolus. The algorithmic complexity of solving LP is discussed in Chapter 11 and in Chapter 13, LP is used to formulate a notion of fairness in the stable matching problem. Our description of LP is minimal and is intended only to familiarise the reader with the basic idea. For a deeper understanding of the area including its algorithmic issues, we refer the reader to Papadimitriou and Steiglitz (1982).

10.1 The Diet Problem

LP is best introduced through a practical example. We start by motivating LP with the so-called diet problem. In this problem, a person wishes to obtain a balanced diet at a minimal cost. The basic idea is that there are several types of nutrients (say, proteins, fats, carbohydrates, minerals, etcetera) and for a healthy diet, a person needs to take in a certain minimum amount of each nutrient. The nutrients are not directly available. Instead, what are available are different kinds of foods (say, rice, wheat, meat, etcetera). Each kind of food contains the basic nutrients in varying proportions. We assume that these proportions can be quantified per unit of each kind of food.

Example of a diet problem: As an example, let us consider the daily requirement of the minerals zinc (Zn), magnesium (Mg) and iron (Fe) by a person. Suppose[1] that 10 units of Zn, 400 units of Mg and 300 units of Fe are required daily. A person wishes to obtain these amounts from three foods, namely, rice, wheat and oats. Further, suppose it is known that 1 gram of rice contains 1, 2, and 3 units; 1 gram of wheat contains 4, 5 and 2 units; and 1 gram of oats contains 5, 6 and 3 units respectively of Zn, Mg and Fe. Also, the prices per unit of rice, wheat and oats are 10, 20 and 15 respectively.

Let us introduce the variables x_1, x_2 and x_3 to denote, in grams, the daily consumption of rice, wheat and oats. Then the cost to the person is $10x_1 + 20x_2 + 15x_3$. The amount of Zn intake is $x_1 + 4x_2 + 5x_3$ units; the amount of Mg intake is $2x_1 + 5x_2 + 6x_3$ units; and the amount of Fe intake is $3x_1 + 2x_2 + 3x_3$ units. To satisfy the daily requirement, the constraints are the following.

$$x_1 + 4x_2 + 5x_3 \geq 10;$$
$$2x_1 + 5x_2 + 6x_3 \geq 400;$$
$$3x_1 + 2x_2 + 3x_3 \geq 300.$$

Clearly, none of the variables x_1, x_2, x_3 can take non-negative values, which gives rise to the constraints $x_1, x_2, x_3 \geq 0$. Hence, the problem now is to find values for x_1, x_2 and x_3 which minimises the cost $10x_1 + 20x_2 + 15x_3$ subject to the inequality constraints mentioned above.

10.2 Formulations of LP

Let us consider the above example in more general terms. The basic set-up is that a person has a choice of n foods and each food has some of

---

[1]The values are only meant for illustration and are not based on any medical recommendation.

each of m nutrients. A healthy diet requires that the person intakes a minimum amount of each of the nutrients. Each food has a certain cost and the person would like to satisfy the nutritional requirements while minimizing the cost. We assume that the following data is available.

1. Consider the i nutrient. The amount of it which is present in a unit of the jth food is $a_{i,j}$, $i = 1, \ldots, m$ and $j = 1, \ldots, n$.

2. For a balanced diet, a person requires r_i amount of the ith nutrient.

3. The cost per unit of the jth food is c_j.

A person will be consuming a certain amount of each food item so that the total nutritional requirement is met. There will, in general, be different ways of meeting the nutritional requirements by varying the amount of each kind of food that is consumed. As a result, the different strategies for satisfying the nutritional requirement will have different costs. The idea is to chose a strategy which minimizes the cost. We now make a more mathematical formulation of the problem.

Suppose x_j, $j = 1, \ldots, n$ be the variable which denotes the number of units of the jth food that is consumed. Then, the cost is $x_1 c_1 + \cdots + x_n c_n$. Let us now consider the restrictions on the variables. Clearly, $x_j \geq 0$. The total amount of the ith nutrient that is consumed is $a_{i,1} x_1 + \cdots + a_{i,n} x_n$ and this should be at least r_i. These constraint can be expressed in a compact form using a matrix.

Let $A = (a_{i,j})$ be an $m \times n$ matrix; $\mathbf{x} = (x_1, \ldots, x_n)^{tr}$ be the vector of variables; $\mathbf{r} = (r_1, \ldots, r_m)^{tr}$ be the vector of nutritional requirements and $\mathbf{c} = (c_1, \ldots, cm)^{tr}$ is the cost vector. Then the problem is the following:

$$\min \quad \mathbf{c}^{tr} \mathbf{x} = c_1 x_1 + \cdots + c_n x_n$$

subject to

$$A\mathbf{x} \geq \mathbf{r},$$

$$\mathbf{x} \geq 0.$$

The constraints captured by $A\mathbf{x} \geq \mathbf{r}$ are called linearity constraints and the constraint $\mathbf{x} \geq 0$ is called the positivity constraint. The function to be minimized is also a linear function of the variables. This is a formulation of the LP problem.

10.2.1   General form

In the above formulation, each of the variables take non-negative values and all the linearity constraints are of the greater than or equal type. Since we have started from the diet problem, the formulation has turned out to be of this form. A more general formulation of the LP problem can also be given.

Suppose A is an $m \times n$ matrix with $n \geq m$; whose row vectors are $\mathbf{a}_1, \ldots, \mathbf{a}_m$; $\mathbf{x} = (x_1, \ldots, x_n)^{tr}$ is a vector of n variables; $\mathbf{c}$ is a cost vector having n components; and let $\mathbf{r} = (r_1, \ldots, r_m)$ be the vector of requirements. Let $\{1, \ldots, m\} = M \cup \overline{M}$ be a disjoint union and similarly, let $\{1, \ldots, n\} = N \cup \overline{N}$ be a disjoint union.

An instance of the *general* LP is defined as follows:

$$\min \ \mathbf{c}^{tr}\mathbf{x}$$

subject to

$$\mathbf{a}_i\mathbf{x} = r_i, i \in M;$$

$$\mathbf{a}_i\mathbf{x} \geq r_i, i \in \overline{M};$$

$$x_j \geq 0, j \in N;$$

$$x_j \gtrless 0 \ j \in \overline{N}.$$

The notation $\gtrless$ denotes that there is no constraint on the corresponding x_j.

In the above general LP formulation, there are n variables and m linearity constraints. Out of the n variables, those whose subscripts are in the set N have positivity constraints while the other variables do not have any constraint. Similarly, out of the m linearity constraints, those which fall in M have equality constraints while the others have greater than or equal constraints.

10.2.2   Canonical form

A linear programming is said to be in *canonical* form if it has the following structure.

$$\min \ \mathbf{c}^{tr}\mathbf{x} = c_1x_1 + \cdots + c_nx_n$$

subject to

$$A\mathbf{x} \geq \mathbf{r},$$

$$\mathbf{x} \geq 0.$$

The LP arising from the formulation of the diet problem is said to be in the *canonical* form.

10.2.3 Standard form

An LP is said to be in the slack form (or standard form) if it has the following structure.

$$\min \quad \mathbf{c}^{tr}\mathbf{x} = c_1 x_1 + \cdots + c_n x_n$$

subject to

$$A\mathbf{x} = \mathbf{r},$$

$$\mathbf{x} \geq 0.$$

All the three formulations are equivalent in the following sense. If there is an algorithm to solve any one formulation of the LP, then with some additional steps, it can be used to solve any of the other formulations. In other words, by suitably introducing new variables and equivalent forms of the equalities and inequalities, any of the formulations can be converted to any of the other formulations. We leave the task of checking this as an exercise.

10.3 Basic Feasible Solution

We make the assumption that the rank of A is m. This is not restrictive and we will discuss this issue later. A basis B of A is a set of m linearly independent columns $\{\mathbf{a}_{*,j_1}, \ldots, \mathbf{a}_{*,j_m}\}$ of A. One can consider B to be an $m \times m$ non-singular matrix B. To B (or B) one can associate a solution in the following manner: drop the columns of A which are not in B and uniquely solve the resulting linear system. More precisely, the *basic solution* corresponding to B is an n-dimensional vector $\mathbf{x}$ such that $x_j = 0$ for $j \notin \{j_1, \ldots, j_m\}$; and x_{j_k} is the kth component of $B^{-1}\mathbf{r}, k = 1, \ldots, m$. The variables $x_{j_1}, \ldots, x_{j_m}$ are called *basic variables* (with respect to B).

A basic solution may or may not be feasible. For example, even in the slack form, it may turn out that some component of a basic solution is negative. A basic solution which is feasible is called a *basic feasible solution* or *bfs* in short. We make a second assumption that an LP has at least one feasible solution. Again, this assumption is not required and an algorithm to solve an LP problem can determine whether a particular instance is feasible or not. Under the assumptions that the rank of A is m and that there is at least one feasible solution, it can be shown that there is at least one bfs.

The third (and also unnecessary) assumption that we make is that the set $B = \{\mathbf{c}^{tr}\mathbf{x} : \mathbf{x} \text{ is feasible}\}$ is bounded from below. Under this assumption, it is possible to show that the set of feasible solutions is bounded. Though this follows from an assumption, an algorithm for solving an LP can detect whether the cost is unbounded and if so, it stops and exits.

Here we have made three assumptions—A has rank m; an LP has at least one feasible solution; and $\mathcal{B}$ is bounded from below. These assumptions help in explaining the problem and the solution. Later, we will show that none of these assumptions are necessary for solving an LP.

10.4 Geometry of Linear Programs

We will now quickly cover some basic concepts from linear algebra. A linear subspace $\mathcal{S}$ of $\Re^d$ is a subset of $\Re^d$ which is closed under vector addition and scalar multiplication. Equivalently, $\mathcal{S}$ can be written as $\mathcal{S} = \{\mathbf{x} \in \Re^d : a_{j,1}x_1 + \cdots + a_{j,d}x_d = 0, j = 1, \ldots, m\}$. The dimension of $\mathcal{S}$ is the maximum number of linearly independent vectors in $\mathcal{S}$ which is equal to $d - \text{rank}\left([a_{i,j}]\right)$. An affine subspace $\mathcal{A}$ of $\Re^d$ is a linear subspace $\mathcal{S}$ translated by a fixed vector $\mathbf{u}$, i.e., $\mathcal{A} = \mathcal{S} + \mathbf{u} = \{\mathbf{x} + \mathbf{u} : \mathbf{x} \in \mathcal{S}\}$.

The dimension of any subset of $\Re^d$ is the smallest dimension of any affine subspace which contains it. For example, a line segment has dimension 1; a set of $\ell \leq d + 1$ points has dimension at most $\ell - 1$. The dimension of a feasible set to an LP in the standard form with an $m \times n$ matrix A is at most $n - m$ (under the assumption that the rank of A is m and that there is at least one feasible solution).

A subset $\mathcal{C}$ of $\Re^d$ is said to be *convex* if for any two $\mathbf{x}_1, \mathbf{x}_2 \in \mathcal{C}$ and any $0 \leq \lambda \leq 1$, the point $\lambda \mathbf{x}_1 + (1 - \lambda)\mathbf{x}_2$ is also in $\mathcal{C}$. It is easy to argue that the intersection of two convex sets is also convex.

An affine subspace of $\Re^d$ of dimension $d - 1$ is called a hyperplane. In other words, a hyperplane is a set $\{\mathbf{x} : a_1x_1 + \cdots a_dx_d = b\}$ where not all the as are zeros. A hyperplane defines two closed halfspaces given by the points satisfying $a_1x_1 + \cdots + a_dx_d \geq b$ and $a_1x_1 + \cdots + a_dx_d \leq b$. Halfspaces are convex sets and hence, the intersection of halfspaces is also convex. The intersection of a finite number of halfspaces, when it is bounded and non-empty, is called a *convex polytope*, or simply a *polytope*. For LP problems in the standard form, we will be interested in polytopes that are included in the non-negative orthant. In other words, d of the halfspaces giving rise to the polytope will be $x_j \geq 0, j = 1, \ldots, d$.

Let P be a polytope of dimension d and HS, a halfspace defined by a hyperplane H. If $f \overset{\Delta}{=} P \cap HS$ is a subset of H, then f is called a face of P and H is the supporting halfplane defining f. In other words, P and HS

just touch in their exteriors. A face of dimension $d - 1$ is called a facet; a face of dimension 0, i.e., a point, is called a vertex; and a face of dimension 1, i.e., a line segment, is called an edge.

It is possible to prove that every point in a polytope is a convex combination of its vertices; in other words, a polytope is the smallest convex set, i.e., the convex hull, of a finite set of points which are its vertices. Alternatively, a polytope can also be viewed as an intersection of halfspaces under the restriction that the intersection is bounded.

Given an LP in the slack form, the constraints are $Ax = r$ and $x \geq 0$. Since A is an $m \times n$ matrix of rank m, we can assume that the equations $Ax = r$ are of the form $x_i = r_i - \sum_{j=1}^{n-m} a_{i,j} x_j$, $i = n - m + 1, \ldots, n$ and therefore, the entire set of restrictions can be written as

$$x_j \geq 0 \qquad\qquad j = 1, \ldots, n - m,$$

$$r_i - \sum_{j=1}^{n-m} a_{i,j} x_j \geq 0 \quad i = n - m + 1, \ldots, n.$$

This describes the intersection of n halfspaces which can be shown to be bounded and hence, defines a polytope $\mathcal{P} \subseteq \Re^{n-m}$. Conversely, it can be shown that given any polytope in $\Re^{n-m}$, it can be seen as the set of feasible solutions of an LP problem.

Denote by $\hat{x}$, the vector $(x_1, \ldots, x_{n-m})$ and extend to the vector $x = (x_1, \ldots, x_n)$ by setting $x_i = r_i - \sum_{j=1}^{n-m} a_{i,j} x_j$, $i = n - m + 1, \ldots, n$. Then, it can be shown that $\hat{x}$ is a vertex of $\mathcal{P}$ if and only if x is a bfs of the corresponding LP. This defines the fundamental relationship between polytopes and linear programs. *A basis uniquely defines a bfs and hence a vertex.* On the other hand, two different bases may correspond to the same bfs. A bfs is said to be *degenerate* if it contains more than $n - m$ zeros. It is easy to prove that if two distinct bases correspond to the same bfs, then it must be degenerate.

The fundamental theorem of an LP is that there is an optimal bfs for any instance of LP. Using the correspondence with polytopes, one can say that the optimal solution to an LP occurs at one of the vertices of the polytope defining the LP instance.

Thus, instead of considering all possible points in the feasible set, one can simply concentrate on the vertices. Unfortunately, the number of vertices can also be too large and simply enumerating them will take too much time. Later, we will consider how the simplex algorithm tackles this problem.

10.5   Duality

Given an LP problem, one can define another optimization problem called the dual. The optimal solutions of the two problems are intimately related. The dual of an LP is simplest to understand if the LP is given in the canonical form. The original problem is called primal.

	Primal	Dual
Objective	$\min c^{tr} x$	$\max y^{tr} r$
Constraints	$Ax \geq r$	$y^{tr} A \leq c$
	$x \geq 0$	$y \geq 0$

In other words, the dual problem is obtained from the primal by swapping the cost and the requirement vectors. *The primal−dual theorem states that if the primal has an optimal solution, then so does its dual and at optimality, their costs are equal.*

Further, it is easy to check that the dual of the dual is the primal. In view of this, the nomenclature of which version is primal and which one is dual is rather artificial. In our formulation, we started by motivating LP with the diet problem and hence, worked with the minimization version as the primal. It is quite common to introduce LP using the maximization version and then, this version becomes the primal.

Let us consider the dual of the diet problem which is given by $\max y^{tr} r$ subject to $y^{tr} A \leq c$ and $y \geq 0$. A possible interpretation is the following. Suppose a manufacturer wishes to market artificial foods at a price y_i per unit of nutrient i. To be competitive with the price of real food, it is required to impose the restrictions $\max y^{tr} A \leq c$. On the other hand, the optimization function captures the idea of maximizing the cost of an adequate diet. By the primal−dual theorem, the optimal cost of a person's primal is equal to the optimal cost of the manufacturer's dual.

The primal−dual formulation provides an easy way to check whether a given solution to an LP is optimal or not. This is based on the so-called *complementary slackness theorem which is stated as follows.*

A pair x and y respectively feasible in a primal−dual pair is optimal if and only if $y_i(a_{i,*}^{tr} x - r_i) = 0$ for all i; and $(c_j - y^{tr} a_{*,j}) x_j = 0$ for all j.

10.6   The Simplex Algorithm

The simplest and perhaps the most popular of all the algorithms to solve the LP problem is the simplex algorithm which was introduced by Dantzig in 1947. In this section, we describe the working of the algorithm through examples. This helps in grasping the algorithm without losing generality.

First let us consider a simple 2-variable example.

max $2x_1 + 3x_2$

subject to

$x_1 + 3x_2 \le 3$

$2x_1 + x_2 \le 2$

$x_1, x_2 \ge 0.$

Figure 10.1 shows the graphical representation of the problem. The polytope bounded by the vertices (or points) $(0,0), (1,0), (3/5,4/5)$ and $(0,1)$ represents the feasible region for the LP. We already know that the optimal will occur at one of the vertices. Hence, one can plug in the values of the vertices into $2x_1 + 3x_2$ and determine the optimal point. In general, however, this method will not be feasible, since the number of vertices will be too many to try out all of them. One needs a systematic method to move from one vertex to another. Recall that a vertex corresponds to a bfs. Therefore, assuming that one already has a bfs, the idea is to improve the solution by moving from bfs to bfs. Later, we address the problem of finding one bfs.

The simplex method works with the slack form of an LP. This is obtained by introducing *slack variables* w_1 and w_2 to convert the two inequalities into equalities with the restriction that both the slack variables are non-negative. The new LP is now the following.

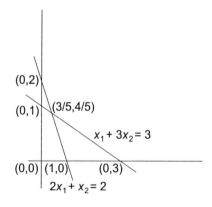

Figure 10.1 Geometrical interpretation of an LP problem.

max $2x_1 + 3x_2$

subject to

$x_1 + 3x_2 + w_1 = 3$

$2x_1 + x_2 + w_2 = 2$

$x_1, x_2, w_1, w_2 \geq 0.$

This is now an LP involving four variables. The rank of the corresponding matrix A is 2 and it is possible to solve for w_1 and w_2 in terms of the variables x_1 and x_2. This gives rise to a bfs where w_1, w_2 are the basic variables and x_1, x_2 are the non-basic variables. Their values in the bfs are 0. We express this by rewriting the LP in the following form.

max $2x_1 + 3x_2$

subject to

$w_1 = 3 - x_1 - 3x_2$

$w_2 = 2 - 2x_1 - x_2$

$x_1, x_2, w_1, w_2 \geq 0.$

At this point, the value of the objective function is 0. Note that the objective function involves only non-basic variables. In general, the $m \times n$ matrix A will have rank m and the dimension of the solution space will be $n - m$. Hence, the m basic variables can be expressed as a linear combination of the $n - m$ non-basic variables. As a result, the objective function can always be written in terms of only the non-basic variables.

In the example, both the coefficients of the non-basic variables in the objective function are positive which indicates that it is possible to increase the value of the function by increasing the values of either x_1 or x_2. If, on the other hand, both these coefficients had been negative, then it would not have been possible to further increase the value of the objective function. The corresponding bfs is optimal. This leads to the first rule for LP.

Rule 1: Write the objective function in terms of only the non-basic variables. If all the coefficients of the variables are negative, then the corresponding bfs provides an optimal solution; if the coefficient of at least one of the non-basic variables is positive, then the solution can be improved.

The improvement is done in the following manner. Out of the several possible non-basic variables with positive coefficients, one is chosen. This is called the pivot. Several strategies are known for pivot selection, one of them being choosing the variable which has the highest positive coefficient. The idea is to move to a different bfs where the pivot is within the basis and another variable is moved out of the basis. The pivot variable is called the entering variable and the variable which leaves the basis is called the leaving variable.

For our example, let us choose x_1 as the pivot (even though the coefficient for x_2 is greater). Now comes the question of how large can we make x_1 while still retaining non-negativity of the variables. If x_1 is increased from 0 to 1, then w_2 becomes zero and w_1 becomes 2, while if x_1 is increased from 0 to 3, then w_1 becomes 0 but w_2 becomes -4 which moves outside the feasible region. Hence, we can increase x_1 to at most 1 and still remain in the feasible region. This brings us to the second rule of LP.

Rule 2: Given a pivot and a fixed basic variable, let δ be the value of the pivot variable such that the basic variable becomes zero. The basic variable corresponding to the minimum of these δs is chosen as the leaving variable. Ties are broken arbitrarily.

Once the leaving variable is determined, the LP is reformulated to express the pivot variable in terms of the leaving variable. In the example, w_2 is chosen to be the leaving variable and we have $x_1 = 1 - w_2/2 - x_2/2$. Using this relation, the LP is reformulated as follows.

$$\max \ 2 + 2x_2 - w_2$$

subject to

$$w_1 = 2 + w_2/2 - 5x_2/2$$

$$x_1 = 1 - w_2/2 - x_2/2.$$

$$x_1, x_2, w_1, w_2 \geq 0.$$

In a nutshell, LP consists of repeatedly applying Rules 1 and 2 until the stopping condition of Rule 1 applies. In this example, we see that the coefficient of x_2 is 2 which by Rule 1 we know that the solution can be further improved. Hence, x_2 is chosen as the pivot variable. Looking at the constraints, we see that increasing x_2 to 4/5 makes w_1 zero (and x_1 positive), while increasing x_2 to 1 makes x_1 zero (but w_1 becomes negative). Hence, by Rule 2, we choose w_1 as the leaving variable and rewrite x_2 as $x_2 = 4/5 + w_2/5 - 2w_1/5$. Using this, the LP is reformulated as follows.

max $18/5 - 4w_1/5 - 7w_2/5$

subject to

$x_2 = 4/5 + w_2/5 - 2w_1/5$

$x_1 = 3/5 - 3w_2/5 - w_1/5.$

$x_1, x_2, w_1, w_2 \geq 0.$

In this LP, all the coefficients of the non-basic variables in the objective function are negative which by Rule 1 shows that the solution cannot be improved further. Hence, the value of the maximum is $18/5$ and is achieved for $x_1 = 3/5$, $x_2 = 4/5$ (and the values of the slack variables w_1 and w_2 are zeros).

Interpreted geometrically, in the example, we started at the vertex $(0,0)$ of the polytope. It turned out that moving along either of the two edges going out of $(0,0)$ improves the solution and we (arbitrarily) chose to move along the x_1-axis to move to the vertex $(1,0)$. Finally, we move along the other edge going out of $(1,0)$ to move to the vertex $(3/5, 4/5)$ which gives the optimal solution to the LP.

10.6.1 Degeneracy and cycling

There are several points that have not arisen in the simple example illustrated here, but, which can arise in a more general LP. The first of these concerns degenerate bfs and arises in the following manner. Suppose that by using Rule 1, we have chosen a pivot variable. Now, it may turn out that increasing the pivot variable to any positive value results in violating the non-negativity constraint of at least one of the other variables. This will happen if the value of some basic variable in the bfs is already zero and therefore, the bfs is degenerate.

Faced with such a situation, we may proceed by choosing one of the basic variables which is zero in the bfs as the leaving variable. Doing this does not change the value of the objective function and we say that the pivot enters the basis at level zero. The resulting bfs may not be degenerate and hence, we can proceed as usual.

It may, however, be true that the resulting bfs is also degenerate and we keep on moving from bfs to bfs without changing the value of the objective function. Even worse, it may turn out that we return to one of the degenerate bfs's and the entire procedure cycles without converging to the optimal solution. For most practical problems, cycling is not an issue since it rarely occurs in practice. On the other hand, it is possible to avoid cycling. Several strategies are known and we mention Bland's rule. Suppose all the variables are numbered as $x_1, \ldots, x_n$. If there is a choice among multiple variables as the entering (or leaving) variable, Bland's rule requires choosing the one with the lowest index. This simple rule ensures that there can be no cycling.

10.6.2 Unbounded feasible region

Suppose we arrive at a bfs where we find that some variable has a positive coefficient in the objective function. This is chosen as the pivot (or the entering) variable. The rule for choosing a leaving variable is to determine a basic variable which decreases to zero when the value of the pivot variable is increased. As mentioned above, degeneracy arises when the value of the pivot variable cannot be increased without violating the non-negativity constraint of one of the basic variables.

In the other direction, it may turn out that it is possible to indefinitely increase the value of the pivot variable, without violating the non-negativity constraints of any of the basic variable. In other words, none of the basic variables decrease when the pivot variable is increased. This means that the value of the objective function can be increased indefinitely without violating the constraints. From this, we can conclude that the feasible region of the LP is not bounded and hence, the algorithm stops at this point.

10.6.3 Finding a bfs

In our description of the simplex algorithm, we have assumed that we start with a bfs. We now address the question of finding the initial bfs to start the algorithm with. Consider the following LP in the general form.

$$\max \ 4x_1 + 5x_2 - x_3$$

subject to

$$3x_1 - 2x_2 \geq 3$$

$$x_2 + 2x_3 \leq -2$$

$$x_4 + x_5 \leq 5$$

$$x_1 + 2x_5 = 3$$

$$x_1, x_2, x_3, x_4, x_5 \geq 0$$

Introducing slack variables z_1, z_2 and z_3, the LP is reformulated in the following manner.

$$\max \ 4x_1 + 5x_2 - x_3$$

subject to

$$3x_1 - 2x_2 - z_1 = 3$$

$$x_2 + 2x_3 + z_2 = -2$$

$$x_4 + x_5 + z_3 = 5$$

$$x_1 + 2x_5 = 3$$

$$x_1, x_2, x_3, x_4, x_5, z_1, z_2, z_3 \geq 0$$

We see that setting $x_1 = x_2 = x_3 = x_4 = 0$ leads to $z_1 = -3$, $z_2 = -2$, $z_3 = 5$ and $x_5 = 3/2$. This violates the non-negativity constraints of z_1 and z_2 and hence, is not a feasible solution. To find a bfs (if one exists), we prepare an alternative LP and apply the simplex method to it.

The form of the linearity constraints is $A\mathbf{x} = \mathbf{b}$. In the above example, one of the components of $\mathbf{b}$ is negative. This is easily adjusted by multiplying the entire row by -1, to get the linearity constraints in the form $A\mathbf{x} = \mathbf{b}$, where $\mathbf{b} \geq 0$. For this example, the resulting form is the following.

$$\max \ 4x_1 + 5x_2 - x_3$$

subject to

$$3x_1 - 2x_2 - z_1 = 3$$

$$-x_2 - 2x_3 - z_2 = 2$$

$$x_4 + x_5 + z_3 = 5$$

$$x_1 + 2x_5 = 3$$

$$x_1, x_2, x_3, x_4, x_5, z_1, z_2, z_3 \geq 0$$

Now we form an alternative LP by introducing artificial variables for each of the equations where the coefficient of the slack variable and the constant have opposite signs. In this example, the artificial variables y_1 and y_2 corresponding to z_1 and z_2 respectively are introduced. The objective function is changed to $-(y_1 + y_2)$ to obtain the following LP.

$$\max \ -y_1 - y_2$$

subject to

$$3x_1 - 2x_2 - z_1 + y_1 = 3$$

$$-x_2 - 2x_3 - z_2 - y_2 = 2$$

$$x_4 + x_5 + z_3 = 5$$

$$x_1 + 2x_5 = 3$$

$$x_1, x_2, x_3, x_4, x_5, z_1, z_2, z_3, y_1, y_2 \geq 0$$

Note that the total number of slack and artificial variables that have been introduced is at most two times m, where m is the number of linearity constraints in the original LP.

In the example, we can now choose $z_1 = z_2 = z_3 = x_1 = x_2 = x_3 = 0$ and $x_3 = 1$ to get $y_1 = 3$, $y_2 = 2$, $x_4 = 7/2$ and $x_5 = 3/2$. which is a bfs for the LP. Now, we can start the simplex method on this LP. If the original LP has a feasible solution, then the new LP has a solution where the artificial variables take the value 0 and the optimal value of the objective function is also 0. Conversely, if the optimal value of the new LP is 0, then the artificial variables must be zero and the values of the other variables give a bfs for the original LP. In view of this, running the simplex on the new LP gives rise to two possibilities: a solution with optimal value 0 in which case we get a bfs for the original LP; or, a solution with optimal value less than 0 or simplex reports that the feasible region for the new LP is unbounded: in both cases, the original LP cannot be solved.

In many situations, it is easy to construct a bfs to start the simplex algorithm. If, on the other hand, a bfs is not immediately evident, then the above method may be used to construct a bfs (if there is one). This is called the first phase of the algorithm. In the second phase, the obtained bfs is used to solve the original LP as explained earlier.

10.7   Overdefined Systems

Suppose that an LP is given in the slack (or standard) form such that the constraints are given by a system of linear *equalities* of the form $A\mathbf{x} = \mathbf{r}$, where the dimension of A is $m \times n$. In the discussion up to now, we have assumed that $m \leq n$ and the rank of A is m. While this has been convenient, this is not a necessary condition for an LP to be solved. If $m > n$, then the number of equations is more than the number of variables and the system is said to be overdefined. In such a situation, the rank of A cannot clearly be m; it is at most n, which is the number of columns in A. Even when $m \leq n$, the actual number of independent equations and hence, the rank of A can be less than m.

The first phase of the simplex method finds a bfs if there is one or many reports that the LP cannot be solved. This phase does not make use of either the fact that $m \leq n$ or that the rank of A is m. Once this phase is executed, one gets to know whether the LP has a solution and if so, a bfs for the simplex method to start. As a result, one can lift the restrictions that $m \leq n$ and that the rank of A is m.

10.8 Core

LP plays an important role in the understanding of the core of a cooperative game (Bondareva 1963; Shapley 1967). Suppose that a game is given by $v : 2^N \to \Re$, where N is the set of players.

Here and in later chapters where we discuss algorithmic issues, the set of players N is taken to be $\{1,\ldots,n\}$. This is for the convenience of describing algorithms. The notation is slightly different from that used in the previous chapters.

Recall that the core of the game is the set of all imputations $\mathbf{x}$ such that $\mathbf{x}(S) \geq v(S)$ for all $S \subseteq N$. Fix a subset $S = \{i_1,\ldots,i_s\}$, $s \geq 0$, of N. The condition $\mathbf{x}(S) \geq v(S)$ can be written out more explicitly in the following manner.

$$x_{i_1} + \cdots + x_{i_s} \geq v(S).$$

Since for a game with n players, i.e., $n = |N|$, there are $2^n - 1$ non-empty subsets of N, each one of these subsets give rise to a condition of the above form. Additionally, we have the non-negativity constraint on the components of the allocation vector, i.e., $x_i \geq 0$ for $i = 1,\ldots,n$. Taken together, these constraints define a polytope. Now, suppose we add the optimization condition of minimizing $x_1 + \cdots + x_n$. This gives us an LP of the following form:

$$\min \quad x_1 + \cdots + x_n$$

subject to

$$\sum_{i \in S} x_i \geq v(S), \text{ for all } S \subseteq N;$$

$$x_i \geq 0, i = 1,\ldots,n.$$

The linear inequality corresponding to N simply says that $x_1 + \cdots + x_n \geq v(N)$. If the optimal solution for the LP is $v(N)$, then there is an imputation in the core and therefore, the core is non-empty. An optimal solution can also be obtained. On the other hand, if the LP has no solution or if the optimal solution of the LP is a value which is greater than $v(N)$, then the core of the game is empty. Conversely, if the core of the game is non-empty, then the above LP has an optimal solution whose value is $v(N)$. Thus, the LP provides a nice way to characterize the (non-)emptiness of the core and to find an imputation in the core if it is non-empty.

This connection to LP can be taken further. The famous Bondareva–Shapely theorem states that the core of a game is empty if and only if the game is balanced. A proof of this statement can be easily derived using the notion of dual of an LP.

To obtain the dual of the above LP, we need to interchange the roles of the cost and the requirement vectors. Writing the linear inequalities in the matrix form, we obtain $A\mathbf{x} \geq \mathbf{v}$, where $\mathbf{v}$ is the vector determining the function v for all the subsets of N. The dimension of A is $2^n \times n$. Therefore, the dual LP will have 2^n variables, one for each inequality in the original LP, i.e., one for each subset of N. The optimization function of the original LP is $x_1 + \cdots + x_n = (1, 1, \ldots, 1)\mathbf{x}$, i.e., the cost vector is $\mathbf{1} = (1, 1, \ldots, 1)$. Hence, the linear inequalities of the dual LP is of the form $\mathbf{y}A \geq \mathbf{1}^{tr}$, where $\mathbf{y} = (y_0, \ldots, y_{2^n-1})$ consists of the variables corresponding to the different subsets of N.

For $0 \leq k \leq 2^n - 1$, we let the n-digit binary representation of k be the characteristic function of a S subset of N. Using this, we can associate a variable y_k to the subset S and we will write $y(S)$ to denote this association. The optimization function of the dual LP can then be written as $\max \sum_{S \subseteq N} y(S)v(S)$. Overall, the structure of the dual LP is the following.

$$\max \sum_{S \subseteq N} y(S)v(S)$$

subject to

$$\sum_{S \subseteq N, i \in S} y(S) \leq 1, \text{ for all } i \in N;$$

$$y(S) \geq 0, \text{ for all } S \subseteq N.$$

Let us now consider the polytope corresponding to the dual LP. The non-negativity conditions restrict the polytope to the non-negative orthant. All the linear inequalities are of the form $y_{j_1} + \cdots + y_{j_\ell} \leq 1$ (where $j_1, \ldots, j_\ell$ are all the integers in the set $\{0, \ldots, 2^n - 1\}$ whose binary expansion have 1 in the ith position). This means that the polytope is contained in the non-negative orthant defined by the hyperplanes corresponding to the non-negativity condition on the variables and the linear inequalities. As discussed earlier, a solution to an LP (if one exists) will be one of the vertices of the polytope. Due to the particular form of the hyperplanes of the dual LP, the vertices of the corresponding polytope are the same as the vertices of the polytope corresponding to the LP where the inequalities are replaced by equalities. Correspondingly, the dual LP has the same set of optimal solutions as the following LP.

$$\max \; \sum_{S \subseteq N} y(S)v(S)$$

subject to

$$\sum_{S \subseteq N, i \in S} y(S) = 1, \text{ for all } i \in N;$$

$$y(S) \geq 0, \text{ for all } S \subseteq N.$$

Often, this form is called the dual of the original LP arising from formulating the emptiness problem of the core. We can interpret the vector $\mathbf{y}$ as a function from 2^N to $[0,1]$. We will denote this function as y. Then, the constraints on $\mathbf{y}$ given by the LP exactly correspond to the notion that the function y is balanced. Hence, a vector $\mathbf{y}$ is feasible for the LP if and only if the corresponding function y is balanced.

By the primal−dual theorem, the primal and the dual LPs have the same optimal value (if they are feasible). The core of the game is non-empty if and only if the optimal value of the primal LP is $v(N)$ if and only if $\sum_{S \subseteq N} y(S)v(S) = v(N)$ for every balanced function y. The last condition is the same as saying that the game is balanced—the Bondareva−Shapely theorem.

10.9 Nucleolus

As we know, the core of a game may be empty or it may contain more than one imputations. A game with an empty core does not have an imputation for the grand coalition to materialize and if the core has more than one imputations, then it becomes difficult to choose a particular imputation as the actual pay-off for the players. This motivated researchers to look for a solution concept which leads to a single imputation as the pay-off vector. The nucleolus is one such notion. Here, for the sake of completeness, we will briefly recap what we learnt before about the nucleolus and outline how it may be obtained using a sequence of linear programs.

Given an imputation $\mathbf{x}$ and a subset S of N, we look at the *excess* that the coalition S can obtain from $\mathbf{x}$ as $e(S, \mathbf{x}) = v(S) - \sum_{i \in S} x_i$. Since the game assigns an amount $v(S)$ to the coalition S, $e(S, \mathbf{x})$ is the extra pay-off that the coalition S can expect to obtain from the imputation $\mathbf{x}$. If this is positive, then the coalition S may have a motivation to break away from the grand coalition.

The excess $e(S, \mathbf{x})$ is defined for each of the possible $2^n - 1$ non-empty coalitions S. Sort the values of $e(S, \mathbf{x})$ in descending order and call the resulting vector as $\theta(\mathbf{x})$ which has $2^n - 1$ components. Given any imputation $\mathbf{x}$, the vector $\theta(\mathbf{x})$ is well-defined. Note however, that for two imputations $\mathbf{x}$ and $\mathbf{x}'$, the sets S and S' which maximize $e(S, \mathbf{x})$ and $e(S', \mathbf{x}')$ respectively need not be equal. The vector $\theta(\mathbf{x})$ by itself does not record the coalitions which correspond to the actual values of the components. These will be required for computational purposes and can be tracked separately. For the vector $\theta(\mathbf{x})$, the ith component will be denoted by $\theta_i(\mathbf{x})$.

Recall that given any two vectors $\mathbf{y}$ and $\mathbf{y}'$ having the same number of components, we define $\mathbf{y} < \mathbf{y}'$ if there is some i such that $y_j = y'_j$ for $j = 1, \ldots, i-1$ and $y_i < y'_i$. This is also described as $\mathbf{y}$ being lexicographically less than $\mathbf{y}'$.

The nucleolus of a game is defined to be the set of imputations $\mathbf{x}$ such that $\theta(\mathbf{x}) < \theta(\mathbf{x}')$ for any other imputation $\mathbf{x}'$. In other words, the nucleolus is the imputation which minimizes the 'excess vector'. It can be shown that the nucleolus contains exactly one element.

Consider the following LP.

$$\min \ \varepsilon$$

subject to

$$\sum_{i \in S} x_i \geq v(S) - \varepsilon, \text{ for all } S \subseteq N;$$

$$\sum_{i \in N} x_i = v(N).$$

In this LP, ε is to be formally considered as a variable. On the other hand, suppose we fix the value of ε and consider the set of all $\mathbf{x}$ which satisfies the linearity conditions. This set is called the ε-core of the game. As we know, even if the core is empty, an ε-core may be non-empty for some value of ε.

If the optimal value of the above LP turns out to be positive, then it indicates that at least one of the linear inequalities $\sum_{i \in S} x_i \geq v(S)$ does not hold. Hence, the game is empty. Conversely, if the optimal value of the LP is non-negative, then there is an imputation which satisfies all the linear conditions and therefore, the core of the game is non-empty. As a result, we obtain a characterization of the emptiness of the core in terms of the sign of the optimal value of the LP.

Let us replace the variable ε by ε_1 and call the corresponding LP, $\mathcal{L}_1$. The optimal value of $\mathcal{L}_1$ provides the value of ε_1 at which the optimal is obtained. All the linear inequalities $\sum_{i \in S} x_i \geq v(S) - \varepsilon_1$ will hold for the optimal value. Some of the inequalities will even hold with equality. Each inequality corresponds to a coalition S. Denote by $\mathcal{S}_1$, the set of all coalitions for which the inequality is actually an equality for the optimal solution.

For the optimal value of ε_1, it holds that for no coalition S can the excess $e(S, \mathbf{x})$ be greater than ε_1. Further, the set $\mathcal{S}_1$ is the set of all coalitions for which the maximum excess is actually attained. Hence, if $\mathbf{x}$ is in the nucleolus, then $\theta_1(\mathbf{x}) = e(S, \mathbf{x})$ for all $S \in \mathcal{S}_1$. This gives the action of $\mathbf{x}$ on certain coalitions. To completely determine $\mathbf{x}$, we need to know its action only on the singleton coalitions. The set $\mathcal{S}_1$ may not contain all (or even any of) the singleton coalitions. Hence, we need to do more work to determine the nucleolus.

If $\mathbf{x}$ is in the nucleolus, then by solving $\mathcal{L}_1$, we obtain the maximum value of the excess that any coalition may have for $\mathbf{x}$ and also the coalitions themselves. The next step then is to fix the maximum value of the excess and look for the next maximum value and the corresponding set of coalitions for which it is attained. This process can be iterated. More formally, let $\mathcal{L}_j$ be the following LP:

min ε

subject to

$$\sum_{i \in S} x_i = v(S) - \varepsilon_1, \text{ for all } S \in \mathcal{S}_1;$$

$$\ldots \ldots$$

$$\sum_{i \in S} x_i = v(S) - \varepsilon_{j-1}, \text{ for all } S \in \mathcal{S}_{j-1};$$

$$\sum_{i \in S} x_i \geq v(S) - \varepsilon, \text{ for all } S \in \mathcal{T}_j;$$

$$\sum_{i \in N} x_i = v(N).$$

Here $T_j = 2^N \setminus \{N\} \setminus \cup_{k=1}^{j-1} S_k$ and ε_k is the optimal value of $\mathcal{L}_k$ for $k = 1, \ldots, j - 1$.

The above expression simply means that starting from the maximum, we successively compute the distinct values of the excess and the corresponding coalitions for the imputation in the nucleolus. Once all the values of the excess are obtained for all the singleton coalitions, the corresponding imputation is the desired imputation in the nucleolus. It can be shown that solving at most n such LPs will provide the desired imputation.

Initial work on computing the nucleolus was done by Aumann and Maschler (1985) and Owen (1978), and later followed by several other authors.

Exercises

10.1 Consider the example of the diet problem in Section 10.1. Suppose it is known that too much of Zn and Mg can cause toxicity in the body. As examples, consider safe limits for daily intake of Zn and Mg to be 40 and 600 units respectively. Modify the LP formulation of the example to also specify these constraints.

10.2 *Production planning problem.* Suppose a company produces an item throughout the year. In month j ($j \in \{1, \ldots, 12\}$), the demand for the item is d_j and the production capacity is m_j; the cost of producing one unit of the item is c_j (we are assuming the the production cost varies over the months) and the cost per unit of inventory-holding for the item is h_j. Assume that there is no initial inventory at the beginning of the first month; units scheduled for delivery in a month are immediately available at the beginning of that month; the inventory-holding cost is incurred at the end of each month; and no shortage is allowed at the end of each month. The target is to minimize the total production and inventory-holding cost over a twelve-month period. Formulate this as an LP problem.

10.3 *Transportation problem.* A company produces a single kind of commodity at several factories and stores them at different warehouses. Suppose there are n factories and m warehouses. The cost of transporting one unit from factory i to warehouse j is $c_{i,j}$, $1 \leq i \leq n$, $1 \leq j \leq m$. Denote by a_i, the amount of production at factory i and by b_j, the amount of demand at warehouse j. The goal is to minimize the transportation cost from the factories to the warehouses. Formulate this as an LP problem. Suppose that there is a upper bound d_j on the amount that can be handled at warehouse j. Modify your LP formulation to take care of this constraint.

10.4 Consider an LP in the general form. This consists of unrestricted variables and both $\leq$ and $\geq$ kind of inequalities.

(i). Let x_j be an unrestricted variable. Define x_j^+ and x_j^- to be two new variables and set $x_j = x_j^+ - x_j^-$ with the constraints $x_j^+, x_j^- \geq 0$. Show that this can be used to obtain an LP where all variables satisfy the non-negativity constraint.

(ii). Suppose $\sum_{j=1}^{n} a_{i,j} x_j \geq b_i$ is a $\geq$ type of inequality in the general LP. Show that by introducing a new variable s_i called a slack variable with a non-negativity constraint, it is possible to convert the inequality into an equality.

(iii). Show that the same can be done if the inequality is of the $\leq$ type.

10.5 In a standard form LP, show that any equality constraint can be replaced by two inequality constraints so that the resulting LP is in the canonical form.

10.6 Consider an LP in the standard form where the linearity constraints are of the form $A\mathbf{x} = \mathbf{b}$. Suppose that $\mathbf{b} \geq 0$ and the linear constraints have been obtained by introducing slack variables to turn inequalities into equalities. Show that it is easy to find a bfs.

10.7 Convert the LP of the diet problem in Section 10.1 into the standard form by introducing slack variables. Find a bfs for this LP.

10.8 Obtain the dual of the LP for the diet problem given in Section 10.1. For this pair of primal–dual LP, verify that at optimality, the optimal values of the two LPs are equal.

10.9 Run the simplex algorithm on the LP obtained by converting the LP for the diet problem in Section 10.1 into the standard form.

10.10 Consider the game (N, v), where $N = \{1, 2, 3\}$ and for any $S \subseteq N$, $v(S) = |S|$. Form the associated LP and determine whether the core of the game is empty.

10.11 For the game in the above problem, determine the nucleolus using the LP method.

CHAPTER 11

Algorithmic Aspects of Cooperative Game Theory

11.1 Introduction

> "What is an algorithm?"

This is an innocuous looking question with a deep answer. We will not attempt to explore the question in its full generality (We refer the reader to Aho, Hopcroft and Ullman (1974) for a comprehensive discussion.). Instead, a high level view will be adopted. An intuitive answer is that an algorithm is a finite sequence of elementary operations with the objective of performing some (computational) task. Let us take this as an acceptable answer and consider several aspects of it in more detail.

Elementary operations: A natural question to ask is how elementary is 'elementary'? The idea of Turing machines formalises an elementary operation as simply reading or writing a symbol and/or moving a tape head one cell to the left or writing on an infinite tape divided into cells where it is possible to write one symbol on any cell. It is possible to start from this simple notion and obtain algorithms for very complex tasks. In fact, it is a hypothesis that Turing machines capture the exact notion of algorithms. We, however, will not work with the Turing machine model. The reason is that the simplicity of the model makes it quite cumbersome to express higher level ideas. Instead, the elementary operations that we will consider will be at a higher level and include arithmetic and logical operations. This is also the usual practice in the study of algorithms. One works at a higher level knowing that, in theory, all algorithms can be reduced to the Turing machine model.

Finite sequence: The finiteness condition of an algorithm implies that it must always halt. Procedures which continue indefinitely will not be considered as algorithms. The notion of Turing machines can be extended to cover such procedures, but, we will not need to consider them here. A word about the sequence of operations in an algorithm will also be in order. The sequential nature of algorithms have been emphasized. Often, however, there are different orderings of the operations which give rise to the same result. Consider the following simple example:

$$t_1 = a + b; t_2 = c + d; t_3 = t_1 * t_2.$$

This is an algorithm consisting of three steps and is equivalent to the following algorithm also consisting of three steps.

$$t_1 = c + d; t_2 = a + b; t_3 = t_1 * t_2.$$

The point here is that the operations $a + b$ and $c + d$ can be executed independently of each other. If these are being executed on a single computing unit (a processor), then they would have to be sequenced in some order. On the other hand, if two computing units are available, then these two operations can be executed simultaneously on the two units. These later considerations gave rise to the study of parallel algorithms. We will not have occasion to consider parallel algorithms.

Inputs and output: The purpose of an algorithm is to perform some task. In the simple example above, the task is to compute $(a + b)(c + d)$. The quantities a, b, c and d are said to be inputs to the algorithm and the quantity $(a + b)(c + d)$ is said to be the output of the algorithm. More generally, an algorithm will take several inputs and produce an output. The relation of the output to the input will define the computational task of the algorithm. In the simplest case, the output of the algorithm will be a binary value.

As an example, consider an algorithm which takes as inputs a list L of integer values; and another value s and determines whether s is present in L or not. The algorithm returns 'yes' if s is present in L; else it returns 'no'. Though binary-output algorithms may appear to be rather simple, much of the sophistication in the field of algorithms can be discovered by studying such algorithms. Later, we will indicate some aspects of this idea.

Resources of an algorithm: We would like to have some way of expressing that an algorithm is 'efficient'. At a very high level, an efficient algorithm is one that does its job while requiring very little 'resources'. To make this more concrete, we need to define precisely what is meant by resources. In the area of algorithm design, the two parameters that are used to quantify resources are the time of execution and the space required by the algorithm.

The time of execution is measured by the number of steps required by the algorithm to produce its output. A simplifying assumption is that each elementary operation requires the same unit of time and hence, the number of steps adequately captures the actual amount of time that is required by the algorithm.

By space, we mean the following. During a computation, an algorithm may need to use some temporary variables (such as t_1, t_2 and t_3 in the above example). Writing down the value of each variable will require a certain amount of memory. The amount of memory that an algorithm requires for its execution is said to be its space requirement.

Apart from time and space, there could be other resources such as power consumption. For algorithms executing on battery-operated devices, this is indeed an important issue. However, for the theoretical study of algorithms, this is usually not taken into account.

Size of input(s): It should be intuitively clear that the amount of time taken by an algorithm will depend on the size(s) of its input(s). For example, in the search problem mentioned above, if the size of the list is long, then one would expect an algorithm to take more time. In view of this, one has to factor in the size(s) of the input(s) while talking about algorithmic efficiency.

The set of all possible inputs to an algorithm is typically infinite. The size of inputs is given by a function from the set of all possible inputs to the set of positive integers. Hence, fixing a positive integer n, fixes the set of all inputs of size n. Typically, the set of all inputs of size n is a finite set. Note that the set of all possible inputs depend on the algorithm and so does the size function. For example, in the search example, the size function returns the size of the list L, while in the arithmetic example, the size function returns the number of bits required to write down the values of a, b, c and d in binary.

Runtime function of an algorithm: Given an algorithm, we would like to define a function $t(n)$ which returns the number of steps required by the algorithm to work on an input of size n. This, however, causes a difficulty. There could be more than one input of size n and the algorithm can take different number of steps on two different inputs of size n. Hence, given n, one cannot define a unique $t(n)$ such that the algorithm requires exactly $t(n)$ steps on any input of size n. There are two ways to tackle this problem.

The first way is to define $t(n)$ as the maximum of the different numbers of steps that the algorithm requires for different inputs of size n. The maximum is taken over all inputs of size n. Such a time measure is called the *worst case* time complexity of the algorithm. In an intuitive sense, this captures the worst case scenario; the algorithm is never going to take more time than its worst case time complexity.

The worst case time complexity may not present a proper picture of the performance of an algorithm. It is possible that there are only a few inputs of size n for which the algorithm requires a rather long time, while, for most inputs of size n, the performance of the algorithm is much better. The inputs which make the algorithm require a long time may be pathological in nature and hardly ever occur in practice. Hence, labelling an algorithm as inefficient based on the behaviour on such inputs is inappropriate. Instead, it may be better to consider the average case behaviour of the algorithm. For each n, the set of all inputs of size n is assumed to be finite and one can define the uniform probability distribution on this set. Then the time function becomes a random variable. The expectation of this random variable is a function of n and is called the *average case* time complexity of the algorithm.

We will not consider average case time complexity; rather, we will focuss only on the worst case time complexity. Later, in the context of linear programming, we will point out how pathological inputs can make an algorithm appear much worse than it really is in practice.

In a manner analogous to the formulation of a runtime function, one can also formulate the worst case and average case space required by an algorithm. There is a relation between the time and space requirement. We will not explore this further and instead only consider the time complexity of an algorithm.

Consider the following simple algorithm to solve the search problem mentioned above.

```
LinearSearch(L[1,...,n], s):
    for i = 1 to n
        if (L[i] = s) return i;
    end for;
    return −1.
```

The algorithm takes as input a list L containing n entries and a value s. It compares s with each of the entries in the list and returns the index of the first position in L where s occurs. If s is not present in the list, the algorithm returns the value -1, indicating that the search is unsuccessful.

The size of the input is taken to be the number of entries in the list L. To assess the time complexity of the algorithm, we count only the comparisons of the type '$L[i] = s$'. The algorithm does other operations, but, the number of such operations is proportional to the number of comparisons and hence, counting only comparisons gives the required picture of the performance of the algorithm. Any unsuccessful search requires n comparisons. A successful search may require between 1 and n operations. Therefore, in the worst case, the algorithm requires n comparisons. This means that the number of steps that the algorithm requires in the worst case is cn for some constant c.

Now, suppose that the list L is sorted in ascending order. The algorithm LinearSearch cannot take advantage of this information. There is another algorithm which can indeed use this information to dramatically speed-up the search procedure. The idea is the following. Compare s to the middle element of L, i.e., make the comparison $s \leq L[n/2]$; if equality holds, then return $n/2$; if $s < L[n/2]$, then search for s in the first half of L, i.e., in $L[1, \ldots, n/2 - 1]$; if $s > L[n/2]$, then search for s in the second half of L, i.e., in $L[n/2 + 1, \ldots, n]$. Using one comparison, it has been possible to either locate the element or to prune down the size of the search space by half. It is not difficult to show that using at most $\lceil \log_2 n \rceil$ comparisons, it is possible to either determine the location of s in L or to determine that s is not present in L. Hence, the time complexity of this algorithm is $c \times \lceil \log_2 n \rceil$ for some constant c. Let us call this algorithm BinarySearch.

Therefore, we see that the problem of searching in a sorted array can be solved using either LinearSearch or BinarySearch. Clearly, BinarySearch is better since it takes lesser time. Using this as a motivating example, one can ask for the best possible algorithm for a given problem. So far, we have talked about algorithms. We have not explicitly considered problems. To discuss best algorithms for a given problem, we need to be able to talk about problems without reference to any particular algorithm. For simplicity, consider decision problems which are of the following kind.

A decision problem Π is a collection of instances and a predicate defined over the set of all instances. The predicate divides the set of instances into two parts—the set of yes-instances and the set of no-instances. Any algorithm to solve Π will take as input an instance of the problem and return the correct answer. Two algorithms for the same problem can be compared by comparing their time complexities. More generally, one can ask for the best possible algorithm to solve Π or show that Π cannot be solved efficiently. Answering such questions form the motivation for the rich field of algorithm design and analysis.

Asymptotic notation: The worst case time complexity $t(n)$ is used to measure the performance of an algorithm. As we have seen, $t(n) = c_1 n$ for LinearSearch while $t(n) = c_2 \lceil \log_2 n \rceil$ for BinarySearch for some constants c_1 and c_2. These constants depend upon many things including impleme-ntation details. It would be convenient to have a method which deals with time complexities without carrying the constants. Asymptotic nota-tion provides this method.

Let g and f be functions from the set of natural numbers to itself. The function f is said to be $O(g)$ (read big-oh of g), if there is a constant c and a natural n_0 such that $f(n) \leq cg(n)$ for all $n > n_0$. Roughly, this means that the function f is dominated by g (modulo the constant c) for all but finitely many naturals. Using this notation, we can say that the worst case time complexity of LinearSearch is $O(n)$ and the worst case time complexity of BinarySearch is $O(\log n)$. This makes the notation lighter and also simplifies the task of comparing algorithms. The caveat is that we lose a lot of detail in making the switch to asymptotics and these details can be indeed important in actual practice.

An algorithm whose time complexity is $O(n^c)$ for some real constant c is said to be a polynomial time algorithm. In other words, this means that for any input of size n, the runtime of the algorithm is upper bounded by a polynomial in n. In contrast, we can have algorithms whose runtime is $O(2^n)$, i.e., for inputs of size n, the runtime is upper bounded by an exponential function of n. Polynomial time algorithms are identified with efficient algorithms. For any given problem, it is of interest to be able to design a polynomial time algorithm to solve it.

Moving again to the notion of problems, one can ask the following question. Given a problem Π, does there exist a polynomial time algori-thm to solve it? This question can be answered by designing an algorithm to solve Π and showing that its runtime is $O(n^c)$ for some constant c. Suppose now that one is unable to obtain any such algorithm. This does not imply that there are no efficient algorithms for Π. Then, the question changes to the following. Given a problem Π, can one show that there is no polynomial time algorithm to solve it? This question is extremely hard to answer. In the current level of knowledge, there are no good techniques to answer this question. Some natural problems, such as the travelling salesman problem do not have any known polynomial time algorithm but, neither has it been proved that no such algorithms exist. Later, we will consider this issue in more detail.

11.2 Computational Intractibility

As mentioned above, algorithms having polynomial run time are considered to be efficient and by extension, problems which have polynomial time algorithms are considered to be computationally easy to solve.   Many problems of practical interest are not known to be polynomial-time solvable.   A rich and systematic theory has been developed to characterize and study such problems. In this section, we provide a brief account of this theory.

Decision versus optimization problems: We will focus only on decision problems, i.e., problems whose instances have yes/no answers. Though this may appear to be a simplifying assumption, it is not overly restrictive. To see this, let us consider an optimization problem and its decision version. The problem that we will consider is that of finding a maximum size clique in a graph as explained below.

Let $G = (V, E)$ be a graph, where V is a set of vertices and E, a set of edges where each edge is an unordered pair of vertices. A clique $H = (V', E')$ in G is a subgraph of G with $V' \subseteq V$ and $E' \subseteq E$ such that for any two vertices $u, v \in V'$, the corresponding edge (u, v) is in E'. In other words, H is a subgraph of G such that any two vertices of H is connected by an edge of G. The size of the clique H is the number of vertices in V'. It is easy to check that if G has no edges, then the maximum size of any clique in G is 1 and at the other extreme, if all possible edges are present in G, then G itself is a clique.

Suppose we are given a graph $G = (V, E)$ and wish to find a clique of maximum possible size in G. This is an optimization problem. Let us now simplify things a bit and consider the following decision problem: Given a graph $G = (V, E)$ and an integer $1 \leq k \leq |V|$, we wish to know whether there is a clique of size at least k in G. The answer will be either yes or no and therefore, this is a decision problem.

Clearly an algorithm to solve the optimization version of the clique problem can be used to solve the decision version. We wish to argue that if there is an algorithm to solve the decision version, then this can be used to efficiently solve the optimization problem. The idea for doing this is simple. Let A be an algorithm which takes as input a graph G and an integer k and returns 'yes' if G has a clique of size at least k; else it returns 'no'. We now construct an algorithm B to solve the optimization version.

Algorithm $B(G = (V,E))$:
   for $k = |V|$ down to 1 do
      run A on (G, k);
      if the answer is 'yes'
         return k and stop;
      end if;
   end for.

The correctness of B is immediate. Let us consider the runtime of B. It calls A a maximum of n times, where n is the number of vertices in G. Hence, if A takes (worst case) polynomial time, then so does B. This shows that if the decision version has a polynomial time algorithm, then so does the optimization version. Such a feature is true for many problems of practical interest which makes the study of decision problems meaningful. Before moving ahead, we would like to point out that the algorithm B can be further improved. The algorithm essentially performs a linear search. It can be modified to perform a binary search so that the run time becomes $O(\log n)$ times the run time of A.

Classes $\mathcal{P}$ and $\mathcal{NP}$: For a systematic study, it is important to classify problems based on the computational difficulty of solving them. Class $\mathcal{P}$ consists of all decision problems that can be solved in polynomial time. More explicitly, a decision problem Π is in class $\mathcal{P}$ if there is an algorithm $\mathcal{A}$ which given an instance of Π correctly answers 'yes' or 'no' and runs in polynomial time. This class captures our notion of efficiently solvable problems.

There are many problems of practical interest which are not known to be in $\mathcal{P}$. The clique problem mentioned above is one such example. There does not seem to be any way to determine in polynomial time whether a given graph has a specific size clique. On the other hand, however, if we are given a subgraph on k vertices, then it is easy to determine whether the subgraph is a clique or not—simply check that each pair of vertices is connected by an edge which can be done in $O(k^2)$ time. Hence, even though determining the presence of a clique may be difficult, it is quite easy to verify whether a given subgraph is a clique. This computational asymmetry is used to define a class of problems.

Class $\mathcal{NP}$ is defined as the collection of all decision problems Π for which the following condition holds. For the problem Π, there is an algorithm A and polynomials $p(n)$ and $q(n)$ such that the following holds. If x is a 'yes' instance of Π of size n, then there is a certificate (or witness) y of size at most $q(n)$ such that $A(x, y)$ returns 'yes'; if x is a 'no' instance of Π of size n, then for all strings of size at most $q(n)$, $A(x, y)$ returns 'no'; and the runtime of $A(x, y)$ is at most $p(n)$. Note that even though A takes both x and y as input, we do not include the size of y in the runtime. This is done without any loss of generality, because y is polynomially bounded in the size of x and by suitably defining the polynomial $p(n)$, it is possible to ensure that the runtime of A is polynomially bounded in the sizes of both its inputs.

As described earlier, the clique problem is in $\mathcal{NP}$. It is also easy to see that any problem in $\mathcal{P}$ is also in $\mathcal{NP}$. This is because any algorithm A to solve a problem Π in $\mathcal{P}$ can be considered to work in the witness verifiability format as required by the definition of $\mathcal{NP}$; the algorithm A simply ignores any witness string and works only with the instance x to determine whether it is a 'yes' or a 'no' instance. The reverse inclusion, i.e., whether $\mathcal{NP}$ is a subset of $\mathcal{P}$ (and so $\mathcal{P}$ equals $\mathcal{NP}$) is one of the outstanding open questions of computer science and mathematics.

Given a decision problem Π, it is possible to define its complement $\overline{\Pi}$ in the following manner. The instance of Π and $\overline{\Pi}$ are the same and x is an 'yes' instance of Π if and only if it is a 'no' instance of $\overline{\Pi}$. This notion can be extended to a class of problems. Let $\mathcal{C}$ be a class of problems. Then, the class co-$\mathcal{C}$ is defined to be the set of all problems Π such that $\overline{\Pi}$ is in $\mathcal{C}$. Specialising this definition to the classes $\mathcal{P}$ and $\mathcal{NP}$, we obtain the classes co-$\mathcal{P}$ and co-$\mathcal{NP}$.

If Π_1 is in $\mathcal{P}$, then there is a polynomial time algorithm A to solve it. By complementing the output returned by A, we obtain an algorithm to solve $\overline{\Pi}$ which shows that $\mathcal{P} =$ co-$\mathcal{P}$. In the case of $\mathcal{NP}$, however, the relation between $\mathcal{NP}$ and co-$\mathcal{NP}$ is not known.

Polynomial time reducibility: Suppose Π_1 and Π_2 are two problems. It may turn out that the ability to solve Π_2 efficiently leads to the ability to solve Π_1 efficiently. We would like to capture this idea more formally. Let A be an algorithm which takes as input an instance x of Π_1 and returns as output an instance $y = A(x)$ of Π_2. Suppose the runtime of A is bounded above by a polynomial in the size of x and the following condition holds: x is an yes instance of Π_1 if and only if y is an yes instance of Π_2. Then the problem Π_1 is said to be polynomial time many$-$one reducible to the problem Π_2 and is written as $\Pi_1 \leq_m \Pi_2$ indicating that problem Π_1 is no harder to solve than problem Π_2.

Suppose Π_1 is polynomial time many–one reducible to Π_2 by an algorithm A and further, there is an algorithm B which solves Π_2 in polynomial time. Then one can build an algorithm C to solve Π_1 by first applying A on an instance x of Π_1 to obtain $y = A(x)$ and then running B on y returning whatever answer is returned by B. Clearly, C is a correct algorithm for solving Π_1. Suppose the runtime of A is $p(n)$ and that of B is $q(n)$. If the size of x is n, then algorithm A running in time $p(n)$ can produce an output of size at most $O(p(n))$, i.e., the size of y is $O(p(n))$. Therefore, running B on y requires time $O(q(p(n))$ and so the overall runtime of C is $O(q(p(n)))$ which is a polynomial since both $p(n)$ and $q(n)$ are polynomials.

Hard problems for a complexity class: Let $\mathcal{C}$ be a class of problems and Π is a problem such that for any Π' in $\mathcal{C}$, Π' is polynomial time many–one reducible to Π. Then, Π is said to be hard for the class $\mathcal{C}$, or $\mathcal{C}$-hard in short. This captures the intuition that no problem in $\mathcal{C}$ is computationally harder than Π.

If a problem Π is $\mathcal{C}$-hard and further, Π is in $\mathcal{C}$, then Π is said to be $\mathcal{C}$-complete. From the above discussion, it is clear that if there is a polynomial time algorithm to solve Π, then every problem in $\mathcal{C}$ is polynomial time solvable. Suppose $\mathcal{C}$ is the class $\mathcal{NP}$ and Π is an NP-complete problem. If Π is polynomial time solvable, then $\mathcal{NP}$ is a subset of $\mathcal{P}$ and hence, $\mathcal{NP} = \mathcal{P}$. This underlines the importance of NP-complete problems.

Many problems of practical interest have been shown to be NP-complete. The first problem which was shown to be NP-complete is the boolean satisfiability (SAT) problem. An instance of SAT consists of a boolean formula in n variables which asks whether the formula is satisfiable under some assignment of truth values 'T' or 'F' to the variables. Once SAT was shown to be NP-complete, the collection of NP-complete problems increased rapidly. Suppose Π is already known to be NP-complete. To show a that new problem Π' is NP-complete, it is sufficient to show that Π' is in $\mathcal{NP}$ and Π is polynomial time many–one reducible to Π'. Using this strategy, it is possible to show that the clique problem (and several other graph problems) is NP-complete.

11.3 Complexity of Linear Programming

We briefly consider the computational complexity of solving LP. See Papadimitriou and Steiglitz (1982) for details. Let us take the simplex method described earlier. We would like to find the (worst case) runtime of the simplex method. As discussed earlier, the runtime is described as a function of the size of the input. Hence, before we can go on to analyze the runtime, we need to have an idea of what is meant by the size of an input to the LP problem.

An instance of LP consists of the n-dimensional cost vector $\mathbf{c}$ and the $m \times n$ matrix A. The entries of $\mathbf{c}$ and $\mathbf{A}$ consists of real numbers. An arbitrary real number cannot be represented by a finite length binary string (due to the fact that reals are uncountable while the set of all finite length binary strings is countable). On the other hand, any finitary method, i.e., a method which halts after a finite number of steps, must work with finite strings. This is where the issue of finite precision comes into play. We will assume that the real numbers appearing in any LP instance are to be represented as ℓ-bit strings for some fixed ℓ. With this assumption, the size of an LP instance becomes $\ell(n + mn)$ bits (In general, real numbers may not have a finite representation, an example being π. However, for computational purposes, one has to work with finite *approximations* of real numbers.).

The arithmetic used during the execution of the simplex method consists of basic addition, subtraction, multiplication and division over the reals which can be expressed using ℓ bits. There is a lot of literature on efficient practical and asymptotic algorithms for such arithmetic. These details are perhaps out of context of the present scenario. Instead, we work at a higher level and consider that basic arithmetic operations takes unit time. This is not correct with multiplication and division requiring substantially more time. For our purposes, however, this distinction is less important as we are more interested in determining the number of basic arithmetic operations as a function of m and n.

Analyzing the runtime of the simplex method boils down to two things. Finding the number of iterations that is required and the number of arithmetic operations executed per iteration. Operating on any particular row of A (or the cost vector $\mathbf{c}$) takes $O(n)$ operations. Since there are a total of $m + 1$ n-dimensional vectors (m rows of A, plus the cost vector $\mathbf{c}$), the total number of arithmetic operations required per iteration is $O(n(m+1)) = O(mn)$. If $m = O(n)$, then this cost comes to

$O(n^2)$. Therefore, the main task is to find the number of iterations required by the simplex method. It would have been nice if it were possible to show that even in the worst case, the number of iterations required by the simplex method is upper bounded by some polynomial in n. Then, the overall worst case runtime of the simplex method would also have been polynomially bounded. This, unfortunately, is not true.

The number of iterations is determined by the pivoting rule and the initial bfs. As mentioned earlier, the initial bfs corresponds to a vertex of the corresponding convex polytope and the simplex algorithm moves from vertex to vertex of this polytope. It is possible to define an instance of LP, a pivoting rule and an initial bfs such that the number of vertices of the polytope is 2^n and the simplex method traverses all the vertices of the polytope. As a result, for this instance, the simplex method requires 2^n iterations for a total of $O(2^n n^2)$ arithmetic operations. Hence, the worst case complexity for the specified pivoting rule is exponential in the input size. It may appear that changing the pivoting rule can require only a polynomial number of iterations. However, till date, for whatever pivoting rule that has been proposed, it has been possible to construct instances for which an exponential number of iterations is required.

Therefore, in the worst case, the simplex method requires an exponential amount of time. Such worst case instances are very rare and have to be artificially constructed to demonstrate the exponential nature of the simplex method. In practice, the simplex method works very well and the number of iterations required is $O(n)$.

The question, of course, remains as to whether the LP problem itself is polynomial time solvable, i.e., whether there is an algorithm whose runtime is bounded above by a polynomial in the input size for any instance. By the above discussion, simplex is not such an algorithm. The first polynomial time algorithm for LP was given by Khachiyan in 1979 using the so-called ellipsoid method with time complexity $O(n^6)$ (improved to $O(n^4)$). Though this is polynomial time, in practice it performed worse than the simplex method. In 1984, Karmarkar gave an $O(n^{3.5})$ algorithm for LP which was hailed as a major achievement. The algorithm was based on the so-called interior point method. Later improvements to the interior point method has resulted in $O(n^3)$ algorithm for LP. In practice, good implementations of both the simplex and the interior point algorithms are used to routinely solve large LP instances.

11.4   Computational Issues in Cooperative Game Theory

The basic motivation of cooperative game theory is to reason about economic costs and benefits in the cooperative processes of coalition formation. Different solution concepts attempt to capture notions of fairness in the sharing of profit or distribution of costs. In this section, we try to motivate the computational aspects of cooperative game theory. Later sections will discuss some actual computational problems and solutions.

There are two kinds of relationships between cooperative game theory and computer science. In the first kind, one considers computational issues associated with solution concepts such as core, nucleolus and the Shapely value. Our attention will be focussed on such issues. The second kind of relation arises from the application of game theoretic techniques in problems arising from computer science. We will not pursue this connection, since it will require a broader pre-requisite in computer science.

For concreteness, let us consider the core of a game. A basic question regarding the core is whether it is empty. Emptiness implies that every imputation is blocked by some coalition. Hence, if the core is empty, the grand coalition cannot form. Thus, given a game $v : 2^N \to \Re$, can it be determined whether the grand coalition will form or not? The key issue here is that of efficiently determining this condition; from a practical point of view, there is hardly any difference in not being able to determine and not being able to do so in a reasonable amount of time. This brings us to the question of obtaining *efficient* algorithms for determining core emptiness.

The emptiness of the core is only one computational question related to the core. Two other immediate questions that can be formulated are the following: Given an imputation, can it be determined whether it belongs to the core or not? Is it possible to find an imputation in the core? The second question is particularly relevant since obtaining an imputation in the core provides a method to share profit among the players. Now, suppose it is known that the core is non-empty, but, it turns out to be very difficult to find a member of the core. Then, there is no way to distribute profits ensuring that the grand coalition will be formed. Again, from a practical point of view, this situation is hardly different from the situation where the core is empty.

In the above discussion, we have considered computational questions related only to the core. Clearly, similar and other questions can be raised regarding other solution concepts. Apart from the core, in the later sections, we will also consider the nucleolus and the Shapely value.

Coming back to the core, some relevant and interesting questions do not seem to have been addressed in literature. We briefly discuss two of these.

1. Suppose we are given a game and it turns out that the core of the game is empty. This means that every imputation is blocked by some coalition. One way to prevent such a situation is to force (perhaps using legislation) certain coalitions not to form. To do this, it will be useful to know how many coalitions needs to be prevented. Hence, given a game with an empty core, one can ask for a minimal number of coalitions such that preventing these coalitions leads to the core of the resulting game becoming non-empty.

2. The issue can also be viewed from the perspective of an individual player. In a given game, can an individual player efficiently determine a coalition (or coalitions) where (s)he will be better off than in the grand coalition? If this question turns out to be hard, then irrespective of whether the core is empty or not, no player will have any motivation to break out of the grand coalition.

In the above discussion, we have tried to argue that computational issues are fundamentally linked to the basic motivation for solution concepts of cooperative game theory. Let us now briefly consider some technical issues. A cooperative game in the characteristic function form is $v : 2^N \to \Re$. Suppose $n = |N|$ is the number of players. Then the domain of v is exponential in n and therefore, representing the function v requires size exponential in the number of players. Assuming that an algorithm has to read its whole input, any algorithm to determine computational questions related to different solution concepts will require time which is exponential in the number of players. Hence, even for a moderate number of players, the runtime of the algorithm becomes impractical.

The way out of the above difficulty is to use a compact representation for a game where v is given implicitly rather than explicitly. Such representations arise in the context of so-called combinatorial optimizatioin games. An example of such a game is the travelling salesman game described earlier. In this game, the players are the cities and the cost of a coalition S is the minimum cost of a tour consisting only of the cities in S.

Therefore, the cost for each coalition need not be given out explicitly—it can be derived from the underlying graph and the weight matrix. Similar formulations can be done using other combinatorial optimization problems.

For such games, it is meaningful to look for algorithms whose runtime is bounded above by a polynomial in the number of players. Of course, it is not guaranteed that the ability to succintly represent a game will necessarily lead to efficient algorithms for the associated computational questions. In the next section, we look at these issues in some more detail. A more complexity theoretic treatment of the subject can be found in Chalkiadakis, Elkind and Wooldridge (2011).

11.5   The Assignment Problem

Suppose there are m tasks each of which can be performed on any one of n machines and each machine can perform exactly one task. Let $c_{i,j}$ be the cost of executing task i on machine j. The problem is to obtain an assignment of tasks to machines in a manner such that the total cost is minimized.

This can be formulated as a linear programming problem. Introduce mn real valued variables $x_{i,j}$ for $i = 1, \ldots, m$ and $j = 1, \ldots, n$. The LP problem is the following.

$$\min \ \sum_{i=1}^{m} \sum_{j=1}^{n} x_{i,j} c_{i,j}.$$

subject to:

$$\sum_{i=1}^{m} x_{i,j} = 1 \text{ for } j = 1, \ldots, n;$$

$$\sum_{j=1}^{n} x_{i,j} = 1 \text{ for } i = 1, \ldots, m;$$

$$x_{i,j} \geq 0 \text{ for } i = 1, \ldots, m \text{ and } j = 1, \ldots, n.$$

Even though the xs can take real values, it can be shown that in an optimal solution, the values of the xs are either 0 or 1. Therefore, an optimal solution to the above LP problem provides an optimal assignment to the orignal problem.

Since this problem is of a particularly simple form, there are simple methods for solving it. One does not require to apply either the simplex or interior point methods for the assignment problem. We provide a brief sketch of the so-called Hungarian algorithm to solve it.

In this algorithm, it is assumed that the number of tasks and the number of machines are the same, i.e., $n = m$. Consider the costs to be given by an $m \times n$ matrix $(c_{i,j})$. The crucial fact utilized by the Hungarian algorithm is the following result. If a fixed quantity is subtracted from all entries of a row or from all entries of a column, then an optimal assignment arising from the resulting matrix is also an optimal assignment for the original matrix. Based on this observation, the Hungarian method proceeds through the following steps.

1. For each row, subtract the smallest entry of the row from all other entries in that row.

2. For each column, subtract the smallest entry of the column from all other entries in that column.

3. Cover all the zeros of the resulting matrix using the *minimum* number r of horizontal and vertical lines. A horizontal line covers all entries of one row and a vertical line covers all entries of a column.

4. If $r = n$, then it is possible to obtain an optimal assignment of zeros.

5. If $r < n$, then determine the smallest entry not covered by any line. Subtract this entry from each uncovered row and then add it to each covered column. Repeat Step 3.

For a medium-sized cost matrix, i.e., if n is around 10 or so, the above method works well and it is possible to work out an optimal assignment by hand calculation. If, on the other hand, n is larger, say around 100 or so, then hand calculation is next to impossible. In particular, the step where the minimum number of covering lines is to be determined becomes a difficult combinatorial problem in itself.

The more general description of the Hungarian method proceeds using a bipartite graph formulation of the assignment problem and considers the problem of finding maximum weighted matching in such graphs. We will not get into the details of this algorithm since it would require getting much deeper into graph theoretic algorithms. Instead, we simply remark that the runtime of the algorithm to find an optimal assignment is $O(n^3)$. See Papadimitriou and Steiglitz (1982) for a detailed exposition of this method.

11.6   Combinatorial Optimization Games

In this section, we take a brief look at several games where the characteristic function is implicitly defined using a combinatorial optimization problem. A more general treatment can be obtained in Deng, Ibaraki and Nagamochi (1981).

11.6.1   Assignment game

Shapely and Shubik (1972) introduced a special class of games called assignment games. Suppose there is a set of m people who wish to sell their homes and a set of n people who wish to buy homes. We will just call them sellers and buyers. The ith seller values his home as c_i and the jth buyer values the ith home as $h_{i,j}$. A sale can take place only if $h_{i,j} \geq c_i$ since, otherwise the ith seller values the home at a price higher than what the jth buyer is willing to pay.

To formulate this as a game, we need to formally define the set of players N and the characteristic function v. The set of players N consists of the sellers and the buyers. For the characteristic function, we first observe that $v(S) = 0$ if either S is empty or a singleton set. Clearly, two persons are required to make a transaction. Extending this idea, if a coalition S consists only of buyers or only of sellers, then also $v(S) = 0$. Hence, it is only a mixed group of buyers and sellers who can hope to assure a profit.

The simplest kind of mixed coalition consists of a single seller i and a single buyer j. In this case, $v(\{i,j\})$ is defined to be $\max(0, h_{i,j} - c_i)$. Let $a_{i,j} = v(\{i,j\})$. Consider a bipartite graph with the sellers on one side and the buyers on the other with seller i joined to buyer j by an arc which is labelled as $a_{i,j}$. Now consider a mixed coalition S having more than two members. Sellers and buyers in the coalition can be matched up (with possibly some sellers or some buyers remaining unmatched). In such a matching, the sum of the labels of the connecting arcs is the value of the matching. It is possible that there are more than one way of matching up sellers and buyers in S. Hence, the value $v(S)$ of the coalition S is the maximum of the values of the different ways in which the buyers and sellers in S can be matched up.

With N and v defined as above, we obtain an example of a cooperative game. Of particular interest is the fact that the characteristic function v is defined implicitly. The definition of v involves an optimization (in this case, maximization) and hence, this game falls within the class of combinatorial optimization games.

Consider the core of the game. An imputation $\mathbf{x}$ in the core is an assignment of values to the sellers and the buyers such that $\mathbf{x}(S) \geq v(S)$ for all coalitions S. The core is non-empty if there is some imputation for which no proper coalition of sellers and buyers can break away and perform better on their own. If an imputation belonging to the core can be obtained, then that will provide a way to maximize the number of actual sales.

A direct LP formulation of the above game can be done but, is inefficient. The crucial point to note is that the characteristic function v is completely defined by the $m \times n$ matrix $(a_{i,j})$. The core can be characterized by formulating the problem as an assignment problem. Let $x_{i,j}$ be real-valued variables for $i = 1, \ldots, m$ and $j = 1, \ldots, n$. Introduce the constraints $\sum_{i=1}^{m} x_{i,j} \leq 1$ for $j = 1, \ldots, n$; $\sum_{j=1}^{n} x_{i,j} \leq 1$ for $i = 1, \ldots, m$; and $x_{i,j} \geq 0$ and let the optimization function be

$$\max \sum_{i=1}^{m} \sum_{j=1}^{n} a_{i,j} x_{i,j}.$$

This is the assignment problem discussed earlier. Even though the variables $x_{i,j}$ are real-valued, an optimal solution will result in these variables getting the values 0 or 1. Hence, the optimal value of the problem will be an assignment of 0 or 1 to the variables $x_{i,j}$ such that the sum $\sum a_{i,j} x_{i,j}$ is maximized. However, this value is exactly the value of the grand coalition, i.e., this is the value $v(N)$ where N is the set of all sellers and buyers.

Now, consider the dual of this problem. The dual will have $m + n$ variables. Let us denote these as $u_1, \ldots, u_m$ and $v_1, \ldots, v_n$. There will be mn constraints of the form $u_i + v_j \geq a_{i,j}$ for $i = 1, \ldots, m$ and $j = 1, \ldots, n$. The objective is to minimize the sum

$$\sum_{i=1}^{m} u_i + \sum_{j=1}^{n} v_j.$$

Consider an optimal solution $(u_1, \ldots, u_m, v_1, \ldots, v_n)$ of the dual. Then the corresponding value $u_1 + \cdots + u_m + v_1 + \cdots + v_n$ is equal (by the primal–dual theorem) to the maximum value $v(N)$ of the primal. This, together with the constraints of the dual problem show that any optimal solution to the dual is an imputation in the core of the associated game.

Due to this elegant relation between the core of the assignment game and the dual of the assignment problem, it is possible to obtain an imputation in the core by solving the assignment problem. As mentioned earlier, assuming the number of sellers and buyers are the same, i.e., $m = n$, the Hungarian method can be used to solve the assignment problem. Since the runtime of the Hungarian method is $O(n^3)$, an imputation in the core of the assignment game can also be found in $O(n^3)$ time. Later work has shown that the nucleolus of an assignment game can be computed in polynomial time.

The above is the first example of a combinatorial optimization game. A later work by Owen (1975a) generalized the assignment game to that of a linear production game. Subsequently, this became a basis for formulating other combinatorial optimization games.

11.6.2   Flow games

A class of games based on the problem of maximizing flows in networks were introduced by Kalai and Zemel (1982; 1982). To discuss this game and its associated results, we first need to briefly describe the notion of a flow.

Let $D = (V, E, \omega)$ be a directed network, where V is a set of vertices, E is a set of directed edges (called arcs) and ω assigns a positive value to each arc, i.e., $\omega : E \rightarrow \Re^+$. If e is an arc, $\omega(e)$ is called the capacity of the arc e. There are two designated vertices s and t in V which are respectively called the source and the sink of the network. All other vertices in V are called intermediate vertices. For any vertex $v \in V$, let $\Gamma_{in}(v)$ be the set of all arcs whose end point is v and similarly, let $\Gamma_{out}(v)$ be the set of all arcs whose start point is v. We assume that $\Gamma_{in}(s) = \Gamma_{out}(t) = \emptyset$, i.e., there is no arc coming into s and no arc going out of t.

A flow in the network is an assignment ψ of non-negative values to each of the arcs of the network satisfying the following conditions:

1. $\psi(e) \leq \omega(e)$ for all $e \in E$, i.e., the assignment to an arc can be at most the capacity of the arc.

2. For all vertices $v \neq s, t$,

$$\sum_{e \in \Gamma_{in}(v)} \psi(e) = \sum_{e' \in \Gamma_{out}(v)} \psi(e').$$

In other words, this constraint requires that the total in-flow into any intermediate vertex equals the total out-flow from it.

The value of a flow ψ is equal to $\sum_{e \in \Gamma_{out}(s)} \psi(e)$. The MAX-FLOW problem is the following: Given a network $D = (V, E, \omega)$, compute a flow with the maximum possible value.

Coming back to the setting of cooperative games, the MAX-FLOW problem can be used to define a game where the characteristic function is defined implicitly. Given a network $D = (V, E, \omega)$, let the players be the elements of E, i.e., the players are the arcs of the networks. This may be interpreted as each player controlling an arc of the network. For each coalition $S \subseteq E$, consider the network $D[S]$ that is obtained by deleting all the arcs from D which are not in S. The value $v(S)$ of the characteristic function v for the coalition S is defined as the value of a maximum flow in the network $D[S]$. This allows for a succint definition of the characteristic function without explicitly giving out its value on all possible coalitions. The resulting game is called the flow game.

An imputation $\mathbf{x}$ in the core of the game is an assignment of values to the arcs (i.e., the players) such that for no subset S of arcs, will the maximum flow in the network $D[S]$ be greater than $\mathbf{x}(S)$. It has been shown (Kalai and Zemel 1982; 1982) that finding an element in the core can be done in polynomial time. In contrast, given a network D and an imputation $\mathbf{x}$, checking whether $\mathbf{x}$ is in the core of the associated game is co-NP-complete.

A network is called simple if the capacity of each arc is equal to 1. For the flow game associated with a simple network, the nucleolus can be computed in polynomial time. This is a rare example of a game where the nucleolus can be computed efficiently. For a general network, however, both the problems of computing the nucleolus and checking whether a core member is the nucleolus is NP-hard.

11.6.3 Other games

There are several other examples of games arising from combinatorial optimization problems. An important and well-understood problem is that of computing the minimum spanning tree of a weighted graph. An associated game can be defined (Granot and Huberman 1981) and the task of finding a core member can be done in polynomial time, though the task of checking membership in the core is again co-NP-complete and computing the nucleolus is NP-hard. We refer the reader to Deng and Fang (2008) for details of other results on algorithmic aspects of cooperative game theory.

Exercises

11.1 Consider the algorithms LinearSearch and BinarySearch described in the chapter. Which algorithm would be preferred and in what situation?

11.2 Design an algorithm which takes as inputs, two matrices A and B of dimensions $m \times n$ and $n \times p$ respectively and provides as output, the product $C = AB$. What is the runtime of your algorithm?

11.3 Let $G = (V, E)$ be a graph. A set $S \subseteq V$ is said to be an independent set in G, if no two vertices in S are connected by an edge in E. The optimization version of the independent set problem is given a graph G to find an independent set of the maximum possible cardinality. The decision version of the independent set problem is given a graph G and an integer k with $1 \le k \le |V|$ to determine whether G has an independent set of size k. Show that a polynomial time algorithm to solve the decision version of the independent set problem gives a polynomial time algorithm to solve the optimization version of the same problem.

11.4 Show that class $\mathcal{P}$ is a subset of class $\mathcal{NP}$.

11.5 Determine the number of arithmetic operations (additions and multiplications) required by the simplex algorithm to move from one bfs to another.

11.6 Suppose there are three sales persons based in cities A_1, A_2, A_3 and it is required to fly them to three other cities B_1, B_2, B_3. Let the cost of flying from city A_i to city B_j be proportional to $2i + 3j$. It is required to get the three sales persons in each of the three cities B_1, B_2 and B_3. Formulate this as an assignment problem.

11.7 Solve the assignment problem in the previous exercise using the Hungarian method.

11.8 In the buyer–seller problem, suppose there are four sellers $S_1, \ldots, S_4$, where S_i values his home as $2i^2$. Further, suppose there are five buyers $B_1, \ldots, B_5$, where for $1 \le j \le 3$, buyer B_j values the house of seller S_i as $(2j - i)^2$; and for $j = 4, 5$, buyer B_j values the house of seller S_i as $(2j + i - 5)$. Formulate this as a cooperative game and determine using the assignment method whether the core of this game is empty.

CHAPTER 12

Weighted Majority Games

The class of weighted majority games is a special case of the class of simple voting games. Both weighted majority games and simple voting games have been discussed in an earlier chapter. One of the key issues for such games is to measure the power of an individual. Several such measures have been introduced and studied in literature. The question that concerns us in this chapter is the following. Given a weighted majority game, is it possible to actually compute the values of the different power indices for this game? We are interested in efficient algorithms and more generally, in the computational complexity of the problem. Before getting into the algorithmic details, we briefly recapitulate some of the basic notions related to weighted majority games.

Recall that a weighted majority game, which we write as $v = (w, q)$ is given by a set of n players N; a list of weights $\mathbf{w} = (w_1, \ldots, w_n) \in \Re^n$, one weight for each player in N; and a quota q. Given a subset S of N, its weight is defined to be $w(S) = \sum_{i \in S} w_i$. As mentioned earlier, the subset S is said to be a winning coalition if $w(S) \geq q$ and a losing coalition otherwise. A minimal winning coalition is a winning coalition S such that if any player is dropped from S, it turns into a losing coalition, i.e., $w(S) \geq q$ and $w(T_i) < q$ for every $i \in S$ with $T_i = S \setminus \{i\}$.

Given a game, the total number of winning coalitions in it and the total number of minimal winning coalitions in it are of interest. For a player i, recall that MW_i is the set of all minimal winning coalitions S such that $i \in S$. For the Deegan–Packel index, it is required to obtain the distribution of the cardinalities of the sets in MW_i.

We now recall the notion of swing. Fix a player i in N. A swing S for i is a winning coalition S such that $i \in S$ and $S \setminus \{i\}$ is losing. In other words, S is a swing for i if $i \in S$, $w(S) \geq q$ and $w(S \setminus \{i\}) < q$. There is some similarity between the concepts of minimal winning coalitions and a swing for a player, though, the two notions are not the same. A minimal winning coalition is a swing for every player in the coalition. On the other hand, a swing coalition for a player need not be a minimal winning coalition, since, there could be another player in the coalition dropping whom does not convert the coalition to a losing one.

The computation of the Banzhaf power index for a player i requires finding the total number of swings of i. On the other hand, the computation of the Shapely–Shubik power index requires more fine-grained information. For player i, let S_i denote the set of all possible swings for i. Then the SS index requires the distribution of the cardinalities of the sets in S_i.

One of the basic questions that we can ask about a voting game is whether a particular player is a dummy player. A player i is dummy if S_i is the empty set. In other words, the player i cannot influence the decision of any coalition. Given a weighted majority game, it is of interest to be able to locate all the dummy players in the game.

In the following, we will discuss algorithms for computing the following aspects of a weighted majority game.

1. The set of all dummy players.

2. The total number of winning coalitions.

3. The total number of minimal winning coalitions.

4. For a player i, the distribution of the cardinalities of the sets in MW_i.

5. For a player i, the total number of swings for i, i.e., the cardinality of S_i.

6. For a player i, the distribution of the cardinalities of the sets in S_i.

With this information, any of the known power indices can be computed.

12.1 Subset Sum Problem

Suppose a set of positive weights $w_1, w_2, \ldots, w_n$ and an integer K is given and the following question is asked: Is there a subset $S \subset \{1, \ldots, n\}$ such that $\sum_{i \in S} w_i = K$? This question clearly has a yes or no answer and hence, it is an example of a decision problem. It is called the subset sum problem.

An algorithm to solve the problem will take as input the tuple $(w_1, \ldots, w_n)$ and K and the output as either yes or no. Given a subset S of

N, it is easy to verify whether $w(S)$ equals K or not. Hence, the problem is in the class $\mathcal{NP}$. In fact, this problem has been shown to be NP-complete and thus, it belongs to a set of problems all of which are believed to be computationally intractable. On the other hand, there is a fairly simple algorithm, which we will shortly discuss, that solves the problem and runs in time $O(nw)$, where $w = w_1 + \cdots + w_n$. This might be perplexing as it might seem that there is a polynomial time algorithm for an NP-complete problem.

The explanation hinges on the size measure of the problem. For the subset sum problem, the size measure is taken to be n which is the number of weights. On the other hand, the runtime of the algorithm is polynomial in both n and w. The actual values of the weights w_is need not be bounded above by a polynomial in n and hence, the overall runtime is not bounded above by a polynomial in n. Thus, the $O(nw)$ algorithm for the subset sum problem is not a polynomial time algorithm. It is called a pseudo-polynomial algorithm. There is a detailed theory about pseudo-polynomial algorithms which we will not get into. Instead, we next discuss the $O(nw)$ algorithm.

12.1.1   Dynamic programming

A broad approach to designing algorithms uses the so-called 'divide-and-conquer' paradigm. The idea is to break the main problem into sub-problems, individually solve the sub-problems and then use the solutions of the sub-problem to obtain the solution to the main problem. A special and very interesting case of this paradigm is the dynamic programming technique. This is a tabular method whereby solutions to the sub-problems are listed in a table and these values are used to solve bigger problems. We illustrate the method by providing a dynamic programming algorithm for the subset sum problem.

Let $(w_1, \ldots, w_n)$ and K be an instance of the subset sum problem. Define a 2-dimensional table $T(i, j)$ with $i = 0, 1, \ldots, n$ and $j = 0, 1, \ldots, w$ with $w = w_1 + \cdots + w_n$ as follows.

$$
\left.
\begin{aligned}
T(i,0) &= 1 && \text{for } 0 \le i \le n; \\
T(0,j) &= 0 && \text{for } 1 \le j \le w; \\
T(i,j) &= T(i-1,j) + T(i-1,j-w_i) && \text{otherwise.}
\end{aligned}
\right\} \quad (12.1)
$$

In the above definition, we have made the assumption that $T(i, j) = 0$ if $j < 0$. This simplifies the description of the recurrence. It is easy to verify that for $1 \leq i \leq n$ and $0 \leq j \leq w$, the entry $T(i,j)$ is the number of subsets S of $\{1,\ldots,i\}$ with $w(S) = j$. The case $T(0,j)$ is a boundary case; $T(i,0)$ is 1 since the empty set is the only subset of $\{1,\ldots,i\}$ having weight 0. For any other i and j, the number of subsets of $\{1,\ldots,i\}$ which have weight j can be divided into two parts—those which are subsets of $\{1,\ldots,i-1\}$ having weight j; and those which contain i and hence, are subsets of $\{1,\ldots,i-1\}$ having weight $j - w_i$.

A simple algorithm to construct $T(i,j)$ is given below.

for $i = 0$ to n, $T(i,0) = 1$;
for $j = 1$ to w, $T(0,j) = 0$;
for $i = 1$ to n do
    for $j = 1$ to w do
        $T(i,j) = T(i-1,j) + T(i-1,j-w_i)$;
    end for;
end for.

Once the table $T(i,j)$ has been prepared, the solution to the subset sum problem is yes if $T(n,K) > 0$; else it is no. Preparation of the table clearly takes time $O(nw)$. As described above, the algorithm requires $O(nw)$ space. However, note that the computation of the ith row is determined entirely from the $(i-1)$th row. Hence, once the ith row has been computed, it is no longer necessary to store the $(i-1)$th row. As a result, at any point of time, storage is required only for two of the rows and hence, it is possible to implement the algorithm using $O(w)$ space.

We provide a small example to illustrate how the table is prepared. Suppose $n = 4$ and $w_1 = 5$, $w_2 = w_3 = 2$ and $w_4 = 1$. The values of $T(i,j)$ are tabulated below.

$i \backslash^j$	0	1	2	3	4	5	6	7	8	9	10
0	1	0	0	0	0	0	0	0	0	0	0
1	1	0	0	0	0	1	0	0	0	0	0
2	1	0	1	0	0	1	0	1	0	0	0
3	1	0	2	0	1	1	0	2	0	1	0
4	1	1	2	2	1	2	1	2	2	1	1

The value $T(i,j)$ records only the *number* of subsets of $\{1,\ldots,i\}$ whose weight is j. Suppose that instead we wish to find the *set* of all subsets of $\{1,\ldots,i\}$ whose weight is j. This can also be done. Define $\mathcal{T}(i,j)$ to be the desired set. Then as above, we define the following.

$$\left.\begin{array}{rll} T(i,0) & = & \{\emptyset\} \\ T(0,j) & = & \emptyset \\ T(i,j) & = & T(i-1,j) \cup T(i-1,j-w_i) \end{array}\right\} \quad \begin{array}{l} \text{for } 0 \le i \le n; \\ \text{for } 1 \le j \le w; \\ \text{otherwise.} \end{array} \quad (12.2)$$

The justification for these relations is very similar to the ones provided for $T(i,j)$ and hence we omit it. Note that the number of subsets in $T(i,j)$ may in general be exponential in n and therefore, listing all these subsets will take time which is exponential in n. Fortunately, such listing of the acutal subsets is usually not required.

Suppose instead of *all* the weight j subsets of $\{1,\dots,i\}$, one is interested only in the distribution of the *cardinalities* of these subsets. In other words, for each $0 \le c \le n$, the requirement is to find the number of subsets of $\{1,\dots,i\}$ having weight j and cardinality c. Denote this quantity by $C(i,j,c)$. There is a simple recurrence for $C(i,j,c)$ which mirrors the recurrence for $T(i,j)$.

$$\left.\begin{array}{l} C(i,0,0) = 1 \\ C(i,0,c) = 1 \\ C(0,j,c) = 0 \\ C(i,j,c) = C(i-1,j,c) \\ \qquad\quad +C(i-1,j-w_i,c-1) \end{array}\right\} \quad \begin{array}{l} \text{for } 0 \le i \le n; \\ \text{for } 0 \le i \le n,\ 1 \le c \le n; \\ \text{for } 1 \le j \le w;\ 0 \le c \le n; \\ \text{otherwise.} \end{array} \quad (12.3)$$

We make the assumption that $C(i,j,c) = 0$ if $j < 0$ to simplify the description of the recurrence. The first three lines provide the boundary conditions. The main recurrence is the last line. Justification for this line is the following. A weight j subset S of $\{1,\dots,i\}$ of cardinality c either has i in it or does not have i in it. If i is not present in S, then S is a weight j subset of cardinality c of $\{1,\dots,i-1\}$; if i is present in S, then $S\setminus\{i\}$ is a weight $j-w_i$ subset of cardinality $c-1$ of $\{1,\dots,i-1\}$.

A simple algorithm to construct $C(i,j,c)$ is given below.

```
for i = 0 to n, C(i,0,0) = 1;
for j = 1 to w, C(0,j,0) = 0;
for c = 1 to n do
    for i = 0 to n, C(i,0,c) = 1;
    for j = 1 to w, C(0,j,c) = 0;
end for;
for i = 1 to n do
    for j = 1 to w do
```

```
for c = 1 to n do
    C(i, j, c) = C(i − 1, j, c) + C(i − 1, j − w_i, c − 1);
  end for;
 end for;
end for.
```

The main loop of the algorithm runs over three nested variables; therefore, the entire algorithm requires $O(n^2 w)$ time. As in the case of $T(i, j)$, it may be noted that the ith row $C(i, \cdot, \cdot)$ is computed entirely from the $(i − 1)$th row $C(i − 1, \cdot, \cdot)$ and thus, at any point of the algorithm, it is sufficient to store only two of the rows. This requires $O(nw)$ space.

12.2   Winning Coalitions and Swings for a Player

All the computational problems of weighted majority games mentioned in the previous section can be solved using dynamic programming methods. The decision problems such as whether a particular player is dummy, are NP-complete while the other problems belong to a computational complexity class of higher difficulty. Due to the applicability of dynamic programming, the algorithms to solve all these problems are actually pseudo-polynomial. In the following sections, we will describe these algorithms. A somewhat dense survey on these algorithms can be found in Matsui and Matsui (2000).

Winning coalitions: Suppose that $(w_1, \ldots, w_n)$ are the weights of the players in a weighted majority game with quota q. The dynamic programming algorithm used for the subset sum problem is used to construct the table $T(i, j)$ from these weights. Then, $T(n, j)$ is the number of subsets of $\{1, \ldots, n\}$ having weight j. As mentioned earlier, a subset S is a winning coalition if and only if $w(S) \geq q$. Hence, the number of winning coalitions in the game is $\sum_{j \geq q} T(n, j)$.

Swings for a player: Let v be a weighted majority game with n players having weights $w_1, \ldots, w_n$ and quota q. Fix a player k. Suppose we are interested in finding the number of swings m_k for k. This number is equal to the number of coalitions S containing k such that S is winning but $S \setminus \{k\}$ is losing. Let $\mathcal{A}_k = \{S : q − w_k \leq w(S) \leq q − 1, k \notin S\}$. Any S in $\mathcal{A}_k$ is a losing coalition, but, adding k to it converts it into a winning coalition. Conversely, given any swing T for k, T is winning while the set $T \setminus \{k\}$ is losing so that $q − w_k \leq w(T \setminus \{k\}) \leq q − 1$. Hence, $m_k = |\mathcal{A}_k|$.

To compute m_k we modify game v to the game v_k by dropping the player k. Denote the corresponding table by $T_k(i,j)$ with $i = 0,\dots,n-1$ and $j = 0,\dots,\omega - w_k$ where, $\omega = w_1 + \cdots + w_n$. Once table $T_k(i,j)$ is prepared, the cardinality of $\mathcal{A}_k$ is given by the following.

$$m_k = |\mathcal{A}_k| = \sum_{j=q-w_k}^{q-1} T_k(n-1,j).$$

This requires invoking the dynamic programming algorithm on an $(n-1)$-player game and hence, the time required to compute the number of swings for a single player is still $O(n\omega)$. By repeating the algorithm for each player, one can find the number of swings for all the players. Doing this requires $O(n^2\omega)$ time. As mentioned earlier, finding the number of winning coalitions can be done using $O(\omega)$ space and hence, this amount of space is also required to find the number of swings for a particular player. Since the space required can be reused, finding the number of swings for all the players also requires $O(\omega)$ space.

Cardinalities of swings for a player: As mentioned earlier, for the Shapely–Shubik power index, it is required to compute the distribution of the cardinalities of the swings for a player k. Let $D(k,c)$ denote the number of swing coalitions of cardinality c for player k. The table $T_k(i,j)$ provides only aggregate information about the number of swings. In particular, it does not contain information about the individual cardinalites of the different subsets having a particular weight. This information is captured by the recurrence $C(i,j,c)$ defined in the previous section. Let $C_k(i,j,c)$ be the recurrence corresponding to game G_k, i.e., $C_k(i,j,c)$ is the number of subsets of cardinality c of $\{1,\dots,i\} \setminus \{k\}$ having weight j. The recurrence $C_k(i,j,c)$ is computed from the $n-1$ weights

$$w_1,\dots,w_{k-1},w_{k+1},\dots,w_n.$$

This requires $O(n^2\omega)$ time and $O(n\omega)$ space. Once $C_k(i,j,c)$ is available, the value of $D(k,c)$ can be obtained as follows.

$$D(k,c) = \sum_{j=q-w_k}^{q-1} C_k(n-1,j,c-1).$$

The justification for this is similar to the justification for the computation of m_k from $T_k(n-1,j)$ with the following modification. A subset S of $\{1,\dots,n\} \setminus \{k\}$ of cardinality $c-1$ and weight j with $q-w_k \leq j \leq q-1$ is a swing for k of cardinality c in the game G.

12.3   Dummy Players and Minimal Winning Coalitions

For a weighted majority game, without loss of generality, we will assume the following condition in this section.

$$w_1 \geq w_2 \geq \cdots \geq w_n. \tag{12.4}$$

Dummy: It is easy to argue that if a player of weight w is a dummy, then any player with weight w' is also a dummy for all $w' \leq w$. Since we are assuming the weights to be sorted in descending order, to find all the dummy players, it is sufficient to find the dummy player with the least index i. Then, any player whose index is greater than i is also a dummy player. Assuming that the game has at least one winning coalition, the first player is never a dummy player.

For $1 \leq i \leq n$, define

$$\alpha_i = \max\{w(S) : S \subseteq \{1, \ldots, i\} \text{ and } w(S) < q\}.$$

In other words, α_i is the maximum weight of any losing coalition which is a subset of $\{1, \ldots, i\}$. Define $\beta_i = w_i + \cdots + w_n$, i.e., β_i is the sum of all the weights from player i onwards.

A useful characterization of when a player becomes a dummy is given in Matsui and Matsui (2000). It states that a player $i > 1$ is a dummy if and only if $\alpha_{i-1} + \beta_i < q$. The justification for this is the following. If i is a dummy, then there is a subset S of $\{1, \ldots, i-1\}$ and a $k \geq i$ such that $w(S) + w_i + \cdots + w_k \geq q$ and $w(S) + w_{i+1} + \cdots + w_k < q$. In particular, this means that S is a losing coalition and hence, $w(S) \leq \alpha_{i-1}$. We have the following:

$$\alpha_{i-1} + \beta_i \geq w(S) + w_i + \cdots + w_n \geq q.$$

Conversely, if $\alpha_{i-1} + \beta_i \geq q$, then it can be argued that i is not a dummy in the following manner. Let $S \subseteq \{1, \ldots, i-1\}$ be such that $w(S) = \alpha_{i-1}$. The condition $\alpha_{i-1} + \beta_i \geq q$ postulates a $k \geq i$ such that

$$w(S) + w_i + w_{i+1} + \cdots + w_k \geq q > w(S) + w_i + w_{i+1} + \cdots$$

$$+ w_{k-1} > w(S) + w_{i+1} + \cdots + w_k.$$

The last inequality follows from the fact that $w_i \geq w_k$. This shows that player i is a swing in the coalition $S \cup \{i, i+1, \ldots, k\}$.

The quantities $\beta_2, \ldots, \beta_n$ are easily computed. If the quantities $\alpha_1, \ldots,$ α_{n-1} can be computed, then it is possible to find all the dummy players. In fact, not all the αs may require to be computed. The first i such that $\alpha_{i-1} + \beta_i < q$ will show that all players $j \geq i$ are dummy players.

Suppose that the table $T(i, j)$ has been computed from the weights $w_1, \ldots, w_n$ (where we are now assuming that these weights are sorted in descending order). Then,

$$\alpha_i = \max\{j : j < q, T(i, j) > 0\}.$$

Recall that $T(i, j)$ is the number of subsets of $\{1, \ldots, i\}$ having weight j. Hence, the maximum value of j such that $j < q$ and $T(i, j) > 0$ is the maximum weight of a losing coalition which is a subset of $\{1, \ldots, i\}$. This is equal to α_i by the definition of α_i.

We would like to point out a subtlety in the computation of α_i. It may appear that α_i is easily obtained from α_{i-1} in the following manner: if $\alpha_{i-1} + w_i \geq q$, then $\alpha_i = \alpha_{i-1}$; otherwise $\alpha_i = \alpha_{i-1} + w_i$. This, however, is not correct as can be seen from the following example. Suppose $w_1 = 5$, $w_2 = 4$, $w_3 = 3$, $w_2 = 2$ and $q = 8$. Then, $\alpha_1 = 5$ and $\alpha_2 = 5$ is easy to see. Now, $\alpha_2 + w_3 = 5 + 3 = 8$ and if we follow the previous rule, then we would have to take α_3 to be 5. However, the correct value of α_3 is 7 which is obtained from the coalition $\{2, 3\}$.

Once the αs have been obtained, it is easy to determine the first i (if one exists) such that $\alpha_{i-1} + \beta_i < q$. Then, all players $k \geq i$ are dummy players.

Minimal winning coalitions: Consider $T(i, j)$ which is the number of subsets of $\{1, \ldots, i\}$ having weight j. We consider coalitions S counted in $T(i, j)$ for j in the range q to $q + w_i - 1$. Suppose i is in S. Then, removing i from S results in a losing coalition. Further, since the weights are sorted in descending order, for any $k < i$ which is in S, removing k from S also results in a losing coalition. Therefore, such an S is a minimal winning coalition which is a subset of $\{1, \ldots, i\}$ and contains i. Let E_i be the number of such Ss.

We claim that $\sum_{i=1}^{n} E_i$ is equal to the number of minimal winning coalitions in G. As already argued, any coalition counted in E_i is a minimal winning coalition and for $i < k$, the coalitions counted in E_i are different from those counted in E_k, since the later coalitions contain k while the former coalitions do not. Conversely, if S is any minimal winning coalition of G, then there is a maximum value i in S. The coalition S is counted in E_i and therefore, we do not miss any coalition in the sum $E_1 + \cdots + E_n$.

We now focus on obtaining E_i. A coalition S is counted in E_i if i is in S and $q \leq w(S) \leq q + w_i - 1$. The quantity $T(i-1, j)$ is the number of subsets of $\{1, \ldots, i-1\}$ having weight j. Hence, for j in the range $q \leq j \leq q + w_i - 1$, the difference $T(i, j) - T(i-1, j)$ is the number of subsets of $\{1, \ldots, i-1\}$ which are losing but, become winning when i is added to the subset. Therefore, summing $T(i, j) - T(i-1, j)$ over all j in the range $q \leq j \leq q + w_i - 1$ gives the number of minimal winning coalitions restricted to the players $\{1, \ldots, i\}$ and necessarily containing i. In other words, this sum gives the value of E_i. Thus,

$$E_i = \sum_{j=q}^{q+w_i-1} (T(i, j) - T(i-1, j))$$

$$= \sum_{j=q}^{q+w_i-1} T(i-1, j - w_i)$$

$$= \sum_{j=q-w_i}^{q-1} T(i-1, j). \tag{12.5}$$

Here we have used the relation $T(i, j) = T(i-1, j - w_i) + T(i, j - w_i)$. The total number of minimal winning coalitions is then obtained as follows.

$$\sum_{i=1}^{n} E_i = \sum_{i=1}^{n} \sum_{j=q-w_i}^{q-1} T(i-1, j).$$

In algorithmic terms, it is not necessary to compute this sum *after* preparing the table $T(i, j)$. The sum can be *incrementally* computed as the table $T(i, j)$ is being prepared.

Minimal winning coalitions containing a player: Fix a player k and suppose that we are interested in obtaining all the minimal winning coalitions containing k. This set has been designated MW_k. It is different from the previous problem, where we were interested in obtaining all the minimal winning coalitions.

Assume without loss of generality that k is the smallest index among all players having weight equal to w_k so that the weights satisfy the following ordering.

$$w_1 \geq w_2 \geq \cdots \geq w_{k-1} > w_k \geq w_{k+1} \geq \cdots \geq w_n.$$

Clearly, if $i < k$, then no minimal winning coalition counted in E_i contains k. On the other hand, coalitions counted in E_k are certainly in MW_k. There could be coalitions in MW_k which are not counted in E_k, but, are counted in E_i for some $i > k$. These are also required to be accounted for. Consider any player $i > k$ and a minimal winning coalition $S \subseteq \{1, \ldots, k\}$ containing both k and i. Denote by $E_{k,i}$ the number of such Ss. Any S in MW_k necessarily contains k and has a highest member which is one of $k+1, \ldots, n$. Therefore,

$$|MW_k| = E_k + E_{k,k+1} + \cdots + E_{k,n}.$$

Computing the individual values will provide $|MW_k|$. The technique to do this is based on removing player k and constructing the table $T_k(i, j)$. A key point to note is that for the first $k-1$ rows, tables $T_k(i, j)$ and $T(i, j)$ are the same, i.e., $T(i, j) = T_k(i, j)$ for $i = 0, \ldots, k-1$ and $j \geq 0$. This is due to the fact that for both the tables, the computations of the first $k-1$ rows involve only the players $\{1, \ldots, k-1\}$ which are the same in both cases. From (12.5), the computation of E_k is based only on $T(k-1, \cdot)$ and therefore, computing E_k from $T()$ or $T_k()$ does not make any difference. This gives the following relation:

$$E_k = \sum_{j=q-w_k}^{q-1} T_k(k-1, j).$$

The quantities $E_{k,i}$ for $i > k$ are to be computed from $T_k()$ as will be described. Hence, only the table $T_k()$ needs to be constructed.

For $i > k$, $w_i \leq w_k$. Consider the coalitions counted in $T_k(i-1, j)$ for j in the range $q - w_k - w_i \leq j \leq q - w_k - 1$. For any such coalition S, if k is added to S, then the weight of the resulting coalition is in the range $q - w_i$ to $q-1$. Further, adding i converts the coalition to a winning coalition. This coalition $S' = S \cup \{k, i\} \subseteq \{1, \ldots, i\}$ contains both k and i and becomes losing if i is removed. Since i is the maximum element of S', the weight of any other member ℓ of S' is at least w_i and hence, $S' \setminus \{\ell\}$ is losing. Therefore, S' is a minimal winning coalition and by its definition, it is counted in $E_{k,i}$. Conversely, for any coalition S' counted in $E_{k,i}$, dropping out both k and i gives a coalition S whose weight is in the range $q - w_k - w_i$ to $q - w_k - 1$. From this it follows that

$$E_{k,i} = \sum_{j=q-w_k-w_i}^{q-w_k-1} T_k(i-1,j).$$

Using this, we obtain

$$|MW_k| = \sum_{j=q-w_k}^{q-1} T_k(k-1,j) + \sum_{i=k+1}^{n} \sum_{j=q-w_k-w_i}^{q-w_k-1} T_k(i-1,j).$$

Since the table $T_k()$ can be computed in $O(nw)$ time and $O(w)$ space, the computation of $|MW_k|$ can also be done in the same time and space.

Cardinalities of minimal winning coalitions containing a player: For the Deegan–Packel index, for each player k, it is required to obtain the distribution of the cardinalities of the minimal winning coalitions containing k, i.e., the distribution of the cardinalities of the sets in MW_k. Let $M_{k,c}$ be the number of minimal winning coalitions in MW_k of cardinality c.

For $1 \leq c \leq n$, we define $E_{k,c}$ to be the number of coalitions in MW_k of cardinality c and having k as the highest element. Similarly, we define $E_{k,i,c}$ to be the number of coalitions in MW_k of cardinality c containing k and having i as the highest element. From what has been discussed earlier, it clearly follows that

$$M_{k,c} = E_{k,c} + E_{k,k+1,c} + \cdots + E_{k,n,c}.$$

Conceptually, the computation of the individual terms is done as above with the difference that we do not compute the table $T_k()$. Instead, we now compute the table $C_k(i,j,c)$ which gives the number of subsets of $\{1,\ldots,i\} \setminus \{k\}$ of cardinality c having weight j. The computation of $C_k(i, j,c)$ is based on the weights $w_1,\ldots,w_{k-1},w_{k+1},\ldots,w_n$ and is done using the algorithm described in Section 12.1.1. This takes $O(n^2w)$ time and $O(nw)$ space. Once the table $C_k()$ is prepared, the quantities $E_{k,c}$ and $E_{k,i,c}$ are computed as follows.

$$E_{k,c} = \sum_{j=q-w_k}^{q-1} C_k(k-1,j,c-1);$$

$$E_{k,i,c} = \sum_{j=q-w_k-w_i}^{q-w_k-1} C_k(i-1,j,c-2).$$

This allows the computation of $M_{k,c}$.

CHAPTER 13

Stable Matching Algorithm

Let $G = (U, V, E)$ be a bipartite graph with $|U| = |V| = n$ and the edges in E have one end-point in U and the other end-point in V. A matching μ in G is a set of vertex disjoint edges, i.e., μ is a set of edges such that no two edges are co-incident on the same vertex. Since the edges in a matching have to be vertex disjoint, no matching can have more than n edges. A perfect matching is a matching containing n edges. There are well-known algorithms to find a perfect matching (if one exists).

In this section, we will address a different matching problem. An instance still consists of two sets U and V, but, the constraints are different. Let $U = \{u_1, \ldots, u_n\}$ and $V = \{v_1, \ldots, v_n\}$. Let $\pi_1, \ldots, \pi_n$ be permutations of the set V and let $\sigma_1, \ldots, \sigma_n$ be permutations of the set U. The problem instance is given by the following relations. For $1 \leq i \leq n$ and $1 \leq j \leq n$,

$$u_i \longmapsto \pi_i; \qquad v_j \longmapsto \sigma_j.$$

The permutation π_i is a linear ordering of the vertices in V and similarly, the permutation σ_j is a linear ordering of the vertices in U. Consider the vertices in U to represent n distinct men and the vertices in V to represent n distinct women. The permutation π_i represents the ranking of the n women by the man u_i; similarly, the permutation σ_j represents the ranking of the n men by the woman v_j.

A matching μ is a pairing of a man and a woman and can be thought of as a marriage. Let the partner of the man u_i be denoted by $\mu(u_i)$ and the partner of woman v_j be denoted by $\mu(v_j)$. Suppose there is a man u_i and a woman v_j such that $\pi_i(v_j)$ precedes $\pi_i(\mu(u_i))$ and $\sigma_j(u_i)$ precedes

$\sigma_j(\mu(v_j))$. This means that u_i prefers v_j to his current partner *and* v_j prefers u_i to her current partner. Then, such a pair is called a *blocking pair*. The matching μ is stable if there are no blocking pairs.

It is of interest to know that stable matchings exist and to be able to find one. This problem and its solution was proposed by Gale and Shapely (1962). Inspite of the complex nature of the problem, the algorithm to find a stable matching is rather simple and intuitive. For each u_i, let $P(u_i)$ be the set of women to whom u_i can possibly propose, i.e., u_i has not yet been rejected by the women in $P(u_i)$.

1. Initially mark all men and women as umatched and set each $P(u_i)$ to be equal to V.

2. Repeat the following until all men have been matched.

   i. Each unmatched man u_i proposes to his first preferred woman in $P(u_i)$.

   ii. For each woman $v_j \in V$, let L_j be the list consisting of her currently matched partner (if any) and including all the men who have proposed in the current round. If L_j is empty, then v_j remains unmatched in the current round; if L_j is not empty, the woman v_j is matched with her most preferred partner in L_j and for each of the other men u in L_j, v_j is deleted from $P(u)$. In other words, v_j selects her most preferred partner and rejects all other men for good, i.e., they cannot further propose to v_j. Note that v_j has the option of rejecting her possible partner in the previous round to a more preferred partner in the current round.

3. Return the final matching.

The first thing we need to ensure is that the algorithm terminates and results in a matching. That it results in a matching is clear, since at no point of time is a woman matched to two men. Further, the terminating condition for the algorithm is that all men (and hence all women) are matched. Therefore, if the algorithm terminates, then certainly all men and women are matched. Arguing termination is easy. If a man is rejected by a woman, then he cannot propose to her in any future round, and hence, there is no cycling. In each round, for each man u_i, either he gets (tentatively) matched, or, $P(u_i)$ reduces by one (It is possible that a man u_i who was matched in the previous round becomes unmatched in the current round, but, in that case $P(u_i)$ reduces by one.). Since $P(u_i)$ cannot decrease indefinitely, ultimately all the men get matched and the algorithm terminates.

We now consider stability. Suppose μ is the matching that is returned and let, if possible, u_i and v_j be a blocking pair. This means that u_i prefers v_j to $\mu(u_i)$ and v_j prefers u_i to $\mu(v_j)$. Since u_i prefers v_j to $\mu(v_j)$, he must have proposed to v_j before proposing to $\mu(v_j)$. At that point, v_j rejected u_i and this will occur only if v_j had received a proposal from a partner whom she preferred to u_i. In subsequent rounds, the partner of v_j may have changed but, such change will only take place when v_j prefers a new partner over her current partner. Using the transitivity of the preferrence relation, this means that v_j prefers her final partner $\mu(v_j)$ over u_i. This contradicts the assumption that v_j prefers u_i over $\mu(v_j)$. Hence, there are no blocking pairs and the matching is stable. The crux of the issue here is that each woman can only improve her preference.

We provide a small example to illustrate the working of the algorithm. Suppose there are 5 men and 5 women and for the sake of convenience, we denote the men as simply 1,2,3,4,5 and the women as A,B,C,D,E. Further suppose the preference relations for each person are as given by the permutation against their names.

Preference relations for men	Preference relations for women
1: ABCDE	A: 54321
2: ACEBD	B: 45123
3: CABED	C: 13425
4: BACDE	D: 51243
5: CDEAB	E: 14523

Initially, for $1 \leq i \leq 5$, L_i is the preference relation for the man i. The computation proceeds in rounds as follows.

Round 1:

    Proposals: 1 → A, 2 → A, 3 → C, 4 → B, 5 → C.
    Choices for the women: A: 2,1; B: 4; C: 3,5; none for D and E.
    Tentative matching: A: 2; B: 4; C: 3.
    Modified L_i: 1: BCDE; 2: ACEBD; 3: CABED; 4: BACDE; 5: DEAB.

Round 2:

> Proposals: $1 \to B$, $5 \to D$.
> Choices for the women: A: 2; B: 4,1; C: 3; D: 5, none for E.
> Tentative matching: A: 2; B: 4; C: 3; D: 5.
> Modified L_j: 1: CDE; 2: ACEBD; 3: CABED; 4: BACDE; 5: DEAB.

Round 3:

> Proposal: $1 \to C$.
> Choices for the women: A: 2; B: 4; C: 1,3; D: 5, none for E.
> Tentative matching: A: 2; B: 4; C: 1; D: 5.
> Modified L_j: 1: CDE; 2: ACEBD; 3: ABED; 4: BACDE; 5: DEAB.

Note that in rounds 1 and 2, C had been matched with 3 but, in this round, it changes to 1, since 1 has made an offer to C and C prefers 1 to 3.

Round 4:

> Proposal: $3 \to A$.
> Choices for the women: A: 2,1; B: 4; C: 1; D: 5, none for E.
> Tentative matching: A: 2; B: 4; C: 1; D: 5.
> Modified L_j: 1: CDE; 2: ACEBD; 3: BED; 4: BACDE; 5: DEAB.

Round 5:

> Proposal: $3 \to B$.
> Choices for the women: A: 2; B: 4,3; C: 1; D: 5, none for E.
> Tentative matching: A: 2; B: 4; C: 1; D: 5.
> Modified L_j: 1: CDE; 2: ACEBD; 3: ED; 4: BACDE; 5: DEAB.

Round 6:

> Proposal: $3 \to E$.
> Choices for the women: A: 2; B: 4,3; C: 1; D: 5, E: 3.
> Final matching: A: 2; B: 4; C: 1; D: 5, E: 3.

So, the algorithm terminates after 6 rounds and results in a stable matching as can be verified.

We would like to point out that a stable matching is not necessarily unique. Further, the description of the Gale–Shapely algorithm that we have given has the proposers to be men. This, of course, is not important to obtain a stable matching. One can also have the proposers to be women and obtain a stable matching. The resulting stable matching from the 'women propose' strategy will in general be different from the stable matching obtained from the 'men propose' strategy. We illustrate this by outlining the workings of the 'women propose' strategy on the preference relations of the example given above.

Initially, for $1 \leq j \leq 5$, L_j is the preference relation for the woman j. The computation proceeds in rounds as follows.

Round 1:

    Proposals: A $\rightarrow$ 5, B $\rightarrow$ 4, C $\rightarrow$ 1, D $\rightarrow$ 5, E $\rightarrow$ 1.
    Choices for the men: 1: C,E; 4: B; 5: D,A; none for 2 and 3.
    Tentative matching: 1: C; 4: B; 5: D.
    Modified L_j: A: 4321; B: 45123; C: 13425; D: 51243; E: 4532.

Round 2:

    Proposals: A $\rightarrow$ 4, E $\rightarrow$ 4.
    Choices for the men: 1: C; 4: B, A, E; 5: D; none for 2 and 3.
    Tentative matching: 1: C; 4: B; 5: D.
    Modified L_j: A: 321; B: 45123; C: 13425; D: 51243; E: 532.

Round 3:

    Proposals: A $\rightarrow$ 3, E $\rightarrow$ 5.
    Choices for the men: 1: C; 3: A; 4: B; 5: D,E; none for 2.
    Tentative matching: 1: C; 3: A; 4: B; 5: D.
    Modified L_j: A: 321; B: 45123; C: 13425; D: 51243; E: 32.

Round 4:

    Proposal: E $\rightarrow$ 3.
    Choices for the men: 1: C; 3: A,E; 4: B; 5: D,E; none for 2.
    Tentative matching: 1: C; 3: A; 4: B; 5: D.
    Modified L_j: A: 321; B: 45123; C: 13425; D: 51243; E: 2.

Round 5:

    Proposal: E $\rightarrow$ 2.
    Choices for the men: 1: C; 2: E; 3: A; 4: B; 5: D.
    Final matching: 1: C; 2: E; 3: A; 4: B; 5: D.

Note that the final matching obtained here is different from the final matching obtained earlier. Both the matchings are stable showing that a stable matching need not be unique.

13.1 Optimality Considerations

A stable matching is desirable from a macroscopic point of view, since, if a matching is not stable, then it is more likely to disintegrate. On the other hand, one can also consider an individual's point of view. Since a stable matching is not unique for an individual, different stable matchings may result in different partners. An individual would have a preference ordering over these possible partners arising out of all the different stable matchings. For an individual w (man or woman), let $\mathsf{Part}(w)$ be the set of all such possible partners and let $\mathsf{best}(w)$ be the person most preferred by w among the individuals in $\mathsf{Part}(w)$.

A stable matching is said to be men-optimal, if for each man u, his partner in the stable matching is $\mathsf{best}(u)$. In other words, this means that in no other stable matching can any man improve upon his current partner. Somewhat surprisingly, the 'men propose' strategy yields a stable matching which is men-optimal (and correspondingly, the 'women propose' strategy yields a stable matching which is women-optimal). The argument for this proceeds as follows.

We will use letters from the English alphabet to denote men and letters from the Greek alphabet to denote women. Suppose the 'men propose' strategy yields the matching μ and let, if possible, that μ not be men-optimal. Then there is a man u who is not matched to $\alpha = \mathsf{best}(u)$ in μ. Let the partner of u in μ be β. Since μ is a stable matching and $\mathsf{best}(u)$ is the most preferred by u among all possible partners that can occur in stable matchings, it follows that u prefers α to β.

Hence, at some point in the 'men propose' algorithm, u would have proposed to α and would have been refused. This happens in a particular round (say k) and without loss of generality, assume that in no earlier round has any man u' being refused by $\mathsf{best}(u')$. Let the partner of α at the end of round k be x. Therefore, in round k, α had a choice between (at least) x and u and she refused u. Hence, α prefers x over u.

Since $\alpha = \mathsf{best}(u)$, there is some stable matching S where u is matched to α. Let γ be the partner of x in S and γ' be $\mathsf{best}(x)$. Then, x prefers γ' over γ.

The claim is that x prefers α over γ' and hence, using the transitivity of preference relation, x prefers α over γ. The argument for the claim that x prefers α over γ' is the following. If x preferred γ' over α, then in the 'men propose' algorithm, x must have proposed to γ' in a round earlier to round k and had then been refused by γ'. Since, $\gamma' = \mathsf{best}(x)$, this contradicts the choice of round k as the first round where a man u' has been refused by $\mathsf{best}(u')$.

At this point, we have the following two relations: α prefers x over u; and x prefers α over γ. In the matching S, u is matched to α and x is matched to γ. Therefore, the pair (x, α) forms a blocking pair in S and hence, S is not a stable matching which is a contradiction. This shows that the 'men propose' algorithm is men-optimal.

Suppose that μ is a men-optimal stable matching. A natural question that arises is how does a woman fare in such a matching? Consider as before the set $\mathsf{Part}(w)$ of all possible partners that a person w may have in stable matchings. Analogous to $\mathsf{best}(w)$, define $\mathsf{worst}(w)$ to be the person least preferred by w in the set $\mathsf{Part}(w)$. A matching μ is said to be women-pessimal if for all women α, her partner in μ is $\mathsf{worst}(\alpha)$. One can similarly define men-pessimal matching.

A stable matching μ which is men-optimal is necessarily women-pessimal. To see this suppose that for some woman α, her partner x in μ is not $\mathsf{worst}(\alpha)$. Let $y = \mathsf{worst}(\alpha)$. Then, α prefers x to y. There is some stable matching S where α is matched to y. In S, suppose x is matched to β. Since μ is men-optimal and x is matched to α in μ, it follows that x prefers α over β. We now have the two relations that α prefers x to y and x prefers α to β; but, in S, α is paired to y and therefore, the pair (x, α) forms a blocking pair for S contradicting the fact that S is stable.

Finally, we get the intriguing result that the 'men propose' algorithm is men-optimal and women-pessimal. This arises due to the fact that in each round when a man proposes, he is free to choose from all women who have not rejected him so far; while a woman has a restricted choice of being allowed to choose only from her current partner (if any) and the men who have proposed to her in the current round. It is this asymmetry that ultimately leads to the best situation for one side and the worst situation for the other.

13.2 Stable Matching Polytope

It is possible to formulate the constraints of stable matching as a linear program (Vate 1989; Rothblum 1992; Roth, Rothblum and Vate 1993). The Gale–Shapely algorithm described above is the best for one side and the worst for the other. By using a suitable cost function, the linear programming formulation of the stable matching problem can be used to obtain stable matchings with some notion of fairness for both sides.

As before, we will denote the men in the set U using letters from the English alphabet and the women in the set V using letters from the Greek alphabet. For each $x \in U$ and $\alpha \in V$, introduce a variable $X_{x,\alpha}$. Consider the following constraints. We use the notation $\alpha \succ_x \beta$ to denote that x prefers α to β, and similarly, the notation $x \succ_\alpha y$ to denote that α prefers x to y.

$$\left.\begin{array}{rcll}
\sum_{\alpha \in V} X_{x,\alpha} & \leq & 1 & \text{for all } x \in U; \\
\sum_{x \in U} X_{x,\alpha} & \leq & 1 & \text{for all } \alpha \in V; \\
X_{x,\alpha} + \sum_{\beta:\alpha \succ_x \beta} X_{x,\beta} + \sum_{y:x \succ_\alpha y} X_{y,\alpha} & \leq & 1 & \text{for all } x \in U \text{ and } \alpha \in V; \\
X_{x,\alpha} & \geq & 0 & \text{for all } x \in U \text{ and } \alpha \in V.
\end{array}\right\} \quad (13.1)$$

The first two constraints along with the fourth one states that each $X_{x,\alpha}$ is between 0 and 1 and for integral solutions: for each $x \in U$, $X_{x,\alpha}$ will be one for exactly one value of α and zero otherwise; for each $\alpha \in V$, $X_{x,\alpha}$ will be one for exactly one value of x and zero otherwise. Therefore, integral solutions to the first two and the fourth constraints specify a matching. Given a matching, the third constraint specifies it to be a stable one. Suppose the third constraint does not hold for some matching. Consider $x \in U$ and $\alpha \in V$: if $X_{x,\alpha} = 1$, then by the first two constraints, the two sums in the third constraint must be zeros and hence, for this choice of x and α, the third constraint holds. Therefore, let $X_{x,\alpha} = 0$. Then, if the third constraint does not hold for this choice of x and α, then each of the two individual sums must be one, i.e., we must have

$$\sum_{\beta:\alpha \succ_x \beta} X_{x,\beta} = 1 \text{ and } \sum_{y:x \succ_\alpha y} X_{y,\alpha} = 1.$$

This means that x is matched to some $\beta \neq \alpha$ and α is matched to some $y \neq x$ while x prefers α to β; and α prefers x to y. Therefore, in this case (x, α) is a blocking pair and hence, the matching is not stable.

Let P be the polytope defined by the linear constraints in (13.1). It can be shown that a vector is an extremal point of the polytope P if and only if it gives a stable matching. With this characterization of stable matchings, it is possible to impose fairness conditions by suitably choosing the optimization function.

Given x in U and α in V, let $\rho(x, \alpha)$ be the rank of α in the preference ordering of V by x; and similarly, let $\rho(\alpha, x)$ be the rank of x in the preference ordering of U by α. Consider the following optimization function:

$$\min \sum_{x \in U} \sum_{\alpha \in V} \rho(x, \alpha) + \rho(\alpha, x).$$

In conjuction with the linear constraints in (13.1), this defines an LP. A solution to this LP is a stable matching which is in some sense fair for both sides.

The above is a brief account of the beautiful Gale–Shapely algorithm. For a detailed algorithmic and combinatorial treatment of the subject we refer the reader to Knuth (1996); Gusfield and Irving (1989); Roth and Sotomayor (1990).

References

Aho, A. V., J. E. Hopcroft and J. D. Ullman. 1974. *The Design and Analysis of Computer Algorithms*. MA: Addison-Wesley.

Albizuri, M. 2001. 'An axiomatization of the modified Banzhaf Coleman index.' *International Journal of Game Theory* 30, 2: 167−176.

Albizuri, M. J. and L. M. Ruiz. 2001. 'A new axiomatization of the Banzhaf semivalue.' *Spanish Economic Review* 3, 2: 97−109.

Alonso-Meijide, J. M. and M. G. Fiestras-Janeiro. 2002. 'Modification of the Banzhaf value for games with a coalition structure.' *Annals of Operations Research* 109: 213−227.

Amer, R., F. Carreras and J. M. Gimnez. 2002. 'The modified Banzhaf value for games with coalition structure: An axiomatic characterization.' *Mathematical Social Sciences* 43, 1: 45−54.

Amer, R., F. Carreras and A. Magaña. 1998. 'Extension of values to games with multiple alternatives.' *Annals of Operations Research* 84, 63−78.

Apostol, T. 1974. *Mathematical Analysis*, second ed. London: Addison Wesley.

Aumann, R. and M. Maschler. 1964. 'The bargaining set for cooperative games.' In *Advances in Game Theory*, edited by M. Dresher, L. Shapley and A. Tucker. Princeton: Princeton University Press, pp. 443−476.

Aumann, R. J. 1974. 'Subjectivity and correlation in randomized strategies.' *Journal of Mathematical Economics* 1, 1: 67−96.

Aumann, R. J. 1976. 'Agreeing to disagree.' *The Annals of Statistics* 4, 6: 1236−1239.

Aumann, R. J. 1987. 'Game theory.' In *The New Palgrave Dictionary of Economics*, edited by J. Eatwell, M. Milgate and P. Newman, first ed., vol. 2. London: Palgrave Macmillan, pp. 202−207.

Aumann, R. J. 1987a. 'Correlated equilibrium as an expression of Bayesian rationality.' *Econometrica* 55, 1: 1−18.

Aumann, R. J. 1989. *Lectures on Game Theory*. Boulder: Westview Press.

Aumann, R. J. 2008. 'Game theory: Introduction.' In *The New Palgrave Dictionary of Economics*, edited by S. N. Durlauf and L. E. Blume, second ed., vol. 3. London: Palgrave Macmillan, pp. 529− 558.

Aumann, R. J. 2010. 'Some non-superadditive games, and their Shapley values, in the Talmud.' *International Journal of Game Theory* 39, 1: 3−10.

Aumann, R. J. and M. Maschler. 1985. 'Game theoretic analysis of a bankruptcy problem from the Talmud.' *Journal of Economic Theory* 36, 1: 195−213.

Banzhaf III, J. F. 1965. 'Weighted voting doesn't work: A mathemati- cal analysis.' *Rutgers L. Rev.* 19: 317−343.

Barua, R., S. R. Chakravarty and S. Roy. 2005. 'Measuring power in weighted majority games.' *Homo Oeconomicus* 22: 459−486.

Barua, R., S. R. Chakravarty and S. Roy. 2005a. 'A new characteri- zation of the Banzhaf index of power.' *International Game Theory Review* 7, 4: 545−553.

Barua, R., S. R. Chakravarty and S. Roy. 2006. 'On the Coleman indices of voting power.' *European Journal of Operational Research* 171, 1: 273−289.

Barua, R., S. R. Chakravarty and S. Roy. 2009. 'A note on the Carreras−Coleman decisiveness index.' *International Game Theory Review* 11, 2: 237−245.

Barua, R., S. R. Chakravarty, S. Roy and P. Sarkar. 2004. 'A charac- terization and some properties of the Banzhaf−Coleman− Dubey−Shapley sensitivity index.' *Games and Economic Behavior* 49, 1: 31−48.

Barua, R., S. R. Chakravarty and P. Sarkar. 2009. 'Minimal-axiom characterizations of the Coleman and Banzhaf indices of voting power.' *Mathematical Social Sciences* 58, 3: 367−375.

Barua, R., S. R. Chakravarty and P. Sarkar. 2012. 'Measuring p-power of voting.' *Journal of Economic Theory and Social Development* 1, 1: 81−91.

Benot, J.-P. and L. A. Kornhauser. 2002. 'Game-theoretic analysis of legal rules and institutions.' In *Handbook of Game Theory*, vol. 3 edited by R. J. Aumann and S. Hart. Amsterdam: North-Holland, pp. 2229−2269.

Bhattacharya, A. 2004. 'On the equal division core.' *Social Choice and Welfare* 22, 2: 391−399.

Bilal, S., P. Albuquerque and M. O. Hosli. 2001. 'The probability of coalition formation: Spatial voting power indices.' *ECSA Seventh Biennial International Conference*. Madison: Wisconsin.

Billera, L. J. 1970. 'Some theorems on the core of an *n*-game without side-payments.' *SIAM Journal on Applied Mathematics* 18, 3: 567−579.

Binmore, K. 1992. *Fun and Games: A Text on Game Theory*. Lexington: D. C. Heath.

Binmore, K., A. Rubinstein and A. Wolinsky. 1986. 'The Nsh bargaining solution in economic modelling.' *The RAND Journal of Economics* 17: 176−188.

Bolger, E. M. 1993. 'A value for games within players and *r* alternatives.' *International Journal of Game Theory* 22, 4: 319−334.

Bolger, E. M. 2002. 'Characterizations of two power indices for voting games with *r* alternatives.' *Social Choice and Welfare* 19, 4: 709−721.

Bondareva, O. N. 1963. 'Some applications of linear programming methods to the theory of cooperative games (in Russian).' *Problemy Kybernetiki* 10: 119−139.

Braham, M. and M. J. Holler. 2005. 'The impossibility of a preference-based power index.' *Journal of Theoretical Politics* 17, 1: 137−157.

Braham M. and F. Steffen. 2002. 'Local monotonicity of voting power: A conceptual analysis.' *University of Hamburg, Mimeographed*.

Brams, S. J. 1975. *Game Theory and Politics*. New York: Free Press.

Brams, S. J. and P. J. Affuso. 1976. 'Power and size: A new paradox.' *Theory and Decision* 7, 1-2: 29−56.

Brams, S. J and P. C. Fishburn. 1995. 'When is size a liability? Bargaining power in minimal winning coalitions.' *Journal of Theore- tical Politics* 7, 3: 301−316.

Brams, S. J., M. A. Jones and D. M. Kilgour. 2002. 'Single-peaked-ness and disconnected coalitions.' *Journal of Theoretical Politics* 14, 3: 359−383.

Branzei, R., D. Dimitrov and S. Tijs. 2008. *Models in Cooperative Game Theory*, second ed. New York: Springer.

Burgin, M. and L. Shapley. 2001. 'Enhanced Banzhaf power index and its mathematical properties.' *WP-797*, Department of Mathema- tics, UCLA.

Carreras, F. 2005. 'A decisiveness index for simple games.' *European Journal of Operational Research* 163, 2: 370−387.

Chalkiadakis, G., E. Elkind and M. Wooldridge. 2011. *Computational Aspects of Cooperative Game Theory*. Morgan & Claypool Publishers.

Chatterjee, K. and W. F. Samuelson, eds. 2001. *Game Theory and Business Applications*. New York: Springer.

Coase, R. H. 1960. 'The problem of social cost.' *Journal of Law and Economics* 3: 1−44.

Coleman, J. 1971. 'Control of collectives and the power of a collectivity to act.' In *Social Choice*, edited by B. Lieberman. New York: Gordon and Breach, pp. 269−298.

Curiel, I. 1997. *Cooperative Game Theory and Applications*. Boston: Kluwer.

Davis, M. and M. Maschler. 1965. 'The kernel of a cooperative game.' *Naval Research Logistics Quarterly* 12, 3: 223−259.

Deegan, John, J. and E. Packel. 1982. 'To the (minimal winning) victors go the (equally divided) spoils: A new power index for simple *n*-person games.' In *Political and Related Models*, edited by S. Brams, W. Lucas and Philip D. Straffin J. Modules in Applied Mathematics. New York: Springer, pp. 239−255.

Deegan Jr, J. and E. W. Packel. 1978. 'A new index of power for simple *n*-person games.' *International Journal of Game Theory* 7, 2: 113−123.

Deng, X. and Q. Fang. 2008. *Algorithmic Cooperative Game Theory*, vol. 17. Springer, pp. 159−185.

Deng, X., T. Ibaraki and H. Nagamochi. 1981. 'Combinatorial optimization games.' In *Proceedings of the Eighth Annual ACM-SIAM Symposium on Discrete Algorithms, 5-7 January 1997*, edited by Michael E. Saks. New Orleans, Louisiana: ACM/SIAM, pp. 720−729.

Derks, J. J. M. 1992. 'A short proof of the inclusion of the core in the weber set.' *International Journal of Game Theory* 21, 2: 149−150.

Diffo, L. L. and J. Moulen. 2002. 'Ordinal equivalence of power notions in voting games.' *Theory and Decision* 53, 4: 313−325.

Dragan, I. 1996. 'New mathematical properties of the Banzhaf value.' *European Journal of Operational Research* 95, 2: 451−463.

Drechsel, J. 2009. *Cooperative Lot Sizing Games in Supply Chains*. New York: Springer.

Drechsel, J. and A. Kimms. 2010. 'The subcoalition-perfect core of cooperative games.' *Annals of Operations Research* 181, 1: 591−601.

Dreyer, J. S. and A. Schotter. 1980. 'Power relationships in the international monetary fund: The consequences of quota changes.' *The Review of Economics and Statistics* 62, 1: 97−106.

Dubey, P. 1975. 'On the uniqueness of the Shapley value.' *Interna- tional Journal of Game Theory* 4, 1: 131−140.

Dubey, P., E. Einy and O. Haimanko. 2005. 'Compound voting and the Banzhaf index.' *Games and Economic Behavior* 51, 1: 20−30.

Dubey, P. and L. S. Shapley. 1979. 'Mathematical properties of the Banzhaf power Index.' *Mathematics of Operations Research* 4, 2: 99−131.

Einy, E. and O. Haimanko. 2011. 'Characterization of the Shapley− Shubik power index without the efficiency axiom.' *Games and Economic Behavior* 73, 2: 615−621.

Felsenthal, D. S. and M. Machover. 1995. 'Postulates and paradoxes of relative voting powera critical re-appraisal.' *Theory and Decision* 38, 2: 195−229.

Felsenthal, D. S. and M. Machover. 1997. 'Ternary voting games.' *International Journal of Game Theory* 26, 3: 335−351.

Felsenthal, D. S. and M. Machover. 1998. *The Measurement of Voting Power*. Cheltenham: Edward Elgar.

Felsenthal, D. S. and M. Machover. 1998a. 'The product paradox of voting power.' *Public Choice* 96, 1-2: 81−92.

Felsenthal, D. S. and M. Machover. 2002. 'Annexations and alliances: When are blocs advantageous a priori?' *Social Choice and Welfare* 19, 2: 295−312.

Felsenthal, D. S. and M. Machover. 2004. 'Analysis of QM rules in the draft constitution for Europe proposed by the European convention, 2003.' *Social Choice and Welfare* 23, 1: 1−20.

Felsenthal, D. S., M. Machover and W. Zwicker. 1998. 'The Bicameral postulates and indices of a priori voting power.' *Theory and Decision* 44, 1: 83–116.

Feltkamp, V. 1995. 'Alternative axiomatic characterizations of the Shapley and Banzhaf values.' *International Journal of Game Theory* 24, 2: 179–186.

Freixas, J. 2005. 'The Shapley–Shubik power index for games with several levels of approval in the input and output.' *Decision Support Systems* 39, 2: 185–195.

Freixas, J. and G. Gambarelli. 1997. 'Common internal properties among power indices.' *Control and Cybernetics* 26, 4: 591–603.

Freixas, J. and D. Marciniak. 2013. 'Egalitarian property for power indices.' *Social Choice and Welfare* 40, 1: 207–227.

Freixas, J., D. Marciniak and M. Pons. 2012. 'On the ordinal equivalence of the Johnston, Banzhaf and Shapley power indices.' *European Journal of Operational Research* 216, 2: 367–375.

Freixas, J. and W. S. Zwicker. 2003. 'Weighted voting, abstention, and multiple levels of approval.' *Social Choice and Welfare* 21, 3: 399–431.

Friedman, J. W. 1986. *Game Theory with Applications to Economics.* New York: Oxford University Press.

Fudenberg, D. and J. Tirole. 1991. *Game Theory.* Cambridge: MIT Press.

Gale, D. and L. S. Shapley. 1962. 'College admissions and the stability of marriage.' *American Mathematical Monthly* 69: 9–15.

Gambarelli, G. 1983. 'Common behaviour of power indices.' *International Journal of Game Theory* 12, 4: 237–244.

Gambarelli, G. and G. Owen. 2004. 'The coming of game theory.' *Theory and Decision* 56, 1-2: 1–18.

Gillies, D. B. 1959. 'Solutions to general non-zero-sum games.' In *Contributions to the Theory of Games IV, Annals of Mathematics Studies,* edited by A. Tucker and R. Luce. Princeton: Princeton University Press, pp. 47–85.

Granot, D. and G. Huberman. 1981. 'Minimum cost spanning tree games.' *Mathematical Programming* 21: 1–18.

Gura, Y.-Y. and M. B. Maschler. 2008. *Insights into Game Theory: An Alternative Mathematical Experience.* Cambridge: Cambridge University Press.

Gusfield, D. and R. W. Irving. 1989. *The Stable Marriage Problem - Structure and Algorithms*. Foundations of Computing Series. MIT Press.

Haller, H. 1994. 'Collusion properties of values.' *International Journal of Game Theory* 23, 3: 261−281.

Harsanyi, J. C. 1967. 'Games with incomplete information played by Bayesian players, part i. The basic model'. *Management Science* 14, 3: 159−182.

Harsanyi, J. C. 1968. 'Games with incomplete information played by Bayesian players, part ii. Bayesian equilibrium points.' *Management Science* 14, 5: 320−334.

Harsanyi, J. C. 1968. 'Games with incomplete information played by Bayesian players, part iii. The basic probability distribution of the game.' *Management Science* 14, 7: 486−502.

Hart, S. 2004. 'A comparison of non-transferable utility values.' *Theory and Decision* 56, 1-2 : 35−46.

Hart, S. and A. Mas-Colell. 1989. 'Potential, value, and consistency.' *Econometrica* 57, 3: 589−614.

Herrero, C. and A. Villar. 2001. 'The three musketeers: Four classical solutions to bankruptcy problems.' *Mathematical Social Sciences* 42, 3: 307−328.

Hoede, C. and R. Bakker. 1982. 'A theory of decisional power.' *Journal of Mathematical Sociology* 8, 2: 309−322.

Holler, M. J. 1982. 'Forming coalitions and measuring voting power.' *Political Studies* 30, 2: 262−271.

Holler, M. J. 1997. 'Power, monotonicity and expectations.' *Control and Cybernetics* 26: 605−607.

Holler, M. J. 1998. 'Two stories, one power index.' *Journal of Theoretical Politics* 10, 2: 179−190.

Holler, M. and X. Li. 1995. 'From public good index to public value: An axiomatic approach and generalization.' *Control and Cybernetics* 24: 257−270.

Holler, M. J. and S. Napel. 2004. 'Monotonicity of power and power measures.' *Theory and Decision* 56, 1-2: 93−111.

Holler, M. J., R. Ono and F. Steffen. 2001. 'Constrained monotonicity and the measurement of power.' *Theory and Decision* 50: 385−397.

Holler, M. J. and E. W. Packel. 1983. 'Power, luck and the right index.' *Zeitschrift für Nationalökonomie* 43, 1: 21–29.

Hurwicz, L. 1972. 'On informationally decentralized systems.' In *Decision and Organization*, edited by B. Mc Guire and R. Radner. Amsterdam: North-Holland, pp. 297–336.

Hurwicz, L. 1973. 'The design of mechanisms for resource allocation.' *American Economic Review*: 1–30.

Ichiishi, T. 1981. 'Super-modularity: Applications to convex games and to the greedy algorithm for LP.' *Journal of Economic Theory* 25, 2: 283–286.

Johnston, R. J. 1978. 'On the measurement of power: Some reactions to Laver.' *Environment and Planning A* 10, 8: 907–914.

Kalai, E. 1977. 'Proportional solutions to bargaining situations: Interpersonal utility comparisons.' *Econometrica* 45, 7: 1623–1630.

Kalai, E. and D. Samet. 1987. 'On weighted Shapley values.' *International Journal of Game Theory* 16, 3: 205–222.

Kalai, E. and M. Smorodinsky, 1975. 'Other solutions to Nash's bargaining problem.' *Econometrica* 43, 3: 513–518.

Kalai, E. and E. Zemel. 1982. 'Generalized network problems yielding totally balanced games.' *Operations Research* 4: 998–1008.

Kalai, E. and E. Zemel. 1982a. 'On totally balanced games and games of flow.' *Mathematics of Operations Research* 7: 476–478.

Kar, A., M. Mitra and S. Mutuswami. 2009. 'On the coincidence of the prenucleolus and the Shapley value.' *Mathematical Social Sciences* 57: 16–25.

Knuth, D. E. 1996. *Stable Marriage and its Relation to Other Combinato- rial Problems*. American Mathematical Society.

König, T. and T. Brauninger. 1998. 'The inclusiveness of European decision rules.' *Journal of Theoretical Politics* 10: 125–142.

Lambo, L. D. and J. Moulen. 2002. 'Ordinal equivalence of power notions in voting games.' *Theory and Decision* 53, 4: 313–325.

Laruelle, A. and F. Valenciano. 2001. 'Shapley–Shubik and Banzhaf indices revisited.' *Mathematics of Operational Research* 26, 1: 89–104.

Laruelle, A. and F. Valenciano. 2004. 'Inequality in voting power.' *Social Choice and Welfare* 22, 2: 413–431.

Laruelle, A. and F. Valenciano. 2005. 'Potential and power of a collectivity to act.' *Theory and Decision* 58, 2: 187–194.

Laruelle, A. and F. Valenciano. 2008. *Voting and Collective Decision-Making: Bargaining and Power*. Cambridge: Cambridge University Press.

Laver, M. 1978. 'The problem of measuring power in Europe.' *Environment and Planning A* 10, 8: 901–905.

Leech, D. 1990. 'Power indices and probabilistic voting assump- tions.' *Public Choice* 66, 3: 293–299.

Leech, D. 2002. 'Designing the voting system for the council of the European union.' *Public Choice* 113, 3-4: 437–464.

Leech, D. 2002a. 'The use of Coleman's power indices to inform the choice of voting rule with reference to the IMF governing body and the EU council of ministers.' *The Warwick Economics Research Paper Series (TWERPS)* 645, University of Warwick, Department of Economics.

Lehrer, E. 1988. 'An axiomatization of the Banzhaf value.' *Interna- tional Journal of Game Theory* 17, 2: 89–99.

Lindner, I. 2002. 'Power measures in large weighted voting games: Asymptotic properties and numerical methods.' *Presented at the Workshop of Voting Power Analysis*, London School of Economics and Political Science.

Littlechild, S. C. and G. Owen. 1973. 'A simple expression for the Shapley value in a special case.' *Management Science* 20, 3: 370–372.

Lorenzo-Friere, S., J. M. Alonso-Meijide, B. Casas-Mendez and M. Fiestras-Janeiro. 1973. 'Characterizations of the Deegan-Packel and Johnston power indices.' *European Journal of Operational Research* 177: 431–444.

Luce, R. D. and H. Raiffa. 1957. *Games and Decisions: Introduction and Critical Survey*. New York: John Wiley & Sons.

Malawski, M. 2002. 'Equal treatment, symmetry and Banzhaf value axiomatizations.' *International Journal of Game Theory* 31, 1: 47–67.

Maschler, M. 1976. 'An advantage of the bargaining set over the core.' *Journal of Economic Theory* 13, 2: 184–192.

Maschler, M. 1992. 'The bargaining set, kernel and nucleolus.' In *Handbook of Game Theory with Economic Applications*, edited by R. Aumann and S. Hart, vol. 1. Amsterdam: Elsevier, pp. 591–667.

Maschler, M. and B. Peleg. 1966. 'A characterization, existence proof and dimension bounds for the kernel of a game.' *Pacific Journal of Mathematics* 18, 2: 289–328.

Maschler, M., B. Peleg and L. S. Shapley. 1979. 'Geometric properties of the kernel, nucleolus, and related solution concepts.' *Mathematics of Operations Research* 4, 4: 303–338.

Maschler, M. B., E. Solan and S. Zamir. 2013. *Game Theory*. Cambridge: Cambridge University Press.

Maskin, E. S. 1999. 'Nash equilibrium and welfare optimality.' *Review of Economic Studies* 66: 23–38.

Matsui, T. and Y. Matsui. 2000. 'A survey of algorithms for calculating power indices of weighted majority games.' *Journal of the Operations Research Society of Japan* 43: 71–86.

McLean, R. 2002. 'Values of non-transferable utility games.' In *Handbook of Game Theory*, edited by R. Aumann and S. Hart, vol. 3, Amsterdam: North-Holland, pp. 2077–2120.

Megiddo, N. 1978. 'Computational complexity of the game theory approach to cost allocation for a tree.' *Mathematics of Operations Research* 3: 189–196.

Mercik, J. W. 2000. 'Index of power for cabinet.' *Homo Oeconomicus* 17: 125–136.

Milnor, J. W. 1952. *Reasonable Outcomes for N-Person Games*. The RAND Corporation, Santa Monica. RM 916.

Muto, S. 1999. 'The Banzhaf index in representative systems with multiple political Parties.' *Games and Economic Behavior* 28, 1: 73–104.

Myerson, R. B. 1977. 'Graphs and cooperation in games.' *Mathema- tics of Operations Research* 2: 225–229.

Myerson, R. B. 1977a. 'Two-person bargaining problems and comparable utility.' *Econometrica* 45, 7: 1631–1637.

Myerson, R. B. 1979. 'Incentive compatibility and the bargaining problem.' *Econometrica* 47, 1: 61–74.

Myerson, R. B. 1980. 'Conference structures and fair allocation rules.' *International Journal of Game Theory* 9, 3: 169–182.

Myerson, R. B. 1981. 'Optimal auction design.' *Mathematics of Operation Research* 6, 1: 58–73.

Myerson, R. B. 1997. *Game Theory: Analysis of Conflict*. Harvard: Harvard University Press.

Napel, S. and M. Widgrn. 2001. 'Inferior players in simple games.' *International Journal of Game Theory* 30, 2: 209–220.

Nash, J. 1950. 'The bargaining problem.' *Econometrica* 18, 2: 155−162.

Nash, J. 1951. 'Non-cooperative games.' *The Annals of Mathematics* 54, 2: 286−295.

Nowak, A. S. 1997. 'On an axiomatization of the Banzhaf value without the additivity Axiom.' *International Journal of Game Theory* 26, 1: 137−141.

Nowak, A. S. and T. Radzik. 1995. 'On axiomatizations of the weighted Shapley values.' *Games and Economic Behavior* 8, 2: 389−405.

O'Neill, B. 1982. 'A problem of rights arbitration from the Talmud.' *Mathematical Social Sciences* 2, 4: 345−371.

Ono, R. 2000. 'Values for multialternative games and multilinear extensions.' *Homo Oeconomicus* 17: 193−214.

Osborne, M. J. 2004. *An Introduction to Game Theory.* New York: Oxford University Press.

Osborne, M. J. and A. Rubinstein. 1994. *A Course on Game Theory.* Cambridge: MIT Press.

Owen, G. 1972. 'Multilinear extensions of games.' *Management Science* 18, 5-Part-2: 64−79.

Owen, G. 1975. 'Multilinear extensions and the Banzhaf value.' *Naval Research Logistics Quarterly* 22, 4: 741−750.

Owen, G. 1975a. 'On the core of linear production games.' *Mathematical Programming* 9: 358−370.

Owen, G. 1978. 'Characterization of the Banzhaf−Coleman index.' *SIAM Journal on Applied Mathematics* 35, 2: 315−327.

Owen, G. 1982. 'Modification of the Banzhaf−Coleman index for games with a priori Unions.' In *Power, Voting, and Voting Power*, edited by M. Holler. Würzburg: Physica-Verlag, pp. 232−264.

Owen, G. 1988. 'Multilinear extension of games.' In *The Shapley Value: Essays in Honor of Lloyd S. Shapley.* Cambridge: Cambridge University Press, pp. 139−151.

Owen, G. 1995. *Game Theory*, third ed. San Diego: Academic Press.

Owen, G. 1999. *Discrete Mathematics and Game Theory.* Boston: Kluwer.

Owen, G. and L. S. Shapley. 1989. 'Optimal location of candidates in ideological space.' *International Journal of Game Theory* 18, 3: 339−356.

Papadimitriou, C. H. and K. Steiglitz. 1982. *Combinatorial Optimization: Algorithms and Complexity.* Dover Books on Computer Science.

Parker, C. 2012. 'The influence relation for ternary voting games.' *Games and Economic Behavior* 75, 2: 867−881.

Peleg, B. 1963. 'Existence theorem for the bargaining set $M_1^{(i)}$.' *Bulletin of the American Mathematical Society* 69, 1: 109−110.

Peleg, B. 1967. 'Existence theorem for the bargaining set $M_1^{(i)}$.' In *Essays in Mathematical Economics in Honour of Oscar Morgenstern*, edited by M. Shubik. Princeton: Princeton University Press, pp. 53−56.

Peleg, B. 1981. 'Coalition formation in simple games with dominant players.' *International Journal of Game Theory* 10, 1: 11−33.

Peleg, B. and P. Sudholter. 2007. *Introduction to the Theory of Cooperative Games*, second ed. New York: Springer.

Penrose, L. S. 1946. 'The elementary statistics of majority voting.' *Journal of the Royal Statistical Society* 109, 1: 53−57.

Perlinger, T. 2000. 'Voting power in an ideological spectrum: The Markov−Plya index.' *Mathematical Social Sciences* 40, 2: 215−226.

Peters, H. 2008. *Game Theory: A Multi-Leveled Approach*. New York: Springer.

Radzik, T., A. S. Nowak and T. S. Driessen. 1997. 'Weighted Banzhaf values.' *Mathematical Methods of Operations Research* 45, 1: 109−118.

Rae, D. W. 1969. 'Decision-rules and individual values in constitu- tional choice.' *The American Political Science Review* 63, 1: 40−56.

Riker, W. H. 1986. 'The first power index.' *Social Choice and Welfare* 3, 4: 293−295.

Roth, A. E. 1977. 'Utility functions for simple games.' *Journal of Economic Theory* 16, 2: 481−489.

Roth, A. E. 1985. 'The college admissions problem is not equivalent to the marriage problem.' *Journal of Economic Theory* 36, 2: 277−288.

Roth, A. E., ed. 1988. *The Shapley Value: Essays in Honour of Lloyd S. Shapley*. Cambridge: Cambridge University Press.

Roth, A. E. and A. Postlewaite. 1977. 'Weak versus strong domina- tion in a market with indivisible goods.' *Journal of Mathematical Economics* 4, 2: 131−137.

Roth, A. E., U. G. Rothblum and J. H. V. Vate. 1993. 'Stable matchings, optimal assignments, and linear programming.' *Mathematics of Operations Research* 18: 803−828.

Roth, A. E. and M. A. O. Sotomayor. 1990. 'Two-Sided Matching: A study in game theoretic modeling and analysis.' *Econometric Society Monographs*. Cambridge: Cambridge University Press.

Roth, A. E. and R. E. Venechaia. 1979. 'The Shapley value as applied to cost allocation: A reinterpretation.' *Journal of Accounting Research* 17: 295−303.

Rothblum, U. G. 1992. 'Characterization of stable matchings as extreme points of a Polytope.' *Mathematical Programming* 54: 57−67.

Roy, S. 2005. 'Essays on individual and collective power in a voting body.' PhD thesis. Kolkata: Indian Statistical Institute.

Royden, H. L. 1968. *Real Analysis*, second ed. London: McMillan.

Rubinstein, A. 1982. 'Perfect equilibrium in a bargaining model.' *Econometrica* 50, 1: 97−109.

Rudin, W. 1976. *Principles of Mathematical Analysis*, third ed. London: McGrawHill.

Rusinowska, A. and H. D. Swart. 2007. 'On some properties of the Hoede-Bakker index.' *Journal of Mathematical Sociology* 31, 4: 267−293.

Saari, D. G. and K. K. Sieberg. 2000. 'Some surprising properties of power indices.' *Games and Economic Behavior* 36, 2: 241−263.

Sanchez, S. 1997. 'Balanced contributions axiom in the solution of cooperative games.' *Games and Economic Behavior* 20, 2: 161−168.

Scarf, H. E. 1967. 'The core of an *n* person game.' *Econometrica* 35, 1: 50−69.

Schelling, T. C. 1956. 'An essay on bargaining.' *The American Economic Review* 46, 3: 281−306.

Schelling, T. C. 1960. *The Strategy of Conflict*. Cambridge: Harvard University Press.

Schmeidler, D. 1969. 'The nucleolus of a characteristic function game.' *SIAM Journal on Applied Mathematics* 17, 6: 1163−1170.

Schotter, A. 1982. 'The paradox of redistribution: Some theoretical and empirical results.' In *Power, Voting, and Voting Power*, edited by M. J. Holler, Würzburg: Physics-Verlag, pp. 324−338.

Selten, R. 1975. 'Reexamination of the perfectness concept for equilibrium points in extensive games.' *International Journal of Game Theory* 4, 1: 25−55.

Serrano, R. 1997. 'Reinterpreting the kernel.' *Journal of Economic Theory* 77, 1: 58–80.

Serrano, R. 2013. 'Lloyd Shapley's matching and game theory.' *The Scandinavian Journal of Economics* 115, 3: 599–618.

Shapley, L. 1953. 'A value for *n*-person games.' In *Contributions to the Theory of Games II, Annals of Mathematics Studies*, edited by A. Tucker and R. Luce. Princeton: Princeton University Press, pp. 307–317.

Shapley, L. and H. Scarf. 1974. 'On cores and indivisibility.' *Journal of Mathematical Economics* 1, 1: 23–37.

Shapley, L. and M. Shubik. 1963. *The Core of an Economy with Non-convex Preferences*. Santa Monica, CA: The Rand Corporation.

Shapley, L. S. 1953a. *Additive and Non-additive Set Functions*. PhD thesis, Department of Mathematics. Princeton: Princeton University.

Shapley, L. S. 1962. 'Simple games: An outline of the descriptive theory.' *Behavioral Science* 7, 1: 59–66.

Shapley, L. S. 1967. 'On balanced sets and cores.' *Naval Research Logistics Quarterly* 14, 4: 453–460.

Shapley, L. S. 1971. 'Cores of convex games.' *International Journal of Game Theory* 1, 1: 11–26.

Shapley, L. S. 1973. 'Political science: Voting and bargaining games.' In *Notes of Lectures on Mathematics in the Behavioral Sciences*, edited by H. Selby. Mathematical Association of America, pp. 37–92.

Shapley, L. S. 1973a. 'On balanced games without side payments.' In *Mathematical Programming: Proceedings*, edited by T. Hu and S. M. Robinson. New York: Academic Press, pp. 261–290.

Shapley, L. S. 1981. 'Discussant's comments: Equity considerations in traditional full cost allocation practices: An axiomatic perspective.' In *Joint Cost Allocation*, edited by S. Moriarity. Tulsa: University of Oklahoma Press, pp. 131–136.

Shapley, L. S. and M. Shubik. 1954. 'A method for evaluating the distribution of power in a committee system.' *American Political Science Review* 48, 3: 787–792.

Shapley, L. S. and M. Shubik. 1966. 'Quasi-cores in a monetary economy with nonconvex preferences.' *Econometrica* 34, 4: 805–827.

Shapley, L. S. and M. Shubik. 1969. 'On market games.' *Journal of Economic Theory* 1, 1: 9–25.

Shapley, L. S. and M. Shubik. 1969a. 'Pure competition, coalition power and fair division.' *International Economic Review* 10: 337−362.

Shapley, L. S. and M. Shubik. 1972. 'The assignment game I: The core.' *International Journal of Game Theory* 1: 111−130.

Smith, J. M. 1982. *Evolution and the Theory of Games.* Cambridge: Cambridge University Press.

Sobolev, A. 1975. 'The characterization of optimality principles in cooperative games by functional equations (in Russian).' *Methods in Social Sciences* 6: 94−151.

Straffin J., Philip. D. 1977. 'Homogeneity, independence, and power indices.' *Public Choice* 30, 1: 107−118.

Straffin J., Philip D. 1982. 'Power indices in politics.' In *Political and Related Models,* edited by S. J. Brams, W. F. Lucas and Philip D. Straffin J., Modules in Applied Mathematics. New York: Springer, pp. 256−321.

Straffin J., Philip D. 1988. *The Shapley Shubik and Banzhaf Power Indices as Probabilities.* Cambridge University Press.

Straffin J., Philip D. 1994. 'Power and stability in politics.' In *Handbook of Game Theory with Economic Applications,* edited by R. Aumann and S. Hart, first ed., vol. 2. Elsevier, pp. 1127−1151.

Sutton, J. 1986. 'Non-cooperative bargaining theory: An introduc- tion.' *The Review of Economic Studies* 53, 5: 709−724.

Suzuki, M. and M. Nakayama. 1976. 'The cost assignment of the cooperative water resource development: A game theoretical approach.' *Management Science* 22, 10: 1081−1086.

Taylor, A. and W. Zwicker. 1992. 'A characterization of weighted voting.' *Proceedings of the American Mathematical Society* 115, 4: 1089−1094.

Taylor, A. D. 1995. *Mathematics and Politics: Strategy, Voting Power and Proof.* New York: Springer-Verlag.

Taylor, A. D. and W. S. Zwicker. 1992. 'A characterization of weighted voting.' *Proceedings of the American Mathematical Society* 115, 4: 1089−1094.

Tchantcho, B., L. D. Lambo, R. Pongou and B. M. Engoulou. 2008. 'Voters power in voting games with abstention: Influence relation and ordinal equivalence of power theories.' *Games and Economic Behavior* 64, 1: 335−350.

Thomson, W. 2003. 'Axiomatic and game-theoretic analysis of bankruptcy and taxation problems: A survey.' *Mathematical Social Sciences* 45, 3: 249–297.

Turnovec, F. 1997. 'Monotonicity of power indices.' *East European Series* 41, Institute for Advanced Studies.

Van den Brink, R. and G. Van der Laan. 1998. 'Axiomatizations of the normalized Banzhaf value and the Shapley value.' *Social Choice and Welfare* 15, 4: 567–582.

Vate, J. H. V. 1989. 'Linear programming brings marital bliss.' *Operations Research Letters* 8: 147–153.

von Neumann, J. 1928. 'Zur theorie der gesellschaftsspiele.' *Mathematische Annalen* 100, 1: 295–320.

von Neumann, J. and O. Morgenstern. 1944. *Theory of Games and Economic Behavior*. Princeton: Princeton University Press.

Weber, R. J. 1988. 'Probabilistic values for games.' In *The Shapley Value: Essays in Honor of Lloyd S. Shapley*, edited by A. E. Roth. Cambridge University Press, pp. 101–119.

Wonham, W. M. 1974. *Lecture Notes in Economics and Mathematical Systems*. New York: Springer-Verlag.

Young, H. P. 1985. 'Monotonic solutions of cooperative games.' *International Journal of Game Theory* 14, 1: 65–72.

Young, H. P. 1988. 'Individual contribution and just compensation.' In *The Shapley Value: Essays in Honor of Lloyd S. Shapley*, edited by A. E. Roth. Cambridge University Press, pp. 267–278.

Young, H. P. 1994. 'Cost allocation.' In *Handbook of Game Theory*, edited by R. J. Aumann and S. Hart, vol. 2. Amsterdam: North- Holland, pp. 1193–1235.

Young, H. P., N. Okada and T. Hashimoto. 1982. 'Cost allocation in water resources Development.' *Water Resources Research* 18, 3: 463–475.

Index